CULTURAL EVENTS ARTISTS AND WRITERS	DATES	WORLD EVENTS POLITICAL LEADERS

MIDDLE AGES AND RENAISSANCE

Gothic cathedrals begun (St. Denis,	**1100**	
Paris, 1144; Chartres, 1145)	**1150**	
	1200	Magna Carta signed by King John (1215)
	1250	Marco Polo leaves for Cathay (1271)
Dante's *Divine Comedy* (1307)	**1300**	Hundred Years' War begins (1337)
Chaucer's *Canterbury Tales* (1386)	**1350**	
Botticelli (1444–1510)	**1400**	Battle of Agincourt (1415)
Gutenberg Bible (1456)	**1450**	Fall of Constantinople (1453)
Michelangelo (1475–1564)		Columbus discovers America (1492)
Raphael (1483–1520)		
St. Peter's begun in Rome (1506)	**1500**	Henry VIII King of England (1509)
		Martin Luther's ninety-five theses (1517)
		Council of Trent (1545–1563)
	1550	Elizabeth I Queen of England (1558)
		Spanish Armada defeated (1588)

BAROQUE

El Greco (1541–1614)		
William Shakespeare (1564–1616)		
Caravaggio (1573–1610)		
Peter Paul Rubens (1577–1640)		
Francesco Borromini (1599–1667)	**1600**	Jamestown settled (1607)
Cervantes, part I of *Don Quixote* (1605)		Thirty Years' War begins (1618)
Rembrandt van Rijn (1606–1669)		Mayflower Compact (1620)
Giovanni Lorenzo Bernini's		Louis XIV King of France (1643)
Ecstasy of St. Theresa (1644)		
Samuel Pepys's *Diary* (1660)	**1650**	Restoration of Charles II in England (1660)
John Milton's *Paradise Lost* (1667)		Reign of Peter the Great begins (1682)
Christopher Wren begins St. Paul's Cathedral (1675)		Salem witchcraft trials (1692)
Isaac Newton's *Principia Mathematica* (1687)	**1700**	War of the Spanish Succession begins (1702)
		Reign of Louis XV begins (1715)
Jonathan Swift's *Gulliver's Travels* (1726)		Age of Enlightened Despots (1740–1796)

CLASSICAL

Francisco Goya (1746–1828)		
Jacques Louis David (1748–1825)		
Pompeii rediscovered (1748)	**1750**	Franklin's discoveries in electricity (1752)
Voltaire's *Candide* (1759)		Seven Years' War; French and Indian War (1756)
William Wordsworth (1770–1850)		Beginnings of the Industrial Revolution (ca. 1770)
J.M.W. Turner (1775–1851)		American Declaration of Independence (1776)
Immanuel Kant's *Critique of Pure Reason* (1781)		French Revolution begins (1789)
Thomas Malthus's *Essay on Population* (1798)		Bill of Rights (1791)
Eugene Delacroix (1798–1863)		Eli Whitney's cotton gin (1793)
Goethe's *Faust, Part I* (1808)	**1800**	Louisiana Purchase (1803)
Jane Austen's *Pride and Prejudice* (1813)		Battle of Waterloo (1815)

ROMANTIC

Edgar Allen Poe (1809–1849)		
Goya's *Witches' Sabbath* (1815)		
Herman Melville (1818–1891)		Monroe Doctrine (1823)
Shelley's *Prometheus Unbound* (1820)	**1825**	Erie Canal opened (1825)
Victor Hugo's *Hernani* (1830)		July Revolution in France (1830)
Claude Monet (1840–1926)		Invention of telegraph (1832)
Ralph Waldo Emerson's *Essays* (1841)		Queen Victoria's reign begins (1837)
Alexander Dumas's *Count of*		California Gold Rush; Revolutions
Monte Cristo (1845)		in Europe (1848)
Karl Marx's *Communist Manifesto* (1848)		
Harriet Beecher Stowe's *Uncle Tom's Cabin* (1852)	**1850**	Opening of Japan to the West (1853)

EXPLORING
MUSIC

Fourth Edition

EXPLORING MUSIC

Robert Hickok

University of California, Irvine

wcb
Wm. C. Brown Publishers
Dubuque, Iowa

Book Team

Editor *Meredith M. Morgan*
Developmental Editor *Raphael Kadushin*
Designer *Laurie J. Entringer*
Production Editor *Harry Halloran*
Photo Research Editor *Marge Manders*
Visuals Processor *Vickie Werner*

wcb group

Chairman of the Board *Wm. C. Brown*
President and Chief Executive Officer *Mark C. Falb*

wcb

Wm. C. Brown Publishers, College Division

President *G. Franklin Lewis*
Vice President, Editor-in-Chief *George Wm. Bergquist*
Vice President, Director of Production *Beverly Kolz*
Vice President, National Sales Manager *Bob McLaughlin*
Director of Marketing *Thomas E. Doran*
Marketing Communications Manager *Edward Bartell*
Marketing Manager *David F. Horwitz*
Manager of Visuals and Design *Faye M. Schilling*
Production Editorial Manager *Colleen A. Yonda*
Production Editorial Manager *Julie A. Kennedy*
Publishing Services Manager *Karen J. Slaght*

Consulting Editor *Frederick W. Westphal*

Interior design by Terri Webb Ellerbach

Cover design by Tara L. Bazata

Cover © Charles Schabes/Journalism Services

The credits section for this book begins on page 475, and is
considered an extension of the copyright page.

Printed in the United States of America by Wm. C. Brown Publishers
2460 Kerper Boulevard, Dubuque, IA 52001

10 9 8 7 6 5 4 3 2

For Roanne, Paul and Laura

CONTENTS

8
MUSIC IN
AMERICA

PREFACE

Exploring Music, fourth edition, is designed for introductory music courses at the college level. The book is structured to suit a variety of course lengths. Coverage is comprehensive enough for a full-year course. At the same time the organization of the text affords considerable flexibility so that instructors in a one- or two-quarter course can use the book selectively to fit the length of time at her or his disposal.

The goal of *Exploring Music* is to help the student acquire informed listening skills which promote the development of a curiosity about, an enthusiasm for, and the enjoyment of many types and styles of music. In its organization and contents, the fourth edition is calculated to enhance the pursuit of this goal.

ORGANIZATION

Part I presents the fundamental elements of music in three easy-to-read chapters. Simple musical examples as well as brief excerpts from musical works covered later in the text are used to illustrate and reinforce concepts. The basic vocabulary necessary for understanding and discussing music is included in these chapters. Part I concludes with a chapter on musical instruments, including the human voice, and explores combinations of instruments in small and large musical ensembles. Part II introduces the music of non-Western cultures, offering the student a global perspective on music before moving to an examination of music in Western society in the remainder of the book. Then, using the material of part I as a foundation, parts III through IX examine in chronological order the periods of music history from the Middle Ages to the twentieth century. Part X focuses on jazz and rock music.

"Preludes," accompanied by full color plates as well as black and white photographs, present historical, philosophical, and artistic background of each major style period. Particular emphasis is given to painting, sculpture, and architecture. These

Preludes may be studied in connection with style periods, they may be assigned as supplemental material, or they may simply be omitted, depending on the instructor's objectives for the course.

Chapters dealing with music of the twentieth century, including jazz and rock, have been revised and updated.

An important new feature of the fourth edition is the inclusion of the contributions to music by such women composers and teachers as Hildegard of Bingen, Barbara Strozzi, Clara Wieck Schumann, Nadia Boulanger, Amy Beach, and Miriam Gideon.

LISTENING GUIDES

The major emphasis of this text and the course of study it presents is on listening. To this end, the fourth edition features succinct *listening guides,* relating to the major instrumental works discussed in the book and included in the recordings which supplement the text. These listening guides are designed to help clarify the form of the piece and to involve the listener in the musical procedures that are taking place. They are not a complete description of the piece; rather, they simply point out certain "cues," easily heard points in the music to help the student keep track of the musical process.

The best way to use these guides is to review the text description of the music before listening, then listen several times while reading the listening guide, and finally just listen to the music with the greater sensitivity and awareness the text description and the listening guide help to foster.

MUSIC NOTATION

The use of music notation in the text neither assumes nor requires that students be able to "read" music as a trained musician does. Rather it is intended that students will "follow" the notation as a visual aid in the listening process.

STUDY AIDS

Several devices have been incorporated in this edition to increase the effectiveness of the book. Musical terms are printed in boldface and defined when they first appear. New terms are also listed at the end of each chapter and are included in a comprehensive glossary at the end of the text.

Summaries at the end of each chapter offer a concise review of the material covered in the chapter. Many students like to read the summary before beginning a chapter in order to get a quick overview of the major points.

This edition includes the texts of all vocal works discussed in the book to enable the student to follow the music by paying attention to the words. For works in foreign languages, both the original and English translations are given.

In addition to the glossary, the back of the book includes an extensive list of suggested readings.

SUPPLEMENTS

Three supplements have been prepared for use with the fourth edition. The recordings prepared by C.B.S. Records contain many of the pieces that are discussed in the text. These recordings provide the basic listening experiences which may be expanded and enriched by the additional listening suggested at the end of each chapter.

The *Instructor's Manual* includes detailed charts showing how the text can be adapted to a one-quarter and a one-semester course. The *Student Workbook and Listening Guide* offers exercises aimed at improving listening skills and questions which test mastery of text material.

ACKNOWLEDGMENTS

It is my happy privilege to acknowledge and express my thanks for the advice and help extended to me in the task of preparing the fourth edition of *Exploring Music*.

The advice of Dr. Franklin S. Miller of the University of Wisconsin–Milwaukee Department of Music was extremely helpful. I am indebted to Robert Kean Turner for providing an understanding of the text of *Dirge* in Benjamin Britten's *Serenade for Tenor, Horn and Strings*. Every imaginable library service was quickly and cheerfully forthcoming from the staff of the Golda Meir Library including William Roselle, Director; Richard E. Jones, Director of Acquisitions; Linda B. Hartig, Music Librarian; and Patricia C. Wiese, Audio Center Supervisor and her staff.

Katherine Busch and Catherine Lutz provided expert research and editorial assistance; and the good natured patience and unfailing skill of Mary Anne McCoy and Laurel Sukup in the preparation of the revised manuscript was indispensable.

R. John Specht of Queensborough Community College prepared the listening guides and provided advice on other aspects of this fourth edition. The work of the staff of Wm. C. Brown Publishers under the leadership of Raphael Kadushin and Meredith Morgan was of a high professional standard from beginning to end in matters great and small.

I am also grateful for the thoughtful criticisms and suggestions of the following reviewers, who read all or portions of the manuscript: Ann C. Anderson, University of Minnesota, Duluth; Al Carnine, Missouri Southern State College; Katherine Charlton, Mt. San Antonio College; Harold E. Griswold, Towson State University; Helen A. Hoff, Colorado State University; James A. Keene, Western Illinois University; William L. Kellogg, University of Southern Colorado; Roy Magers, Winthrop College; Alan G. Schmidt, Erie Community College South; John Specht, Queensborough Community College; Elizabeth Weber, Chicago State University.

Robert Hickok
Irvine, California

EXPLORING MUSIC

FUNDAMENTALS OF MUSIC

© Susanne Kaspar/Leo de Wys, Inc.

1 : MUSICAL SOUND

W e are a people surrounded by sounds. The roar of airplanes, the rumble of automobiles, the blare of horns, the screech of sirens, and many other types of sounds constitute an ever-present aspect of the day-to-day environment in which most of us live. In addition to these random sounds, the average American is subjected to a constant flow of music. We experience music almost continuously—the phonograph as we chat, the radio while driving, Muzak in the supermarket, the restaurant, and place of employment. What student lounge is without music? Indeed, from playpen to funeral parlor, we are bombarded by the sounds of music. Although we hear these sounds, we often hear them only as a vague background against which more immediate activity takes place. Most of us do not really understand or respond to such music, which is merely part of the atmosphere. To be fully alive to music, we must learn to listen with curiosity and care, with attention to the flow of musical sound. An important aid in developing skill at this kind of listening is some understanding of the nature of the materials out of which music is made.

Music is built from particular elements and described by a particular vocabulary. In these first chapters, then, we will introduce the elements of music and establish the vocabulary used to explore and discuss them.

Musical sound is not like the random noise we experience. Rather, it is highly organized and displays four general characteristics—**pitch,** its highness or lowness; **duration,** its longness or shortness; **volume,** its loudness or softness; and **timbre,** its tone quality.

PITCH

A sound, any sound, is the result of vibrations set in motion by the activation of a sounding body—the slamming of a door, the ringing of a bell. In the case of a *musical* sound, the rate of vibrations is definite and steady, producing a **tone.** The precise pitch, the exact highness or lowness of the tone, is determined by the *frequency* of its vibration—the *faster* the frequency, the *higher* the pitch and, conversely, the *slower* the frequency, the *lower* the pitch.

For instance, if we pluck a string, it vibrates at a certain rate of frequency and produces a tone of a certain pitch. If we *shorten* the string, the tone it produces will be *higher;* if we *lengthen* the string, the pitch of the tone will be *lower.*

While the human ear is capable of perceiving pitches ranging from sixteen vibrations to twenty thousand vibrations per second, the outer limits for musical purposes range from about twenty to five thousand vibrations per second and most of the music we hear normally employs a much narrower pitch range. The piano, for instance, ranges in pitch from 27 vibrations per second, the lowest tone, to the highest tone with 4,186 vibrations per second.

Other things, such as volume and duration, being equal, two tones sound different because they have different pitches. The *distance* between two pitches is called an **interval.** Intervals can be small or large depending upon the pitches involved.

Example 1.1

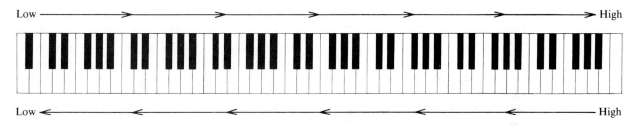

Each key of the piano represents a specific pitch which is sounded when the key is pressed. If you begin with any key and press successive keys to your *right,* each tone produced is slightly *higher* than the one before it—the interval between the two tones is small. If you skip a few keys, the interval between the two is larger. Beginning on any *white* key (such as key 1 in example 1.2) and moving upward (to your right) on the white keys, you will discover that the tone produced by the eighth key sounds very much like the tone produced by key number 1. These two tones are so much alike that the upper tone is heard as a higher *duplicate* of the lower tone and vice versa and are referred to by the same name (see pitch notation on pages 6–9). The interval formed by these two tones is called an **octave.** If we continue the process, starting with the eighth key, we come to the same result—another tone that sounds the same on a higher pitch level—an octave higher.

Example 1.2

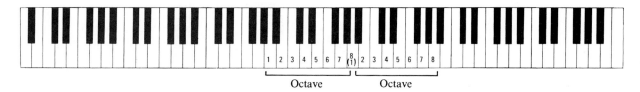

Each and every pitch has its upper and lower octave duplicates—a fact that makes the interval of the octave very important.

Returning to the piano keyboard, we find that *within* the octave there are other pitches represented by the black and white keys. The tones produced by the succession of white and black keys fills the octave with twelve different pitches, the thirteenth being an octave duplicate of the first.

The distance between each pair of tones in example 1.3 is the interval of the **half step (semi-tone),** the smallest interval used in most music in Western society. These twelve pitches and their upper and lower octave duplicates constitute the total pitch resource out of which composers select their materials and fashion them into melody and harmony which we will examine in the next chapter.

Example 1.3

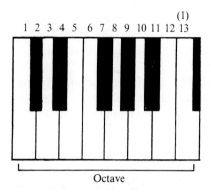

Octave

Notation of Pitch

Pitches are named using the first seven letters of the alphabet ABCDEFG, this sequence being repeated over and over through upper and lower octaves. These letter names apply to the white keys of the piano as shown in example 1.4. (The key labeled **"middle C"** is located approximately in the middle of the keyboard as a point of reference.)

Example 1.4

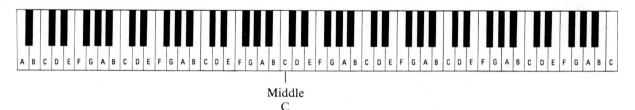

Middle
C

In musical **notation,** the pitch of a tone is indicated by the position of a symbol (𝅝 or 𝅗𝅥 or 𝅘𝅥, for example) called a **note** on a graph-like structure called a **staff,** consisting of five lines and four spaces. Each line and each space represents a different note.

Example 1.5

The higher the position of the note on the staff, the higher the pitch of the tone:

Example 1.6

Pitches which are too high or too low to be written on the staff are notated by using **ledger lines** above or below the staff:

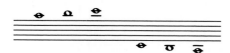

Example 1.7

The staff location of specific pitches is indicated by a **clef** sign placed at the beginning of the staff. The G clef or **treble clef** (𝄞) is used for higher pitches and designates the second line of the staff as the pitch "G."

G A B C D E F G

Example 1.8

The F clef or **bass clef** (𝄢) is used for lower pitches and designates the fourth line as the pitch "F":

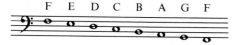

F E D C B A G F

Example 1.9

The treble clef is used to notate music for the violin, flute and other instruments that play in the higher pitch-ranges; the bass clef is used for instruments that play in lower ranges such as the violoncello and bassoon.

For keyboard music, *both* clefs are used on what is called the **grand staff:**

Example 1.10

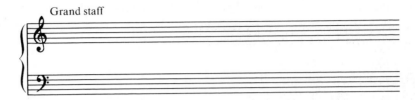

Grand staff

The notes written in the treble clef are usually played by the right hand; the bass clef used by the left hand.

Example 1.11 shows notes on the grand staff correlated with the white keys of the piano:

Example 1.11

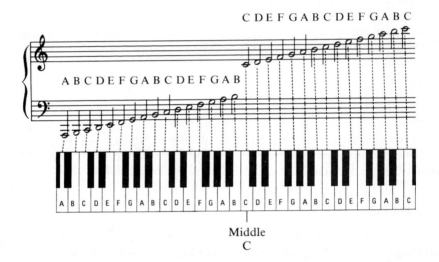

Middle
C

Pitches represented by the *black* keys of the piano are notated by the use of two symbols: the **sharp** (♯) which *raises* the pitch of the note to which it is applied and the **flat** (♭) which *lowers* the pitch.

For instance, the black key between the white keys C and D is regarded as either a raised C, (C♯) or a lowered D, (D♭). C♯ and D♭, therefore, are two ways of designating the *same pitch:*

Example 1.12

C sharp or D flat

or   (Same pitch)

The same is true of the other black keys and the pitches they represent: D sharp or E flat; F sharp or G flat; and A sharp or B flat.

Example 1.13

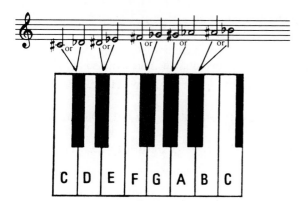

(The symbol called a **natural** (♮) is employed to cancel the effect of a sharp or a flat.)

DURATION

The element of *time* is extremely important in the art of music. The flow of music creates the illusion of the passage of time—a very special kind of time that exists on many levels as we shall discover when we consider *rhythm* in the next chapter.

On its most fundamental level, musical time has to do with the relative longness or shortness of individual sounds.

Notation of Duration

The principle underlying duration and its notation is fairly simple. Time values are expressed in *relative* terms. A **whole note** (𝅝) lasts twice as long as a **half note** (𝅗𝅥). A half note lasts twice as long as a **quarter note** (𝅘𝅥) which lasts twice as long as an **eighth note** (𝅘𝅥𝅮) and so on:

1 whole note

𝅝

Example 1.14

2 half notes

𝅗𝅥 𝅗𝅥

4 quarter notes

𝅘𝅥 𝅘𝅥 𝅘𝅥 𝅘𝅥

8 eighth notes

𝅘𝅥𝅮 𝅘𝅥𝅮 𝅘𝅥𝅮 𝅘𝅥𝅮 𝅘𝅥𝅮𝅘𝅥𝅮 𝅘𝅥𝅮𝅘𝅥𝅮

16 sixteenth notes

𝅘𝅥𝅯 𝅘𝅥𝅯 𝅘𝅥𝅯 𝅘𝅥𝅯 𝅘𝅥𝅯𝅘𝅥𝅯𝅘𝅥𝅯𝅘𝅥𝅯 𝅘𝅥𝅯𝅘𝅥𝅯𝅘𝅥𝅯𝅘𝅥𝅯 𝅘𝅥𝅯𝅘𝅥𝅯𝅘𝅥𝅯𝅘𝅥𝅯

Notice that eighth notes that look like quarter notes with single **flags** attached may be written separately (♪♪) or may be grouped together by a connecting **beam** (♫). The same is true of sixteenth notes (♫♫) which have two flags when written separately and are grouped by a double beam (♬♬). Further subdivision is used such as thirty-second (♫) and sixty-fourth (♫) notes.

So far we have considered the division of each successive "long" note by two: a whole note = two half notes; a half note = two quarter notes and so on. Divisions by three are indicated by adding a "3" above the *shorter* notes producing a **triplet:**

Example 1.15

The length of a note can be extended by the use of a **tie** (‿)

Example 1.16

or by placing a **dot** (•) to the right of the note. The dot extends the note by half its original length.

Example 1.17

The duration of *silence* is just as important as the duration of sound and is indicated by the use of a symbol called a **rest:**

Example 1.18

Whole rest   Half rest   Quarter rest   Eighth rest   Sixteenth rest

These rests are equivalent to the note values discussed previously.

VOLUME (DYNAMICS)

Musical dynamics have to do with the relative degree of loudness or softness in the flow of music. Along with pitch and duration, the relative shades of volume, loudness and softness, are important in determining the character of music.

Notation of Volume (Dynamics)

Written indication of the dynamic aspect of music is less precise than that relating to pitch and duration because there is no absolute standard for degrees of loudness and softness. The *performer* has a great deal of latitude in the interpretation and execution of dynamic indications provided by the composer.

These dynamic indications consist of a set of words and signs placed below or above the staff. By tradition most dynamic instructions are indicated by the use of terms in Italian.

pianissimo (*pp*) very soft
piano (*p*) soft
mezzo piano (*mp*) moderately soft
mezzo forte (*mf*) moderately loud
forte (*f*) loud
fortissimo (*ff*) very loud

Intensified extremes of dynamic levels are indicated by *ppp* or *pppp* and *fff* or *ffff*.

To indicate *gradual* change from one dynamic level to another the following signs and terms are used:

crescendo (cresc.)   ◁—————   gradually louder

decrescendo (decresc.)
diminuendo (dim.)   —————▷   gradually softer

TIMBRE (TONE COLOR)

Each type of musical instrument has its own distinct kind of sound. A melody played on the oboe sounds different from the same melody played on the trumpet because the sound quality of the trumpet is clearly different from that of the oboe. As we mentioned earlier, the distinctive sound quality of an instrument is called tone color or **timbre**. The elements that contribute to the tone color of an instrument are various and include the nature of the material out of which the instrument is constructed and the method by which it is made to sound (such as a plucked instrument as opposed to one into which air is blown).

Instruments differ from each other in regard to tone color on several levels. The most obvious difference is between families of instruments. As a group, brass instruments (trumpet, French horn, trombone, and tuba) sound quite unlike the woodwinds (flute, oboe, clarinet, and bassoon), and both these instrument groups contrast sharply in sound with the string family (violin, viola, cello, and string bass). Within each instrument family there is a certain similarity of sound which distinguishes that family as a whole.

While the difference between the tone color of one instrument family and that of another is fairly obvious, there is a more subtle contrast in timbre among instruments in a single family. For instance, the flute and the oboe, both of which are woodwinds, sound quite distinct from each other; similarly, the violin and cello each sound unique. On a still more subtle level, a considerable variety of tone colors can be produced on a single instrument. For example, the flute can be manipulated to produce shades of tone color ranging from "bright" to "velvety" and from "piercing" to "warm."

Nineteenth-century composers were especially intrigued by the uses of tone color. It was during the romantic era that color came to be regarded for the first time as an element as important as melody, harmony, and rhythm. Many modern composers share this view and continue to explore the expressive possibilities of tone color, using not only conventional instruments, but also electronic media and nonmusical sounds as well.

SUMMARY

In the preceding pages we have described the qualities of musical sound—those properties that distinguish musical sounds from simple, random noises. Musical sounds have pitch, the quality of being high or low; they exist in durations of varying lengths; they can be produced at varying levels of intensity, or volume; and they are imbued with distinctive tone colors. The desired pitch, duration, and intensity of musical sound can be expressed, though not always with precision, in a system of written notation.

Thus far we have been dealing with the raw material of music, not music itself. Individual sounds achieve musical significance only when one tone relates to another and groups of tones relate to other groups, organized in the time flow they create. The next two chapters will consider musical relationships and musical organization.

NEW TERMS

duration
volume
timbre
pitch
    tone
    interval
    octave
    half step (semi-tone)
    middle C
notation of pitch
    note
    staff
    ledger lines
    clef (bass; treble)
    grand staff
    sharp
    flat
    natural

notation of duration
    whole note
    half note
    quarter note

eighth note
flag
beam
triplet
tie
dot
whole rest
half rest
quarter rest
eighth rest
sixteenth rest
volume (dynamics)
    pianissimo
    piano
    mezzo piano
    mezzo forte
    forte
    fortissimo
    crescendo
    decrescendo (diminuendo)
timbre (tone color)

2 : MUSICAL ELEMENTS

|| I || n chapter 1 we concentrated upon the characteristics of musical sounds. This chapter deals with the various kinds of relationships *among* sounds and the resulting musical elements known as **melody, harmony, tonality** and **rhythm.** These are the primary ingredients out of which a piece of music is fashioned.

MELODY

When we listen to music, we are usually drawn first to a melody. We tend to follow the melodic flow with the greatest interest and ease, and, in general, it is the melody that lingers with us. When we think of a piece of music, we tend to recall the melody or melodies that for us represent the piece.

We can define a melodic line or **melody** as a series of pitches and time values that sound one after another. Melody gives music a sense of movement up and down through space as it moves forward in time. Different melodies follow different patterns of movement. For example, the melodic line in example 2.1 gives the impression of moving upward.

Example 2.1 Handel, *Messiah,* "Every valley."

On the other hand, a melody—even one with some upward skips—can also give a sense of moving downward (example 2.2):

shall be re - veal - ed

Example 2.2 Handel, *Messiah,* "And the Glory of the Lord."

In comparison, the following melody seems anchored. Its movement is evenly distributed around a particular tone (example 2.3).

for the mouth of the Lord hath spo - ken it.

Example 2.3 Handel, *Messiah,* "And the Glory of the Lord."

Melodic movement can be smooth and even, as the preceding examples show. It can also be jerky and angular, leaping over a wide span of pitches (example 2.4):

the crook - ed straight, the crook - ed straight and rough pla-ces plain

Example 2.4 Handel, *Messiah,* "Every Valley."

A melody consists of two inseparable, interacting elements: a succession of *pitches* and a succession of *time values* (durations). The "highs and lows" of pitch and the "longs and shorts" of duration combine to give a melody its particular shape and form, its "personality."

The character of melody is an extremely important aspect of any piece of music. In a long piece of music some melodies assume a greater importance than others. Melodies that contain central musical ideas are called **themes.** In the course of a musical composition important themes may be stated and restated in many different forms. Later in this text we will see how themes are developed in a variety of musical works.

HARMONY

While a piece of music consisting of a single melodic line can be complete in and of itself (see Gregorian chant, p. 89), most Western music depends heavily on harmony to help give it structure and to enhance its expressiveness. We speak of melody as the horizontal aspect of music since it consists of pitches sounding one after another, in a linear fashion. Harmony, on the other hand, involves the vertical aspect of music, the tones that sound together. A **harmony** is a composite sound made up of two or more tones of different pitch that sound simultaneously. The smallest harmonic unit is one consisting of two tones. A harmony of three or more tones is called a **chord.**

The tones that make up a chord are heard not only individually; they also blend together into a composite sound that has its own distinctive qualities.

Chords can appear in "solid" form (example 2.5) or in "broken" form, with the notes played in rapid succession (example 2.6).

Example 2.5

Example 2.6

A broken chord is called an **arpeggio.**

As a musical element harmony functions in a variety of ways. Harmonies are often used to support and amplify melodic lines. A particularly distinctive series of harmonies, or *harmonic progression,* often becomes an important element in its own right. In addition, the harmonic qualities of **consonance** and **dissonance** contribute to the energy and interest of a piece of music.

Consonance and Dissonance

One important quality of a given harmony is its degree of consonance or dissonance. A consonant harmony imparts a sense of stability, simplicity, and repose. In contrast, a dissonant harmony creates a feeling of complexity, instability, and the necessity of movement.

Dissonance is important in creating a feeling of tension in the musical flow. Without points of tension the music would quickly become boring and lifeless. Dissonance usually occurs as a transient tension in a harmonic progression. This tension is immediately relieved by the resolution of the dissonant harmony into a consonant harmony. Thus, the movement from dissonance to consonance contributes to the balance between movement and rest that makes music vital and coherent.

The general character of some pieces is consonant, even though some dissonance may be employed. Haydn's String Quartet in C, op. 33, no. 3 (side 4, selection 1) is a good example. Other works are predominantly dissonant, such as Schoenberg's Variations for Orchestra, op. 31 (side 13, selection 1). As we move through music history from century to century, we find that the relationship of consonance and dissonance begins to change, with a gradual increase in the importance or prevalence of dissonance as we approach the twentieth century. Indeed, most of the serious concert music written today is predominantly dissonant.

TONALITY (KEY)

One of the striking characteristics of Western music is its reliance on **tonality** as an organizing element. *Tonal music* is characterized by the presence of a central tone called the **tonic** and the chord built on that tone, called the **tonic chord.** The tonic chord acts as the musical center of gravity, a kind of "home base" in a piece of music. It is the point of rest from which the musical flow departs and to which it returns, creating a sense of convincing conclusion.

Although there are several ways of establishing a tonal center, the most familiar method is embodied in the **major-minor system** of scales.

A **scale** (sometimes called a *mode*) is a series of ascending or descending pitches in a certain pattern. What is called the **major scale** consists of eight notes filling the octave with the following pattern between notes:

whole step, whole step, half step, whole step, whole step, whole step, half step

as illustrated using only the white keys of the piano in example 2.7.

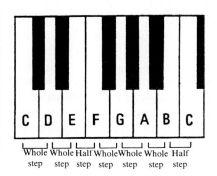

Example 2.7

This is the C major scale. It begins and ends on the note C, its tonic. The tonic chord of a major scale is a *major chord.* A stretch of music written on the basis of this scale is said to be in the tonality or **key** of C major.

The major scale can be built on any one of the twelve pitches (white and black keys) using the fixed pattern of whole steps and half steps previously mentioned.

The **minor scale** also consists of eight tones filling an octave but in a different arrangement of whole steps and half steps producing a quality which is quite different from the major scale. The third tone in the minor scale is a *half step* rather than a whole step above the second tone, making the tonic chord a *minor chord* and imparting a distinctive character. The upper part of the minor scale assumes different forms depending upon the musical context.

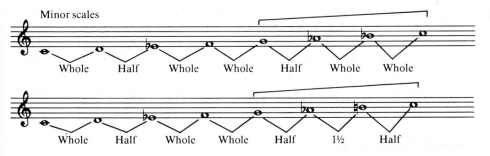

Example 2.8

This is the C minor scale. It begins and ends on the note C which is its tonic. The tonic chord of a minor scale is a *minor chord*. A stretch of music written on the basis of this scale is in the tonality or key of C minor. The minor scale can be constructed beginning with any one of the twelve tones contained in the octave.

Major and minor scales and the music constructed from them differ considerably in character but they have in common the strong sense of tonality—a clearly felt tonal center. The tonic note and the chord built upon it are supported by the other tones and chords in the scale. Melodically, the seventh tone in the scale, called the **leading tone** has a strong "pull" into the tonic—it *leads* to the tonic. If we play the scale of C major and stop on the seventh tone,

Example 2.9

the listener is left with an unsettling feeling of incompleteness. The ear expects to hear the tonic tone. Without it, no sense of finality is achieved. Once the C is played, however, "home base" has been reached and there is a convincing sense of completeness.

While the *leading tone* is the strongest *melodic* force supporting the tonic, the **dominant chord** (the chord built on the fifth note in the scale) performs the same function in the realm of *harmony*. The dominant chord demands *resolution* to the tonic chord in the same way the leading tone creates the need for the tonic tone. The dominant to tonic harmonic progression is an important force in most of the musical styles we will deal with later.

Modulation

In addition to the relationships among tones and chords *within* a key, tonality also refers to the relationship *among keys*. A piece of music of any appreciable length seldom stays in one key. When we say that a piece of music is "in C major," we actually mean that the piece *begins* and *ends* in that key. Within the piece different keys are introduced, thereby providing an important aspect of variety. The process of shifting from one key to another is known as **modulation.** The diagram below illustrates one of the most frequent modulations found in Western music, that growing out of the tonic-dominant relationship.

Section A	Section B	Return of Section A
C major (tonic key)	G major (key of the dominant)	C major

RHYTHM

All the elements discussed thus far come together and interact to create the sense of movement in time. Everyone has had the experience of being so caught up in an enjoyable activity that time seems to fly by. Similarly, the same amount of time spent doing something we dislike can seem interminable. Thus the way we experience time is on the basis of the events that occur during the course of an hour or a day. Without these events there would be less sense of the passage of time. Musical time is similar to this kind of "personal" time. It is perceived and experienced on the basis of musical events that occur. If we play a single tone over and over again for two minutes, it may seem as though a long period of time has elapsed. However, if we fill that two minutes with a cheerful and interesting melody, the same length of time will seem quite short. Although the length of time is the same, the experiences differ because the quality and character of the time are structured differently by the musical events that take place.

Like "personal" time, the passage of musical time is created by change. One tone leading to another in a melody, the progression from one harmony to another, the movement from one key to another—these and many other musical "incidents" work together to create the sense of musical time. The element that encompasses all aspects of musical time is called **rhythm.** Musical time consists of two different aspects—*regularity* and *diversity*.

Beat

If you clap along while singing or listening to the familiar patriotic song "America the Beautiful," it is probable that you would clap as follows, (X = clap):

Example 2.10

In doing so, you are instinctively responding to the **beat** of the music. Beats are the most basic units of musical time. Instead of measuring the duration of individual tones in seconds or fractions of seconds by the clock, we use the beat as a measuring device. Each tone is judged as lasting one beat, several beats, or a fraction of a beat. Once we have picked out the beat at the beginning of the composition, we became accustomed to it and expect that it will continue. The regular beat is fundamental to our response to music.

Against this background of regularly occurring pulsations, notes of varying lengths make some beats more prominent than others.

Meter

As you sing or listen to the beginning of "America the Beautiful," you will find that certain beats have more "weight" than others:

Example 2.11

Oh beau - ti - ful   for   spa - cious skies   for   am - ber waves of grain

Because of their longer duration and placement, the notes marked ⊗ stand out. The fact that these prominent notes happen at *regular intervals* creates a new kind of regular pulsation which groups the beats into equal units of four beats each.

Example 2.12

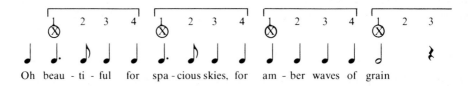

Oh beau - ti - ful   for   spa - cious skies, for   am - ber waves of grain

This grouping of beats into equal units is called **meter** and the units themselves are called **measures.** There are several types of meter defined by the number of beats in the measure. The most common are:

Two beats to the measure (**1**2,**1**2) *duple meter* ("Yankee Doddle")
Four beats to the measure (**1**234,**1**234) *quadruple meter* ("America the Beautiful")
Three beats to the measure (**1**23,**1**23) *triple meter* ("Star Spangled Banner")

More complicated meters with more beats to the measure are also used. Inherent in all meters is the fact that the first beat in the measure is stressed or **accented.**

Notation of Meter

Two notation devices are used to indicate meter: the **time signature** and the **bar line.**

The time signature consists of two numbers, one above the other. The top number indicates the number of beats per measure; the bottom number indicates the kind of note getting the beat. For instance:

3 ———— Three beats to the measure
4 ———— Quarter note (♩) equals one beat

4 ———— Four beats to the measure
2 ———— Half note (♩) equals one beat

6 ———— Six beats to the measure
8 ———— Eighth note (♪) equals one beat

The bar line is a vertical line drawn through the staff separating one measure from the next. (Note: the beat *before* the bar line is called the **up-beat;** the beat after the bar line is called the **down-beat.**)

Example 2.13

Oh   beau - ti - ful   for   spa-cious skies, for   am - ber waves of   grain

Syncopation

Ordinarily the first beat of a measure is stressed or *accented*. A piece in triple meter, for example, has a *one*-two-three accentual character. When the accent falls somewhere other than on the first beat—on another beat or in between beats where it is *unexpected*—the rhythm is **syncopated.** Syncopation is a favorite device in jazz.

Tempo

All aspects of musical time are very much affected by the **tempo** of the music. The tempo is determined by the rate of speed of the beat—if the beat is quick, the tempo is *fast;* a slow beat results in a *slow* tempo.

Tempo Indications

Indications concerning tempo are usually given in Italian at the beginning of the piece or section of the piece:

Very slow:	*Largo* (broad)
	Grave (grave, solemn)
Slow:	*Lento*
	Adagio (leisurely; literally, at ease)
Moderate:	*Andante* (at a walking pace)
	Moderato
Fast:	*Allegretto*
	Allegro (faster than allegretto; literally, cheerful)
Very fast:	*Vivace* (vivacious)
	Presto (very quick)
	Prestissimo (as fast as possible)

These basic terms can be modified by adding such words as *molto* (very), *meno* (less), *poco* (a little), and *ma non troppo* (not too much). For example, *allegro molto* is very fast; *poco adagio* is somewhat slow; and *allegro non troppo* is fast but not too fast. Gradual changes in tempo are indicated by such words as *accelerando* (getting faster) and *ritardando* (becoming slower). To reestablish the original tempo, the term *a tempo* is used.

Tempo can be altered in other ways. The term **rubato** indicates freedom to move ahead and fall behind the tempo and the symbol ⌢ (**fermata**) tells the performer to hold the note longer than its normal time value—suspending the meter and tempo for the moment.

As was the case with dynamic indications, tempo indications are approximate and relative, leaving a great deal of discretion to the performer.

LEVELS OF TIME

As we have seen, musical time exists simultaneously on different levels; on the most fundamental level—the *beat.* On a higher level, the grouping of beats into longer units of equality—the *measure.* On yet still a higher level are longer segments of musical time consisting of groups of measures. These larger units are called **phrases.** If we examine the entire melody of "America the Beautiful," we find that it consists of four phrases, each consisting of eight measures:

Example 2.14

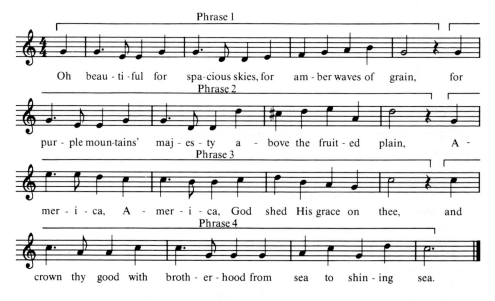

With the concept of the musical **phrase,** we enter the realm of musical form, a major subject in our next chapter.

SUMMARY

Melody is the element of music we tend to follow with the greatest ease. A melody consists of two inseparable, interacting elements: a succession of pitches and a succession of time values. Moving in a linear fashion through space and forward in time, melody represents the horizontal aspect of music.

Harmony is an expressive and structural element, representing the vertical aspect of music. The tones of a harmony are heard not only individually, but as a composite sound. The smallest harmony consists of two tones; chords are harmonies of three or more tones. Harmonies are usually described as consonant (in repose) or dissonant (in a state of tension).

Tonal music is characterized by the affirmation of a central tone, the *tonic,* which is the first degree of the scale. The principle of tonality involves relationships among tones and chords *within* a key and also relationships *among* keys. Modulations, or shifts from one key to another, are usually employed in larger works of music as one means of providing musical interest and variety.

Rhythm encompasses all aspects of musical time. It includes, but is not confined to, meter—the grouping of beats into regular units. Meter imposes equality and regularity by providing the basic groupings within which the listener organizes sound. Rhythmic variation lends diversity and inequality.

NEW TERMS

melody (melodic)
  theme
harmony (harmonic)
  chord
  arpeggio
  consonance
  dissonance
tonality (tonal)
  tonic
  tonic chord
  major-minor system
  scale (mode, major, minor)
  key
  leading tone
  dominant chord
  modulation

rhythm
  beat
  meter (metrical)
  measure
  accent
  time signature
  bar line
  up-beat
  down-beat
  syncopation
  tempo
  rubato
  fermata
  phrase

MUSICAL ORGANIZATION

We have seen that combinations of individual sounds produce the basic elements of music: melody, harmony, tonality and rhythm. In this chapter we explore the ways these elements are combined to create musical texture, musical form, and musical style.

MUSICAL TEXTURE

Like cloth, music is woven of horizontal and vertical strands. We think of melody as moving horizontally, because one tone follows the next along the flow of time. We describe harmony as vertical because it is based upon sounds that happen simultaneously—on top of one another.

Musical **texture** is created by the ways that these vertical and horizontal strands are interwoven. There are three basic musical textures: **monophony, polyphony,** and **homophony.**

Monophony

Monophonic music (monophony literally means "one sound") consists of a single melodic line with no accompaniment. If you sing or hum by yourself, you are creating monophonic music (example 3.1).

Example 3.1
Monophony, single voice.

Similarly, when many people sing exactly the same notes at the same time (in unison) or the same note an octave apart, the texture is also monophonic (example 3.2).

Monophony, two voices an octave apart.

A good example of monophony is the chant, "Salve Regina," discussed in chapter 6.

SALVE REGINA
SIDE 1/SELECTION 1

Polyphony

Music consisting of two or more "independent" melodic lines that are roughly equal in their melodic and rhythmic interest has a texture known as **polyphony.**

In example 3.3, both voices sing the same melody. But because the lower voice begins later than the first, we hear two *independent* lines of music. It can be said that the second voice *imitates* the first—it sings exactly the same melody immediately after the first voice. Music that uses this device is known as **imitative polyphony.** Examples of imitative polyphony are the motet, *Ave Maria* by Josquin des Prez in chapter 6, and Fugue in G Minor by J. S. Bach, discussed in chapter 8.

AVE MARIA
SIDE 1/SELECTION 3
FUGUE IN G MINOR
SIDE 2/SELECTION 2

Independence and equality of voices are the defining characteristics of polyphony. A **voice** is a single line of music; independence is its ability to compete with other melodic strands for the attention of the listener.

In polyphonic music we are interested in the relationship of the independent, simultaneous melodies. Our attention will shift from one melodic line to another, depending on which is most important at any given moment. The melodic lines thus enhance and enrich each other, contributing to the expressiveness of the overall sound. The interplay of melodies which characterizes polyphonic music is known as **counterpoint,** and polyphonic music is also termed **contrapuntal.**

Example 3.3 Polyphony.

Homophony

In **homophonic** music, a *single* melodic line predominates, while the other voices or instruments provide harmonic **accompaniment.** The listeners' attention is focused on the melody; the harmonic accompaniment is heard as a kind of musical background.

In example 3.4 the voices sing the melodic line while the piano provides harmonic accompaniment.

Example 3.4
Homophony.

MUSICAL INSTRUMENTS AND ENSEMBLES

|T| he musical instruments available to the composer offer a wide variety of pitch ranges, modes of articulation and tone colors. They are traditionally grouped into six categories or families—**voices, strings, woodwinds, brasses, percussion, keyboard, and electronic.**

VOICES

Because it is part of the human body, the voice is in many respects our most fundamental musical instrument, the expressive qualities of which are greatly enhanced by its ability to combine music and words.

Individual voices vary in pitch range, but male and female voice types are generally divided into high, middle and low **registers.** Arranged from highest to lowest pitch register, the basic vocal categories are:

Female*
{
Soprano
Mezzo Soprano
Contralto (Alto)

Male
{
Tenor
Baritone
Bass

*The "female registers" are also sung by young boys with unchanged voices.

STRINGS

The string family has two branches—those that are *bowed* and those that are *plucked*.

Bowed Instruments

From highest to lowest pitch register the bowed instruments are:

> **Violin**—noted for its lyric expressiveness. The neck is held by the left hand, the tail rests beneath the player's chin.
> **Viola**—produces a more sombre tone quality than the violin. Held in the same way as the violin.
> **Violoncello**—usually referred to as simply *cello*. Because of its size, it rests on the floor and is held upright between the player's knees.
> **Double Bass**—or *string bass* is the largest and lowest voiced member of the family. Because of its size, the player stands or sits on a stool to play it.

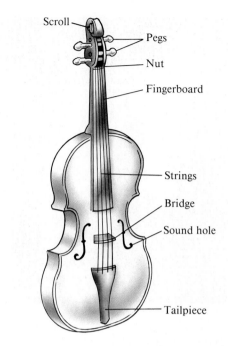

Scroll

Pegs

Nut

Fingerboard

Strings

Bridge

Sound hole

Tailpiece

Tip

Bow-stick

Hairs

Frog

With the exception of size, these instruments are similar in construction as illustrated by the violin in figure 4.2.

Each of its four strings is stretched between two fixed points, with one end attached to a *peg* on the neck of the instrument and the other to the *tailpiece* at the base of the instrument's body. The strings pass over the *bridge* which holds them away from the *fingerboard* allowing them to vibrate. The strings are tuned to specific pitches by adjusting the tension by tightening or loosening the pegs to which the strings are attached.

The instrument is made to sound by drawing the *bow* (fig. 4.3) across the string causing it to vibrate.

The player determines the pitch produced by the string by using the fingers of the left hand to press the string against the fingerboard, thereby adjusting the length of the string. This is known as **stopping** the string.

A variety of musical effects can be achieved by using different bowing techniques.

Figure 4.4 Itzhak
Perlman, violinist.

Legato—smooth and connected up and down strokes of the bow
Staccato—short and detached strokes of the bow
Tremolo—very rapid strokes of the bow

The tone quality of the instrument can be made richer or warmer by the use of **vibrato,** rapid vibration of the left hand while pressing the string against the finger board. And a subdued, velvety tone is produced by the use of a **mute,** a device clamped onto the bridge.

When the player plucks the string, the result is short, crisp notes. Plucking is called **pizzicato.**

The violin, viola, cello, and string bass are among the most important instruments in the history of Western music. They constitute the backbone of the symphony orchestra and are used extensively in chamber music. All of them, particularly the violin, are used as solo instruments and the double bass ("bass fiddle") is frequently used in jazz ensembles.

Figure 4.5 The violoncello.

Figure 4.6 The largest and lowest-voiced member of the violin family, the double bass (or string bass) is played standing.

During the Renaissance and Baroque periods of music history, the five members of the *viola da gamba* family were the basic string instruments. They are similar to the violin family in appearance but they produce a much lighter and more nasal tone quality. All of them are played in the cello position, between the player's knees.

Plucked Instruments

Today the prominent instruments in this branch of the string family are the **harp** and the **guitar.**

The harp is used as a solo instrument and is a member of the symphony orchestra. The modern harp has forty-seven strings stretched vertically in a triangular frame. Seven pedals at its base are used to adjust the pitch of the strings. The guitar has become popular as a solo instrument and is used widely in folk, jazz, rock, and country and western music.

Figure 4.7 A stringed instrument played by plucking, the harp has foot pedals that alter the pitch of the strings.

WOODWINDS

Woodwind instruments produce sound when air is blown through the tube-like body of the instrument. The length of the vibrating air column is controlled by opening or closing small holes along the side of the instrument with fingers or pads activated by a key mechanism. In closing or opening the *fingerholes,* the player lengthens or shortens the air column thereby lowering or raising the pitch of the tones produced.

The most commonly used woodwind instruments from highest to lowest in pitch-range are the **flute*, clarinet, oboe,** and **bassoon.** The difference in tone quality among these instruments is more pronounced than that among the members of the string family. Each has its own very distinctive sound caused, in part, by the different ways of blowing air into the instrument.

The flute is **edge blown.** The player activates the column of air inside the instrument by blowing across a hole called the embouchure hole. The other instruments use a vibrating **reed**—a small strip of cane—through which the player blows air into the instrument.

Clarinets use a *single reed.* Oboes and bassoons use a *double reed,* two pieces of cane fastened together. The flute, oboe, clarinet, and bassoon are used as solo instruments in chamber music groups and as members of larger performing groups such as wind ensembles, bands, and the symphony orchestra.

Figure 4.8 The flute is highest in pitch-range among the most commonly used woodwind instruments.

---

*In the twentieth century, this instrument came to be made of metal rather than wood.

Figure 4.9 (a) The oboe, being played by the late Marcel Tabuteau, and (b) English horn.

(a)   (b)

Figure 4.10 Fuller in tone than the oboe, the clarinet is capable of producing rapid runs and trills.

In the symphony orchestra and concert wind ensembles, this basic group of woodwinds is often expanded to include other instruments in order to provide a greater overall pitch range and an expanded variety of tone color. Often included in this expanded group are the **piccolo** (little flute), the **English Horn** (a lower version of the oboe), the **bass clarinet,** and the **contrabassoon** (the lowest pitch range among woodwinds).

(a)

(b)

Figure 4.11 (a) The bassoon and (b) contrabassoon.

From highest pitch range to lowest this expanded woodwind group is:
    piccolo
    flute
    oboe
    English Horn
    clarinet
    bass clarinet
    bassoon
    contrabassoon

The **recorder,** in its various sizes and pitch ranges, was popular in the Renaissance and baroque eras. It is **end blown** and produces a tone similar in quality to that of a flute.

The **saxophone,** invented in the mid-nineteenth century by Adolphe Sax of Brussels, is a single reed instrument with a body made of brass. Although it is most commonly encountered as a jazz instrument, it is sometimes employed as a solo instrument in the symphony orchestra and as a member of bands and wind ensembles. In the twentieth century it has been developed as a solo concert instrument.

Figure 4.12 The saxophone is important in jazz and dance bands.

Figure 4.13 The Candadian Brass Quintet, consisting of Ronald Romm (left) and Fred Mills on trumpets, David Ohanian, French horn, Charles Deallenbach, tuba, and Gene Watts, trombone.

BRASSES

The most commonly used brass instruments, from highest to lowest in pitch range, are the **trumpet, French horn, trombone, and tuba.**

Like the woodwinds, brass instruments produce sound by sending a vibrating column of air through tubing. (In brass instruments the tubing is coiled in order to facilitate handling the instrument by reducing its overall length.) At one end of the tubing is a **mouthpiece;** at the other end the tube is flared to form a bell. Pitch adjustments are made by a combination of adjusting the tension of the lips of the player and by a mechanism which extends or shortens the length of the tube.

In the trumpet, French horn, and tuba this mechanism is a set of **valves** operated by the fingers. In the case of the trombone, the mechanism is a **slide,** a U-shaped piece of tubing operated by the right hand of the player. The *tenor* and *bass trombone* are most frequently seen in the modern orchestra, while the *alto trombone* is encountered less often.

Other brass instruments such as the *cornet* (similar to the trumpet), the *baritone horn* (which looks like a small tuba), and the *euphonium* (also of the tuba family) are used in both concert and marching bands. Both the trumpet and trombone are popular jazz instruments.

PERCUSSION INSTRUMENTS

The **battery,** a term used to refer to the collection of percussion instruments in the symphony orchestra, can range in membership from a single pair of drums to a large array of instruments that produce sound when struck, shaken, or rubbed. Our exploration of these instruments will focus upon those most commonly used. They fall into two categories; those of *definite* pitch and those of *indefinite* pitch.

Figure 4.14 The timpani are available in a number of different sizes.

Definite Pitch

Timpani, also known as kettledrums, are the most commonly used percussion instruments. Sound is produced by the vibration of a calf skin *head* stretched over a kettle-like base. The pitch of the drum is determined by the degree of tension of the head which can be adjusted by screws around the rim of the drum or by foot pedals. Timpani are made in a number of sizes. One percussionist plays a number of drums.

The *glockenspiel* consists of two rows of steel bars. The sound produced by striking the bar with a mallet is crisp and bell-like.

The *celesta* is a keyboard glockenspiel that looks something like a small upright piano.

The *vibraphone* (also called vibraharp) has metal bars and an electrical mechanism that produces its characteristic vibrato.

Figure 4.15 The glockenspiel.

Figure 4.16 The vibraphone.

FUNDAMENTALS OF MUSIC

The *xylophone* has tuned wooden bars that produce a dry hollow sound when struck by a mallet.

The *marimba* is a softer-sounding xylophone.

Chimes are a set of tuned metal tubes suspended vertically in a frame. Played by striking with one or two mallets, they are often used to represent church bells.

Indefinite Pitch

Among the drums that produce sounds of indefinite pitch are the **side drum** (snare drum) and the **bass drum.**

The other instruments that produce sounds of indefinite pitch are: the **tambourine,** played by shaking and striking the head; the **castanets,** clicked together; the **triangle,** which is struck by a metal rod; the **gong,** which is struck with a soft-headed stick; and the **cymbals,** struck together or hit by a stick.

Figure 4.17 Chimes.

Figure 4.18 The bass drum.

Figure 4.19 The side drum.

Figure 4.20 Tambourine.

In the mid-eighteenth century, the orchestra became more standardized. The strings remained dominant, but the woodwinds took on an increasingly important role.

In the early decades of the nineteenth century, many of the woodwind and brass instruments underwent significant technical improvements. Composers were quick to take advantage of the greater versatility of these instruments. In the second half of the nineteenth century, the orchestra grew extensively in both size and makeup. Today's symphony orchestra consists of a nucleus of about one hundred players, with additions and subtractions being made to suit the requirements of individual pieces. The players are distributed according to the plan shown in figure 4.27.

Bands and Wind Ensembles

The word "band" has many applications. Marching band, military band, stage band, jazz band, hillbilly band, and the rhythm band that many of us played in as children give an idea of the variety of bands possible. For much of its history the band has been associated with summer concerts in the park. Today the term is most often applied to two types of musical organizations: the marching band and the concert band.

We are all familiar with the **marching bands** that play at high school and college sports events, march in military parades, and participate in municipal celebrations. The **concert band,** often referred to as a **symphonic band** or **wind ensemble,** is perhaps less familiar. It became an important musical force in the years following World War I. It differs from the marching band in its smaller size, its emphasis on performing original compositions, and the fact that it was intended for indoor concerts. The wind ensemble, with its lighter sound, has attracted the attention of several serious modern composers: Darius Milhaud, Paul Hindemith, and Ralph Vaughan Williams are among those who have written original works for wind ensemble.

Whereas the members of the violin family form the mainstay of the symphony orchestra, concert bands rely primarily on woodwind, brass, and percussion instruments to produce their unique tone colors. Concert bands generally contain no violins, violas, or cellos, but do employ the string bass.

Vocal Ensembles

Chamber vocal ensembles vary in size and makeup in much the same way that chamber instrumental ensembles do. There are vocal trios, quartets, quintets, sextets, and so on. The vocal quartet usually consists of soprano, alto, tenor, and bass. So long as only one or two singers sing each part, the ensemble is essentially of chamber music proportions. However, when there are four or five or more singers in each section, the ensemble is referred to as a **chorus** or **choir.** Several types of choruses are possible. A *women's chorus* usually consists of two soprano parts (first and second) and one or two alto sections—SSAA. A *men's chorus* is made up of two tenor sections (first and second), baritone, and bass—TTBB. The mixed chorus consists of both female and male voices, divided into soprano, alto, tenor, and bass—SATB. In church choirs before the nineteenth century, female voices were not generally used; soprano and alto parts were sung by boys whose voices had not yet changed.

Choral music is sometimes intended for voices alone, without instrumental accompaniment, a style of performance called **a cappella.** But choral music is also frequently performed with instruments, for example, piano, organ, or orchestra.

Conductor

Large ensembles usually require the leadership of a **conductor.** Standing in front of the orchestra or chorus, usually on a podium, the conductor directs the ensemble and is reponsible for all aspects of the performance. The craft of conducting is a complex one, and conducting techniques and styles are highly individual and vary widely. In general, the conductor's right hand indicates the tempo and basic metrical structure of the music. With the left hand, the conductor cues the entrances of instruments, guides the shadings or dynamics, and indicates other nuances relating to the expressive character of the music.

Figure 4.28 Joan Sutherland singing with the Atlanta Symphony Orchestra, conducted by Richard Bonynge.

THE MUSIC OF
WORLD CULTURES

© Eastcott/Momatiuk/The Image Works

THE MUSIC OF WORLD CULTURES

AN INTRODUCTION

E ach of us is, to some extent, a product of the culture into which he or she is born. Our physical, intellectual, and emotional lives are affected continuously by our surrounding social environment. The foods we consider most succulent, the art we enjoy, our patterns of friendship, family solidarity, and group identity are influenced by the cultural standards we absorb.

The same is true of music. A people's sense of their history, of their relationship to a deity, of their joy in life and sorrow in death are revealed by the use they make of musical materials. And ideas of what music should be—how it should sound, when it should be heard, and who should perform it—are related directly to cultural backgrounds. In short, the "ear" of the listener is very much conditioned by his or her culture.

SOME PRELIMINARY COMMENTS

In this chapter we will consider examples of musical cultures outside the Western European tradition. Although there are many fundamental differences between Western and non-Western music, certain similarities appear to be a common heritage of all humanity. In every culture music plays an important role in rites and ceremonies; and for all people music has an emotional content that satisfies certain deeply felt needs. Yet the resulting sounds are often so diverse that the music of one group may not be recognized as music at all by other groups. A significant degree of contrast also exists between the relative positions of music in the social fabric of various cultures. For example, the traditional work music of some African tribes is so closely integrated into daily life that it is not even recognized by its members as basically

The revision of Chapter 5 was contributed by Dr. Carolyne Jordan of Salem State College.

the same phenomenon as the European-derived music which they hear on transistor radios. Thus, any study of the music of non-Western cultures must include a description of not only its technical nature, but also its role and function in society.

Let us begin by clarifying some terms. The music described in this chapter is variously called "ethnic," "folk," and "traditional." Although these terms are not synonymous, the distinctions among them are sometimes unclear. *Ethnic* music usually refers to the music of a group of people who have shared a common cultural history over many generations. *Traditional* music, which can also be considered "classical" or "sophisticated," is classified by its use. In this category are included official music, such as the imperial court music of ancient China, Japan, and Vietnam, and ceremonial music used in all cultures for specific rites and festivals. Traditional (or classical) music is often formal, following more or less rigorous principles of content, style, and performance. It is usually performed by artists who have refined the music through continued use or disciplined training. *Folk* music is the music of everyday life—work songs, children's songs, lullabies, love songs, and ballad-story songs sung and played by ordinary people. In contrast to traditional music, folk music is available for all to learn, enjoy, and modify as occasion demands. In this chapter we will consider representative examples of both traditional and folk types of ethnic music.

Written and Oral Traditions

The music we will spend most of our time exploring in this text—the concert music of Western Europe and the United States—is based on a tradition of written notation through which the artistic expression of individual composers is carefully preserved. This written music is usually recreated in performance by highly trained musicians at scheduled concerts and recitals. While the performer may take some liberties with the score, using a variety of musical techniques and resources to interpret and enrich the music, the final role of performance is to recreate sounds as intended by individual composers.

The musical heritages of many world cultures, by contrast, are usually transmitted orally. Young musicians learn by carefully listening to, observing, and imitating elder musicians. While music composition is treated with seriousness and reverence, in many cultures the name of an individual composer is not attached to the piece. In ancient cultures music was linked with supernatural beings and mythical gods and was considered a reflection of universal order and spiritual purity.

MUSICAL ELEMENTS IN NON-WESTERN MUSIC

Part I discussed many of the elements common to all music, emphasizing how these elements are organized in the practice of Western music. Now let us look briefly at how some of these elements are organized in non-Western music.

Pitch and Scale Systems

The scales employed in many non-European cultures are unfamiliar and strange to Western ears. While certain cross-culture similarities do occur, such as the significance applied by many cultures to the intervals of the octave and the fifth, octaves frequently have more, or fewer, than twelve subdivisions, and the smallest pitch differences found in non-European music may be larger or smaller than the European semi-tone (half step).

One of the most prevalent combinations of pitches is the **pentatonic scale**—a series of five tones. Pentatonic scales are found in the music of North and South American Indians and in African and Far Eastern cultures. If we play the pentatonic scale CDEGA(C) on the piano, we Westerners will quickly hear a characteristic "oriental" quality. It is the same scale structure as that produced by playing the five black keys of the piano. A subtle difference will be noted if we play instead the scale CDE♭GA♭. This scale is one of several pentatonic scales used commonly in Japanese music, while the first scale is typical of Chinese music.

African cultures south of the Sahara use, in addition to pentatonic scales, a variety of **tritonic** (three-tone) and **heptatonic** (seven-tone) scales, including patterns of whole and half steps that are common in Western music. Japanese music also employs heptatonic scales. In the classical music of India, sequences of pitches known as **ragas** are employed. The basic tones of a raga are modified by the use of **microtones**—intervals smaller than a half step. Microtones cannot be played on the piano, but can be produced on any stringed instrument such as a guitar, violin, or Indian sitar.

Harmony

In most cultures there is some use of simultaneous sounds. As we shall see in succeeding chapters, Western music is governed by a long tradition of rules of harmonic organization. In non-Western music there is little use of harmony per se, particularly in countries such as India, where melodic intricacies are far more important. One prominent form of harmonic texture in Indian music is provided by a **drone**— a stationary tone or tones of constant pitch played throughout a piece. The four-stringed dulcimer used in performing Appalachian folk music also makes use of the drone, sustaining a continuous tone on one of its strings. Some cultures employ **heterophony:** two or more individuals perform a single melody, adding their own rhythmic or melodic modifications. And in some non-Western cultures textural variety is provided by changes in tone quality and vocal inflection. Such vocal or instrumental variations as slides, trills, and vibrato are among the techniques through which the effect of varying textures is achieved.

Rhythm

Much Western music is based on symmetrical rhythmic patterns and uniform time intervals. Many world cultures, however, use complex, irregular, and free rhythms. Many cultures use primarily vocal forms; in these cultures rhythms conform to the stress patterns of the words sung. In African music, **polyrhythms**—two or more contrasting and independent rhythms used at the same time—are common, and the sophistication of use of rhythm in Africa is unmatched in any other culture. Polyrhythms have increasingly fascinated and influenced Western jazz and concert music composers. A good example of their adaptation in Western music is Stravinsky's *The Rite of Spring* (see pages 352–57).

EXAMPLES OF TRADITIONAL AND FOLK MUSIC

Rarely have any cultures lived in complete isolation for many centuries. As a result, the music of the dominant culture of a region has often been influenced by contacts through trade, exploration, and migration. Thus, the music in world cultures today has often been transformed to some degree from its original character. The examples we will survey here represent music of ancient origin in which many indigenous characteristics have been preserved.

Music of China

Background

From its beginnings, Chinese music was conceived of as a system that would reflect the order of the universe. Musicians and philosophers in ancient China believed in the existence of one true "foundation tone" upon which the whole edifice of musical composition should be built. This foundation tone, or *huang chung,* was thought to have social, cosmological, and mystical significance. For many centuries, the disappearance of a dynasty was attributed to its inability to find the true *huang chung.* Several methods were used to discover the elusive tone. One method prescribed that the correct height of the pipe that would produce the true *huang chung* would be equal to ninety average-size grains of millet laid end to end. From this tone the pitches of the other tones in the Chinese musical system were derived. Small bamboo tubes, sized through an exact mathematical formula, were used to produce twelve tones, or *lü,* which were roughly comparable to the twelve months of the year, so that each month had its tone. Musicians selected five tones from these twelve to form a pentatonic scale based on the hours of day and night and the revolving cycle of months in the yearly calendar.

Because each tone was invested with mystical significance, Chinese music developed as a system in which the perfect performance of individual tones was regarded as the highest art. The philosopher Confucius (ca. 551–479 B.C.) played a stone slab on which only one note could be produced. Yet he is said to have played it with such a full heart that its sound was captivating. The sophistication needed to enjoy subtle colorations and inflections on only one tone was, of course, not a universal gift among the ancient Chinese. Popular discontent with "scholarly music" led to the development of more accessible forms that could be enjoyed by everyone. The most enduring secular form was Chinese opera.

Chinese Opera

Presented originally in teahouses or outdoor arenas, Chinese opera evolved in an atmosphere of noisy informality. Today, the uniform loudness with which the operas are performed is thought to be a stylistic holdover from the days when players had to compete with squalling babies and clattering rickshaws for audience attention. To involve the audiences emotionally, singers and musicians presented operas in which characterization was the overriding concern.

To portray three basic emotional moods, three corresponding musical styles became customary. For scenes involving agitated emotions such as happiness, gaiety, or temporary distress a quick, light style was employed. Music written in another style portrayed subdued, contemplative moods, whereas a character's despair or depression was conveyed through a third style of composition.

Similarly, various dramatic situations came to be associated with certain melodic patterns. These stereotyped melodic formulas are still available to any composer who wishes to communicate one of the standard dramatic incidents common to Chinese operatic plots. Consequently, in a number of operas the same melodic material forms the basis for any set aria (vocal piece) describing the anguish of the abandoned wife, a villain's intended vengeance, or the final triumph of good over evil.

The vocal quality and range in these arias also depends, to a large extent, on the type of character to be portrayed. Heroes are required to sing wth a tight, controlled rasp, whereas heroines often produce a high, nasal sound that originated with the male singers who until recently played the female roles.

The scenes of an opera generally begin with percussion overtures. Percussive devices are used to accompany the recitative (dialogue that is half spoken and half sung) and to mark off one character's words from another's. In melodic passages, instruments of the orchestra—bowed and plucked lutes, fiddles, and flutes—play the main melody either in unison or at various pitches. The crashing of cymbals emphasizes the end of a melody. As the Chinese opera form developed, energetic acrobatic displays and dances were introduced, adding greatly to audience enjoyment.

In modern China, the traditional music, which was associated with the old aristocratic society, has been systematically suppressed. Classical Chinese instruments are very rarely played today and it is feared that much knowledge of the traditional

Figure 5.1 Chinese operas today have rejected traditional themes for themes of the Communist revolution, such as the struggles of peasants against oppressive landlords. Costumes and sets are simple, in keeping with socialist ideology.

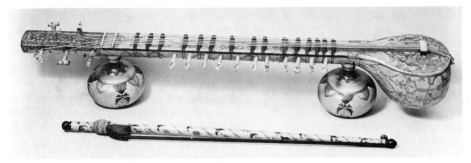

Figure 5.3 Vina, with two gourds added as resonates; movable threads. The vina is the oldest of the Indian stringed instruments. It is used today in southern India, but in the north it is supplanted by the smaller sitar. (Courtesy The Metropolitan Museum of Art; gift of Alice E. Getty, 1946.) (46.34. 3ab)

Figure 5.4 Drum; brown, with red, yellow, and green bands. Wood (body); skin (head); braced by strips of skin on sides. H. 10 in., Diam., 7½ in. 8 small cylinders L.3 in. Diam. A tabla of northern India. (Courtesy The Metropolitan Museum of Art; The Crosby Brown Collection of Musical Instruments, 1889.) (89.4.166)

of movable bridges. The main playing strings are pulled sideways on the frets to produce the characteristic ornamentation. Two hemispheric resonators fashioned from gourds amplify the sound. When played, the vina is either placed horizontally across the performer's knee or laid slanting against the left shoulder (see fig. 5.3).

In the northern regions of India the vina has been supplanted by the *sitar*, which is smaller and simpler to play. The sitar has a track of twenty metal frets, above which are the seven main strings. Below the frets, a set of thirteen "sympathetic" strings can be tuned to the pitches that will most advantageously pick up the main notes of the raga to be performed.

The drums of India are fashioned so that they will reinforce the most important tonal pitches of the raga. In the south, the *mridanga*, a single-piece drum with two heads, is treated with tuning pastes so that various areas on the playing surface produce differing pitches. The *tabla* of the north (fig. 5.4) is a right-hand drum which is often tuned to the tonic. A single performer plays the tabla simultaneously with the *banya*, a left-hand bass drum.

Music of Africa

Background

In this discussion we shall be concerned only with those cultures found in the area south of the Sahara Desert (see fig. 5.5). Many diverse cultures inhabit this vast area, representing a wide variety of musical styles. Nowhere in the world is music more a part of the very process of living than in Africa. Almost all communal activities are accompanied by singing, dancing, and drumming. These three are rarely separated: they are interdependent. As a whole the music is characterized by sophisticated and complex rhythmic structures, a wide range of indigenous instruments, a strong oral tradition of songs, and a vast store of dances to accompany and celebrate all aspects of life.

Figure 5.5 Africa, showing countries whose music is discussed in the text.

These African cultures are based on the power of the spoken word, which is believed to be the "life force" called *nommo* in Bantu languages. The languages are often inflective, and common speech assumes musiclike qualities. Musical sounds produced most often are percussive and players use bodily gestures to enhance a performance. Polyphonic textures are employed and polyrhythms are common.

Uses of African Music

The abundance of songs may be classified into two broad categories: secular (non-religious) and sacred (religious). Secular music is usually a common property of the people and may be performed for pure entertainment (fig. 5.6) or as an accompaniment to daily tasks. Religious music may be either ceremonial or *esoteric*. Ceremonial music is heard on such diverse occasions as the end of harvest or fishing season; at weddings and funerals, and at installations of heads of state or rulers. Esoteric music is played only by the particular religious cult for which it is designed. These cult organizations have a repertoire of drummings, dances, and songs which are performed only by their members.

Much African music is meant to be heard by the deity. The Dagon of Mali believe that music, specifically that of the drums, is the vehicle through which the sacred word is brought to humans. More commonly, music is used to lift up prayers to a divinity. To ensure the delivery of a healthy baby, special songs are sung during the hours of childbirth. After birth, thankfulness of the family finds expression in chants and dancing. The naming of the baby, the loss of a first tooth, and other incidents in the life of the child from infancy through puberty are celebrated with music.

In addition to marking the stages of life, music also deepens and defines African existence. Through songs and dances young men and women are taught the language of the tribe, the traditions of family living, the obligations they will be expected to

Figure 5.6 African dancers.

fulfill, even the "facts of life." Communal holidays and festivals are celebrated through seasonal musical offerings. In some West African cultures, political music is considered so important to the general welfare that select groups of musicians, known as *griots,* specialize in songs of governmental and social information. Each event has a consciously selected musical program, the use of which is strictly adhered to. For example, among the Banum people of the Cameroons, a specific piece of music is traditionally performed only at the hanging of a governmental minister.

To ease the strain of monotonous labor, people everywhere have sung work songs. Today in Africa work songs coordinate communal efforts such as the closing of the fishnet after a day's harvest, counter the dreariness of repetitive agricultural tasks, and provide diversions from the dangers of gold and diamond mining.

Tonality and Styles of African Music

Africa's vocal and instrumental music exhibits a variety of styles and scale patterns. Much music is composed on a foundation of pentatonic (five-tone) or heptatonic (specially derived seven-tone) scales. In addition, a large body of African songs is based on the diatonic pattern found in Western music. A characteristic song style is based on the repetition of a short melodic phrase. This style, known as **call and response,** is found in much West African music. Repetitions of a phrase sung by a leader alternate with repetitions of the responding phrase of the chorus. Call and response singing is done in unison or with two and three parts sounded simultaneously in the chorus. The following example of call and response style is a song of exhilaration of the Akan people.

Example 5.1

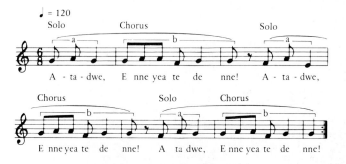

African harmony differs from Western harmony. Where it occurs, it exists mainly as a by-product of melodic elaboration. Some African folk songs carry over into a round type of polyphony or a simple harmonic structure in which one group of performers sustains the key tone of a melody while another group repeats the tune. At times both groups will sing the same melody at different pitches in heterophonic style. While the interval of the third is common, harmonic intervals of a fourth, fifth, sixth, seventh, and octave may be heard in *kple* music of the Ga people (a music also based on the pentatonic scale).

Master drummer says: "Ahgo" (Are you ready?) } *three times*
Group answers: "Ameh" (We're ready)

Gankogui (bell)

> End on accent

Axatse (rattle)

Played against left hand

Played against thigh

Dundun (drum)

Gankogui (bell)
2nd & 3rd players

Kagan (drum)

Atsimewu
(master drum)

Figure 5.11 Typical fragment of music performed by an Ewe drum orchestra, as transcribed into traditional staff notation. Note the varying rhythmic patterns assigned to the instruments. The master drummer plays all these parts as well as variations and improvisations. In addition, he is responsible for starting, stopping, and coordinating the performance of the entire ensemble.

Performance Styles

Africans are far more apt to play an instrument or sing *with* others than *for* them. It is this ease of coming together to make music that results in the characteristic group performance of African music. Although there is solo singing and playing in the music of Africa, the most typical musical expression involves any number of singers and players. The melodies that form the basis for ensemble singing or playing are generally quite short. This shortness of the melodic unit helps to keep the phrase easily workable and open to improvisation.

In every ensemble there is a master drummer. The master drum is capable of great range of expression and is most often played by true artists with a genius for improvisation. The master drummer signals the group to begin and end and is essentially the conductor of the orchestra. The master drummer's repertoire includes any number of standard phrases with which he improvises to enhance, articulate, accentuate, and modulate the music at appropriate points. The expression of mood and true feeling of the occasion is left to the dancers.

Music of North American Native Americans

Background

In the United States today music is highly diversified. In addition to sophisticated concert music and many types of popular music there are considerable repertoires of folk and ethnic music, including folk ballads, black spirituals, blues, and Native American tribal music. These latter types, which have their roots in the cultural identities of generations of large ethnic groups, form the core of what may be called traditional American music. They have three broad cultural sources: the folk music of Europe (especially England), the tribal music of the West Coast of Africa, and the music of aboriginal America. We will consider the Afro-American contribution to music in chapter 22. Our focus here will be on the music of the Native Americans.

The Character of Native American Music

The fact that there are approximately two hundred different Native American tribes in the United States today is evidence of the enormous variety and diversity of American Indian culture. The tribes were scattered over a vast geographic area, and each tribe had its own way of life, its own customs and traditions; yet a fundamental belief shared by the many Native American nations was the importance of song and ceremony to all aspects of life. Songs were part of every act of worship, every important ritual to mark the passing of time and the coming of death. Native American songs were also associated with the routines of daily life: hunting, praying for rain or successful harvest, coming of age, curing of ills, preparing for war, or celebrating peace.

The Native Americans believed that every living thing had power—the buffalo, the eagle, the tree (see fig. 5.12), even the ant. Power also resided in the unseen things, in powerful spirits who could be called upon to help supply whatever was needed to sustain the life and health of the tribe. Songs were the means of invoking the aid of these seen and unseen beings; thus, songs were imbued with almost supernatural powers.

An important source of new songs was the "vision quest," a trancelike ritual in which a member of the tribe was "given" a new piece of music through supernatural means. He became, temporarily, a mouthpiece through which powerful beings spoke. A song revealed in a dream was always used to improve the life of the people in some way, for example to heal the sick or achieve victory in war. An interesting aspect of these dream songs was that they became the personal property of the dreamer. The singing of the song gave him power, power which would be lost if the song were sung by someone else, especially without the agreement of the owner.

Another type of individual expression was the song of praise sung to honor a powerful chieftain, a courageous warrior, or a loyal friend. A third type of song was associated with the rituals and ceremonies of the tribe. Such songs belonged to everyone and were sung during various kinds of ceremonies.

Figure 6.1 Gregorian chants continue to be a part of monastic worship.

Gregorian Chant

The chants, also known as *plainsong* or *plainchant,* are monophonic, or single line melodies. Their texts are in Latin and many are derived from the Bible, particularly the Book of Psalms.

The rhythm of the chants is unmeasured and the tempos are flexible. The melodic material is based upon a system of scales now referred to as **church modes.** They are similar to the major and minor scales developed in the baroque period (see page 112). However, they are different in that the church modes do not express as strong a tonal center (tonic) as do the scales that make up the later major-minor system.

The melodies achieve their aesthetic beauty with the most modest means. They have an undulating, wavelike quality, and a simplicity that is wholly in keeping with their religious intent as a functional part of worship. Generally, chant melodies follow the implied inflections of the text with its stressed and unstressed syllables.

"Salve Regina," a chant written by Hermannus Contractus, a Benedictine monk, is a hymn to the Virgin Mary. It was sung as part of evening worship (vespers) during a specified portion of the church year.

SALVE REGINA
SIDE 1/SELECTION 1

The chant is made up of six sections. The first section (A) consists of a melodic phrase and its immediate repetition with different words. Each subsequent section (B through F) consists of a line of text with its own individual melody. Two types of phrases are employed: **syllabic,** in which each syllable is given one note, and **melismatic,** in which one syllable is spread over several notes. The concluding section (F) is of particular interest because of the expressiveness resulting from the extended phrases on "O," the last of which is the longest **melisma** in the entire piece.

Example 6.1
(Hermannus Contractus,
"*Salve Regina*")

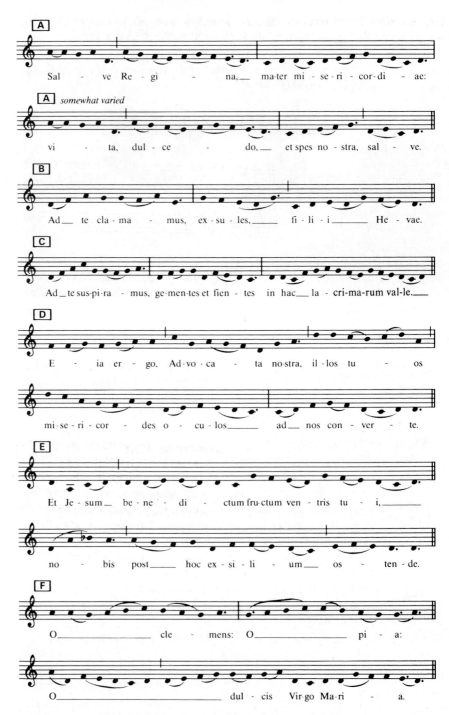

Hail, Holy Queen, Mother of mercy, our life, our sweetness, and our hope. To thee do we cry, poor banished children of Eve. To thee do we send up our sighs, mourning and weeping in this valley of tears. Turn then, most gracious advocate, thine eyes of mercy toward us; and after this our exile, show unto us the blessed fruit of thy womb, Jesus. O clement, O loving, O sweet Virgin Mary!

By the fifteenth century the motet had evolved full circle. Once again it became primarily a religious form, using one text for all voices. The text was almost always taken from the Bible. One of the leading motet composers of the fifteenth century was Guillaume Dufay (ca. 1400–1474).

RENAISSANCE SACRED MUSIC

The Renaissance in literature and the visual arts began in the fourteenth century and centered in Italy. The Renaissance in music began in the fifteenth century in what is today northern France, Holland, and Belgium. The Franco-Flemish style developed in these countries and spread to all parts of the Continent.

In addition to Guillaume Dufay, the outstanding members of this early Flemish school were Johannes Ockeghem (ca. 1430–1495), Jacob Obrecht (1452–1505), and Josquin des Prez (ca. 1450–1521). In their Masses and motets, four-part writing became standard. An independent bass part was added beneath the chant for the first time, so that the chant was no longer the lowest voice part. In addition, the use and treatment of the chant as a basic material became much freer and at times was abandoned altogether. The practice of using secular tunes (rather than chant) as the musical raw material for sacred compositions became extremely popular. The polyphonic style emphasized the true independence of each of the four parts.

Josquin Des Prez

The greatest representative of the Franco-Flemish school was Josquin des Prez, who spent most of his creative life outside his native country, Belgium. In 1475 he was a member of the choir at the court of the Duke of Szorfa in Milan and later he joined the Papal Choir in Rome. He was also active in the Italian cities of Florence, Ferrara, and Modena. In the last years of his life he returned to northern Europe.

Josquin was acknowledged by his contemporaries to be the greatest master of the time, and he developed the complex Franco-Flemish style to its highest point. In much of his secular music he employed a lighter, more homophonic style, then popular in Italy. His polyphonic style is distinguished by the use of *imitation,* wherein a melodic fragment stated in one voice is repeated or imitated by another voice a measure or two later. Examples of imitative polyphony appear earlier than Josquin, but he was the first to apply the principle consistently.

Josquin's motet *Ave Maria* (*Hail Mary*; a portion is shown in example 6.2) is typical of his motet writing in the following ways:

AVE MARIA
SIDE 1/SELECTION 3

1. The melodic material is freely based on a Gregorian chant, in this case *Ave Maria, gratia plena.*

2. It is a four-part composition in which the voices are often paired, the two upper voices being pitted against or alternating with the two lower voices.

Example 6.2 (Josquin des Prez, *Ave Maria*)

Hail Mary, full of grace, the Lord (is with thee

3. The music is **through-composed,** that is, each unit of text is given a different musical setting. (This contrasts to strophic music, where each stanza of text is sung to the same melody.) A feeling of continuity is achieved through overlapping phrases: before one phrase ends, another voice begins a new phrase, so that there is seldom a cadence when all four voices come to a stop. This continuous flow is characteristic of later Renaissance polyphony.

4. Contrapuntal passages alternate with homophonic sections, another hallmark of Josquin's style. Despite the complexity of the contrapuntal writing, the text remains clear, for Josquin assigns to the homophonic sections the expressive parts of the text, particularly at the very end where Josquin adds an unusual personal note—*O Mater Dei, memento mei* (O Mother of God, remember me).

Josquin left many motets, many Masses, and a considerable amount of secular music. He was also a gifted teacher, and many of his pupils became outstanding figures in the next generation of composers.

Giovanni Pierluigi da Palestrina

One of the most distinguished of Josquin's successors was Giovanni Pierluigi da Palestrina (1524–1594), who spent the greater part of his life as choirmaster of St. Peter's in Rome. Palestrina's great contribution was to return church music to the simplicity and purity of earlier times. Although his motets are masterpieces of composition, his Masses constitute his most important work.

Palestrina lived and worked during the Counter-Reformation, the reaction by the Catholic church to the spread of Protestantism. Central to this reaction was the Council of Trent, which met from 1545 to 1563 to formulate and execute the means by which church reform could be accomplished. The Council investigated every aspect of religious discipline, including church music. It was the opinion of the Council that sacred music had become corrupted by complex polyphonic devices that obscured the text and diverted attention from the act of worship. To remedy this situation the Council called for a return to a simpler vocal style, one that would preserve the sanctity of the text and discourage frivolous displays of virtuosity by the singers.

Legend has it that Palestrina, in order to prevent the Council from abolishing the polyphonic style entirely, composed a Mass of such beauty and simplicity that he was able to dissuade the cardinals from taking this drastic step. Without abandoning polyphony, Palestrina created a style that was less intricate and more direct than that of his predecessors.

A prolific composer, Palestrina wrote more than a hundred Mass settings. One of his relatively late Masses was based on the chant melody "Salve Regina." The *Missa salve regina,* which is an excellent example of late Renaissance polyphony, employs elements of the chant in each movement.

MISSA SALVE REGINA
SIDE 1/SELECTION 2

Notice in example 6.3 that the notes of the chant, marked with an x, are used as the basic melodic material. The Mass also exhibits the following characteristics:

1. All the voice parts (five in this case) are of equal importance. Each participates fully in singing the text.

2. The general style is imitative polyphony, with occasional homophonic sections.

3. Strong cadences set off sections from each other.

Example 6.3
(Palestrina, *Missa salve regina*)

Lord have mercy on us.
X = notes of chant incorporated into each vocal part.

Palestrina's sacred music was performed *a cappella,* without instruments, but this was the exception rather than the rule. Although no instrumental parts were written, it is well known that instruments frequently played along with or substituted for a voice in one or more of the parts.

RENAISSANCE SECULAR MUSIC

In addition to being a period of great piety, the sixteenth century was also a period of bawdy earthiness, irreverent humor, and celebration of sensual love. The same composers who created works "for the greater glory of God" also wrote compositions of an entirely different character. In Italy and England the principal form of secular music was the *madrigal;* in France it was the *chanson;* in Germany it was the *lied.*

The Madrigal

The Renaissance **madrigal** is a poem set to music. It had its beginnings in the fourteenth century among the aristocrats of the small Italian courts. The texts, written in the vernacular, were often twelve-line poems whose subject was sentimental or erotic love. The early madrigal was written in a predominantly homophonic style. It was usually in three, but sometimes four, parts, and its expressive qualities were subdued and restrained. The so-called *classical madrigal* of the mid-sixteenth century was written usually for five and sometimes for four or six voices. Its texture was more polyphonic than the early madrigal, and a greater attempt was made to capture in the music the expressive possibilities of the words.

The final flowering of the madrigal took place during the closing decades of the sixteenth century. The late madrigal was an elaborate composition, invariably nonstrophic, with a mixture of homophonic and polyphonic textures. It used notes from the chromatic scale (all twelve notes in the octave) for bold effects, often to express sadness. The compositions also used coloristic and dramatic effects. One of the most interesting elements of the madrigal style was **word painting,** which attempted to represent the literal meaning of the text through music. Thus, the melody would ascend for the word "heaven," and a wavelike melody would depict the word "water."

Around the middle of the sixteenth century the Italian madrigal was brought to England. There it flourished under a variety of names—song, sonnet, canzonet, and ayre. William Byrd (1543–1623) and Thomas Morley (1557–1603) were the first English composers to cultivate the genre. Morley wrote simplified versions of the madrigal, known as *balletts.* Adapted from the Italian *belletti,* they were usually characterized by a *fa-la-la* refrain of the type that appears in the English carol "Deck the Halls." Enlivened by accents and a regular beat, the music was largely homophonic.

Figure 6.4 During the Renaissance, music became a popular leisure time activity for both the educated middle class and the aristocracy. This detail of a fresco in the Este palace, Ferrara, Italy, depicts the musical and sensual delights of spring.

The Chanson

In the sixteenth century the **chanson** (the French word for "song") was to France what the madrigal was to Italy and England. Early chansons developed with the work of Clement Jannequin (ca. 1485–ca. 1560), Claudin de Sermisy (ca. 1490–1562), and Pierre Certon (ca. 1510–1572).

Chansons modified the motet style with strong accented rhythms, frequent repetitions, and short phrases ending simultaneously in all parts. They were usually sung by three, four, or five voices, and sections of simple imitation alternated with sections that were essentially homophonic.

CHANT DES
OISEAUX
SIDE 1/SELECTION 4

Word painting occurred frequently in the early chansons. Jannequin wrote several *program chansons,* in which the music imitates a nonmusical idea. An example is his *Chant des oiseaux* (*Song of the Birds*), in which the singers' voices imitate the sounds of birds such as the cuckoo.

The Waverly Consort (New York). This ensemble of ten men and women, directed by Michael Jaffe, is a leading American group specializing in the performance of medieval and Renaissance music. (Vanguard and Columbia Records.)

Choir of the Monks of the Abbey of Saint Pierre de Solesmes (Solesmes, France). The performances of chant by this Benedictine Order are considered by many scholars to be among the best, historically as well as musically. (Deutsche Grammophon Geselischaft, DGG, Archive series.)

Medieval Secular Music

John Dunstable, *O Rosa bella.* Though Dunstable was an English composer, he spent much of his life on the Continent; some of his vocal works employ French or Italian texts.

Medieval Sacred Music

Guillaume de Machaut, *Messe de Nostre Dame (Mass of Our Lady).* One of the earliest and best-known polyphonic settings of the Ordinary of the Mass. The five interrelated movements demonstrate most of the important compositional techniques of the late medieval period.

Renaissance Secular Music

Roland de Lassus, *Matona, mia cara (Matona, Lovely Maiden).* One of the best-known of Renaissance satirical pieces, this madrigal for four voices makes fun of the German soldiers occupying much of sixteenth-century Italy by—among other things—mocking their pronunciation of Italian ("Matona" for "Madonna").

Orlando Gibbons, *The Silver Swan.* One of the loveliest vocal compositions ever written, this melancholy work is an outstanding example of English madrigal style.

Thomas Morley, *My Bonnie Lass She Smileth.* Using both homophonic and polyphonic textures, swift changes from the major to minor, and a "*fa la la*" section, this song is typical of Morley's balletts.

Renaissance Sacred Music

Guillaume Dufay, *Missa Se la face ay pale (Mass on "If My Face Is Pale").* A classic example of early Renaissance polyphonic style, this four-voice setting of the Ordinary takes its rather odd name from the title of the chanson melody upon which it is based.

Josquin des Prez, *Missa Pange lingua (Mass on "Sing, My Tongue").* One of the great masterpieces of the Renaissance, this work is based on the plainsong hymn for the Feast of Corpus Christi.

Giovanni Pierluigi da Palestrina, *Sicut cervus desiderat (Like as the Hart Desireth).* One of Palestrina's most expressive and technically perfect works, this motet, its text taken from Psalm 42, is a classic example of Palestrina-style harmonic and melodic construction.

Hildegard of Bingen, *Ordo Virtutum.* Harmonia Munchic–20395/96. Hildegard's music represents the transition from chant to polyphony.

Plate 1 This Cross Page from the Lindisfarne Gospels (A.D. 700) was painted by Irish monks and demonstrates the movement of Christianity into northern Europe in the early Middle Ages. The interlace design shows distinguished craftsmanship but no interest in representing the visible world. (Scala/Art Resource.)

Plate 2 Sainte Chapelle, the royal chapel in Paris, is a culmination of the Gothic style of the thirteenth century. Between 1140 and 1240, French designers developed a system of supports and pointed arches that made masonry merely a skeleton for colored glass. The result was highly spiritual and elegant. (© Ciccione/Photo Researchers.)

Plate 3 This fifteenth-century Flemish *Annunciation,* center panel of the Merode Alterpiece (ca. 1425–28), shows a setting similar to a contemporary townhouse. It is not abstract like earlier medieval painting, but its lack of linear perspective and its distorted figures make clear the difference between "late Gothic" painting in Flanders and the Renaissance style being developed at that time in Italy. (The Metropolitan Museum of Art; The Cloisters Collection, Purchase 1956.)

Plate 4 *The Small Cowper Madonna,* by Raphael (1505). This masterpiece displays the quiet, powerful dignity of the High Renaissance style as well as the clarity, stability, draughtsmanship, and subtle emotions that made Raphael a paragon of artists of succeeding generations. (The National Gallery of Art, Washington; Widener Collection.)

Plate 5 The sculpture on the west portals of Chartres Cathedral, done in the middle of the twelfth century, demonstrates the greater order and realism of Gothic design as compared with Romanesque work. The three-dimensionality of the figures suggests the growing independence of sculpture from architecture. (Scala/Art Resource.)

Plate 6 The west façade of the cathedral at Reims, built in the thirteenth century, exemplifies the height, grandeur, and sculptural magnificence of Gothic architecture. The nave of the cathedral is 125 feet high, with a drive upward that is reinforced by the slenderness of its proportions. (Scala/Art Resource.)

Plate 7 Andrea Palladio's Villa Rotunda (begun 1550) exhibits the balance, symmetry, and simplicity of Renaissance architecture in the fifteenth and sixteenth centuries. Inspired by the architectural structures and details of Roman antiquity, proponents of this new style rejected the soaring towers, flying buttresses, sculptured pinnacles, and pointed arches of the Gothic era. (Scala/Art Resource.)

Plate 8 *The Annunciation,* by Botticelli (1490). In this Florentine painting the beautiful, linear figures interact in a nearly bare room drawn through the principles of perspective. This kind of design resulted in a more accurate and more naturalistic image than in earlier centuries. (Scala/Art Resource.)

Plate 9 Michelangelo dominated Italian art during the sixteenth century. His athletic figures, often in highly imaginative, complicated poses, were copied and paraphrased by later artists throughout Europe. *The Dying Slave* (1513–16), shown here, was meant for a papal tomb that was never completed. (Scala/Art Resource.)

Plate 10 Caravaggio's *The Conversion of St. Paul* (1600–1601) not only demonstrates the theatrical lighting for which he is famous but also shows his rejection of the idealism of the High Renaissance. Caravaggio declared early in his career that nature—not tradition—would be his teacher. (Scala/Art Resource.)

Plate 11 *The Rape of the Daughters of Leucippus* (ca. 1618), by Peter Paul Rubens. Rubens created a highly charged style full of color, energy, voluptuous and powerful figures, and complex, dynamic composition. (Scala/Editorial Photocolor Archives.)

Plate 12 Nicholas Poussin's *Rape of the Sabine Women* (1636–37) exemplifies the classical style of the most influential of seventeenth-century French artists. While Poussin exploited the drama of his subject, he presented it with balance and restraint, with figures based on Roman statuary rather than on Rubens's flashy nudes. (The Metropolitan Museum of Art; Harris Brisbane Dick Fund, 1946.)

Plate 13 Bernini's *Ecstasy of St. Theresa* (1646) demonstrates the baroque attempt to involve the spectator in art through highly dramatic, emotional presentations. Here, the fluid interaction of space and stone belie the marble's hardness. (Scala/Art Resource.)

Plate 14 Despite its diminutive size, Borromini's San Carlo alle Quattro Fontane (1662–67) is highly baroque in its undulating, sculptural façade, which engages the passer-by with its complicated architectural detail. (Scala/Art Resource.)

Plate 15 Rembrandt's *The Blinding of Samson,* done in 1636, indicates the impact outside Italy of Caravaggio's modeling though light and shadow. Likewise, its passionate energy and violence are unmistakably Rubenesque. Later in his career, Rembrandt developed a more individual style. (© Städelsches Kunstinstitut, Frankfurt, West Germany.)

Plate 16 Baroque opera achieved a synthesis of many different arts in one grand spectacle to thrill its audience. The opera at Versailles was built for Louis XIV (1638–1715), the most grandiose of the French kings and one of the chief patrons of the new art form. (Scala/Art Resource.)

Plate 17 Thomas Jefferson's Monticello (1770–84; 1796–1806) was modeled after
Palladio's Villa Rotunda (see plate 7) in brick and painted wood. It is an excellent example
of the impact of the European neoclassicism on architecture in the American colonies and
the new United States. (Virginia State Library and Archives.)

Plate 19 *Are They Thinking About the Grape?* by François Boucher (1751). Boucher was the most popular painter at the court of Versailles in the middle of the eighteenth century. His style is consummately rococo—light, delicate, playful, and colorful. Its innocence and sensuality were dismissed by later generations as frivolous and trivial. (© 1988 The Art Institute of Chicago, Martha E. Leverone Endowment.)

Plate 18 Sir Joshua Reynolds, the most powerful and respected English painter of the eighteenth century, portrayed a distinguished actress of the time in *Mrs. Siddons as the Tragic Muse* (1784). His discourses on an academic approach to art had immense impact on English and American students. (Henry E. Huntington Library and Art Gallery.)

Plate 20 This reconstruction of an eighteenth-century French interior is a magnificent example of the elegant decoration of the rococo. Tapestries, mirrors, chandeliers, curved woods, and gilt all contributed to the luxury of the Parisian townhouses. (Scala/Art Resource.)

Plate 21 Jacques Louis David's *The Death of Socrates* (1787) was exhibited in Paris just two years before the French Revolution broke out. It exemplifies the neoclassical style in its classical subject matter. It was also a political statement, memorializing the heroism of a great man who died for ideas that an oppressive state could not accept. (The Metropolitan Museum of Art; Wolfe Fund, 1931.)

Plate 22 Jean Antoine Houdon was the most renowned of late eighteenth-century French sculptors. He was commissioned to produce this sculpture (1788–92) of George Washington, first president of the United States and a model of the republican hero to many French revolutionaries. (Virginia State Library and Archives.)

MUSIC OF THE BAROQUE ERA

"The Lute Player" Orazio Gentileschi, ca. 1610. The
National Gallery of Art, Washington. The Ailsa Mellon
Bruce Fund.

THE TRIUMPH OF THE BAROQUE STYLE

B aroque is a word that eludes easy definition. It refers to a special approach to the arts that dominated all of the European continent in the seventeenth and eighteenth centuries—an approach that sought consciously to move the emotions and arouse the feelings of an audience through spectacular displays of sight and sound.

The early baroque is grounded in Italian art and reflects the recovery of the Roman Catholic church after the Protestant challenge of the sixteenth century. In 1517, Martin Luther had openly defied the authority of the Pope and the legitimacy of Church doctrine. He and his followers wanted to reform and "purify" the Christian religion; in doing so they set into motion a religious controversy that shattered European stability for more than a century. In the 1500s, large blocs of anti-Romanists threatened to bring about the utter collapse of Catholicism.

The Catholic response to the Protestant heresy is called the Counter-Reformation. It included a far-reaching "housecleaning" within the Church to stamp out clerical abuses and to shore up the faith where it was crumbling. Between 1545 and 1563 church leaders at the Council of Trent drew up a broad program that included tighter discipline for the clergy and a strong denial of the individual's right and ability to interpret the Bible. The Church reexamined its rituals. The Jesuit Order was established as an international force for teaching, missionary work, reconversion, and protection of the faith. By the seventeenth century the Counter-Reformation had paid its dividends: most of Europe remained bound to Catholicism and Rome.

After 1600, the arts were used by the Italians to celebrate the power and glory of the Church. The Italian artist became a narrator of the Christian spectacle. All over the peninsula painters and sculptors reworked ceilings and chapels. Architects built new churches and palaces, and craftsmen decorated them with rich gilding and ornament. The energy of Italian design was imitated throughout the continent, and Rome became an unparalleled cultural center where artists from many different countries came to admire the classical ruins and modern wonders of the city. Pilgrims and noblemen returned to their lands with marvelous tales of "the first city of the world."

The baroque style grew out of Renaissance forms that were employed in dynamic and grand ways to trumpet churchly prestige. The "look" was sparkling, exciting, and new: it is not surprising that the new Roman style was immediately and immensely popular, that it rapidly spread to the north and became an international style.

In the case of painting, the most radical of early baroque artists in Italy was Caravaggio, whose striking contrasts of light and shadow and whose vigorous realism in figures and settings redirected the course of all European painting (plate 10). But the two greatest baroque painters who followed him were Rubens, who was Flemish, and Poussin, who was French. In different ways these artists both depended on Italian sources. Rubens traveled in Italy as a young man and was influenced by Michelangelo's powerful figures and Venetian color as well as by Caravaggio. Poussin lived more than forty years in Rome.

The differences between Rubens and Poussin reveal the breadth of the baroque style in painting during the seventeenth century. Rubens's complicated compositions, full of rich color and straining movement, packed with gesturing figures and dramatic emotions, are one kind of baroque (plate 11). Poussin, who had tremendous impact on French contemporaries, was much more reserved, crisp, and logical in his design. He was deeply affected by classical sculpture and anxious to achieve a baroque that was more balanced and elegant in its drama (plate 12).

Bernini, another of the great baroque artists, was aided by a large group of assistants. He produced, over a very long career, an extraordinary amount of sculpture whose appearance set the style of work in stone and metal in the seventeenth century. His most famous work was the exquisite Ecstasy of St. Theresa (plate 13). To present this radiant moment Bernini showed the instant when the saint was pierced by an angel's golden arrow. His cutting of the marble is so delicate and fluid, the drapery sweeping in such magnificent folds, that the saint appears to float in absolute exaltation in the clouds of heaven itself. The drama of the scene makes apathy or detachment on the part of the observer unlikely. Like so much baroque work, Bernini's sculpture meant to force the onlooker into active participation with the image.

Bernini was also a great architect. He finished the great basilica of St. Peter's, begun 150 years earlier, and gave it his masterful colonnade in front of the facade, a monumental pair of arms that reach out toward the faithful and almost compel them to move toward the church itself. The most inventive of baroque architects, however, was Borromini, a designer whose work was the culmination of baroque ingenuity. The most radical of his buildings was San Carlo alle Quattro Fontane. Full of weirdly undulating surfaces, the walls of the church protrude and recede, creating a wavelike effect, and the contrasting planes of stone produce sculptural patterns of light and shade. The church seems built not of stone but of some pliable material (plate 14).

Borromini had great influence on the building of the late baroque churches of Germany and Austria (a more delicate eighteenth-century style usually called rococo). The baroque fondness for ornate decoration reached its greatest emotional extremes here in gilded altars with carved scrolls and garlands, and in gold and white walls with pastel-painted ceilings—all calculated to awe and delight. Critics of these beautiful churches too easily disregard their sincerity and dismiss them unfairly as "gaudy" and "vulgar" interiors with "false fronts." To their builders they were magical syntheses of painting, sculpture, and architecture that mirrored the magnificence of the Roman Catholic church.

Music played an important role in the life of the churches. Sound, perhaps more than the visual arts, could move, elevate, and involve a congregation and thus intensify the spiritual experience. While Protestants were skeptical of visual displays and the veneration of images, they warmed to the use of music in church services. In the seventeenth century, major churches began to form orchestras and choirs and to hire organists, soloists, and music masters. The greatest of baroque church musicians was Johann Sebastian Bach, who spent a major part of his career at Leipzig, leaving a vast treasure of sacred music, vocal and instrumental, at the time of his death in 1750.

It is wrong, however, to think of the baroque arts as exclusively religious. In France they were used to enhance the position of Louis XIV and his court. The efforts of architects, stonemasons, sculptors, painters, furniture makers, and gardeners were carefully coordinated to remake the royal palace at Versailles in the latter half of the seventeenth century. By 1700, the visitor to Paris would have been overwhelmed by French monuments to the power of the Crown, in a style codified and taught by a Royal Academy, a style increasingly fashionable throughout the continent. In the eighteenth century, Paris replaced Rome as the leader in European culture and design.

Because the seventeenth century was fascinated with the natural world, baroque art could also celebrate the ordinary and commonplace. In Dutch painting a brilliant artist like Rembrandt might craft biblical scenes (plate 15) but the predominant taste in baroque Holland sought paintings of the familiar world of town and country. Walls were decorated with landscapes, still lifes, and scenes from everyday life. There was a rage for portraiture among bankers and businessmen, prominent civic leaders, and well-heeled families. Citizens, soldiers, and peasants, their daily occupations and amusements, their gardens and taverns, all became the subjects of works of art. This naturalism reminds us of the scientific investigation of the century, when basic laws of the physical and biological sciences were uncovered. In 1702 a primitive steam engine was developed.

The best example of the worldly side of the baroque spirit is perhaps in opera, a medium developed to entertain royalty and aristocrats of highly discriminating taste (plate 16). This kind of theater integrated scene painting, costuming, dancing and choreography, and vocal and instrumental music. Opera thus achieved the synthesis of many different arts in one grandiose spectacle to thrill its audience. It is this elevating exploitation of the senses that is the hallmark of the baroque style.

BAROQUE VOCAL MUSIC

||T|| he baroque era, spanning the century and a half between the composition of the first opera in 1600 and the death of Johann Sebastian Bach in 1750, is a period of vast significance in the history of Western music. This period witnessed fundamental changes in musical thinking and practice that resulted in new forms including the opera, cantata, and oratorio in vocal music, and the concerto, the concerto grosso, and the sonata in instrumental music, which gradually achieved a place of equal importance to that of vocal music. The intensified interest in harmony and tonality that characterized the beginning of the period eventually led to the development of the major-minor system of musical organization which dominated Western music for the next three hundred years. The baroque period saw the emergence of the virtuoso performer in both vocal and instrumental music—a fact which had a profound effect on the course of music throughout the baroque and subsequent historical periods.

THE NEW MUSIC

The fundamental change in attitude toward music which laid the foundation for baroque style occurred in Italy around 1600 and focused on the relationship between words and music in vocal compositions. In Florence a group of scholars and musicians calling themselves the *Camerata* rejected the polyphonic style of the late Renaissance on the grounds that the elaborate contrapuntal texture obscured the words and diluted their emotional impact.

The Renaissance preoccupation with the polyphonic relationship between the voice parts often meant that the various voice parts sang different words at the same time with the result that no words were heard distinctly. In a single voice part, a word frequently was stretched out over so many tones that its indentity and meaning were lost to the listener.

The members of the *Camerata* insisted that the words must be clear and that the music should serve the meaning and emotional content of the text. They sought to recapture the spirit of Greek drama as they understood it by creating a new kind of music capable of expressing emotional extremes with powerful impact. Their concepts led to the development of the **monodic style** in which a single-voice part was predominant and was supported by harmonies played by a combination of instruments called **basso continuo.**

Basso Continuo

The monodic style consisted of a single vocal line accompanied by a bass instrument (cello or bassoon) and a keyboard instrument (harpsichord or organ). The composer wrote a two-part structure consisting of a melodic line for the singer and a simple bass. The bass was played by the cello or bassoon and the left hand of the keyboard player. Above this bass the keyboardist improvised chords according to a musical shorthand called **figured bass.** Figures (numbers) written below the notes of the bass line indicated the chord to be played. But the keyboard player had wide latitude as to the manner in which the chord was executed and was guided in doing so by the nature of the words being sung by the solo voice. Both the melodic line for the singer and the realization of the figured bass reflected and intensified the meaning and emotional quality of the words.

While the basso continuo (or simply **continuo**) originated in the vocal music of the early baroque, it came to be applied to virtually all music throughout the period, both vocal and instrumental. So prevalent was the continuo practice that the baroque was later nicknamed the "continuo period."

The Major-Minor System

The flow of music in the homophonic style of the early baroque depended upon a single predominant melodic line with strong harmonic support supplied by the basso continuo. The progression of one harmony to the next was of fundamental importance. The desire to make the harmonic aspect of music more effective led to the reduction in the number of modes (scales) from many in the Renaissance to just two—the *major* mode and the *minor* mode—in the baroque.

While these modes and the music based upon them differ in character, they share the important aspect of imparting the sense of a strong tonal center or *tonic*. The establishment of a clear tonic, movement away from it through the use of other chords, and the return to it, usually through the dominant chord, brought into being important new structural and expressive possibilities. And the device of *modulation,* the establishment of one or more secondary tonal centers within a composition, opened up a new way of organizing musical time-flow. It permitted the development of larger structures, for the expectation of eventual return to the original tonic could support long excursions away from it. Also included in this new harmonic approach to music was an expanded use of *dissonance* as an expressive element.

The monodic style became the basis for the vocal forms of the baroque period.

Recitative

The **recitative** is a kind of singing speech in which the musical rhythm is dictated by the natural inflection of the words. In contrast to the Renaissance idea of an even flow of music, the recitative is sung in free, flexible rhythm with continuo accompaniment. The tempo is slowed down or speeded up according to the performer's interpretation of the text.

Within baroque opera and oratorio, the recitative primarily served to heighten dramatic impact or to further the action of the story. As it evolved, the recitative acquired greater dramatic importance. The recitative with only continuo accompaniment, known as **secco recitative,** usually introduced an aria or appeared in the less dramatic moments of a piece. The **accompanied recitative,** in which the voice is accompanied by instruments in addition to continuo, produced a more powerful effect and was used for dramatic situations.

Arioso and Aria

While the general character of the recitative is declamatory, that of the **arioso** is essentially lyrical. The tempo in the arioso is steady. Unlike the recitative which can portray swift dramatic change, the arioso is comparatively static and tends to dwell on a single emotional state. In the early baroque, it is not uncommon to find these two styles side by side within the same movement depending upon the progression of dramatic events.

The arioso was later expanded into the **aria** which is a three-part form, ABA. The first section (A) was followed by a contrasting section (B) at the end of which appeared the words **"da capo"** instructing the performers to return to the beginning and repeat section A. It was intended that the A section differ in its repeated version. Singers would decorate, ornament, and embellish the original melody of the A section the second time around to further intensify the spirit of the words and to add excitement to the performance by a display of vocal virtuosity. This style of performance became an inherent part of the opera and, to a lesser extent, the oratorio.

The recitative (both secco and accompanied), the arioso, and the da capo aria were the principal ingredients for the important forms of baroque vocal music—the **opera,** the **oratorio,** and the **cantata.**

The early baroque **opera** was a dramatic form based on secular themes and written in Italian. Sung primarily by solo voices, operas were fully staged with costuming, scenery, acting, and instrumental ensembles.

The early **oratorio** was a dramatic work for chorus, solo voices, and orchestra. Unlike opera, it did not include scenery, costuming, or stage action. Texts were usually taken from the Old Testament and sung in Latin. A singing narrator helped to explain the dramatic action, which unfolded in a series of arias, recitatives, choral movements, and instrumental sections.

Figure 7.1 Leontyne Price, world-famous opera singer, performs at the Metropolitan Opera House.

The **cantata** was shorter and used fewer performers than the opera and oratorio. Either sacred or secular, it was usually written in Italian rather than Latin and emphasized solo voices with continuo.

OPERA

The earliest surviving opera was written by a member of the Camerata named Jacopo Peri (1561–1633), whose *Eurydice* dates from the year 1600. Based on the Greek legend of Orpheus and Eurydice, it consists almost entirely of recitative with continuo. In accordance with the principles of the Camerata, Peri wrote in the foreword to his opera that its style was intended to "imitate speech in song."

Claudio Monteverdi

The first master of operatic composition was the Italian Claudio Monteverdi (1567–1643) whose treatment of the Orpheus legend, *La favola d'Orfeo,* marks the beginning of opera as a major art form. First performed in Mantua in 1607, *Orfeo* had elaborate costuming, staging and lighting, an instrumental ensemble of forty players, and a chorus of singers and dancers.

In addition to *Orfeo,* Monteverdi wrote several other operas. Among the most successful were *Il ritorno di Ulisse in patria* (*The Return of Ulysses to His Homeland,* 1641) and *L'Incoronazione di Poppea* (*The Coronation of Poppea,* 1642). Like those of his contemporaries, Monteverdi's operas were written in Italian. They drew mainly upon Greek and Roman legends for their plots, which were adapted by poets into **libretti,** or operatic texts.

Originally performed for aristocratic gatherings, opera gradually became a popular form of entertainment for the middle class. Public opera houses were built and composers and librettists adapted their operas to a wider and more varied audience. The popularity of many opera singers was as intense as that of today's movie and TV "stars."

Opera, with its concentration on secular subjects, greatly increased the professional opportunities for women, whose role in the music of the church had been and continued to be quite limited.

During the baroque period, Italian opera spread throughout Europe, reaching its heights in the Italian operas of Handel in England. The Italian style had less influence in France, where the composer Jean-Baptiste Lully (1632–1687), ironically an Italian, headed the group that created and supported French opera.

SECULAR CANTATA

The secular cantata was a popular form of musical entertainment in baroque Italy. Prominent composers such as Luigi Rossi (1597–1653), Giacomo Carissimi (ca. 1605–1674), and Antonio Cesti (ca. 1623–1669) wrote numerous cantatas for performance at social gatherings in the homes of wealthy aristocrats. The earliest secular cantatas were comparatively short and consisted of contrasting sections of recitatives, ariosos, and arias.

One of the most prolific composers of secular cantatas was Barbara Strozzi (1619–ca. 1664). Between 1644 and 1664, Strozzi published eight volumes of vocal works containing about one hundred pieces, most of which were individual arias and secular cantatas for soprano and basso continuo. The texts of many of her cantatas center on unrequited love, a favorite theme among seventeenth-century composers. In all probability, Strozzi performed these pieces for the Accademic degli Unisoni, a Venetian fellowship of poets, philosophers, and historians who met in the home of her father.

ORATORIO

Early baroque oratorio appeared in two forms—the *Latin oratorio* and the *oratorio volgare*, which used Italian texts. The Latin oratorio included the roles of narrator and chorus in addition to the central characters. It reached its peak in the works of the Roman composer Giacomo Carissimi (1605–1674). The finest of his many oratorios, *Jepthe* (ca. 1649), was based on an Old Testament story from the Book of Judges.

Carissimi's pupil Alessandro Scarlatti (1660–1725) was one of the principal composers of the *oratorio volgare*. In the hands of Scarlatti, the oratorio became musically indistinct from opera. While the themes were still religious, the texts were in Italian, the role of the narrator was eliminated, and the chorus was abandoned. Actually, the oratorio was little more than a substitution for opera, theatrical performances of which were banned by the church during Lent.

The oratorio spread from Italy to the other countries of Europe. Henrich Schütz (1585–1672), who studied in Italy, introduced the oratorio to Germany, and Marc-Antoine Charpentier (1634–1704), a pupil of Carissimi, was the principal oratorio composer in France. But the oratorio rose to its height in England in the monumental works of George Frideric Handel.

Figure 7.2 An engraving of Handel.

George Frideric Handel was born in Halle, a trading center some eighty miles southwest of Berlin, the son of a prosperous barber-surgeon attached to the court of the duke of Saxony. His father had in mind a legal career for the boy but did allow him to begin music study at age eight with the organist of the town's principal Lutheran church. Aside from learning to play the organ, harpsichord, violin, and oboe, young Handel also studied composition, writing church cantatas and numerous small-scale instrumental works.

Out of respect for his father's wish, Handel enrolled at the University of Halle in 1702. At the end of his first year, however, he withdrew from the university and went to Hamburg to pursue his interest in music.

Musical activity in Hamburg, as in most cosmopolitan cities of the time, centered around the opera house, where Italian opera thrived. Soon after Handel arrived in Hamburg in 1703, he obtained a position as violinist in the theater orchestra and industriously set about learning the craft of opera composition. His first opera, *Almira* (1704), reflected the curious mixture of native German and imported Italian musical styles then prevalent in Hamburg: the recitatives were set in German, the arias in Italian. The work was a popular success and three other operas soon followed. In 1706, feeling that he had learned all that Hamburg had to offer, Handel decided to go to Italy.

His three-year stay in Italy was amazingly successful. Traveling back and forth between Florence, Venice, Rome, and Naples, he met many of Italy's greatest composers and was the frequent guest of cardinals, princes,

HANDEL'S WORK

Handel's fame today rests largely on the half-dozen oratorios—particularly *Messiah*—still in concert repertory, several *concerti grossi* (see chapter 8), some organ concertos, and two orchestral suites, *Water Music* and *Royal Fireworks Music*. These amount to only a fraction of his total work.

With few exceptions, Handel's operas followed the pattern laid down by Italian composers of the seventeenth century. Their plots, drawn from classical mythology, were developed through a series of paired recitatives and arias. His gifts for melody and his imaginative, resourceful orchestration were acclaimed in his own time, and his ability to dramatize in music the psychological and emotional states of his characters was unexcelled.

and ambassadors. Much of his popularity stemmed from the success of his operas *Rodrigo* (Florence, 1708) and *Agrippina* (Venice, 1709).

Through one of the friends he met in Italy, Handel obtained the position of musical director to the Electoral Court of Hanover, Germany. He had just taken up his duties in 1710, however, when he asked permission from Elector Georg Ludwig to visit London. Italian opera was then in great vogue with the English aristocracy, and the success of his opera *Rinaldo* (1711) led Handel to ask permission for another leave of absence the following year. Though promising to return "within a reasonable time," Handel stretched out his second London visit indefinitely.

In 1714 Queen Anne died, and Elector Georg Ludwig of Hanover ascended to the throne as George I of England. How Handel settled the embarrassing problem of his long-neglected contract with the Electoral Court is unknown. But the annual pension Queen Anne had given him was continued and even increased by George I, and within several years he was in high favor at the royal court.

During his years in England (he became a subject in 1726) Handel was involved in no less than four operatic enterprises. The most significant of these, the Royal Academy of Music, was organized by British nobility under the sponsorship of the king. During its eight-year existence (1720–1728), Handel's career as an opera composer reached its highest point.

Despite Handel's many personal successes, each of his four opera companies collapsed. A major reason for their collapse was the declining taste of the English for Italian opera. The enormously successful production, in 1728, of John Gay's *The Beggar's Opera* undoubtedly hastened the extinction of Italian opera in England. A parody of Italian style, *The Beggar's Opera* was widely imitated and a new form of light, popular musical entertainment was created in English.

Though Handel continued to compose Italian operas for more than a decade after the appearance of *The Beggar's Opera*, he turned increasingly to the oratorio.

His first English oratorio, *Haman and Mordecai* (later revised and renamed *Esther*), was composed in 1720. Others followed during the 1730s, but it was not until 1739, with the completion of *Saul* and *Israel in Egypt*, that he seemed to sense the full musical and dramatic possibilities of this form. Neither of these works was an immediate success, but others that followed were. In 1742, *Messiah* received high critical praise after its first performance in Dublin. By 1746, with the performance of *Judas Maccabaeus*, Handel had found a new public in the growing English middle class.

In his last years Handel was universally recognized as England's greatest composer. His popularity with all segments of English society steadily grew, and the royal patronage of George I was followed by that of George II. Despite declining health and the eventual loss of his eyesight, Handel continued to maintain a heavy schedule of oratorio performances, which he conducted himself from the keyboard. While attending a performance of *Messiah* on March 30, 1759, he suddenly grew faint and had to be taken home. He died two weeks later and was buried with state honors in Westminster Abbey. His will revealed that he had accumulated a substantial private fortune, which was dispersed—along with his music manuscripts—among friends.

The bulk of Handel's oratorios are dramatic, with specific characters and plots. Although most of them, including *Samson, Saul, Solomon, Belshazzar,* and *Jeptha,* are based on stories drawn from the Old Testament, they were not written as church music. Instead, they were intended to be performed for the public in music halls and auditoriums.

Handel's two nondramatic oratorios are *Israel in Egypt* and *Messiah.* In *Israel in Egypt* the chorus dominates, narrating and describing the events. The solo voices do not represent specific characters as they would in a dramatic oratorio. Instead, they complement and act as a foil for the chorus. The unusually large orchestra is used brilliantly to depict the plagues that were inflicted upon Egypt, particularly in the sections representing the buzzing of the flies, and the fire and hailstones.

Handel's other nondramatic oratorio, *Messiah,* is based on the life of Christ. In *Messiah* the solo voices do not represent specific characters (with the exception of the passage in which the angel appears to the shepherds) nor is the orchestra used for pictorial narration. Although we might expect that the text for this oratorio would come from the Gospels of the New Testament, where the life of Christ is recorded, the bulk of the libretto consists of prophetic passages from the Old Testament. As a result, the events in Christ's life and his role as Redeemer are suggested symbolically rather than portrayed dramatically.

Messiah was composed in only twenty-four days. It was a success in Handel's lifetime and has become one of the most loved and popular pieces of music in the history of Western civilization. At its first London performance in 1743, King George II was so moved by the opening of the "Hallelujah" chorus that he stood during its performance, a precedent that most audiences follow still.

Altogether, *Messiah* represents about three hours of music for four solo voices (SATB), chorus, (SATB), and orchestra. The onatorio is in three parts comprising fifty-three movements. (A **movement** is an independent section of a larger composition.) The movements include arias, recitatives, choruses, and orchestral sections. Part I deals with the prophecy of the coming of the Messiah and his birth. Part II treats the sacrifice of Jesus and the salvation of humanity through his suffering and death; part III, the certainty of eternal life through faith in the risen Christ.

Aria

The aria received ingenious treatment in the oratorios of Handel. He modified the standard da capo form (ABA), often avoiding the expected return to the A section. In *Messiah* the arias are rich in expression and marvelously varied in mood. Among the many vocal gems are the joyous contralto aria "O Thou that tellest good tidings to Zion," followed immediately by a choral version of the same musical material; the stirring aria for bass "The trumpet shall sound"; and the serenely beautiful "I know that my Redeemer liveth."

Recitative   In *Messiah,* Handel employs both secco and accompanied recitatives. The secco recitatives are quite short and function merely as brief introductions to ensuing arias. The accompanied recitatives, are longer and achieve a higher level of musical interest, at times even rivaling the expressiveness of the arias they introduce. This is true of such recitatives as "Thus saith the Lord," "For, behold, darkness shall cover the earth," "Thy rebuke hath broken His Heart" and "Comfort ye," the recitative that initiates the action of *Messiah* immediately after the overture.

Chorus

A primary factor that stamps Handel's oratorios as historically unique is the use of the chorus as a major element in the dramatic and musical structure. Certainly this is true of *Messiah*. In *Messiah,* choral movements perform a variety of functions. They serve as the climatic element in a three-part complex consisting of a recitative, an aria, and a chorus. A second use of the chorus is as a structural "frame" beginning and ending a large section. Part II of *Messiah,* for example, begins with the restrained and sorrowful "Behold the Lamb of God" and concludes with the joyous and triumphant "Hallelujah." These two choruses constitute a frame for the entire middle section of the oratorio. Occasionally, Handel joins two or more choruses into a larger unit in which each chorus depends upon the one preceding or following it. This is the case in part II of *Messiah* with "Surely, He hath borne our griefs," "And with His stripes we are healed," and "All we like sheep have gone astray."

Many of *Messiah's* choral movements have an extra-ordinary emotional impact and musical appeal. Such well-known choral movements as "And the glory of the Lord," "For unto us a child is born," and the magnificent "Hallelujah" help account for the tremendous popularity of *Messiah.*

Orchestra

Because of the limited orchestral resources available to him in Dublin, where *Messiah* had its premiere, Handel employed a modest instrumental ensemble consisting of oboes, bassoons, trumpets, timpani, strings, and continuo. Two movements in the oratorio were written for orchestra alone—the overture that begins the work and the short, eloquent *"Pastorale"* that sets the scene in part I in which the angel appears to the shepherds.

Organization

Part of the genius of *Messiah* derives from Handel's ability to unify a complex musical structure consisting of numerous individual movements. Frequently he employed the pattern recitative-aria-chorus to organize a long stretch of music. The recitative introduces the aria, which progresses to a culminating choral movement. Each movement possesses its own internal organization and interest but also contributes to the larger structure. This organizational procedure dominates the first part of *Messiah* and is well illustrated by the movements that immediately follow the overture:

Overture	Recitative	Aria	Chorus
	Comfort ye	*Every valley*	*And the glory of the Lord*

The first movement (recitative) displays Handel's masterful handling of baroque techniques. The text is divided into two parts. *SIDE 1/SELECTION 5*

A: Comfort ye, comfort ye my people, saith your God; speak ye comfortably to Jerusalem, and cry unto her, that her warfare is accomplish'd, that her iniquity is pardon'd.

B: The voice of him that crieth in the wilderness, Prepare ye the way of the Lord, make straight in the desert a highway for our God.
ISAIAH 40:1–3.

Part A, in the key of E major, is very much like an arioso in that it is quite lyrical and its tempo is steady. Both the orchestra and the tenor voice convey the feelings inherent in the words. This is evident from the tenor's opening motive:

Example 7.1

Com-fort ye

which not only matches the rhythmic inflection of the text but also conveys the feeling of serenity of the first part of the movement.

Another example of musical treatment of words to reflect their expressive quality is shown in the phrase:

Example 7.2

and cry un-to her

The large upward leap on "and cry" and the long note on "cry" reinforce the drama of the joyful announcement.

This part of the movement is unified by the statement and reappearance of material played by the orchestra:

Example 7.3

The first portion of this material (sometimes only the first five notes) reappears several times, either giving way to the tenor voice:

Example 7.4

Tenor

Speak ye com

or coming in "on top" of it:

Example 7.5

that her war - fare, her war -

The last appearance of the material is a full statement which, after the various fragment versions, imparts a feeling of completion and concludes the first part of the movement.

In the second part of the movement the decisive emotional change in the text is reflected in the musical structure. The lyricism and serenity of the "comfort" section give way to dramatic assertiveness in the B section. The voice executes short, clipped phrases while the orchestra punctuates with short, isolated chords:

Example 7.6

the voice of him that crieth in the wil - der-ness pre - pare

This procedure is typical of the recitative style, as is the ending, with its downward motion of the voice followed by two concluding chords (dominant to tonic) from the orchestra:

Example 7.7

for our God

Thus Handel uses both arioso and recitative in one movement to exploit the contrasting character of the two sections of text. In addition, the recitative portion not only brings the movement to a close, but leads naturally into the next movement, the aria "Every valley."

Every valley shall be exalted and every mountain and hill made low, ISAIAH 40:4 the crooked straight, and the rough places plain.

Probably the most immediately striking aspect of this aria is its use of word painting, a device we encountered earlier in our discussion of Renaissance secular music. The word "exalted" is set to a long ascending sixteenth-note melisma which gives a feeling of rising:

Example 7.8

shall be_____ ex - alt - - - - -

_ _ _ _ _ _ _ - ed.

The words "crooked" and "plain" (meaning "level") also receive musical treatment which reflects their meaning and spirit:

Example 7.9

the crook-ed straight, the crook-ed straight and rough pla-ces plain _____

The angular figure on "crooked" contrasts sharply with the static, simple melody on "plain."

Word painting is used again in the setting of the phrase "and every mountain and hill made low," in which the melody rises to a peak on "mountain" and then descends to a tone an octave below on "low":

Example 7.10

and ev-'ry moun-tain and hill _____ made low.

The use of individualized musical figures to reflect the emotional feeling or physical characteristics of a word or phrase was common in the baroque period and, indeed, is found in music of virtually every baroque composer. Extended melismas and highly ornamented figures provided the perfect vehicle for virtuoso soloists to display their remarkable vocal skills.

"Every valley" is followed immediately by the allegro choral movement in A major, "And the glory of the Lord."

> And the glory of the Lord shall be revealed, and all flesh shall see it ISAIAH 40:5 together, for the mouth of the Lord hath spoken it.

This choral movement is based upon four melodic ideas, each with its own set of words:

Example 7.11

Handel contrasts these ideas in a variety of ways, perhaps the most striking of which is the use of both polyphonic and homophonic textures. The first polyphonic section of the movement is based upon "a" and a combination of "a" and "b."

Example 7.12

Here the texture is very thin, with no more than two voice parts singing at the same time and with the orchestra reduced to continuo only. This thin polyphonic texture is maintained until the climactic point when all four parts of the chorus and the full orchestra join in a *homophonic* phrase, which brings the first section of the movement to a close (example 7.13). The change from thin texture to full chorus and orchestra and the sudden switch from polyphony to homophony provide a powerful climax.

Example 7.13

The rest of the movement consists of several sections organized in roughly the same manner. Each is characterized by imaginative and flexible use of the four melodic ideas and their combinations. And each involves the same alternation between polyphonic imitation and strong homophonic endings, each more powerful than the one before. The movement culminates in a passage of almost breathtaking force:

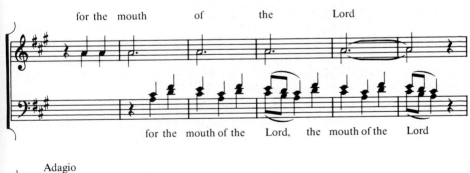

Example 7.14

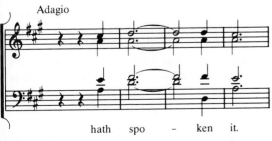

Just before the final statement of "hath spoken it," Handel brings the music to a sudden and surprising halt, followed by silence, creating a feeling of excitement and suspense. This suspense is resolved by a prolonged cadence on "hath spoken it," as all parts of the chorus and the full orchestra combine to provide a stirring conclusion to the entire three-movement complex.

Of course, we have discussed only a small portion of this work. The rest of *Messiah* is full of equally glorious music, masterfully crafted. Certainly, it is no wonder that *Messiah* is one of the world's most beloved pieces of music.

LUTHERAN GERMANY

While the seed of baroque style sown in Italy at the beginning of the seventeenth century came to fruition in England in the operas and oratorios of Handel, it grew and flowered differently in Germany, culminating in the music of Johann Sebastian Bach.

The traditions of the Lutheran church into which Bach was born and for which he composed almost all of his vocal music rested heavily upon the principle of direct and active participation by the congregation in church ceremonies. To this end, religious services were conducted in the *German* language as opposed to *Latin* in the case of Catholicism. And to this end there needed to be a kind of religious music sufficiently simple and direct that the congregation could sing regardless of the degree of musical talent or training.

Martin Luther (1483–1546) began the development of a body of such music as part of the reforms that began the Protestant movement. The **chorale,** a simple hymn tune with spiritual words provided this kind of music not only as part of the church service but also for devotional activity in the home.

Chorale melodies came from a variety of sources. Some were adapted from Gregorian chants, others came from secular tunes, and many were newly composed. Luther himself is responsible for many chorales and his still famous "Ein' Feste Burg ist Unser Gott" ("A Mighty Fortress is Our God") typifies the simplicity and strength of the chorale.

By Bach's time these well-known chorale melodies and their texts functioned not only as the basis for congregational singing, but they also provided a rich body of materials from which larger and more complex vocal and instrumental musical structures could be built. Thus, they were used in much the same way as the Gregorian chant had been during the Renaissance.

The most important forms of vocal music in baroque Germany were the cantata, the opera, and the Passion. The Italian influence that spread throughout Europe was felt in Germany. Italian music and Italian musicians held sway particularly in the field of opera. So strong was this influence that early attempts to establish opera in the German language failed, and it was not until the later part of the period that German opera enjoyed any sustained popularity and then only for a brief span of time.

The Italian style also influenced German Protestant religious music but to a lesser extent. The polyphonic tradition was never completely abandoned and remained a strong element in the music of the church particularly among the more conservative composers such as J. S. Bach.

The Passion

The **Passion** is a musical setting of the story of the suffering and crucifixion of Jesus Christ as told in the Bible by the gospels. The Passion was particularly important during Holy Week, especially on Good Friday. The early settings of the Passion text, for instance those of the great German master of the early baroque, Heinrich Schütz (1585–1672), employed only the Biblical text with an introductory and concluding chorus. By Bach's time, musical settings of the Passion had expanded to include *nonbiblical* texts in the form of commentary about the events described in the Gospel.

In Bach's monumental *Passion According to St. Matthew,* the Gospel account of the betrayal, arrest, trial, and crucifixion of Christ is told by soloists in recitative, secco for all characters but Christ, who is accompanied by a string quartet. The chorus assumes various roles such as the crowd and the disciples. The nonbiblical contemplations are interspersed between sections of the Gospel story in the form of da capo arias sung by soloists and numerous chorales in which the congregation joins the choir and orchestra.

Bach's *St. Matthew Passion* joins Handel's *Messiah* in representing the culmination of baroque vocal music.

The Cantata

Like the opera and the oratorio, the cantata went through considerable transformation from early to late baroque, reaching its height in Germany in the works of Dietrich Buxtehude (ca. 1637–1707) and J. S. Bach. By Bach's time, the sacred cantata often included the standard baroque elements of recitative, aria, chorus, and instrumental ensemble. Frequently, cantatas were built upon one of the many well-known chorale tunes.

Cantata texts related to specific feast days of the church year and for church musicians such as Bach, the writing of cantatas was a routine professional obligation. Between 1704 and 1740, Bach composed cantatas on a regular basis for the churches he served. He is believed to have written more than 300, although only 195 have been preserved.

Bach's Cantata no. 4 was written early in his career and does not employ the recitative and da capo aria that typify his later compositions. Using as its theme the chorale tune and text, *Christ Lag in Todesbanden,* it is an example of Bach's contrapuntal technique, a skill that ultimately marked him as one of the great musical craftsmen in history. The cantata was intended to be performed as part of the Easter Sunday service.

CANTATA NO. 4: CHRIST LAG IN TODESBANDEN (CHRIST LAY IN DEATH'S BONDAGE)

The work is scored for four solo voices (SATB), chorus (SATB) doubled by four brass instruments, and a string ensemble with continuo. It consists of seven movements (one for each verse of the chorale text) and a **sinfonia,** a short instrumental introduction, according to the following plan:

Sinfonia	Verse I	II	III	IV	V	VI	VII
	chorus	duet	solo	quartet	solo	duet	chorus
	SATB	SA	T	SATB	B	ST	with congregation

CHRIST LAG IN TODESBANDEN

VERSUS I

Christ lag in Todesbanden
Für unsre Sünd gegeben,
Er ist wieder erstanden
Und hat uns bracht das Leben;
Des wir sollen fröhlich sein,
Gott loben und ihm dankbar sein
Und singen Halleluja,
Halleluja!

VERSUS II

Den Tod niemand swingen kunnt
Bei allen Menschenkinden,
Das macht alles unsre Sünd,
Klein Unschuld war zu finden.
Davon kam der Tod so bald
Und nahm über uns Gewalt,
Hielt uns in seinem Reich gefangen,
Halleluja!

VERSUS III

Jesus Christus, Gottes Sohn,
An unser Statt ist kommen
Und hat die Sünde weggetan,
Damit dem Tod genommen
All sein Recht und sein Gewalt,
Da bleibet nichts denn Todsgestalt,

Den Stachl hat er verloren.
Halleluja!

VERSUS IV

Es war ein wunderlicher Krieg,
Da Tod und Leben rungen,
Das Leben behielt den Sieg,
Es hat den Tod verschlungen.
Die Schrift hat verkündigt das,
Wie ein Tod den andern frass,
Ein Spott aus dem Tod ist worden.
Halleluja!

CHRIST LAY IN DEATH'S BONDAGE

VERSE I

Christ lay in death's bondage,
For our sins given;
He is again arisen
And has brought us life;
For which we should rejoice,
Praise God and give him thanks,
And sing Hallelujah,
Hallelujah!

VERSE II

No one could overcome Death
Among all mortal children;
This was caused by all our sins,
No innocence was to be found.
Hence came Death so soon
And over us achieved dominion,
Held us in his realm imprisoned,
Hallelujah!

VERSE III

Jesus Christ, God's Son,
In our stead has come
And has done away with sin;
Thus from Death seizing
All its prerogatives and power;
There remains nothing but Death's
image,
Its sting has been lost.
Hallelujah!

VERSE IV

It was a wondrous war,
With Death and Life embattled;
Life achieved the victory,
It swallowed up Death.
The scripture has proclaimed this,
How one Death consumed another;
A mockery has Death become.
Hallelujah!

Example 7.19

Bach's penchant for giving selected ideas special musical treatment is present in this movement. "Kreuzes" (cross) is emphasized by a lengthening and decoration of

Example 7.20

the note on which the word occurs. Of particular interest is the setting of the words

Example 7.21

"dem Tode für" with the extreme downward leap to and elongation of "Tode" (death). And the elongation of the first syllable of "Würger" (destroyer) is very dramatic.

Example 7.22

Verse VI, scored for soprano, tenor, and continuo, expresses very beautifully the light-hearted joy embodied in the text of this movement. The chorale tune is passed back and forth between the two solo voices, and the end of each phrase is extended and decorated by a melismatic triplet figure.

SIDE 2/SELECTION 1 In verse VII, the last movement, we finally encounter the chorale tune in its pure form. The melody is located in the soprano voice and the first violin part, the rest of the chorus, doubled by instruments, providing simple harmonic support.

Example 7.23

In comparison to the elaborate settings in the previous movements, the final verse is considerably less complex, allowing the congregation to join the choir in singing the last verse of the cantata. This active participation provides the climactic religious and spiritual fulfillment of the experience as a whole.

SUMMARY

The baroque era began in Italy around the year 1600. Fundamental style changes were brought about by a reaction against Renaissance vocal polyphony and a desire to make music serve and reflect the mood and meaning of the words. This attitude resulted in the monodic style, in which a single voice is accompanied by a group of instruments called basso continuo. The new prominence of the major and minor modes, the establishment of a tonic, and the devices of modulation and dissonance permitted the development of larger musical structures.

Many new vocal forms developed during the baroque, notably the speech-like recitative and the lyrical arioso. The da capo aria is an expansion of the arioso and is characterized by an ABA form. These became important features of the large vocal forms of the baroque—the opera, the oratorio, and the cantata.

The opera is an elaborately staged dramatic form based on secular themes. The first great opera was *Orfeo,* written by the Italian, Claudio Monteverdi. The oratorio is a sacred dramatic work presented without scenery or stage action. It reached its height in the works of George Frideric Handel, particularly with his *Messiah.* The cantata is smaller in scale than either the opera or oratorio and used both sacred and secular texts.

The Protestant movement in Germany promoted the use of simple hymn tunes for congregational singing. These tunes, known as chorales, formed the basis for larger, more elaborate vocal works. Such works as *St. Matthew's Passion* and the numerous cantatas by Johann Sebastian Bach represent the finest in German baroque vocal music.

NEW TERMS

monodic style	**opera**
figured bass	**oratorio**
basso continuo (continuo)	**cantata**
recitative	**libretto (libretti)**
secco recitative	**movement**
accompanied recitative	**chorale**
arioso	**Passion**
aria (da capo aria)	**sinfonia**
da capo	**basso ostinato**

SUGGESTED LISTENING

Bach, Johann Sebastian

Magnificat in D. This setting of the Latin canticle of the Virgin Mary is one of Bach's finest and most melodious works. It is scored for soloists, chorus, and orchestra.

Cantata 140, *Wachet auf, ruft uns die Stimme* (*Sleepers Awake*). Movements one, four, and seven are based upon the chorale melody. Movements three and six are duets in ABA form. Each duet is introduced by a short recitative (movements two and five).

Carissimi, Giaccomo

Jepthe. An oratorio that tells the Old Testament story of Jepthe's pledge to God. If allowed to return from battle victorious, he will sacrifice the first person who greets him upon his return. The first person turns out to be his daughter. The piece ends with a lament sung by the daughter, followed by a moving chorus.

Handel, George Frideric

Israel in Egypt. An oratorio based upon the Old Testament account of the flight of the Jews from captivity in Egypt. Of particular interest is the description of the plagues.

Monteverdi, Claudio

L'Orfeo. An opera based upon the Orpheus legend. Probably the finest opera of the early baroque.

Purcell, Henry

Dido and Aeneas. Purcell wrote this opera to be performed by a school for young gentlewomen—all but one of the roles are for female voices. The music is faithful to the mood of the libretto; for example, it mixes major and minor modes to heighten emotional tension and creates the sounds of laughter and echoes.

Schütz, Heinrich

Historia von der Geburt Jesu Christi (*The Christmas Story*). One of the earliest masterpieces of baroque oratorio, this work is divided into eight sections with opening and closing choruses. The recitatives are written in a masterful, flowing style, and the vocal arias and ensembles have very colorful instrumental accompaniments.

Strozzi, Barbara

Cantatas found in *Harmonia Mundi 1114.* Interesting music by a prolific composer of baroque secular cantatas.

BAROQUE INSTRUMENTAL MUSIC

T he baroque era was not only a period of magnificent achievement in vocal composition but it also saw the gradual development of a significant body of instrumental music. The baroque was the age of the great violin makers, among them the members of the Stradivari family. Improvements were made in the construction of virtually every wind and brass instrument, and the organ and the harpsichord became the basic keyboard instruments. By the end of the baroque era, instrumental music had gradually equalled and surpassed vocal music in importance, and the style of vocal music itself was very much influenced by the instrumental idiom.

KEYBOARD MUSIC

A large body of music for keyboard instruments—the organ and harpsichord (the piano had not yet been invented)—was written during the baroque period. These pieces appeared with various titles—**fantasia, prelude, toccata,**—that were carryovers from the names given to lute music in the sixteenth century. The terms described the style and character of a piece rather than its form, for pieces bearing these titles were cast in "free form," with no standard formal design.

The term toccata derives from the Italian verb *toccare* ("to touch") and implies a piece full of scale passages, rapid runs and trills, and massive chords. The fantasia was a piece characterized by displays of virtuosity. The prelude customarily introduced another piece or group of pieces.

The prelude, fantasia, and toccata were improvisatory in nature and were often used as an introduction to a **fugue,** one of the great intellectual musical structures of the baroque era.

Figure 8.1 Vast technical improvements in wind, brass, and keyboard instruments, and the development of the violin encouraged the growth of instrumental music during the baroque era. Pictured here is an imaginary instrument-maker's workshop.

FUGUE

A fugue is a piece of music consisting of the polyphonic development of a melodic phrase called the **subject.** Fugues are composed for a certain number of voice parts—two-voice fugue, three-voice fugue, and so on. The precise manner in which the subject is developed among these voice parts varies from piece to piece. However, the initial section of virtually every fugue follows a plan that is more or less standard. This section is called the **exposition.**

The exposition begins with a single voice part stating the subject. As the subject ends, a second voice part enters in imitation stating the subject while the first voice continues with contrasting melodic material called the **countersubject.** This process of imitative entrances of each voice part in turn continues until all voice parts have stated the fugue subject, at which point the exposition has been accomplished. Without pause the piece continues with a number of sections that function either as new statements of the fugue subject or some variation of it, or as transitions between statements of the subject. The transition sections are called **episodes,** and most frequently modulate from the key of one statement of the subject to the key of the next statement. The melodic material in the episodes may be derived from the subject, the countersubject, or entirely different material.

A number of techniques were available for the development of the fugue subject. For example, the subject can be elongated—stretched out with longer note values—**augmentation.** Or just the opposite, condensed through the use of shorter note values—**diminution.** It can be turned upside down (**inversion**) or even played backward (**retrograde**). Sometimes statements of the subject overlap—before one voice finishes, another enters—a device known as **stretto.**

In listening to a fugue, the primary interest lies in following the life of the fugue subject as it appears and reappears in different surroundings and in different forms throughout the course of the piece.

The fugue was a very popular form utilized in both choral and instrumental literature. Although it originated in the baroque period, it has held a high place in all musical eras after the baroque, up to and including the present time. The unchallenged master of the baroque fugue was Johann Sebastian Bach.

BACH *(1685–1750)*

Johann Sebastian Bach was the most distinguished member of a family of musicians that reached back four generations before him and was carried forward by three of his sons. His father, Johann Ambrosius, was a musician in service to the town council of Eisenach, a small community in Thuringia—now part of East Germany. Little is known about Bach's early life, but it seems that his father, an excellent violinist, taught him to play stringed instruments, and another relative, the organist of Eisenach's leading church, began instructing him at the organ.

Orphaned when he was only ten, Bach was sent to live with his eldest brother, Johann Christoph, an organist at the nearby town of Ohrdruf. He remained there five years, taking organ and harpsichord lessons from his brother, earning some money as a boy soprano, and studying at the town's famed grammar school. He did so well at the school that he was offered a scholarship at St. Michael's, a secondary school in Luneburg, a city in northern Germany.

In 1703 Bach obtained his first musical position, as violinist in the small chamber orchestra of the ducal court of Weimar, but when a post as church organist became available in Arnstadt in August of 1703, he accepted the position. Dissatisfied with working conditions in Arnstadt and the poor state of the church choir, Bach left in 1707 to become organist at the church of St. Blasius in the Free Imperial City of Muhlhausen. In that same year he married a cousin, Maria Barbara Bach.

Soon entangled in a feud between factions within the Lutheran church, he left Muhlhausen in 1708 to become court organist, and later concertmaster, in the ducal chapel of Weimar. His nine years in Weimar constitute his first major creative period. Here he composed a number of cantatas and many of his greatest organ works, and he worked intensively with singers and instrumentalists as a conductor.

Because of his evident talent as a composer, performer, and conductor, Bach expected to be offered the top position of *Kapellmeister* (chapelmaster) at Weimar when it became available in 1716. However, he was passed over in favor of another. The following year he accepted the position of court conductor to the small principality of Anhalt-Cöthen.

Bach had enjoyed a growing reputation as an organist and composer of church cantatas and had made annual performing tours to important centers such as Kassel, Leipzig, and Dresden. His duties at Cöthen, as conductor and composer for the eighteen-member court

Figure 8.2 Johann Sebastian Bach.

orchestra, led to a shift in emphasis toward intrumental music. Much of his finest orchestral music dates from this period, including the six Brandenburg Concertos.

The happy and productive years at Cöthen were marred by the death of his wife in 1720. Bach soon remarried, however, and his new wife, Anna Magdalena, proved to be a hardworking, cheerful companion who raised Bach's four children by Maria Barbara along with her own. She gave birth to thirteen children in all, six of whom survived.

In 1723 Bach was offered the position of cantor (director of music) at St. Thomas Church in Leipzig, one of the most important musical posts in Protestant Germany. However, it was not a completely auspicious beginning for Bach, as the city council turned to him only after it had received refusals from two other composers. His duties included composing cantatas for St. Nicholas Church as well as St. Thomas Church, supervising the musical programs in all the municipal churches, and teaching Latin in the St. Thomas choir school.

Despite the irksome nature of some of his duties and his uneasy relationship with his superiors, the Leipzig town council, Bach remained in Leipzig for the rest of his life. He personally supervised the musical education of his most gifted sons, Wilhelm Friedemann, Carl Philipp Emanuel, and Johann Christian, and saw them embark on promising musical careers. Though, like Handel, he went blind in old age, his creative powers remained undimmed. His last composition, dictated to a son-in-law a few days before his death, was a chorale prelude, "Before Thy Throne, My God, I Stand."

Figure 8.3 Bach at the organ in St. Thomas Kirche Leipzig. This superb instrument stimulated Bach's musical genius for more than a quarter of a century.

BACH'S WORK

Bach's profound genius extended to nearly every form of musical composition prevalent in the baroque period. His vocal music is best represented by his B Minor Mass, his Passions, and his many cantatas. In his instrumental music he was equally prolific and far-ranging in style.

His consummate skill is clearly seen in the Fugue in G Minor (ca. 1709), subtitled "The Little" to distinguish it from his longer fugue in the same key.

BACH:
FUGUE IN G MINOR
("THE LITTLE")
SIDE 2/SELECTION 2

Example 8.1

The Fugue in G Minor is a four-voice piece for organ based upon the following subject:

MUSIC OF THE BAROQUE ERA

Voice I (in this case the highest, or soprano voice) states the subject in the tonic key of G minor and continues with the countersubject where voice II enters in imitation with the subject in D minor.

Example 8.2

After a brief modulation back to G minor, voices III and IV follow the same pattern of stating the subject and countersubject as indicated in example 8.3.

Exposition of the Fugue in G Minor

Example 8.3

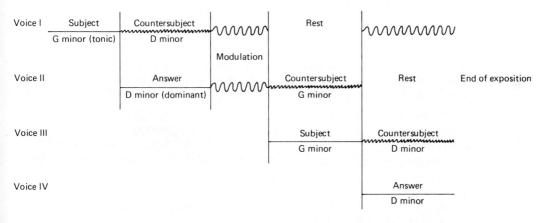

Note that this musical organization is heavily dependent upon the device known as imitation—voice II imitates voice I, and each voice in turn imitates the one before it in stating the subject.

There is no pause at the conclusion of the exposition. The flow of music is continuous. After a modulation back to the key of G minor, there appears to be an entry of the subject in voice III. However, after the first few notes, voice III continues not with the subject but the countersubject, while voice I "steals" the subject and goes on with a full statement. Aside from this "fake entry," the piece consists of a number of sections in which episodes prepare for and lead to statements of the subject in a variety of keys, ending with the final statement of the subject in the bass voice in the tonic of G minor.

Example 8.4

| Episode | False entry (Voice III), full statement (Voice I) | Episode | Subject (Voice II) | Episode | Subject (Voice IV) |

| Episode | Subject (Voice I) | Episode | Final statement of subject (Voice IV) |

Aside from the structural fugal procedures, this little piece illustrates a major stylistic feature of much baroque instrumental music—namely, an unbroken, uninterrupted steady flow of music from the first note to the last chord. Quite unlike later styles, in which sections of music are separated by pauses, the polyphonic instrumental style of the baroque is characterized by continuous motion and progression from beginning to end.

Baroque organ literature included many works intended for performance in conjunction with religious ceremonies and many of these pieces were based upon chorale melodies. For instance, as an introduction to the service, the organist would play a work based upon the particular chorale tune appropriate for the specific day in the church year—hence the *chorale prelude, chorale partita,* and *chorale fantasia.*

SUITE

A popular form among composers of music for the harpsichord was the **suite,** a series of movements with each movement based upon a particular dance rhythm and style. Usually it included the German **allemande,** the French **courante,** the **sarabande** (originally from Spain), and the English or Irish **gigue** (jig). Many suites also included the **gavotte** and at times nondance movements such as the prelude were employed. This series of movements was designed to offer interesting contrasts in meter, tempo, and texture.

The dance movements of the suite were not intended to accompany actual dancing. Composers simply adapted the rhythm and character of the dances, turning them into well-wrought compositions for listening.

While harpsichord suites were very popular in the late baroque (J. S. Bach's so-called *English* and *French Suites*), the suite was by no means confined to the keyboard. Rather, suites were written for a wide range of solo instruments, chamber ensembles, and orchestra. Handel's orchestral suites—The *Water Music* and *Music for the Royal Fireworks*—remain popular today.

BAROQUE SONATA

In the beginning of the baroque period, the term **sonata** was applied to instrumental pieces that varied greatly in structure, character, and the number and type of instruments. Usually it was a multimovement work but the number of movements varied from piece to piece.

MUSIC OF THE BAROQUE ERA

Gradually there developed a distinction between the sonata written for the church, **sonata da chiesa,** and that intended for the chamber, **sonata da camera.** The sonata da camera became essentially a dance suite, and the sonata da chiesa a four movement work in which the movements alternated in tempo: slow-fast-slow-fast.

Toward the later part of the baroque, three types of sonatas were predominant: the sonata for unaccompanied instrument; the **solo sonata** for one solo instrument (usually the violin) and continuo; and the **trio sonata** usually employing two violins for the upper voices and a cello and keyboard instrument for the continuo. Corelli, Vivaldi, Handel, and Bach all made important contributions to the sonata literature.

At the very end of the baroque, the emphasis shifted to the solo sonata, setting the stage for its development as a primary musical form during subsequent periods of music history.

CONCERTO

Baroque innovations in the realm of instrumental music included the **concerto,** a type of musical form based upon the contrast between relatively large and small bodies of sound. This principle of contrast manifested itself in the **solo concerto** and the **concerto grosso.**

Concerto Grosso

The concerto grosso is a multimovement work in which a small group of solo instruments, the **concertino,** and the full ensemble called the **ripieno** (Italian for "full") are contrasted. The basic outlines of the concerto grosso were established by Arcangelo Corelli (1653–1713) whose *Christmas Concerto* remains a favorite today. Corelli's concertino consisted of two solo violins and violoncello with either organ or harpsichord (continuo), contrasting with a small string orchestra (with its own continuo) playing the role of ripieno. The actual contrast between the solo group and the string orchestra in Corelli's concerti was slight in comparison to the concerti of later composers and the number of movements employed by Corelli varied from piece to piece.

Giuseppe Torelli (1658–1709) established a three-movement pattern—allegro-adagio-allegro (fast-slow-fast)—and the **ritornello form** as the structure of the first movement. In general, ritornello form follows the pattern outlined below:

A   B   A   C   A

ritornello   concertino   ritornello   concertino   ritornello   etc.

The thematic material given to the ripieno (the "ritornello") returns between sections played by the solo group of instruments—an example of alternation (see page 28). The ritornello statements *within* the movement are often fragmentary, consisting of only part of the original material, and are in different tonalities. Nevertheless, the returns of the ritornello theme, even though somewhat changed, give the movement a great sense of unity. The final ritornello is usually complete and is always in the same tonality in which the movement began.

Antonio Vivaldi (1669–1741) was a great master of the concerto grosso. He adopted the three movement form and the ritornello pattern described above. He also made a greater distinction between the ripieno and the concertino in terms of the increased degree of complexity of the musical material played by the concertino. Vivaldi's music had a strong influence on J. S. Bach.

In 1721 Bach completed six works for orchestra dedicated to Christian Ludwig, the Margrave of Brandenburg. Although Bach referred to these pieces as "concertos for several instruments," they have come to be known as the Brandenburg Concertos. Three of them (nos. 2, 4, and 5) follow the tradition of Vivaldi in that they contrast a group of solo instruments (concertino) against a full ensemble (ripieno).

BACH:
BRANDENBURG
CONCERTO NO. 5

The Brandenburg Concerto is scored for a concertino consisting of flute, violin, and harpsichord contrasting with a string orchestra with continuo as the ripieno. By his choice of instruments for the concertino, Bach created a contrast in timbre *within* the solo group as well as *between* the solo group and the ripieno. He maintains the fast-slow-fast three movement structure established by earlier composers.

First Movement

SIDE 2/SELECTION 3
SEE LISTENING, GUIDE
ON P. 147

The first movement is in ritornello form using as the returning thematic material the following:

Example 8.5

At the beginning, in the middle, and at the end of the movement, the ripieno presents a complete statement of this material in the key of D major, the tonic key of the movement. These full statements act as thematic and harmonic pillars providing the movement with a solid and unified structure. In between these complete statements, the solo instruments of the concertino develop and expand upon melodic and rhythmic ideas derived from the ritornello theme, punctuated by the ripieno with periodic fragmentary statements of the ritornello theme itself in a variety of keys.

As the movement progresses, the equality among the three solo instruments gradually gives way to the almost total predominance of the harpsichord. In fact, toward the end of the movement the violin, the flute, and the ripieno cease altogether, and the harpsichord is heard as a solo instrument in passages that require great virtuosity such as:

Example 8.6

The long solo section by the harpsichord climaxes in the final entry of the ritornello theme played by the entire ensemble ("tutti").

Like much baroque instrumental music, this entire movement is characterized by a constant spinning out of music with no stopping points or pauses of any kind—a relentless rhythmic drive from beginning to end.

Second Movement

In accordance with the concerto grosso plan, the second movement contrasts markedly. It is in a different key (B minor), it is slow in tempo (marked *affettuoso*—"tenderly") and it employs only the three solo instruments of the concertino, the harpsichord performing the dual function of solo instrument and continuo. The essence of this short movement is drawn from two distinction rhythmic motives:

Example 8.7

Example 8.8

They are contrasted and combined in a variety of ways by the three solo instruments.

Third Movement

The third movement returns to the tempo (allegro) and key (D major) of the first movement. It is very much in the spirit of a *gigue* based upon:

Example 8.9

It features the solo instruments, particularly the harpsichord with the ripieno devoted to light accompanying support except in a few climactic places where it joins with or rivals the concertino. Structurally the movement is a large three part form ABA. It has the same kind of continuous rhythmic drive as the first movement with the exception of an obvious stop and pause immediately before the return of the A section—quite a surprise in this style!

This work, along with the second and fourth Brandenburg concertos, represent the culmination of this fascinating form.

Solo Concerto

The solo concerto is organized along the same lines as the concerto grosso with the notable exception that it is written for only *one* solo instrument—contrasting with a full instrumental ensemble. Vivaldi wrote hundreds of solo concertos which became the models for later baroque composers, including Handel and Bach.

Of all Vivaldi's concertos, the group called *Le quattro stagione (The Four Seasons)* is perhaps the most interesting because of the extramusical basis of its inspiration. Vivaldi was one of the first to try to depict by musical means the feelings and sounds of the changing seasons. His four concertos are an early form of baroque descriptive or *program music,* and the music for the solo violin, which calls for virtuoso playing, demonstrates Vivaldi's skill at writing for the instrument.

Each of the four concertos bears the title of one of the seasons—spring, summer, winter, fall—and each is preceded by a sonnet describing that particular season. For instance, the concerto entitled *Spring* has the following introduction:

Spring has come, and the birds greet it with joyous songs, and at the same time the streams run softly murmuring to the breathing of gentle breezes . . .

The song of the birds, the murmuring streams, and the gentle breezes all are vividly represented by the solo violin and the full ensemble. But all of this takes place within the three movements of the basic concerto structure. And the ritornello structure of the first and last movements is also maintained.

Program music has attracted composers of every age. We have already mentioned the program chansons of Jannequin in the Renaissance, and an entire chapter (chapter 14) is devoted to program music in the romantic period.

The fates of the solo concerto and the concerto grosso beyond the baroque were quite different. The concerto grosso ceased to occupy the attention of composers to any appreciable extent while the solo concerto thrived during subsequent stylistic periods.

LISTENING GUIDE

J. S. Bach: *Brandenburg Concerto no. 5*

First Movement: fast
quadruple meter
ritornello form

Concertino: flute, violin, harpsichord

Ripieno: string orchestra with continuo

Review: Example 8.5 (the ritornello theme)
Example 8.6 (virtuoso passage on harpsichord)

Ritornello theme *Ripieno*	1a	complete statement in tonic; vigorous melody surges upward, setting rhythmic drive in motion
Contrasting section *Concertino*	b	fragments from ritornello theme; imitation between flute and violin, with harpsichord an independent third part in constant motion
Ritornello theme	2a	partial statement from beginning of theme
Contrasting section	b	continued imitation between flute and violin; more extended than *1b*
Ritornello theme	3a	partial statement, begins where *2a* left off
Contrasting section	b	harpsichord enters; flute and violin echo in single notes, then develop other fragments
Ritornello theme	4a	partial statement, taken from where *3a* left off
Contrasting section	b	interplay between violin and flute; fast notes, virtuosic display, draw attention to harpsichord
Ritornello theme	5a	partial statement from middle of theme
Contrasting section	b	figures tossed back and forth between flute and violin; new melodic fragment introduced and developed; extended length; final trills lead to:
Ritornello theme	6a	partial statement from beginning of theme
Contrasting section	b	continued imitation between violin and flute
Ritornello theme	7a	full statement in tonic key
Contrasting section	b	continued imitation between flute and violin moving smoothly into:
Ritornello theme	8a	partial statement from middle of theme
Contrasting section	b	the longest contrasting section; virtuosic display draws attention to harpsichord; flute and violin drop out, leaving harpsichord, with trills and passage work, long preparation on dominant for return of:
Ritornello theme	9	complete statement in tonic

SUMMARY

The baroque era saw the rise of instrumental music of all kinds, due in part to the development and improvement of existing instruments.

The harpsichord and the organ were the chief keyboard instruments of the baroque. Single movement works written for them include the fantasia, the prelude, and the toccata. Chorale tunes formed the basis for a large body of literature written for the organ. The suite is an example of the multimovement keyboard form that became popular for other solo instruments and ensembles. A form which often appears in keyboard, instrumental, and vocal works is the fugue. The fugue, in which a melodic subject is presented and developed in a variety of ways, is one of the most significant forms of the baroque.

The baroque sonata is a multimovement work for one or more instruments. Two of its early forms are the sonata da camera and the sonata da chiesa. Later developments include the sonata for unaccompanied instrument, the solo sonata, and the trio sonata.

The concerto grosso is a multimovement work that pits a small group, the concertino, against a full ensemble, the ripieno. A solo concerto differs from the concerto grosso in that the concertino is reduced to a single instrument. The three-movement pattern of the concerto (fast-slow-fast) and the use of the ritornello form in the first movement, influenced the development of subsequent musical forms.

Arcangelo Corelli, Giuseppe Torelli, and Antonio Vivaldi all contributed to the development of instrumental music in the baroque, especially in the areas of the solo concerto and the concerto grosso. An acknowledged master of baroque instrumental music is Johann Sebastian Bach.

NEW TERMS

fantasia
prelude
toccata
fugue
   subject
   exposition
   countersubject
   episode
   augmentation
   diminution
   inversion
   retrograde
   stretto

suite
   allemande
   courante
   sarabande
   gigue
   gavotte
sonata (da chiesa, da camera)
   solo sonata
   trio sonata
concerto (solo, grosso)
   concertino
   ripieno
   ritornello

country that had become the leading cultural center of the continent. Fashion, in dress, design, and ideas, radiated from Paris and Versailles. It was the aristocracy rather than the busy entrepreneurs of the middle class that had the money and time for the cultivation and refinement of life.

It is wrong, however, to imagine the members of the upper class as wicked pleasure-seekers. In townhouse and palace, they strove for worldly perfection in art and thought as well as in manners. In fact, the eighteenth century was a period of vigorous intellectual activity. Scientific advance continued with even greater velocity; more important, the century was energized by the active philosophical debate over the nature of reform and progress.

Some thinkers believed that the human race could attain perfection through the application of common sense to social problems, a viewpoint eloquently championed by the German mathematician Leibnitz and brutally satirized by Voltaire in Candide. *Diderot and other brilliant French* philosophes *undertook the* Encyclopedia, *a massive enterprise of twenty-four volumes that tried to codify accumulated knowledge from the past and current ideas in the present. Rousseau, a harbinger of nineteenth-century romanticism, challenged the ultra-refined world around him. He believed that human beings enjoyed a god-like character that had been corrupted and deadened by civilization. He wanted to abandon the cerebral world of logic and analysis and return to the more natural, instinctual, primitive world of the aborigine. All these different points of view appear contradictory on the surface; they all assumed, however, that the human condition could be improved or perfected. The eighteenth century glorified the power of the individual to control and order the world, a viewpoint that nurtured both economic growth and the notion that governments should reflect the will and interests of the people.*

For much of this period the visual arts, dominated by the late baroque style called rococo, did not mirror the rising tide of reason and simplicity. The rococo style emphasized elegance rather than clarity, delicacy rather than strength, softness rather than severity, and playfulness rather than solemnity. French interiors were decorated with beautiful gold-and-white curved woods, crystal chandeliers, and gilt ceilings (plate 20). The French painters Boucher and Fragonard, who idealized the joy and sweetness of aristocratic life, were deluged with commissions (plate 19).

Rococo art, though, became less popular in the last decades of the eighteenth century. Cream colors and rich velvet grew less fashionable. The "new taste" of the 1770s and later, called neoclassicism, borrowed from the seventeenth-century French artist Poussin (plate 12) as well as from Greek temples and Roman statuary. In short, the last quarter of the eighteenth century rejected baroque design and began to work from "more noble" classical models.

Music, with all its evocative powers, held a high position in the ancien régime *("the old order," a phrase later used to summarize the elegance and grandeur of France before 1789). The two greatest composers of the late eighteenth century were both Austrian—Wolfgang Amadeus Mozart (1756–1791) and Franz Joseph Haydn (1732–1809). Both depended on commissions in their early careers, Mozart as a concertmaster to the Archbishop of Salzburg and Haydn as a music director for a Hungarian prince.*

Both Mozart and Haydn ended their careers in Vienna. This eastern city, the seat of the Hapsburgs and the capital city of the Holy Roman Empire, was a magnet for first-rate musicians, since the Hapsburg court and the Viennese townspeople placed a very high premium on musical achievement and excellence. The prestige of the composer, musician, and performer—from whatever background—was high. The demand for new composition, frequent concerts, and the competition between the private orchestras of the nobility made it the first city of European music by the end of the eighteenth century.

THE FRENCH REVOLUTION AND ITS AFTERMATH (1798–1825)

In the first half of the eighteenth century royal governments were able to exercise tremendous power over their subjects. In 1776, however, leaders in England's North American colonies, convinced that London no longer represented their economic interests and infuriated that it was trying to extinguish their local political rights, declared their independence from George III and his Parliament. Thirteen years later, the French bourgeoisie acted to wrest law-making power from Louis XVI. This was the beginning of a political struggle that in the 1790s reduced France to a state of anarchy and made for war throughout Europe.

The progress of the French Revolution is confusing and (like most revolutionary periods) often irrational. In the first stage the bourgeoisie established a limited monarchy; later, after Louis XVI tried to escape to the company of royalists and fight against the rebels, the monarchy was abolished and the king was executed for "treason." In the 1790s revolutionaries argued among themselves while they tried to stamp out aristocratic and peasant opposition to their programs: the result was a busy guillotine and political chaos.

At the same time, a revolutionary French army battled the armies of a more conservative European continent. From these contests there emerged a new French hero and leader—Napoleon Bonaparte. Napoleon's mind was tenacious and perfectly ordered; his spirit was dazzling. By 1799, he had enough power to take over the French government. In the next fifteen years he came to control almost all of Europe.

In the last quarter of the eighteenth century the visual arts underwent as radical a change as European politics. The rococo faded entirely, to be replaced by that neoclassicism which idealized ancient Athens and Rome and attempted to recreate a heroic world based on antiquity. In the 1790s Napoleon's counterpart in the arts was Jacques-Louis David (1748–1825), a painter who became a kind of art dictator during the Revolution and whose style was undisputed before the 1820s. David avoided the "capricious ornament" of earlier art. Instead, he built solemn scenes of noble sacrifice and great historical moments in a clear, balanced, linear style (plate 21). To David and his fellow revolutionaries, the excellence of antiquity was a guide to the perfection of the human race: in politics and art the French Revolution was a culmination of the spirit of reform of the generations that preceded them.

In some respects the use of the term "classical" to describe the milieu of the late 1700s and early 1800s is misleading. Classical suggests clarity, harmony, evenness, and tranquility—all qualities for which this period is not known. It was an age of ferment, of differing values, of change. Nevertheless, the music of the classical period attaches great importance to balance and clarity of structure. The symphonic form reached its zenith and became a kind of music that later composers could only elaborate on or reject.

No musician of the nineteenth century could ignore the impact of Beethoven (1770–1827), who came to Vienna as a young man to play under Mozart and study under Haydn. It was Beethoven who brought the classical musical style to completion; moroever, for many musicians and critics of the nineteenth century, he served as a model and a beacon of musical perfection.

MOZART AND HAYDN

he term "classical" is applied to music in several different ways. In one sense,
we speak of a "classic" as any work of lasting value. "Classical" sometimes
designates so-called *serious* or concert music, as opposed to *popular* music. In this
case the term is applied without regard to historical or stylistic factors, so that composers of different style periods—Bach, Beethoven, and Tchaikovsky, for example—
may all be considered "classical" composers. In a narrower and more accurate sense,
the term is applied to music in either of two meanings. First, it describes those periods
in music history when style emphasized formal clarity, balance and structure, lucid
design, objectivity, and traditionalism, as opposed to the romantic qualities of sen-
timentalism, exaggerated emotionalism, subjectivism, and experimentation. (Seen in
this light, the late Renaissance and late baroque periods, when the art of polyphony
was brought to its greatest heights, were periods of classicism.) Second, it designates
the music of the Viennese classic school (that is, the music of Haydn, Mozart, and
to an extent, Beethoven and Schubert) from about 1770 to 1830. It is the second
meaning that is intended when we refer to the "classical era."

As we discussed in chapters 7 and 8, the style of the baroque period began as a
reaction against the vocal polyphony of the late Renaissance. Gradually the homophonic style of early baroque music was transformed into a new kind of polyphony
based upon the major-minor harmonic system and shaped by the maturing instrumental idioms.

Similarly, the style of the classical era was the result of a reaction to the instrumental polyphony that we encountered in the late baroque, particularly in the music
of Johann Sebastian Bach.

The new style, the classical style, was essentially homophonic rather than polyphonic; it was based upon the idea of successive *contrasting* thematic ideas rather
than the contrapuntal expansion of *one* germinal melodic idea. Classical musical forms

are sectional with clear divisions between the sections as opposed to the baroque manner of one continuous flow of music without pauses and stopping points from beginning to end.

Although the basso continuo was gradually abandoned in the classical era, the major-minor system with its reliance on the dominant-tonic relationship continued to be a fundamental structural element. These major stylistic features are embodied in the sonata style of the classical period.

THE CLASSICAL SONATA

The meaning of the word "sonata" varies from age to age in music history. Originally "sonata" meant something to be *played,* as opposed to "cantata," something to be *sung.* The term had various applications throughout the baroque period, but in the classical era it took on very specific and important meaning.

The classical **sonata** is a multimovement work in one of two schemes:

Three-movement plan

First movement	*Second movement*	*Third movement*
Fast tempo	Slow tempo	Fast tempo
Key of tonic	Contrasting key	Key of tonic

Four-movement plan

First movement	*Second movement*	*Third movement*	*Fourth movement*
Fast tempo	Slow tempo	Minuet and trio	Fast tempo
Key of tonic	Contrasting key	Key of tonic	Key of tonic

Sonata-Allegro Form

In both plans, the first movement is invariably cast in what has become known as **sonata-allegro form.** Sonata-allegro form (often referred to as simply **sonata form**) is based upon the scheme of the statement of musical materials; the exploration and manipulation of the materials; and the restatement of the materials. This general scheme is realized in three specific sections of the movement: (1) the **exposition,** (2) the **development,** and (3) the **recapitulation.**

Exposition

The exposition introduces the thematic material that forms the basis of the entire movement. This thematic material usually consists of two contrasting themes or groups of themes connected by a **bridge.** The first theme establishes the overall tonality for the movement as a whole; the second theme is always in a different key. If the first

Figure 9.1 Sonata-
allegro form.

Exposition	Development	Recapitulation
Theme I (tonic)	Transformation of expositional material	Theme I (tonic)
Bridge (modulates to new key)	Rapid modulations	Bridge (extended)
Theme II (new key)		Theme II (tonic)
Codetta to cadence		*Coda*
Exposition repeated		Final cadence (tonic)

theme is in a major key, the second theme will almost always be in its *dominant* key. If the first theme is in a *minor* key, the second theme will usually appear in the relative *major* key. In some cases, sonata-allegro movements contain only *one* melody which functions as *both* first *and* second themes. In such cases the key relationships explained above are maintained. The bridge serves the function of modulating from the key of the first theme to the new key of the "second theme." Usually there is a clear and definite cadence and/or pause separating the bridge and the second theme. Frequently, a short section called a **codetta** is employed after the second theme to bring the exposition to a close.

In almost all cases the exposition is immediately repeated so that the basic thematic ideas are firmly established, enabling the listener to follow the use of these ideas in the development section.

Development

The development concentrates on some of the materials of the exposition and manipulates them in a variety of ways. Themes may be fragmented, small melodic or rhthmic motives expanded, or counterpoint added. Changes in timbre, rhythm, and dynamics are among the many devices that may be employed. No two development sections are the same; however, what is common to all of them is the process of *modulation*. Frequent and often extreme modulation is the rule.

Recapitulation

The recapitulation is a restatement of the whole exposition with one important change—the second theme appears in the *tonic* rather than in a contrasting key as in the exposition. This reaffirmation of the tonic key and the return of the melodic material in its original form lends great unity to this formal structure. In some pieces a concluding section, the **coda** ("tail") is added as an extended conclusion of the movement, as shown in figure 9.1.

Occasionally the sonata-allegro movement is preceded by a slow introduction. The introduction, however, is *not* part of sonata-allegro form and is *not* included in the repetition of the exposition nor in the recapitulation.

First movement	Second movement	Third movement	Fourth movement
Sonata-allegro form	Theme and variations, alternating form, or sonata-allegro form	Minuet and trio or scherzo and trio	Rondo or sonata-allegro
Fast tempo		Triple meter (minuet)	Fast tempo
Dramatic	Slow tempo		Spirited, playful
	Lyrical	Fast tempo (scherzo)	Key of first movement
	Key contrasts with first movement	Light, cheerful	
		Key of first movement	

Figure 9.2 The complete classical sonata.

Other Sonata Movements

The second movement of the sonata is slower and often more lyrical than the first. It always contrasts in key with the first movement. Theme and variations or an alternating form such as ABA or ABACA is commonly used, although sonata-allegro form is occasionally employed.

In the four-movement sonata plan, the third movement is usually a **minuet-and-trio** in the key of the first movement. It is in the stately style of the minuet in triple meter and cast in ternary form:

A	B	A
Minuet	Trio	Minuet

Typically there are repeated small sections within the first minuet and the trio but not the second minuet:

A	B	A
Minuet	Trio	Minuet
aabb	ccdd	ab

The term *trio* is a carryover from the seventeenth century during which the second of two alternating dances was scored for three instruments. In the classical sonata the trio is rarely a three-voice piece but does contrast with the minuet in a variety of ways.

The minuet-and-trio plan described above is typical of works by Haydn and Mozart, and of early works by Beethoven. However, Beethoven experimented with this movement a great deal and eventually adopted, in place of the minuet, a much faster type of piece known as a **scherzo.** As we shall see, the scherzo and trio became a movement of great power and drama in the works of Beethoven.

The last movement of the sonata returns to the general quality of the first movement. It is fast and in the key of the first movement. It is often a **rondo,** an extended alternating form in fast tempo, usually ABACA or ABACABA. It is generally spirited and often playful. Occasionally the last movement of a sonata employs the sonata-allegro form.

The sonata principle just outlined and presented in figure 9.2 was an all-pervasive concept that served as a procedure for the composition of thousands of works of music during the classical and romantic periods. The four-movement plan became the basis for the **symphony** (sonata for orchestra) and the **string quartet** (sonata for four stringed instruments). The three-movement scheme, omitting minuet-and-trio, was typical of works for solo piano (piano sonata), for solo instruments and the piano (e.g., sonata for violin and piano), and for the **concerto** (sonata for solo instrument and orchestra).

PIANOFORTE

In the classical period, the harpsichord of the baroque gave way to the new **pianoforte** (or simply **piano**) as the preferred keyboard instrument. The greater dynamic range and ability to sustain sounds for a longer period of time made the piano popular as a solo instrument, a chamber music participant, and as a concerto instrument. The change of sound quality represented by the piano was an important element in the nature of classical style and influenced the course of music history in later stylistic periods. Equally important was the development of the orchestra.

THE CLASSICAL ORCHESTRA

In the baroque era instrumental music had become an independent idiom, and a vast literature for instrumental ensembles was produced. But the baroque orchestra, aside from the usual complement of strings, had no fixed makeup.

In the classical era the makeup of the orchestra became standardized to a great extent. Its development was largely the work of Johann Stamitz (1717–1757), a violinist, composer, and conductor of the orchestra at the German city of Mannheim. Under his direction it became the most celebrated musical ensemble in Europe. The excellence of its playing was praised by the leading composers of the day.

By baroque standards the Mannheim orchestra was of large dimensions. In 1756 it consisted of twenty violins, four violas, four cellos, and four basses. The wind section included four horns in addition to pairs of flutes, oboes, clarinets, and bassoons. Trumpets and timpani were also used. The German poet and musician D. F. D. Schubert (1739–1791) recorded his impressions of the orchestra in his *Essay on Musical Esthetics:*

> *No orchestra in the world ever equalled the Mannheimers' execution. Its forte is like thunder, its crescendo like a mighty waterfall, its diminuendo a gentle river dissappearing into the distance, its piano is a breath of spring. The wind instruments could not be used to better advantage; they lift and carry, they reinforce and give life to the storm for violins.*

While the technical improvement of the instruments during the baroque period contributed to the creation of a significant body of solo and chamber music, the development of this collective instrument, the orchestra, enabled the growth of a vast body of symphonic compositions. Symphonic composition centered in the cities of Berlin, Mannheim, and Vienna. The Berlin or North German composers, of whom C. P. E. Bach was the leading figure, retained the more conservative three-movement structure and preserved elements of the contrapuntal style. The Mannheim group, under the leadership of Stamitz, employed the four-movement structure. The Viennese symphonists also favored the four-movement form. One of the greatest of the Viennese composers was Wolfgang Amadeus Mozart.

MOZART *(1756–1791)*

Born in Salzburg, Austria, Wolfgang Amadeus Mozart began his musical career as one of the most celebrated child prodigies in eighteenth-century Europe. His father, Leopold, a highly respected composer and violinist, recognized his son's extraordinary talent and carefully supervised his musical education. Mozart began harpsichord lessons when he was four and wrote his first compositions when he was five. At the age of six he and his older sister, Maria Anna ("Nannerl"), were taken by their father on a concert tour of Munich and Vienna.

From this first public performance until he was fifteen, Mozart was almost constantly on tour, playing prepared works and improvising. While the harpsichord and later the piano remained Mozart's principal instruments, he also mastered the violin and the organ. In addition to keyboard pieces, he wrote church works, symphonies, string quartets, and operas. In 1769, on a long trip to Italy, Mozart composed his first major opera, *Mitridate,* which was performed in Milan in 1770. His success in Italy, as triumphant as Handel's had been some sixty years earlier, brought him a number of commissions for operas.

His father, court composer and vice chapelmaster to the Archbishop of Salzburg, obtained a position for his son as concertmaster in the Archbishop's orchestra. But the new Archbishop of Salzburg, installed in 1772, failed to appreciate Mozart's genius. Relations between the haughty churchman and the high-spirited young composer steadily deteriorated until, in 1781, despite his father's objections, Mozart quit his position and settled in Vienna.

The first years in Vienna were fairly prosperous. Mozart was in great demand as a teacher; he gave numerous concerts, and his German **Singspiel**—a German comic opera with spoken dialogue—*Die Entführung aus dem Serail (The Abduction from the Harem,* 1782), was a success. He married Constanze Weber, a woman he had

Figure 9.3 This portrait of Mozart at the clavier shows the young prodigy in his early teens.

met several years earlier on a concert tour, and looked forward to a happy family life. But Constanze was a careless housekeeper, and Mozart was a poor manager of finances. Intrigues at the Viennese court kept him from obtaining a permanent post. Public taste changed and his teaching began to fall off. Except for occasional successes—his opera *Le Nozze di Figaro (The Marriage of Figaro,* 1786) and the *Singspiel, Die Zauberflöte (The Magic Flute,* 1791)—the last ten years of his life were spent, for the most part, in poverty.

In 1788 he gave up public performances, relying on a meager income from teaching and loans from various friends to sustain himself and his family. In spite of these troubles he continued to compose, but his health began to decline. When he died in 1791 at the age of thirty-five, he was buried in an unmarked grave in a part of the cemetery reserved for the poor.

MOZART'S WORK

Unlike the meticulous Haydn, who kept a chronological list of all his compositions, Mozart never bothered to organize his musical papers in any consistent fashion. In the nineteenth century, Ludwig von Köchel compiled a roughly chronological listing of Mozart's music (numbering up to 626). This catalogue, along with substantial revisions and additions by later musicologists, remains in use today.

The most recent edition of Köchel's catalogue, in which the number of each piece is preceded by the initial "K," includes twenty-one stage works, twenty-seven concert arias, fifteen Masses, over fifty symphonies, twenty-five piano concertos, twelve violin concertos, some fourteen concertos for other instruments, twenty-six string quartets, seventeen piano sonatas, forty-two violin sonatas, and numerous works for miscellaneous chamber-sized ensembles.

Religious Music

Mozart composed almost all of his church music at the beginning of his career, when he was working in Salzburg. His two greatest choral works, unfortunately, were left incomplete. The first of these was the gigantic Mass in B Minor (1782), intended as an offering of thanks for his marriage to Constanze. The second is also his last work, the Requiem in D Minor. In 1791 Mozart accepted a commission to write this work on behalf of a nobleman who wished to remain anonymous. Mozart died before the work was finished. On his deathbed Mozart extracted a promise from his wife that Franz Süssmayr, his favorite pupil, would be selected to finish the piece. Süssmayr did so, making some additions of his own.

Opera

Mozart's operas are the only eighteenth-century works in this genre that have remained consistently in general repertory. For the most part, they fall into one of three categories: (1) Italian *opera seria,* based on serious plots, including *Mitridate* (1770), *Idomeneo* (1781), and *The Clemency of Titus* (1791); (2) comic Italian opera, including *The Marriage of Figaro* and *Cosi fan tutte* (1790); and (3) German *Singspiel,* including *The Abduction from the Harem.* Two of Mozart's most popular and significant operas resist such classification. *Don Giovanni* (1787), subtitled "humorous drama," vacillates between high comedy and genuine tragedy in following the career of the legendary Don Juan. *The Magic Flute,* though cast in the form of a *Singspiel* with intermittent spoken dialogue, might better be considered a morality play bound up in a fairy tale setting. In many ways *Don Giovanni* may be regarded as the greatest of the eighteenth-century Italian operas; *The Magic Flute* may be considered the first great German opera.

Instrumental Music

The amazing fluency with which Mozart composed his operas is also evident in his instrumental music. He was able to carry around finished compositions in his head, once remarking that "the committing to paper is done quickly enough. For everything is already finished, and it rarely differs on paper from what it was in my imagination."

Many of the twenty-three piano concertos were composed for Mozart's own use in his public performances. These concertos demonstrated many of Mozart's most progressive ideas. His string quartets, at first influenced by Haydn's, also reveal Mozart's mastery of musical forms.

His final three symphonies—nos. 39, 40, and 41 (the *Jupiter* Symphony)—were composed during the summer of 1788, three years before his death. Little is known about the circumstances of their composition, but these three works stand among Mozart's finest contributions to instrumental music.

Mozart's G Minor Symphony follows the four-movement plan outlined earlier: fast-slow-medium-fast. It is scored for an orchestra consisting of flute, two oboes, two clarinets, two bassoons, two horns, and strings.

First Movement (Allegro): Sonata-Allegro Form

Exposition   The opening theme centers on two phrases.

MOZART:
**SYMPHONY no. 40 IN
G MINOR**
*SIDE 3/SELECTION 1
SEE LISTENING GUIDE
ON PAGES 180–81*

Example 9.1

They are the same *length;* they are identical in *rhythm;* but they differ in melodic shape. Melodically the first phrase is static until the end when it leaps upward, the second is active until the end when it becomes static, repeating the same tone. These paired phrases and elements drawn from them—especially the rhythmic motive   —are crucial to the spirit and structure of the entire first movement.

The first theme begins with this pair of phrases played softly by the violins against an agitated background in the lower strings. The phrases are stated and repeated and then interrupted by a new phrase which is stated and extended by the woodwinds with a crescendo to a half-cadence in the dominant key of D major.

Example 9.2

MOZART AND HAYDN   **163**

There is an immediate return to the key of G minor and the paired phrases. Again they are stated and repeated, this time to be interrupted by a sudden forte and the beginning of the *bridge* which modulates to the key of B♭ major.

Example 9.3

After an emphatic cadence and a pause, the second theme appears. The first part of the theme is a soft, lyrical, and expressive melody shared by the strings and woodwinds.

Example 9.4

The strings and winds exchange roles in a repetition of this melody which is extended through a long crescendo leading to the second part of the second theme in which the rhythmic motive from the first phrase is employed.

Example 9.5

Closing material brings the exposition to a definite ending and the entire exposition is then repeated, followed by the development section.

This figure, almost unnoticeable when it first occurs, gradually assumes more and more importance as the exposition progresses. It becomes more noticeable as the first theme draws to a close; it permeates the bridge:

Example 9.10

it is integral to the tender second theme in B♭ major:

Example 9.11

and it is included in the codetta which brings the exposition to a close.

In fact this small chirp-like motive is included in every part of the exposition—sometimes barely noticeable, sometimes dominating the melodic material—tying together the entire exposition and unifying the movement as a whole.

Third Movement: Menuetto (Allegretto)

This movement returns to the original key of G minor and conforms to the general formal outline—minuet-trio-minuet—described earlier. It is unusual in its character and in the striking contrast between its two major sections.

The minuet is in G minor. Its loud dynamic level, constant use of the full orchestra, syncopated rhythms, and use of pronounced dissonances gives it a driving and intense character that is unusual in this type of movement.

Example 9.12

The trio provides a calming contrast. In addition to the change from G minor to G *major,* the trio is soft in dynamic level (piano) and has a graceful flowing mood that is enhanced by striking alternations between the strings and winds of the orchestra. The serenity of the trio makes even more pronounced the agitated character of the minuet when it returns to conclude the movement.

Fourth Movement: Allegro Assai

The last movement of this symphony confirms the key of G minor, is fast in tempo and is cast in sonata-allegro form.

Exposition The first theme consists of two melodic ideas: the triad of G minor played in a rapidly rising "rocket" figure, which is played *piano,* and a contrasting figure, which is played *forte.*

Example 9.13

After the theme is repeated several times, a new element adds dynamic contrast, moving from loud to soft. A bridge leads to a cadence and pause, and the second theme begins, played by reduced orchestra, first only the strings and then only the woodwinds. A closing, based on the bridge material, leads to a repetition of the exposition.

Development and recapitulation The "rocket" motive of theme 1 and an extensive modulation are the basis of the short development section. Passed from one section of the orchestra to another, the motive is treated polyphonically with overlapping entrances. Gradually it leads to a pronounced pause that separates the development from the recapitulation. Mozart intended that the entire development, recapitulation, and coda be repeated.

The G Minor Symphony not only provides a superb example of Mozart's craft, but also illustrates general characteristics of the classical style and the classical symphony.

1. The four-movement plan of the sonata (fast-slow-medium-fast) is followed, the first movement being cast in sonata-allegra form.

2. There is *no thematic relationship* among the movements; each movement is self-contained and none of the materials of one movement appears in any other movement.

3. Structurally, the main unifying force is *key;* movements 1, 3, and 4 are in the common key of G minor, creating *tonal unity.*

4. Within individual movements, clarity and balance are probably the most pronounced stylistic features. Contrasting materials and sections are for the most part clearly and carefully set off from each other—often with the help of such musical devices as changes in dynamics, cadences, and pauses—without the blurring of relationships we will encounter in later periods of music.

HAYDN (1732–1809)

*F*ranz Joseph Haydn was born in Rohrau, a small Austrian village located near the Hungarian border southeast of Vienna. His parents, both of peasant stock, seemed to have encouraged their son's musical ability and entrusted his earliest musical training to a relative, Johann Franck, a schoolteacher and choirmaster in the nearby town of Hainburg. At age six, Haydn was already singing in Franck's church choir and had begun playing the *clavier* (an early keyboard instrument) and violin.

In 1740, the composer and choirmaster at St. Stephen's Cathedral in Vienna stopped in Hainburg to recruit singers for his choir. Impressed with Haydn's voice, he arranged to take the young boy back with him to Vienna.

For the next nine years Haydn immersed himself in the routine of a Catholic choirboy. He received a smattering of elementary education at St. Stephen's choir school and continued with violin and voice lessons, but his training in composition and theory was erratic and largely self-taught. In 1749, when his voice began to mature, Haydn was abruptly dismissed and turned out into the street.

The following years were hard ones. At first Haydn made his living teaching clavier by day and playing in street bands and serenading parties by night. His reputation as a teacher and vocal accompanist, however, gradually spread, and he started serious composition. In 1759 he was appointed *Kapellmeister* and chamber composer to a Bohemian nobleman, Count Morzin. He composed his first symphonies for the count's small orchestra.

In 1760 Haydn married Maria Anna Keller, but the marriage, which lasted forty years, was a tragic mistake. They were incompatible in temperament and finally separated.

The unhappy marriage was offset by his appointment in 1761 as assistant music director to Prince Paul Anton Esterhazy, head of one of the most powerful and wealthy Hungarian noble families. Haydn's contract stipulated that he was to compose whatever music was required of him (which would become the property of his patron), to keep the musical instruments in good repair, to train singers, and to supervise the conduct of all of the musicians.

Despite the rigid and burdensome requirements of his contract, Haydn enjoyed his work and was to say later, "My prince was pleased with all my work, I was commended, and as conductor of an orchestra I could make experiments, observe what strengthened and what weakened an effect and thereupon improve, substitute, omit, and

Figure 9.4 Portrait of Haydn.

try new things; I was cut off from the world, there was no one around to mislead and harass me, and so I was forced to become original."

Haydn remained in the employ of the Esterhazy family for almost thirty years, serving first Prince Paul Anton and then his brother, Prince Nikolaus. Despite his isolation at their country estate, his fame gradually spread throughout Europe. He was able to fulfill commissions from other individuals and from publishers all over the Continent. When Prince Nikolaus died in 1790, Haydn was retained as nominal *Kapellmeister* for the Esterhazy family, but he was now independent. Moving to Vienna, he resumed his friendship with Mozart, whose talent he had admired since their first meeting in 1781. Haydn also gave lessons to a young, rising composer named Ludwig van Beethoven. He made two successful trips to London (1791–1792, 1794–1795), where he conducted a number of his own symphonies, written on commission for the well-known impresario Johann Salomon. After his second London visit, he ceased writing symphonies, turning instead to the composition of Masses and oratorios. After 1800 his health began to fail, and he lived in secluded retirement. He died in 1809 at the age of seventy-seven.

Mozart's symphony demonstrates the organizing power and wonderful flexibility of sonata-allegro form. Three of the work's four movements are organized by this formal procedure, all of them solid in design, yet completely different from each other in their expressive qualities.

CHAMBER MUSIC

Even after the orchestra had emerged, music for smaller ensembles continued to thrive as wealthy patrons commissioned works to be performed in their salons for private audiences.

The multimovement sonata structure that we encountered in the symphony was also used in chamber music for a wide variety of instrumental combinations. The string quartet, consisting of a first and second violin, a viola, and a cello, became, in the classical era, the most important chamber music medium. Its popularity continued well into the twentieth century in the works of Bartók, Hindemith, and others.

Franz Joseph Haydn was the first great master of string quartet composition, which occupied him throughout most of his long and creative life.

HAYDN'S WORK

The great majority of Haydn's work was composed during his service to the Esterhazy princes. The biweekly concerts and opera performances at Esterhaz, Prince Nikolaus's country estate, engendered a prodigious flow of instrumental and vocal music. Most of Haydn's 104 symphonies were written for the small but excellent Esterhazy orchestra.

Symphonies

The symphonies form a remarkably complete record of Haydn's development as a composer, ranging in unbroken continuity from his earliest, somewhat crude efforts to the rich and masterful works of the 1780s and 1790s. Many of the more popular symphonies bear identifying nicknames: the *Horn Signal* (no. 31, 1765), the *Farewell* (no. 45, 1772), the *Surprise* (no. 94, 1791), and the *Drumroll* (no. 103, 1795) are but a few. His greatest works in this genre are the last twelve symphonies, called the *London* Symphonies, which were written for his two London visits.

Chamber Music

While many of Haydn's experiments with musical form were carried out in the symphonies, his chamber music, particularly the string quartets, was equally significant in his development as a composer. In his eighty-three quartets, Haydn laid down many of the fundamental principles that were taken up by younger composers such as Mozart

Figure 9.5 Haydn, shown here directing the rehearsal of a string quartet, spent many of his most productive years composing for and conducting the orchestra of the Esterhazy princes.

and Beethoven. The six works making up opus 20* (the *Sun* Quartets, 1772) are among his masterworks in this genre. The later sets of opus 33 (the *Scherzo* or *Russian* Quartets, 1781) and opus 50 (1787) represent still further advances in Haydn's musical development.

Among Haydn's other chamber works are more than twenty *divertimenti*. As their title suggests, these were light "diversionary" pieces written in a simple, popular style. Other chamber music included a multitude of trios and sonatas for various instruments. Of some sixty sonatas written for piano, fifty-two survive.

Though he was a good string player, Haydn did not consider himself a virtuoso performer. Consequently his solo concertos are few. A good many concertos have been lost, and still others attributed to Haydn have not yet been authenticated as coming from his hand.

Operas

Opera was a highly important part of musical activity at the Esterhazy palace, and Haydn was for a long time quite proud of his more than twenty stage works. The Austrian Empress, Maria Theresa, reputedly said, "If I want to hear a good opera,

---

* The term opus refers to a musical composition numbered to show its place in the composer's published work.

I go to Esterhaz." When Haydn became familiar with Mozart's incomparable genius for opera composing, however, he realized that his own works were of lesser quality. Today they are all but forgotten.

Masses and Oratorios

Haydn's Masses and oratorios present a different story. The last six of his twelve Masses, composed between 1796 and 1802, are his crowning achievement as a church composer—works of old age demonstrating a mastery of form and technique accumulated over more than fifty years of composing. Several of them—*Missa in tempore belli (Mass in Time of War,* 1796), the *Missa in Augustiis (Nelson Mass,* 1798), and the *Harmoniemesse* ("Wind-blown" Mass, 1802)—rank among Haydn's masterworks. Stimulated by Handel's oratorios, some of which he had heard during his London visits, Haydn produced two of his own. Titled *The Creation* (1796–1798) and *The Seasons* (1798–1801), they have remained in concert repertoire to this day. Contemporary with these major vocal works was Haydn's gift to the Austrian people, the national anthem, *Gott erhalte Franze den Kaiser (God Save the Emperor Franz,* better known as the *Austrian Hymn).* He wrote it on his own initiative as a patriotic gesture when Napoleon's armies invaded Austrian territory in 1796. During the French bombardment of Vienna in 1809, he played it to comfort himself. It was the last music he heard before he died.

HAYDN: STRING QUARTET OP. 33, NO. 3 ("THE BIRD")

Haydn developed the string quartet from the eighteenth-century *divertimento,* giving more substance to the light, popular form and scoring it for two violins, a viola, and a cello. His eighty-three quartets, written over the course of his creative lifetime, evolved slowly into a sophisticated form. Together they constitute one of the most important bodies of chamber music literature.

The quartets of Haydn's opus 33 are collectively known as *Gli Scherzi (The Scherzos)* because Haydn uses the more rapid scherzo rather than the minuet-and-trio. Number 3 of this set became known as "The Bird," owing to the bird-like trills and ornaments in the first, second, and fourth movements.

Example 9.14

"Bird" motive

First Movement

Exposition The clarity and balance that we encountered in the music of Mozart are again evident here in the clearly separated, repeated phrases, the sudden contrast and extension of one phrase, and the use of dynamics to reinforce structure.

The "bird" ornaments heard in the first theme provide a unifying element among the contrasting sections of the movement.

With the entrance of the piano the orchestra drops out altogether until the strings take over the answering function first performed by the winds.

The alternation between piano and orchestra, in which one is silent while the other is active, is a device favored by Mozart and typifies this particular movement. In the previous example we saw how the orchestra and piano alternate in rather large blocks of music; in other parts of the movement they often "share" a phrase. In example 9.18 the piano begins a phrase which is completed by the flute; in example 9.19 the reverse is true: the orchestra initiates the phrase, which is finished by the solo piano.

Example 9.18

Example 9.19

In this movement the solo instrument and the orchestra rarely work together for any appreciable length of time. When they do, the solo instrument is almost always dominant. The most obvious place where the solo piano "shines" is the cadenza, which occurs after the recapitulation and leads into the closing material. The cadenza that is usually played is one written by Mozart himself. It exhibits all the qualities outlined earlier and provides a convincing and exciting conclusion to the first movement.

Second Movement

The second movement is a glorious example of Mozart's lyrical use of the piano as a "singing" instrument. The movement is slow in tempo (larghetto) and in the contrasting key of E-flat major. Its structure is a large ABA form with each section containing a rich variety of melodic materials.

SIDE 3/SELECTION 2
SEE LISTENING GUIDE
ON P. 183

The B section features the solo instrument, supported throughout by unobtrusive orchestral accompaniment. The A section that frames the movement is more elaborate, both in the variety of its materials and in the relationship between the orchestra and the piano. As in the first movement, the solo instrument and orchestra tend to alternate rather than work together.

The most important thematic material is the simple melody played by the solo piano at the beginning of the movement (example 9.20). The flowing beauty of this short melody sets the mood for the entire movement.

Example 9.20

Third Movement

The third movement returns to the key of B-flat major and is fast (allegro), conforming to the three-movement plan of the classical concerto. Its brisk tempo is intensified by a jocular dance-like rhythm, giving the piece a lively quality:

Example 9.21

The movement, which begins with solo piano, is essentially a rondo but includes developmental sections which impart a flavor of sonata-allegro form. Of particular interest is the fact that the movement includes *two* cadenzas, both of which function to reintroduce the principle theme.

Mozart's last piano concerto is one of his most serene and sublime works, well deserving of its honored place in the repertoire.

CHARACTERISTICS OF CLASSICAL MUSIC

Texture
Largely homophonic, but flexible, with shifts to polyphony

Tonality
Major-minor system with frequent modulations to related keys; heavy dependence on tonic-dominant relationship

Rhythm
Variety of rhythmic patterns within a work

Melody
Composed of short, balanced phrases; melodic phrases often contrasted with each other
Melodies often lyrical and expressive; less ornamentation of notes

Mood
Expression of variety of moods within a work and sudden changes of mood

Dynamics
Gradual dynamic changes

Large Works
Sonata, symphony, concerto, string quartet, Mass, oratorio, opera

Instruments
Piano and violin favored for solo concerto; makeup of orchestra becomes standardized; development of orchestra favors growth of symphonic works

Formal Structures
Sonata principle (multimovement structure for long pieces); sonata-allegro form (first movement form); rondo; minuet-and-trio; scherzo and trio; theme and variations; cadenza and double exposition used in concertos

Symphonic Style
Follows four-movement plan, with first movement in sonata-allegro form
Each movement self-contained
Key is main unifying device
Clarity and balance are major stylistic features

LISTENING GUIDE

Mozart: Symphony no. 40 in G Minor

First Movement: Allegro (fast)
duple meter
sonata form

Classical Orchestra

Review: Example 9.1 (theme 1, two phrases)
Example 9.2 (half-cadence, middle of theme 1)
Example 9.3 (theme 1 interrupted by bridge)
Example 9.4 (theme 2)
Example 9.5 (second part of theme 2)
Example 9.6 (contrapuntal passage from development)
Example 9.7 (composite of two previously separate phrases)
Example 9.8 (static reduction of ex. 9.7)

Exposition

Theme 1	1a	agitated accompaniment; violins state symmetrical melody, phrase leaping upward and phrase moving downward; similar phrases answer with extension; woodwinds answer, loud chords
Bridge	b	violins begin symmetrical melody
	2	forte, upward-leaping motive in violins; rushing string scales, emphatic close
Theme 2	3a	flowing melody mostly in violins; woodwind answer begins, moves in new direction
	b	strings take over, crescendo, build twice to high point; soft descending scale
	c	rhythmic motive from symmetrical melody traded among woodwind instruments and strings, alternating soft and loud
Closing	4	rushing downward string scales, emphatic closing chords

(Exposition may be repeated)

Development

	1	piano, symmetrical melody in violins, new harmonies
	2	sudden forte, symmetrical melody traded between low strings, violins, low strings; violins extend with composite of two phrases into one
	3a	soft, static version of phrase traded between violins and woodwinds
	b	woodwind answer reduced to three-note motive
	c	sudden forte, three-note motive traded between violins and low strings
	4	no strings, flute and clarinets trade three-note motive descending into:

Recapitulation
Theme 1

	1a	violins state symmetrical melody piano, second phrase extended; woodwinds answer, loud chords
	b	violins begin symmetrical melody, move in new harmonic direction

Bridge

	2a	forte, upward-leaping motive in violins; upward-leaping motive in low strings; motive tossed between low strings and violins; violins take over
	b	rushing string scales, emphatic close

Theme 2

	3a	flowing melody mostly in violins; woodwind answer begins, moves in new direction
	b	string take over, crescendo, build twice to high point; soft descending scale
	c	rhythmic motive from symmetrical melody traded among woodwind instruments and strings, alternating soft and loud

Coda

	4a	rushing string scales, build to woodwind chord
	b	violins begin symmetrical melody, answered by violins, violas, woodwinds; sudden forte, emphatic closing chords

LISTENING GUIDE

Haydn: String Quartet op. 33, no. 3 ("The Bird")

Fourth movement: Presto (very fast)
duple meter
sonata-rondo form

String quartet

Review: Example 9.18 (return of A theme after unexpected pause)

A	a a	bouncy theme, staccato, repeated
	b b	repeated-note bird calls, motive from bouncy theme accompanies; repeated, clear stop at end
B	c c	minor theme, more flowing, repeated; goes directly into:
Development		opening motive of bouncy theme and repeated-note fragment developed in rapid-fire polyphony; four-note motive tossed back and forth, reduced to two-note motive; sudden pause
A	a	bouncy theme
	b	repeated-note theme, goes directly into:
B	c	flowing minor theme, goes directly into:
Recapitulation		long notes in first violin, bouncy-theme motive accompaniment; minor-theme motive repeated, reduced to repeated monophonic note, transition back to:
A	a	bouncy theme
	b	repeated-note theme, clear stop at end
Coda		two-note motive and bouncy motive tossed back and forth, move quickly to pause; moves further to apparent emphatic closing; piano, bouncy motive and repeated-note motive to actual quiet close

LISTENING GUIDE

Mozart: Piano Concerto no. 27 in B-flat Major

Second Movement: Larghetto (slow)
                      quadruple meter
                      ternary form

Solo piano; Classical orchestra

Review: Example 9.22 (opening theme)

A   a a   simple, quiet theme stated by solo piano, then by orchestra *[handwritten: French Horns, bassoon on bottom]*
            b   second part of melody by solo piano
            a   first half returns, solo piano
                repeated-note figure begins orchestral transition; continues based on 3-note fragment:

Example 9.22

                moving to clear pause

B   c c   piano sings melody accompanied by orchestra; repeated
            d   second part of melody begins with repeated note, also by piano with orchestra
            e   piano melody moves gently up and down with long notes by instruments; piano trills prepare for:

A   a   simple melody by piano solo; short orchestral transition
            b   second half by piano with orchestra; piano and orchestra echo each other; orchestral chord then piano transition
            a   simple melody in flute and violin accompanied by piano

                repeated-note figure begins coda; material based on three-note transition fragment as piano and orchestra together move gradually toward gentle, unadorned close

· ·

SUMMARY

Instrumental music arrived at a new level of maturity during the classical period. The ranges and technical capabilities of many instruments were improved greatly and composers began to score their works for standard groupings. The makeup of the orchestra also became standardized and included an increased number and variety of instruments. Because of the social customs of the day, chamber music also flourished and encouraged sophisticated compositions in which each player performed an individual part.

Sonata-allegro form and the multimovement structure became the main basis for music composed in the early classical period. The two great masters of the classical era—Haydn and Mozart—developed and refined sonata-allegro form in their symphonies, string quartets, and concertos.

NEW TERMS

sonata
sonata-allegro form (sonata form)
   exposition
   bridge
   codetta
   development
   recapitulation
   coda
minuet-and-trio

scherzo
rondo
symphony
string quartet
concerto
pianoforte (piano)
double exposition
Singspiel
cadenza

SUGGESTED LISTENING

Haydn, Franz Joseph

Symphony no. 45 in F-sharp Minor (*Farewell*). One of Haydn's most dramatic and unorthodox symphonies. The opening movement introduces an extended new theme in place of the usual development section; and in the final movement, the tempo suddenly changes from presto to adagio and the instruments drop out (say farewell) one by one, leaving only two violins to conclude the work.

Mozart, Wolfgang Amadeus

Symphony no. 41, K.551. The *Jupiter* was the last of Mozart's symphonies and is often lumped with symphonies no. 39 and 40 as the finest examples of Mozart's symphonic compositions.

Eine Kleine Nachtmusik (A Little Night Music). This string serenade was written as outdoor entertainment. Its character is light.

CLASSICAL VOCAL MUSIC

T he classical era was predominantly a period of instrumental music. The new instrumental style and forms became the area of greatest concentration for the major composers of the time. Vocal music occupied a position of lesser importance. The lieder (songs) written by Haydn, Mozart, and Beethoven are considered a relatively secondary part of their compositional efforts. The operas composed by Haydn to entertain the guests at Esterhazy have vanished into history, and Beethoven wrote only one opera, *Fidelio.* However, the age was not without significant and lasting achievements in the area of vocal music. Specifically, some of the large choral works of Mozart, Haydn, and Beethoven and many of Mozart's operas made lasting contributions to the body of vocal literature.

CHORAL MUSIC OF HAYDN

Of the three giants of the classical era, Haydn contributed the largest number of compositions to the choral music repertoire. Two of his oratorios, the *Creation* and the *Seasons,* are still widely performed; together with his Masses, they constitute his most important contribution to vocal music.

Haydn's *Missa in Angustiis* (*Mass in Time of Peril*) is one of the choral masterpieces of the classical period. Better known as the *Nelson Mass,* it was written in 1789 during the naval Battle of the Nile. When Lord Nelson visited Eisenstadt Castle in 1800, this Mass was among the works performed in his honor.

HAYDN: MISSA IN ANGUSTIIS (NELSON MASS)

The orchestration of Haydn's masses varied from work to work according to the instruments and players available to him at the time. The *Nelson Mass* is scored for a comparatively small orchestra consisting of three trumpets, timpani, organ, and strings, together with four solo voices (SATB) and four-part chorus (SATB). The organ is used alternately as a continuo instrument, merely filling in chords—a carryover from baroque practice—and as an ensemble or solo instrument.

The text is divided into six main sections and five subdivisions, constituting eleven movements in all:

Kyrie	*Credo*	*Benedictus*
Gloria	*Et incarnatus*	*Agnus Dei*
Qui tollis	*Et resurrexit*	*Dona nobis*
Quoniam tu solus	*Sanctus*	

Kyrie

The prevalence of sonata-allegro procedure in instrumental music has been well established in the previous chapter, but its organizing force was by no means confined to instrumental music. The first movement of the *Nelson Mass* is an example of how the sonata-allegro principle was applied to vocal composition.

The first theme, in D minor, is characterized by short, emphatic pronouncements by the chorus on the text *"Kyrie eleison"* ("Lord have mercy"). The trumpets and timpani sound a prominent figure (♫♫ ♫♫♫ | ♩), which alternates with sharp chords in the strings. The organ, meanwhile, plays sustained chords. The second theme is dominated by the soprano solo voice, singing elaborate virtuoso passages, quite instrumental in character.

Example 10.1

Chri - ste e - lei   -   son, e - lei - son

The light texture, the *piano* dynamic level, the key change (to the relative F major), and the concentration on the individual voice are in marked contrast to the driving force of the first theme.

Ky - ri - e e - lei - son

The prominent elements of the development are sung by the chorus. The solo part from the second theme is now played by the violins. Imitative entrances in the chorus lead to a climax where all four parts come together. The drive that results from these insistent overlapping entrances of the voices is enhanced by constant modulation.

The key returns to D minor for the recapitulation. Here the second theme resembles the original theme in texture, dynamics, and the relationship of the solo soprano voice to the orchestra, but new melodic material is involved.

The coda ends with the entire orchestra hammering out the rhythmic figure (♫♫ ♫♫♫ ♩) on which the movement began in the orchestral introduction.

Gloria, Qui Tollis, and Quoniam Tu Solus

Although the second, third, and fourth movements each appear to be self-contained, they are actually parts of one three-movement complex.

The driving tension and restlessness that characterized the *Kyrie* are immediately SIDE 4/SELECTION 1 dispelled at the striking beginning of the *Gloria*. The important thematic material of the A section, on the text *"Gloria in excelsis deo"* ("Glory to God in the highest"), is introduced in dialogue fashion between the soprano soloist and the chorus.

Glo-ri-a in ex - cel-sis De-o, glo-ri-a in ex - cel-sis De-o, in ex - cel-sis De - o.

Example 10.2

The dynamic level drops to *piano* for the contrasting B section, *"et in terra pax hominibus"* ("and on earth peace to men"). The emphasis is on the solo tenor and bass parts, whose imitative entrances grow into a moving, expressive duet.

The chorus enters in octaves in the C section, loudly proclaiming in short, clipped statements *"laudamus te"* ("we praise Thee"), *"adoramus te"* ("we adore Thee"), and the section builds to an ending on an extended setting of *"glorificamus te"* ("we glorify Thee").

A kind of development begins with successive statements of the A melody, utilizing new words and modulating into different keys. It opens with the solo alto, who is answered by the soprano, and then, more fully, by the chorus. After expanded statements of B by the solo voices, the chorus brings the movement to a rather abrupt close, without the expected return of the A theme.

The slow, quiet *Qui tollis* movement is, structurally, a straightforward example of alternating themes. The solo bass has the dominant part, often paired with the first violins. Frequently the bass voice and first violins answer each other back and forth. The organ is used as a solo instrument in conjunction with the choral entrances, and while the choral entrances are expressive in themselves, they also constitute a considerable "surprise" element in the movement. It is impossible to anticipate either when they will occur or whether they will occur softly in unison or loudly in full harmony on statements of *"miserere nobis"* ("have mercy on us") and *"deprecationem nostram"* ("our prayer").

The *Qui tollis* has no real conclusion, but ends instead on a chord of suspense, the dominant. Its resolution comes in the opening measures of the *Quoniam tu solus* movement, which, in addition, returns to the melody from the *Gloria*. Thus the lack of conclusion in the preceding movement, coupled with the reappearance of the original theme of the *Gloria*, acts as a powerful unifying element in the three-movement complex.

Example 10.3

Solo Soprano

Quo-ni-am tu so-lus, so - lus sanc-tus.

After the solo and choral statements of the A theme, a quiet transition section on the words *"cum sancto spiritu"* ("with the holy spirit"), leads to a long, vigorous fugue. The coda, which uses material from the *Gloria* movement, creates further unity and builds to one of Haydn's brilliant and exhilarating endings on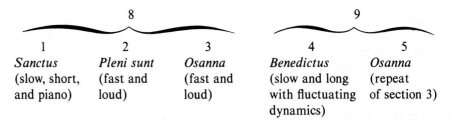

Credo

The *Credo* is divided into three parts, which constitute the fifth, sixth, and seventh movements. The fifth movement, which begins with *Credo in unum Deum* ("I believe in one God"), is a two-part canon. The sopranos and tenors sing the first part against the altos and basses on the second. The tempo is fast; and there is a driving rhythm throughout, with much activity in the orchestra.

In contrast to the fifth movement, the sixth, *Et incarnatus* ("and was incarnate"), is slow and quiet. An atmosphere of lyricism and melodic grace pervades. The first theme is stated in turn by the orchestra, the solo soprano, and the chorus. A concluding coda adds weight to the movement's mood of loss.

The seventh movement, *Et resurrexit tertia dia* ("and on the third day He arose"), bursts forth *forte,* in a fast tempo, and with great musical activity to convey the atmosphere of triumph and resurrection. This movement is particularly interesting for the abundance of technical devices employed to organize it: imitative entrances are used to build momentum; homophonic texture and choral declamation set off the meaning of the text, and striking differences in dynamics and pitch contrast the *vivos* ("living") with the *mortuos* ("dead"). The movement ends with a brilliant "Amen."

Sanctus and Benedictus

The eighth and ninth movements consist of five subsections:

	8			9	
1	2	3	4	5
Sanctus (slow, short, and piano)	*Pleni sunt* (fast and loud)	*Osanna* (fast and loud)	*Benedictus* (slow and long with fluctuating dynamics)	*Osanna* (repeat of section 3)

The *Sanctus* is a slow introductory section. The *Pleni sunt* is an allegro choral section with an active orchestral background. This section merges without a break into the *Osanna.*

The *Benedictus,* which follows, is very much like the sonata-allegro movement of a concerto. It consists of a double exposition (the first in the orchestra, the second in the solo soprano and chorus), a short development section, a genuine recapitulation, and a dramatic coda. The *Benedictus* stops on a dominant chord, followed by a pause. The resulting suspense is dispelled when the *Osanna* returns, bringing the entire complex to a stirring ending.

Figure 10.1 Count Almaviva (Thomas Hampson) rages at his wife the countess (Elizabeth Soederstrom) in a recent production of *The Marriage of Figaro.*

An examination of a portion of act 3 illustrates Mozart's use of these musical forces to portray the dramatic action and reveal and underscore its character. At the beginning of act 3, Susanna and the Countess arrange for Susanna to meet the count that night. Their dialogue, and the subsequent conversation between the count and Susanna, are in secco recitative. In the duet that follows, the count rejoices at Susanna's agreement to meet him, while she (in an aside to the audience) asks forgiveness for her lie. Each one has distinctive music, so that it is quite clear that they are singing about two different things.

SIDE 4/SELECTION 2

The next recitative ends with Susanna mentioning to Figaro, as they leave, that he has won his case. The count overhears her remark and sings a recitative expressing his fury and plotting to force Figaro to marry Marcellina. This recitative is accompanied by the full orchestra and includes many sudden changes of key, tempo, and dynamics. It leads to an aria by the count in which he explains how jealous he is of his happy servant Figaro, how he will get revenge, and how happy the thought of revenge makes him. The aria is in two large sections; the second section is faster than the first and is repeated with an extended and ornamented cadence. The style of the accompaniment changes frequently, to reflect the count's different thoughts.

As the count finishes, he meets the judge, Don Curzio, who has just upheld Marcellina's right to repayment or marriage. Figaro mentions that he cannot get married without his parents' consent, and he has not been able to locate them, since he was kidnapped as a child. He describes the circumstances, and Marcellina and Dr. Bartolo realize that he is their child. This dramatic action is covered quickly in recitative, and then a large ensemble begins: the reunited family rejoices together ("beloved son," "beloved parents").

Susanna enters, sees Figaro embracing Marcellina, and misunderstands the situation. During the next section, a sextet, Susanna and the count both rage furiously, with a jagged, dotted musical line,

Example 10.5

Fre-mo, Sma-nio dal fu - ro - re

("I fret, I rave with fury"), while Figaro and his parents calmly note that Susanna's jealousy is a sure sign of her love. The judge joins the count, making the balance in the sextet even—three against three. Finally Susanna listens to their explanation that Marcellina is Figaro's mother. Scarcely believing it, she questions each one of them in turn: *"Sua madre?"* Each one answers *"Sua madre!"* and the pitch level rises with each statement. The same device is used when Dr. Bartolo is introduced as Figaro's father.

The sextet ends with all characters singing, but the balance has changed from three and three to four and two, since Susanna has changed sides and is no longer angry. The musical setting makes their different feelings perfectly clear. The happy four sing smoothly and lyrically, with Susanna (the highest soprano) expressing her joy with an ornamented musical line. The count and the judge sing another jagged, dotted line to express their anger. At the end, where both groups have identical words, the different meanings are expressed by the speed of the notes: the angry men sing much faster than the others.

Example 10.6

or sà,   re   -   si   -   ster   or sà.

or   sà,   quest' a - ni-ma ap-pe-na re -si-ster or   sà.

or   sà,   re   -   si   -   ster   or sà.

MUSIC OF THE CLASSICAL ERA

Bartolo
Resistenza la coscienza
Far non lascia al tuo desir.

Curzio *(tra sé)*
Ei suo padre, ella sua madre:
L'imeneneo non può seguir.

Conte *(tra sé)*
Son smarrito, son stordito: Meglio è
assai di qua patir. *(Il Conte fa per
partire, Susanna l'arresta)*

Marcellina e Bartolo
Figlio amato!

Figaro
Parenti amati!

Susanna
Alto, alto, signore Conte, Mille doppie
qui son pronte. A pagar vengo per
Figaro, Ed a porlo in libertà.

Conte e Curzio
Non sappiam come'è la cosa. Osservate
un poco là.

Susanna *(si volge e vede Figaro che
abbraccia Marcellina)*
Già d'accordo colla sposa? Giusti dei;
che infedeltà! Lascia, iniquo! *(vuol
partire)*

Figaro *(la trattiene; ella lo forza)*
No, t'arresta Senti, o cara.

Susanna *(dà uno schiaffo a Figaro)*
Senti questa!

Marcellina, Bartolo, e Figaro
È un effetto di buon core, Tutto amore
è quel che fa.

Conte e Curzio
Fremo, smanio dal furore, Il destino
me la (gliela) fa.

Susanna
Fremo, smanio dal furore, Una vecchia
a me la fa.

Bartolo
*Do not let conscience stand in the way
of your desire.*

Curzio *(aside)*
*He's his father, she's his mother: the
wedding can't go forward.*

Count *(aside)*
*I'm astounded, I'm amazed: to leave
here would be for the best. (He makes
to leave, but Susanna detains him)*

Marcellina and Bartolo
My beloved son!

Figaro
My beloved parents!

Susanna
*Just a moment, pray, my lord. I have
the money ready here. I've come to
pay for Figaro and set him free.*

Count and Curzio
*We don't know where we are. Just
look over there.*

Susanna *(turns and sees Figaro embracing
Marcellina)*
*Already reconciled to her as wife?
Great heaven, how faithless! Leave
me, wretch! (She starts to go.)*

Figaro *(detains her; she struggles)*
Stay a moment. Listen, my dearest.

Susanna *(boxes Figaro's ears)*
Listen to that!

Marcellina, Bartolo, and Figaro
*It's the result of her full heart; what
she did, she did for love.*

Count and Curzio
*I rage, I burn with fury; fate has
overcome me (him).*

Susanna
*I rage, I burn with fury; this old
woman has overcome me.*

Marcellina

Lo sdegno calmate, Mia cara figliuola,
Sua madre abbracciate, Che vostra or
sarà. *(Marcellina corre ad abbracciare
Susanna)*

Susanna

Sua madre?

Tutti

Sua madre.

Figaro

E quello è mio padre,
Che a te lo dirà.

Susanna

Suo padre?

Tutti

Suo padre.

Figaro

E quella è mia madre,
Che a te lo dirà *(Corrono tutti e quattro
ad abbracciarsi)*

Susanna, Marcellina, Bartolo, e Figaro

Al dolce contento
Di questo momento, Quest' anima
appena
Resistere or sa.

Conte e Curzio

Al fiero tormento
Di questo momento Quest' anima
appena
Resistere or sa.

Marcellina

*Dearest daughter, calm your
bitterness, and embrace his mother,
who now will be yours too. (She runs to
embrace Susanna)*

Susanna

His mother?

All

His mother.

Figaro

*And this is my father,
who'll tell you it's true.*

Susanna

His father?

All

His father.

Figaro

*And this is my mother,
who'll tell you it's true. (All four
embrace)*

Susanna, Marcellina, Bartolo, and Figaro

*My heart
scarcely can support
the bliss
of this moment.*

Count and Curzio

*My heart scarcely can support
the raging torment
of this moment.*

SUMMARY

Although the main area of concentration for most classical composers was instrumental music the age did produce lasting achievements in vocal music as well.

Haydn's *Nelson Mass* well represents the classical treatment of the Mass. In the six main sections, comprising eleven movements, the listener is carried from themes of driving force to adagio passages of light texture, from exhilarating and dynamic movements to slow and expressive sections. Considered a masterpiece, this work is a favorite in contemporary choral repertoires.

The greatest composer of opera in the classical era was Mozart. His first comic opera, *The Marriage of Figaro,* stands out among opera buffa for its realistic characters, amusing libretto, delightful solo and ensemble music, and skillful use of orchestral devices to enhance the characterization.

NEW TERMS

opera seria
opera buffa

SUGGESTED LISTENING

Haydn, Franz Joseph

Die Schöpfung (The *Creation*). This oratorio (one of three by Haydn) depicts and tells the story of the creation of the world. From the overture (Representation of Chaos) to the final triumphant chorus, Haydn uses soloists, chorus, and orchestra to impart the story vividly and dramatically.

Mozart, Wolfgang Amadeus

Requiem in D Minor K.626. In spite of the fact that Mozart died before he could finish this piece (it was completed by a student), it became and still is one of the great settings of the Requiem for the Dead. It is scored for soloists, chorus, and orchestra.

Exsultate, Jubilate. This motet is written for soprano soloist and an orchestra consisting of strings, oboes, and French horns. Its last movement, *Alleluja,* calls for brilliant vocal technique on the part of the soprano.

Don Giovanni. The story of Don Juan, the Spanish lover, and his downfall in what many consider to be Mozart's best opera.

11 | THE MUSIC OF BEETHOVEN

||P|| robably no single composer has influenced the course of musical events more than Ludwig van Beethoven. His evolving style had a profound effect on the musicians of his time, and the music he left to the world has continued to influence musicians and to have great public appeal. In 1970, concert halls around the world presented programs of his music to commemorate the two hundredth anniversary of his birth in 1770. Athough he is considered a representative of the classical era, Beethoven in many ways was a precursor of romanticism. His life bridged two centuries almost equally, and his spirit seemed more in tune with the upheaval that followed the French Revolution than with the relative stability of the Age of Reason. While he injected a new freedom into the classical forms, Beethoven continued to adhere to them. His great contribution was to carry forward the tradition of Mozart and Haydn, building on the structures they had developed and elevating them to new heights of power and expressiveness.

BEETHOVEN'S WORK

In comparison to the production of Mozart and Haydn, Beethoven's works seem surprisingly few. This is partly due to his method of composing. Mozart never lacked musical inspiration, and ideas flowed from his pen with miraculous ease; Haydn confessed to the necessity of resorting to prayer at difficult moments, but he kept to a regular schedule of composition. Beethoven, however, had to struggle. Ideas did not come easily, and he filled innumerable pages with slowly evolving sketches. Even his finished compositions were continually rewritten and revised (see fig. 11.2). The second reason for limited production was his attitude toward composition. He regarded music, above all, as art, and he generally took on only those commissions that he personally wished to fulfill.

BEETHOVEN (1770–1827)

Ludwig van Beethoven was born in the Rhineland city of Bonn, the son of a singer in the Electoral Court chapel. His musical education was taken over by his father, who hoped to make his boy into a child prodigy like Mozart. Though never fulfilling his father's hope, young Beethoven did learn piano and violin quickly. He received instruction from several musicians at the court, and by the age of twelve he was substituting at the chapel organ. In 1784 he was appointed to a permanent position as assistant organist and had already begun to make his mark because of his virtuoso improvisations at the piano. After his mother died, in 1787, his father's alcoholism grew worse, and Beethoven's home life became increasingly unbearable.

The year 1790 marked a turning point in the young composer's career. Haydn, passing through Bonn on his way to London, urged the Elector to send Beethoven to Vienna for further study. Two years later, at the age of twenty-two, Beethoven moved to Vienna, where he remained the rest of his life. At first he studied composition with Haydn; but, unsatisfied with the older man's methods, he turned to other composers for instruction. Though he was a frequent performer at musical evenings held by prominent Viennese nobility, Beethoven did not play in public until 1795, when he performed one of his early piano concertos.

Unlike Mozart, he always retained his popularity with both the general public and the aristocracy of Vienna; and unlike Haydn, he never had to endure the rigors of the eighteenth-century system of musical patronage. Though he may have yearned at times for the prestige and security of a court position, he remained proudly and fiercely independent throughout his life. During most of his career he was able to count on annual stipends from a small circle of aristocratic friends and admirers. He seemed to enjoy moving about in the upper echelons of Viennese society, remarking that "it is good to mingle with aristocrats, but one must know how to impress them." He was one of the first composers to demand and obtain an equal footing with this aristocracy solely on the basis of his genius. It was his fortune to come upon the world in a time of rapidly changing values and increasing social mobility. The emerging middle-class audience and the growth of public concerts provided ample opportunities for performance of his music. The rising demand for his works enabled him to live off the sale of his music to publishers.

During the first years of the nineteenth century, when Beethoven seemed to be approaching the height of his career, he became aware that he was growing deaf. He

Figure 11.1 Beethoven's music encompasses both the classical love of form and the fiery passion of romanticism. The force and intensity of his stormy personality are evident in this engraving.

became deeply depressed when he realized that his career as a performer would end. In a moving letter to his two brothers, written from the small town of Heiligenstadt outside Vienna and intended to be read after his death, Beethoven confessed:

My misfortune pains me doubly, in as much as it leads to my being misjudged. For me there can be no relaxation in human society, no refined conversations, no mutual confidences: I must live quite alone and may creep into society only as often as sheer necessity demands; I must live like an outcast. If I appear in company I am overcome by a burning anxiety, a fear that I am running the risk of letting people notice my condition. . . . Such experiences almost made me despair, and I was on the point of putting an end to my life—The only thing that held me back was my art. For indeed it seemed to me impossible to leave this world before I had produced all the works that I felt the urge to compose, and thus I have dragged on this miserable existence.*

After his affliction became painfully obvious, he gave up conducting and playing in public. His principal means of communication became a notebook in which his few visitors were invited to write their remarks. As he withdrew into his art, his works became more complex, more abstract, and more incomprehensible to his fellow musicians. He never married, and when total deafness set in after 1820, he became almost a recluse. Beethoven died in 1827 at the age of fifty-seven.

*Emily Anderson (ed. and transl.), *The Letters of Beethoven*, 3 vols. Vol. 3, p. 1352. Copyright © 1961 St. Martin's Press, New York. Reprinted by permission of MacMillan Publishing, London.

Figure 11.2 This
manuscript for a piano
sonata shows signs of the
struggle and painstaking
reworking that marked
Beethoven's composing
sessions.

If his works took longer to write than was usual at the time, they were also more
substantial, both in content and length. His works include nine symphonies; nine concert overtures; five piano concertos; one violin concerto; sixteen string quartets; ten
sonatas for violin and piano; five sonatas for cello and piano; thirty-two sonatas for
solo piano; twenty-one sets of variations for piano; one opera, *Fidelio;* an oratorio,
Christus am Olberg, (Christ on the Mount of Olives); Choral Fantasia for piano,
chorus, and orchestra; and two Masses, one in C major, the other, entitled the *Missa
solemnis,* in D major.

Most musical scholars divide Beethoven's career into three periods: the first extending to about 1802, the second extending to 1814, and the last ending with his
death in 1827. The first period was a time of assimilation of the classical tradition of
Mozart and Haydn and includes the string quartets of opus 18 (1798–1800), the First
Symphony (1799), and his first three piano sonatas.

The second period was perhaps the happiest of his life; it was certainly the most
productive. During it he wrote masterpiece after masterpiece; seven more symphonies, including the gigantic *Eroica* (no. 3, 1803) and the Fifth (1805); the *Ra-
soumovsky Quartets* of opus 59 (1806); his opera *Fidelio* (with no fewer than three
versions appearing from 1805 through 1814); and the "Waldstein" and "Appassionata" piano sonatas of 1804.

His last creative period, a time of great personal troubles including his deafness, was less productive, but in many ways it was the most important of the three. It culminated in his monumental Ninth Symphony (1823), the equally immense *Missa solemnis* (completed in 1824), and increasingly abstract late quartets and piano sonatas. In these works he developed many of the musical ideas that influenced the coming romantic movement. The innovations they contained in form and harmonic structure were not fully understood or appreciated until almost half a century after his death.

ELEMENTS OF HIS STYLE

Beethoven's music reveals several original stylistic characteristics. One that is immediately apparent is size. His works tend to be much longer than those of Haydn or Mozart.

Another striking characteristic is the prevalence of the developmental process. Beethoven lengthened the development section of sonata-allegro form, giving it a weight equal to that of the exposition and recapitulation, and used development in other parts of the movement, especially in the coda. In many of his works the coda is not a short, tacked-on ending but is extended into a second development section, sometimes followed by a second coda that acts as a genuine coda—a short, concluding section.

In general, Beethoven adhered to the schemes of separate, self-contained movements, unrelated thematically. But there are exceptions: the Sixth Symphony (the *Pastoral*) has five movements, and there is no break between the last two. And the Fifth Symphony, which we shall discuss below, was a striking departure from the principle of thematic independence among the movements.

Within the four-movement scheme, he radically transformed the *third* movement. The short, stately minuet and trio was replaced by a scherzo and trio movement of an entirely different character. Swift of tempo, and fully proportioned in their length, Beethoven's scherzos are the equal of the other movements, performing an important structural and expressive role in the overall scheme of the work.

His music is characterized by an intense, dramatic use of fluctuating dynamics. Frequently he used special dynamic effects, such as a crescendo that is not allowed to climax, but is aborted by a sudden change to pianissimo. He also used long crescendos for structural and expressive purposes. A crescendo slowly builds momentum and energy culminating in the appearance of an important event, such as the beginning of the recapitulation. Under these circumstances, the beginning of the recapitulation would also serve as a climactic ending of the development section.

Beethoven was ingenious in the use of *silence*. In his music, silence functions both as a structural element, separating sections, and as an expressive element, building suspense.

The qualities that we have outlined here are characteristic of Beethoven's work in general. Other, more specific, qualities can be seen in his orchestral works.

Orchestral Style

Beethoven's orchestral sound is more powerful and dramatic than that of Mozart or Haydn. This increased intensity was the result of both larger orchestra and a change in the ways in which the instruments were used. More players were added to the string section, and two horns (sometimes four), two trumpets, and timpani were included as standard parts of the orchestral ensemble. The normal woodwind section comprised two flutes, two oboes, two clarinets, and two bassoons. For extra color and power, Beethoven occasionally added piccolo, contrabassoon, and three trombones. The trumpets, horns, and trombones assumed a greater role than they had previously and the timpani, which formerly merely reinforced the trumpets, were used independently, even as solo instruments.

Working with this expanded orchestra, Beethoven made important contributions to the craft of **orchestration**—writing and arranging music for orchestra to achieve the most effective overall combinations. In this area he greatly influenced later composers in the romantic era for whom orchestration became a major component of musical composition.

The increased dimensions, extended use of development, advanced exploitation of dynamics, employment of suspense-building devices, and powerful use of an expanded orchestra are among the most important stylistic features of Beethoven's symphonies. Beginning with the Third and culminating in the Ninth, they revolutionized orchestral writing and playing.

BEETHOVEN: SYMPHONY NO. 5 IN C MINOR

Beethoven's Fifth Symphony, which he began in 1804, was first performed in Vienna in December, 1808. It is probably the most popular of Beethoven's symphonies, not only for its terse and memorable themes, but also for its unity.

SIDE 5/SELECTION 1 LISTENING GUIDE ON PAGES 219–20

First Movement

The first movement of the symphony is an excellent example of Beethoven's skill at building a large structure out of a small motive, in this case the famous ♪♪♪|𝅗𝅥

Its stark and forceful announcement, played fortissimo by all strings and clarinets, stands at the beginning of the movement.

Example 11.1

After these two statements, there is a change to *piano* as the motive is used to create the initial phrase of the first theme, in the principal key of C minor.

Example 11.2

The theme is soon abruptly driven to a dramatic halt by a crescendo, leading to three loud, separated chords. The last chord lingers on a long-held note in the first violin, creating a feeling of suspense that is dispelled when the full orchestra, fortissimo, hammers out the motive. This dramatic and isolated statement of the motive draws attention to it, interrupting the flow of the theme. With another extreme change, from full orchestra playing fortissimo to strings playing piano, the theme is resumed, building on the motive.

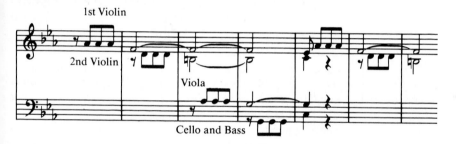

Example 11.3

Shortly after the resumption of the theme, several important features of Beethoven's style appear. The intensity increases, underlined by the gradual addition of instruments, stepped-up rhythmic activity, and climbing pitch level, all combining in a mighty crescendo that envelops the bridge and culminates in two sharp chords separated by silence and followed by silence, dramatically setting off the appearance of the second theme.

The second theme, in E-flat major, is launched by the four-note motive announced by the horns.

Example 11.4

The second theme continues with a lyrical legato melody in the first violins and the woodwinds. The basic motive is still present as a kind of punctuation in the lower strings.

Example 11.5

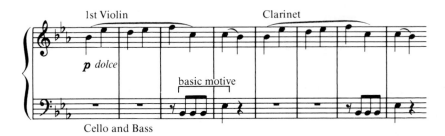

As the rhythmic activity of the theme increases, the basic motive reasserts itself, commanding full attention in the closing material ending the exposition, which is then repeated.

Example 11.6

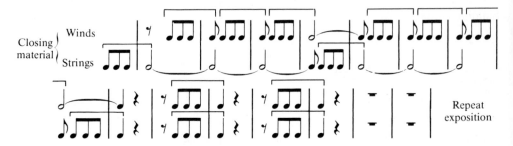

The first phase of the development concentrates on the basic motive, in a manner similar to theme 1, gradually leading to the winds and strings answering each other.

The second phase of development begins with the opening phrase of theme 2 and turns it into one of the most intense examples of suspense building in the history of musical composition. After the violins state the phrase twice, each time followed by rhythmic punctuations in the winds and lower strings, the phrase

The motive is not used in theme 3, although later in the movement the material from this theme is used in association with the motive.

Example 11.15

The bridge between themes 1 and 2 is exceptionally long, and its melodic importance rivals that of the themes themselves.

Example 11.16

It modulates from C to G major, ending with repetitions of the motive as it leads to the second theme.

After the repeat of the exposition (many conductors do not make this repetition), the closing section flows directly into the development section—indeed, there is almost no indication of where one ends and the other begins.

The development section makes forceful use of the orchestra, with emphasis on winds and brasses, extended use of dynamics and modulation. Toward the end of the development section a loud, fanfare-like section leads to a remarkable phase of development. There is a direct quote of the end of the *third* movement. Using this quote the development builds through a long crescendo to the recapitulation. Again, as in the beginning of the fourth movement, because of the way it is approached, the first theme produces a "victorious" effect.

The piece does not end with the conclusion of the recapitulation. Instead, there is a long coda which is actually a new development section. It is characterized by an exhilarating increase in tempo leading to what is without question one of the longest and most emphatic endings in music history—bringing to a close one of the most remarkable compositions of all time.

Compositions for Piano

A significant portion of Beethoven's output was devoted to works for the piano. For this instrument he wrote thirty-two solo sonatas, five piano concertos, and a host of other works for solo piano including the *Thirty-Three Variations on a Waltz by Diabelli*. Added to this list are many works in which the piano was employed as a collaborating instrument such as sonatas for violin and piano, cello and piano, and horn and piano.

All of the stylistic elements noted previously are evident in his writing for the keyboard. In his hands the piano became a more dramatic and dynamic instrument than was the case in the keyboard works of Mozart and Haydn.

Both as a virtuoso pianist and as a composer, Beethoven preferred the heavier piano developed in England to the lighter Viennese instrument played by Mozart. The English design and construction resulted in an instrument of great brilliance and dynamic power which Beethoven exploited to the fullest extent, as illustrated in his Piano Sonata op. 57 to become known as the "Appassionata."

The sonata maintained the three movement plan—fast, slow, fast—without, however, the usual break between the second and third movements.

First Movement (Allegro assai)

The first movement, in the key of F minor, is in sonata-allegro form, including two contrasting themes, the first ominous:

BEETHOVEN: PIANO SONATA OP. 57 ("APPASSIONATA")

SIDE 5/SELECTION 2 LISTENING GUIDE ON PAGE 221

Example 11.17

the second, flowing:

Example 11.18

The abrupt changes of mood, sudden and frequent change in dynamic level, dramatic pauses, and suspense building we encountered in much of the Fifth Symphony are in abundance in this movement. In addition, Beethoven makes full use of the extremes of pitch level—very high to very low—of which the piano is capable:

Example 11.19

MUSIC OF THE CLASSICAL ERA

Example 11.20

Example 11.21

Two stretches of music in this movement are very much like cadenzas. One ends the development and introduces the recapitulation, and the second ends the recapitulation and introduces the allegro finale. The closing coda is a tour de force for the virtuoso pianist, as it races at breakneck speed and with fortissimo dynamics. The theme is doubled in octaves and sounded in the most brilliant register of the piano. In a gesture typical of Beethoven, it then progresses from its point of climax to one of repose. In the last measures, the dynamic level drops from fortissimo to pianissimo to triple piano. The theme is sent soaring to the heights of the keyboard, then plummeting to a final whispered cadence five octaves below.

Second Movement

The second movement is a lyrical theme and variations in D-flat major. In this movement Beethoven exploits the lower range of the piano and creates striking effects by juxtaposing high and low sections. The initial somber theme is stated in the rich and sonorous lower register of the keyboard. The theme is in two parts, each of which is repeated.

The first variation preserves the theme's contour but alters the rhythm. The right hand transforms the legato articulation into short, detached notes. The left hand, meanwhile, syncopates the rhythm of the theme, so that notes now appear slightly after the beat.

The second variation returns to the smooth legato of the opening, with the right hand playing chordal figures while the left hand retains the original bass line with slight rhythmic alterations. The material in both hands has been transposed one octave higher than in the original, thus creating a lighter, less massive texture.

In the first two variations the repetition structure of the theme is retained, but in the final variation this is no longer the case. Beethoven uses a motive based on the opening of the theme as a superstructure around which he weaves rapid chordal and scale figurations; here again we witness his exploration of development possibilities.

The magic that sometimes results from the juxtaposition of high and low registers emanates from the last simple statement of the theme at the close of the movement. The first three chords of each phrase are high, the next low, and this continued alternation between high and low registers gives the theme itself a quiet, fragmented quality of suspense. This feeling is heightened by the fact that the movement doesn't "end"; rather it pauses in anticipation on two long, arpeggios—one very soft, the second very loud—that call for resolution—

Example 11.22

a resolution which comes only with the beginning of the concluding movement with a return to a fast tempo.

Third Movement (Allegro ma non troppo)

The beginning of the last movement constitutes a continuation of the introductory character of the end of the second movement. Not until twenty measures into the movement does the theme of the last movement appear.

Example 11.23

This passage, or some variant of it, seems omnipresent throughout the entire movement, blurring the distinctions between exposition and development and development and recapitulation. The movement sounds like one continuous development of this material, with other thematic elements imbedded within or grafted onto it. The movement ends with a presto finale in a climax of brilliance and excitement.

MUSIC OF THE CLASSICAL ERA

LISTENING GUIDE

Beethoven: Symphony no. 5 in C Minor

First Movement: Allegro con brio (fast, fiery)
                     duple meter
                     sonata form

Classical orchestra

Review: Example 11.1 (opening, with basic motive)
         Example 11.2 (initial phrase of first theme)
         Example 11.3 (continuation of first theme)
         Example 11.4 (horns announcing second theme)
         Example 11.5 (legato second theme with basic motive in basses)
         Example 11.6 (closing material of Exposition)
         Example 11.7 (two-note Development pattern)
         Example 11.8 (reduction to one-note pattern)

Exposition		
Theme 1	*1a*	basic motive stated twice, forte
	b	piano, motive sounds throughout strings; crescendo, three forte, separated chords, long-held note by violins on last chord
	c	motive, fortissimo; piano, motive builds theme in strings; instruments gradually enter, crescendo, pitch rises; two separate chords, fortissimo
Bridge		
Theme 2	*2a*	horn call, basic motive with extension, fortissimo
	b	legato theme in violins, then clarinet, then flute; basic motive in low strings; fragment of theme in strings, other instruments gradually enter, crescendo
Closing	*3a*	loud chord, strings in strong descending passage, repeated
	b	basic motive descends in winds answered by strings; repeated; two separate statements of motive

(Exposition may be repeated)

Development	*1*	basic motive in horns, strings, fortissimo; motive developed among instruments, piano, slight crescendo, return to piano for further development
		strings and winds toss motive back and forth, crescendo to strings hammering on repeated note

THE MUSIC OF BEETHOVEN

	2a	horn call from theme 2 developed, with answer from low strings; reduced to two-note fragment echoed between winds and strings; reduced to one-note echo, suspense builds through diminuendo to pianissimo
	b	horn call erupts in full orchestra; one-note echo resumes; basic motive repeated fortissimo, directly into:
Recapitulation *Theme 1*	1a	trumpets and timpani added for two statements of basic motive
	b	motive through strings with countermelody in oboe, piano; three separated chords, oboe cadenza concludes countermelody on last chord
	c	motive, fortissimo; piano, motive builds theme in strings; instruments gradually enter, crescendo, pitch rises; two separate chords, fortissimo
Theme 2	2a	horn call (bassoon in some recordings), basic motive with extension, fortissimo
	b	legato theme traded between violins and flute, basic motive in low strings; fragment of theme divided between strings and flute, crescendo in strings as other instruments gradually enter
Coda	3a	loud chord, strings in strong descending passage, repeated
	b	basic motive descends in woodwinds answered by strings; repeated
Second Development	4	separate statements of motive extended fortissimo to hammer on repeated note, basic motive piano, repeated note forte, motive piano horn call from theme 2 in cellos and violas, new countertheme in violins; repeated; countertheme vigorously developed, full orchestra fragment of countertheme tossed between winds and strings; repeated note leads directly into:
Second Coda	5a	basic motive stated twice, fortissimo
	b	piano, basic motive in strings; fortissimo, full orchestra states basic motive three times with final chords

●●

SONG AND PIANO MUSIC

T he romantic period in music roughly coincides with the nineteenth century. In some respects it was a logical extension of the principles established during the classical era. In other respects, however, it represented a fundamental departure from those principles. Even within the outlines of the basic musical structures of the classical period—the sonata-allegro form, theme and variations—formal balance and clarity of structure gave way to spontaneity, to emotional depth and richness, qualities foreshadowed in the later works of Beethoven. In addition, the romantic era saw the classical forms abandoned altogether by some composers. Instead, there was a heavy reliance on literature, nature, visual images, and the supernatural as sources for musical inspiration and as frameworks for musical forms.

ROMANTIC INNOVATIONS

Romantic composers made some of their most remarkable achievements in harmony and tone color, and the harmonic vocabulary became increasingly rich during the nineteenth century. Chromatic harmonies, modulations to distant keys, complicated chords, all tended to blur the outlines of the harmonic system of major and minor keys. Harmony became as much a means of expression as an element of musical structure.

The romantic interest in tone color is shown by the phenomenal growth of the orchestra during this period. For the first time, instrumental color was regarded as an important element of music, on a par with melody, harmony, and rhythm. Instruments were improved, new ones were invented, new combinations were discovered, and the art of orchestration became a prime preoccupation for many composers of the age.

Figure 12.1 The short piano piece was tremendously popular during the romantic period. The social intimacy created by this smaller musical form is well illustrated by this romanticized painting entitled, *A Schubert Evening in a Viennese Home.*

The romantic period is often described as the age of the art song and the short piano piece, since these two genres constitute some of the most interesting musical literature of the nineteenth century. This fascination with the smaller forms is one of the two major aspects of the romantic spirit; the other aspect centered upon the larger forms, which offered greater scope in which to expand and develop. (We will discuss the larger forms in succeeding chapters of this unit.) These small pieces had an intimate quality, as though the composer were speaking directly to a small group of friends. The media that seemed most suitable to them were the piano and the solo voice.

ART SONG

The **art song** is a musical setting of a poem for solo voice and piano. The German words **lied** and **lieder** (plural)—which we previously encountered in chapter 6—became the standard terms for this type of song. The lied became an important musical genre in the work of major composers early in the nineteenth century.

In the mid-eighteenth century the lied had been a simple song with keyboard accompaniment. The musical setting used **strophic form,** with the same melody repeated for every stanza (or strophe) of the poem. The text was treated syllabically (one note for each syllable) and the accompaniment served merely to support the singing voice.

Toward the end of the eighteenth century, the **ballad**—a narrative poem set to music—became popular in Germany. The ballad was long, emphasized dramatic situations, and alternated in structure between narration and dialogue. These characteristics required greater musical resources than the strophic procedure offered. Hence the ballads were **through-composed;** that is, each section of the text had new music that was different from the music preceding and following.

Both the strophic and through-composed procedures were used in the nineteenth-century lied. The earliest and, in many respects, the most important of lieder composers was Franz Schubert.

SCHUBERT *(1797–1828)*

*I*n many ways the circumstances of Franz Peter Schubert's life were the very essence of the romantic's view of an artist's condition. During his brief and troubled lifetime, Schubert lived in poverty and was unrecognized, except by a small circle of friends; only after his death was his genius more widely acknowledged. He was born in a suburb northwest of Vienna, the fourth surviving son of an industrious and pious schoolmaster. His formal musical training, never very systematic, began with violin lessons from his father and piano instruction from an older brother.

In 1808, at the age of eleven, Schubert obtained a place in the choir of the Imperial Court Chapel and was thereby privileged to attend the *Stadt-Konvict* (City Seminary), one of Vienna's most prestigious boarding schools. In addition to his regular studies and music lessons, he became a violinist in the school orchestra, later assuming the duties of conductor on various occasions. The numerous works he composed during these years at the *Konvict* include songs, overtures, religious works, an operetta (light opera), and six string quartets. His first symphony was written in 1813, the year in which he left the *Konvict,* and his first Mass was successfully performed in 1814.

After leaving the *Konvict* Schubert returned home to live, first attending a training college for primary school teachers and then teaching at his father's school. The regimen of the classroom was not suited to his temperament, and he applied for the musical directorship of the new State Normal School at Laibach (now Ljubljana in Yugoslavia) in 1816, but was turned down. Unable to find any other permanent employment at that time, he resolved to earn his living by taking music students, selling his compositions, and writing for the theater. In 1817 he moved to Vienna.

During the early 1820s, performances of Schubert's solo songs and vocal quartets for male voices aroused considerable public interest, and his name became widely known throughout Vienna. Two of his operettas were produced with moderate success, and a number of songs and piano works were published. These successes were offset by his continuing inability to obtain a salaried position. In 1822, a serious illness, probably syphilis, necessitated a

Figure 12.2 Schubert's lieder exemplifies the spontaneity and lyricism of the Romantic movement.

stay in the hospital and a prolonged period of recuperation. The following year, *Rosamunde,* a play with incidental music by Schubert, failed dismally, closing after only two performances. It was his last work for the theater.

The last four years of his life were a continual battle against ill health and poverty. Though his music, particularly the songs, continued to draw high praise from fellow musicians, including Beethoven, it was not until 1828 that a public concert of his works was given. He was unable to live on the pitifully small income from his music publications, but he continued to compose at a feverish pace. Despite his weakening health, he seemed at the height of his creative power. In the fall of 1828 he became ill and died on November 19, at the age of thirty-one. His last wish, to be buried near Beethoven, was granted, and on his tombstone was written: "The art of music here entombed a rich possession but even far fairer hopes."

Schubert's Work

During the seventeen years between 1811, when he was fourteen, and 1828, the year of his death, Schubert composed about one thousand works. They include nine symphonies, fifty chamber works and piano sonatas, a large number of short piano pieces, several operas and operettas, six Masses and about twenty-five other religious works, nearly one hundred choral compositions, and more than six hundred songs.

Schubert's symphonic style displays a romantic gift for lyric melody and a love of interesting patches of color and harmony. Nevertheless, his symphonies were written in the classical forms. His famous Symphony no. 8 in B Minor was written in 1822, when the composer was twenty-five years old, but he never chose to extend it beyond the original two movements. Nicknamed "The Unfinished," the work was not performed until 1865, forty-three years after his death.

Schubert is best known, however, for his abundant body of lieder. He set to music the poetry of the great literary figures of his time, Goethe and Schiller among them. In addition to settings of individual poems, Schubert wrote two **song cycles** (a series of art songs that tell a story), *Die schöne Müllerin* (*The Maid of the Mill,* 1823), and *Die Winterreise* (*Winter Journey,* 1827).

Schubert employed both the strophic (which he used with considerable flexibility) and through-composed forms with great imagination. His songs also reflected the supremacy of the poem as the generating force. The shape and quality of the melodic line, the choice of harmonic progressions, the rhythmic character of the work, and the entire structure were fashioned to serve the poem. And the piano accompaniment, now no longer a mere harmonic background for the voice, joined with the voice, virtually as a full partner, bringing to musical life the essence of the poem.

SCHUBERT:
GRETCHEN AM
SPINNRADE (1814)

One of the finest examples of the use of the piano is found in "Gretchen am Spinnrade" ("Gretchen at the Spinning Wheel"). Gretchen, who in Goethe's play has fallen in love with Faust, sings as she sits at her spinning wheel.

GRETCHEN AM SPINNRADE	**GRETCHEN AT THE SPINNING WHEEL**[*]
Meine Ruh ist hin,	*My peace is gone,*
Mein Herz ist schwer;	*my heart is heavy;*
Ich finde sie nimmer	*never, never again*
Und nimmermehr.	*Will I find rest.*
Wo ich ihn nicht hab;	*Where I am not with him*
Ist mir das Grab,	*I am in my grave,*
Die ganze Welt	*the whole world*
Ist mir vergällt.	*turns to bitter gall.*
Mein armer Kopf	*My poor head*
Ist mir verrückt,	*is in a whirl,*
Mein armer Sinn	*my poor thoughts*
Ist mir zerstückt.	*are all distracted.*

[*]From *The Penguin Book of Lieder* edited and translated by S. S. Prawer (Penguin Books, 1964), copyright © S. S. Prawer, 1964.

Meine Ruh ist hin,	*My peace is gone,*
Mein Herz ist schwer,	*my heart is heavy;*
Ich finde sie nimmer	*never, never again*
Und nimmermehr.	*Will I find rest.*
Nach ihm nur schau' ich	*I seek only him when I look*
Zum Fenster hinaus,	*out of the window,*
Nach ihm nur geh'ich	*I seek only him when I leave*
Aus dem Haus.	*the house.*
Sein hoher Gang,	*His noble gait,*
Sein' edle Gestalt,	*his fine stature,*
Seines Mundes Lächeln,	*the smile of his lips,*
Seiner Augen Gewalt,	*the power of his eyes,*
Und seiner Rede	*and the magic flow*
Zauberfluss.	*of his speech,*
Sein Händedruck,	*the pressure of his hand,*
Und ach, sein Kuss!	*and oh, his kiss!*
Meine Ruh ist hin,	*My peace is gone,*
Mein Herz ist schwer,	*my heart is heavy;*
Ich finde sie nimmer	*never, never again*
Und nimmermehr.	*Will I find rest.*
Mein Busen drängt	*My bosom yearns*
Sich nach ihm hin!	*towards him.*
Ach dürft' ich fassen	*If only I could seize him*
Und halten ihn,	*and hold him*
Und küssen ihn,	*and kiss him*
So wie ich wollt',	*to my heart's content—*
An seinen Küssen	*under his kisses*
Vergehen sollt'!	*I should die!*
An seinen Küssen	*under his kisses*
Vergehen sollt'!	*I should die!*
Meine Ruh ist hin,	*My peace is gone.*
Mein Herz ist schwer . . .	*My heart is heavy. . . .*

The piano accompaniment, which represents the spinning wheel, mirrors her growing agitation. As Gretchen conjures up her lover, a running sixteenth-note figure (the sound of the wheel) gradually intensifies. As the voice rises higher and higher, the sound of the whirling wheel crescendos, stops, and Gretchen cries out *"und ach, sein Kuss!"* ("and oh, his kiss"). Gretchen sits transfixed by her passion, as does the listener.

It is not the voice but the piano that tells us that Gretchen returns to her senses. The spinning motive in the piano (pianissimo) makes two false starts; then with the third, the song is in motion again, with the spinning reintroducing the voice on *"Meine Ruh ist hin"* ("My peace is gone").

The words *Meine Ruh ist hin* and their melody begin each verse and act as a unifying element throughout the song. Gretchen repeats these words once more at the end of the song in a sigh of resignation. As the sound of her voice fades away, the whirring of the piano's spinning motive closes the piece as it began it.

The romantic love of nature is evident in "Die Forelle" ("The Trout"), one of Schubert's shorter lieder. The poem concerns the struggle between a fish and a fisherman; typically the romantic poet's sympathy lies with the fish.

DIE FORELLE

In einem Bächlein helle,
Da schoss in froher Eil'
Die launische Forelle
Vorüber wie ein Pfeil.
Ich stand an dem Gestade
Und sah in süsser Ruh
Des muntern Fischleins Bade
Im klaren Bächlein zu.

Ein Fischer mit der Rute
Wohl an dem Ufer stand,
Und sah's mit kaltem Blute,
Wie sich das Fischlein wand.
So lang' dem Wasser Helle,
So dacht ich, nicht gebricht,
So fängt er die Forelle
Mit seiner Angel nicht.

Doch endlich ward dem Diebe
Die Zeit zu lang. Er macht'
Das Bächlein tückisch trübe,
Und eh' ich es gedacht,
So zuckte seine Rute,
Das Fischlein zappelt' d'ran,
Und ich mit regem Blute
Sah die Betrogne an.

THE TROUT*

*In a bright little stream,
in joyous haste,
a playful trout
flashed past me like an arrow.
I stood by the shore
and in sweet contentment I watched
the little fish bathing
in the clear stream.*

*A fisherman with his rod
stood on the bank
and coldly watched
the trout's windings.
So long as the water
—I thought—remains clear,
he will not catch the trout
with his line.*

*But at last the thief
grew impatient. He
treacherously dulled the clear stream,
and before I could think it
his rod quivered
and the fish was struggling on his hook.
I felt the blood stir within me
as I looked at the cheated trout.*

In form "Die Forelle" is almost strophic. The first two verses have identical music: a simple melody with a very simple harmonic background. The accompaniment makes use of a short, rising figure that seems to sparkle and babble like a brook, conveying a mood of cheerful calm.

The third verse of the poem is much more excited, as the fish is caught. Schubert echoes this change of mood by putting aside the strophic form. The new melody is backed by a more agitated, more chromatic accompaniment. For the last two lines of the song, however, Schubert returns to the original melody and accompaniment. Although the text of the poem does not repeat the opening lines, the reappearance of the first melody rounds out the form of the song. In 1819 Schubert used this song as a basis for a set of variations in the Quintet in A Major (op. 114), the famous "Trout" Quintet for Piano and Four Strings.

*From *The Penguin Book of Lieder* edited and translated by S. S. Prawer (Penguin Books, 1964), copyright © S. S. Prawer, 1964.

While two of the romantic period's favorite themes, nature and painful love, occupy "Die Forelle" and "Gretchen am Spinnrade," the supernatural is involved in Schubert's setting of "Erlkönig" ("King of the Elves"). The poem, a ballad by Goethe, tells the story of a father riding through a storm on horseback carrying his sick child in his arms. As they hurry through the stormy night, the delirious boy imagines that the Erlkönig (who symbolizes death) appears and tries to entice him away with promises of fine games and pleasures. When the father and son finally arrive home, the boy is dead in his arms.

SCHUBERT:
ERLKÖNIG (1815)
SIDE 5/SELECTION 3

The poem has four separate characters, all sung by one voice with piano accompaniment: the narrator, who introduces and closes the song, the frightened child, the frantic father, and the sinister Erlkönig.

ERLKÖNIG (GOETHE)	KING OF THE ELVES*
Narrator	
Wer reitet so spät durch Nacht und Wind?	*Who rides so late through the night and the wind?*
Es ist der Vater mit seinem Kind;	*It is the father with his child.*
Er hat den Knaben wohl in dem Arm	*He holds the boy in his arm, grasps*
Er fasst ihn sicher, er hält ihn warm.	*him securely, keeps him warm.*
Father	
"Mein Sohn, was birgst du so bang dein Gesicht?"	*"My son, why do you hide your face so anxiously?"*

*From *The Penguin Book of Lieder* edited and translated by S. S. Prawer (Penguin Books, 1964), copyright © S. S. Prawer, 1964.

Son

"Siehst, Vater, du den Erlkönig nicht?
Den Erlenkönig mit Kron' und
    Schweif?"

*"Father, do you not see the Elf-King?
The Elf-King with his crown and
    train?"*

Father

"Mein Sohn, es ist ein Nebelstreif."

"My son, it is only a streak of mist."

Elf King

"Du liebes Kind, komm, geh' mit mir!
Gar schöne Spiele spiel' ich mit dir;
Manch' bunte Blumen sind an dem
    Strand,
Meine Mutter hat manch' gülden
    Gewand."

*"Darling child, come away with me!
I will play fine games with you.
Many gay flowers grow by the shore:*

my mother has many golden robes."

Son

"Mein Vater, mein Vater, und hörest
    du nicht,
Was Erlenkönig mir leise verspricht?"

"Father, father, do you not hear

*what the Elf-King softly promises
    me?"*

Father

"Sei ruhig, bleibe ruhig, mein Kind:
In dürren Blättern säuselt der Wind."

*"Be calm, dear child, be calm—
the wind is rustling in the dry leaves."*

Elf King

"Willst, feiner Knabe, du mit mir
    gehn?
Meine Töchter sollen dich warten
    schön;
Meine Töchter führen den nächtlichen
    Reihn'
Und wiegen und tanzen und singen
    dich ein."

*"You beautiful boy, will you come
    with me?
My daughters will wait upon you.*

*My daughters will lead the nightly
    round,
they will rock you, dance to you, sing
    you to sleep."*

Son

"Mein Vater, mein Vater, und siehst
    du nicht dort
Erlkönigs Töchter am düstern Ort?"

*"Father, father, do you not see
the Elf-King's daughters there, in
    that dark place?"*

Father

"Mein Sohn, mein Sohn, ich seh' es
    genau:
Es scheinen die alten Weiden so grau."

"My son, my son, I see it clearly:

*it is the grey gleam of the old
    willow-trees."*

Elf King

"Ich liebe dich, mich reizt deine
    schöne Gestalt;
Und bist du nicht willig, so brauch'
    ich Gewalt."

Son

"Mein Vater, mein Vater, jetzt fasst
    er mich an!
Erlkönig hat mir ein Leids gethan!"—

Narrator

Dem Vater grauset's, er reitet
    geschwind
Er hält in den Armen das ächzende
    Kind,
Erreicht den Hof mit Müh' und Not;
In seinen Armen das Kind—
                  war tot.

"I love you, your beauty allures me,

*and if you do not come willingly, I
    shall use force."*

"Father, father, now he is seizing me!

The Elf-King has hurt me!"—

Fear grips the father, he rides swiftly,

*holding the moaning child in his arms;
with effort and toil he reaches the
    house—
the child in his arms—*
                  was dead.

In form, "Erlkönig" is through-composed. As in "Gretchen am Spinnrade," the piano is a crucial element. It sets the atmosphere at the beginning: the wild wind, the galloping horse, and the anxiety of the father.

Example 12.1

The triplet figure in the right hand occurs in various forms throughout, sustaining the highly charged atmosphere until the final moments of the song. The figure in the left hand appears periodically to indicate the running horse and to unify the piece musically.

Schubert portrays the characters and sets them off from each other by a number of devices, particularly by manipulating the piano accompaniment. Whenever the Erlkönig enters, for example, the dynamic level drops to pianissimo, the accompaniment changes, the vocal line becomes smooth and alluring.

Schubert reflects the son's mounting terror by repeating the same melodic material at successively higher pitch levels each time he cries out to his father. An upward leap on *"Mein Sohn"* and *"Sei ruhig"* marks the father's utterances that act as modulatory bridges linking the passages of child and Erlkönig.

The father's final statement ends with the strong drop of the interval of a fifth doubled by the left hand of the piano. The same figure recurs as the Erlkönig utters his last words as he seizes the boy,

Example 12.2

and is repeated once more in the boy's cry as he is taken in death.

Example 12.3

The last verse shows Schubert's sense of drama and the manipulation of the song's elements to heighten the emotional impact. The piano is silent as the narrator sings "the child in his arms," a single chord sounds, increasing the feeling of suspense, and the narrator concludes "was dead."

PIANO MUSIC

The piano which had replaced the harpsichord as the basic keyboard instrument in the classical era and was written for extensively by such composers as Mozart and Beethoven increased in importance during the romantic period. The huge body of romantic piano music falls into two broad categories; one consists of short, intimate, lyrical pieces similar in scope to lieder, while the other includes larger, more brilliant exhibition pieces written for virtuoso performers. Virtually every major composer of the nineteenth century contributed to the piano repertory.

Three composers stand out as major contributors to the piano literature and the development of piano technique—Robert Schumann, Franz Liszt, and Frédéric Chopin.

ROBERT SCHUMANN (1810–1856)

*A*long with Chopin and Liszt, Schumann was one of the creators of modern piano technique. Almost all of his most popular and greatest works for piano date from his early years as a composer, up to 1840. They range from miniature **character pieces** (pieces portraying a single mood, emotion, or idea) whose titles establish them as wholly romantic—*Papillons (Butterflies), Carnaval, Kinderscenen (Scenes from Childhood)*—to large, classically oriented works such as the three piano sonatas, the Fantasy in C Minor, the Symphonic Etudes, and the Piano Concerto in A Minor. Schumann considered the *Fantasiestücke* (Fantasy pieces) to be among his best works for piano.

Much of Schumann's music was inspired by poetry and the titles of his piano pieces are often derived from extramusical sources. His style is very free and flexible, almost kaleidoscopic, with rapid alternations between the characteristic Romantic extremes of intimacy and brilliance.

In addition to his works for piano Schumann composed four symphonies, several song cycles of which *Dichterliebe (Poet's Love)* ranks with those of Schubert, a goodly amount of chamber music and the oratorio, *Das Paradies und die Peri (Paradise and the Peri)*.

Clara Wieck (1819–1896) married Robert Schumann in 1840 over the violent objections of her father. Clara had received extensive musical training in her youth and became widely recognized as a virtuoso pianist including among her admirers Felix Mendelssohn, Frédéric Chopin and Schumann, her future husband. She also demonstrated promise as a composer.

Figure 12.4 Robert and Clara Wieck Schumann.

Her marriage to Schumann and the subsequent birth of eight children placed considerable limitations on her musical activities. Nevertheless, she continued to perform, teach, and compose, leaving behind a sizeable collection of songs, piano pieces, and chamber and orchestral works. After the death of Robert, she toured extensively as a pianist, championing the music of her husband and her close friend and companion, Johannes Brahms.

CHOPIN *(1810–1849)*

*F*rédéric Chopin was one of the most creative and original composers in the history of music. Almost none of his mature works relies on traditional devices or forms; he created an entirely new musical idiom. His style is unique and easy to identify; every phrase is characteristically his. Chopin's art is inescapably linked to the sonority of the piano, the only possible means of expression for him. Chopin suffered neither the privation and neglect that Schubert experienced nor the corroding mental illness that tormented Schumann. But although his life was marked by fame and the friendship of some of the greatest artists of the time, it ended in a mortal illness and an early death. When he died at the age of thirty-nine, he left behind him a literature for the piano unequaled before or since, and his critics, borrowing a character from Shakespeare's *The Tempest,* dubbed him the "Ariel of the piano." He followed no national school of romanticism, and one can be no more specific than to call him a European composer.

Chopin was born near Warsaw on February 22, 1810, of a French father and a Polish mother. His father, Nicolas, had come to Poland to teach French to the sons of the Polish nobility, and it was in these surroundings that young Frédéric received his formal education. He studied piano at the Warsaw School of Music, showing an early talent for the instrument. He gave his first public concert at the age of seven. By the age of fifteen, he had already published some compositions, and by nineteen he had achieved eminence in both composition and performance. He traveled widely through Europe and was received enthusiastically wherever he played. So cordial was the reception at Chopin's first concert in Paris, in 1831, that he decided to make that city his home and never again returned to Poland.

The public and his peers immediately recognized his genius, and he was in constant demand as a teacher and performer. He played frequently in Parisian salons, which had become the meeting places of the artists, musicians, and writers devoted to romanticism. His circle of friends included the writers Victor Hugo, Honoré de Balzac, and Alexandre Dumas, the composers Liszt, Berlioz, and Schumann, and the painter Delacroix. Reviewing some of Chopin's works, Schumann wrote of him that he was the "boldest and proudest poetic spirit of the time." His admirers were legion and he was the recipient of almost fanatical acclaim.

Figure 12.5 An engraving of Chopin.

Among the influential members of Parisian society was a woman novelist, Mme. Aurore Dudevant, who wrote under the name of George Sand. Through Liszt, Chopin met George Sand in 1837, when he was twenty-eight and she was thirty-four. It was a relationship that was to have a profound effect on his life, and though happy at first, their relationship became increasingly bitter. By the time Chopin developed tuberculosis in 1847, their once deep affection had deteriorated completely.

In 1848, with the full knowledge that he was in failing health, Chopin traveled to England and Scotland, where he stayed for seven months. There his concerts and strenuous activities sapped his fast-ebbing strength. Heartbroken over the bitterness that accompanied the conclusion of his relationship with George Sand, his energies exhausted, he returned to Paris, where he spent his remaining months. The funeral following his death on October 17, 1849, was attended by the elite of Paris society, artists as well as aristocrats; only Mme. Sand was absent from among the mourners. As a final gesture to his homeland, he wished his heart to be returned to Poland, while his body was buried in Père Lachaise Cemetery in Paris.

With few exceptions Brahms composed in all the familiar instrumental and choral idioms of the nineteenth century. He was a careful and disciplined composer who frequently revised his earlier works.

Brahms did not attempt to compose symphonies until quite late in his life. His first symphony (in C minor) took him twenty-one years to write and was not finished until 1876. Three others followed during the next nine years: no. 2 (in D major, 1877), no. 3 (in F major, 1883) and no. 4 (in E minor, 1884–1885). These works remain as some of the most frequently performed symphonies in modern times.

Brahm's masterful symphonic style was developed through the composition of serenades, concertos, and overtures. His first orchestral composition was a Serenade in D Major (1857–1858), followed by his first piano concerto (in D minor, 1858). His other concertos include the renowned Violin Concerto in D Major (1878), the second piano concerto (in B-flat major, 1878–1881), and the Double Concerto in A Minor for violin and cello (1887). His overtures include the *Academic Festival Overture* (1880) and the *Tragic Overture* (1880–1881). Falling into none of these categories is the very popular *Variations on a Theme by Haydn* (1873).

Choral music, both sacred and secular, attracted Brahms throughout his career. His *Ein Deutsches Requiem* (*A German Requiem,* 1857–1868), discussed in chapter 16, ranks as one of the choral masterpieces of the nineteenth century.

Brahms's contributions to chamber music repertory were the most substantial of those made by any nineteenth-century composer after Beethoven. Among them are duos, trios, quartets, and quintets for a variety of instrumental combinations. His piano works reveal a mastery of contrapuntal texture and require virtuoso performance technique. They include variations on themes by Schumann, Paganini, and Handel, three sonatas, and a number of short lyric pieces including ballades, rhapsodies, fantasies, and intermezzi.

His Symphonic Style

Brahms retained the traditional four-movement structure of the late classical symphony: fast, slow, scherzo-like, fast. In many ways his style is a direct outgrowth of the symphonic style of Beethoven: he continued to expand sonata-allegro form, enlarge the orchestra, and use dynamics and sonorities as structural elements.

Brahms's use of sonata-allegro form involves some changes, primarily in the treatment of the bridge section and the coda. The bridge becomes much more important; its material often sounds like a genuine theme, and it is often difficult to distinguish between the bridge and second theme on first hearing. The first and second themes are still contrasted in the classical manner, but there is often no noticeable separation (such as a rest) between them.

The beginning of the recapitulation is sometimes obscure because Brahms tends to lead into it unobtrusively; frequently the exposition material reappears with different instrumentation, a device Beethoven used. The coda is extended, as in Beethoven's works, and used as a second development section. In contrast to Beethoven, however, Brahms often ends movements very quietly.

One of Brahms's favorite structural devices is to build new themes out of short motives taken from earlier material. This brings an additional element of unity to a movement, beyond that provided by sonata-allegro form. Brahms often incorporates the motive into themes in a subtle way, and it appears in many rhythmic variations.

Brahms uses a larger orchestra than Beethoven but much smaller than that used by Berlioz in the colossal works described in chapter 14. His orchestra consisted of two flutes, two oboes, two clarinets, two bassoons, four horns, two trumpets, three trombones, tuba, timpani, and strings. In his use of the orchestra, the lower strings, woodwinds, and brasses are given important roles. Timpani are often treated independently from the brass instruments and even have solo passages.

His second symphony beautifully illustrates Brahms's symphonic skill and expressiveness.

The symphony conforms to the basic sonata outline of the classical tradition. It has four movements in the traditional fast, slow, scherzo-like, fast pattern. The first and last movements are in D major, the middle movements are in contrasting keys.

**BRAHMS:
SYMPHONY NO. 2 IN
D MAJOR**
*SIDE 6/SELECTION 2
LISTENING GUIDE ON
PAGES 264–65*

First Movement (Allegro non troppo)

The standard outlines of sonata form as we encountered it in the works of Mozart, Haydn, and Beethoven are clearly evident in this movement with its exposition (repeated), development, and recapitulation. Brahms also uses a short motive to unify the thematic material.

Example 13.1

Theme 1 is divided between groups of instruments. It begins with the basic three-note motive in the cellos and basses and continues first in the horns and bassoons and then in the upper winds.

Example 13.2

It is typical of Brahms to dispense a theme among several instruments or instrumental groups. Their instrumental colors become part of the character of the theme itself and thus the theme can be effectively varied by changing its instrumentation.

The second theme, which is longer than the first theme and the bridge combined, consists of sharply contrasting thematic materials in an ABA form. The A section is flowing and serene, only at the end increasing in volume with a crescendo that introduces the second section (B) which is loud, vigorous, and rhythmically complex. At its conclusion there is an abrupt and unexpected return to the calmer A section followed by a short codetta, ending the exposition that Brahms indicates should be repeated.

Development   The development section concentrates on materials drawn from the first theme and the bridge. In it Brahms applies all the technical and dramatic tricks of the development trade. There is frequent modulation to a great variety of keys; themes are fragmented; motives are expanded, melodic elements are inverted (turned upside down), polyphonic treatment of themes, dramatic changes in volume, in articulation, and in orchestral color—all producing the dramatic tension characterized by the developmental process.

Toward the end of the section, Brahms plays a "trick" on his listeners by introducing what at first appears to be the recapitulation—but it is a **false recapitulation** and goes on to more development which prepares the way for the genuine recapitulation.

Recapitulation   In typical romantic fashion, Brahms produces a recapitulation section which is *not* an exact replica of the exposition. The character of the music is altered in a variety of ways. The first theme is reorchestrated and the bridge is quite different from that found in the exposition. Only the second theme, with its ABA structure, is more or less intact.

While Beethoven habitually used the coda for further *development* of the movements' thematic materials, Brahms often introduced *new* themes in the coda. Such is the case with the first movement of this symphony; the coda of which includes two very beautiful new themes—one for horn,

Example 13.3

the other played by the first violins accompanied by the original basic motive in the bass.

Example 13.4

The quiet intensity of these themes enriches the movement.

Second Movement (Adagio non troppo)

The second movement is a wonderful example of romantic symphonic lyricism of which Brahms was a master. In character, it provides the kind of contrasts traditionally expected of a second movement—it is slower in tempo and in a contrasting key. However, in terms of structure, it follows no standard formal procedure, such as sonata form, or theme and variations. Rather, it is rather freely based upon the principle of contrasting themes and the development process.

A long flowing melody played by cellos (A) begins the movement.

Example 13.5

MUSIC OF THE ROMANTIC ERA

The horn begins theme B which is treated polyphonically with imitative entrances of the melody in the oboe, flute, and cello following the horn.

The winds and strings alternate in presenting theme C with its prevailing syncopated triplet pattern.

Example 13.6

And, finally, the intensely expressive theme D,

Example 13.7

with its push into a stretch of music given over to the development of themes A, C, and D. A short coda based on material from theme A provides a quiet conclusion.

Third Movement (Allegretto Grazioso—Presto ma non troppo)

With this movement Brahms has cleverly produced a kind of cross between the minuet of the earlier classical symphony and the scherzo of Beethoven. It is organized into a five-part alternating form:

A   B   A   C   A

and the sections are clearly distinguishd by marked changes in meter and tempo. This movement is further offset from the rest of the symphony by the fact that Brahms employs a reduced orchestra, leaving out trumpets, trombones, tuba, and timpani.

Fourth Movement (Allegro con spirito)

The final movement of the Second Symphony is one of the most confident and jubilant movements Brahms ever wrote. It returns to the key of D major, its tempo is fast, and the full orchestra is brought back into play. Sonata-allegro form is followed and the contrast between the two major themes is striking—the first is brisk and sparkling—the second theme is lyrical and expressive.

Both themes and the bridge make subtle use of the three-note basic motive from the first movement thereby providing an added degree of unity to the entire work. This desire to make a single entity out of a multimovement work is typical of much romantic music. After a rather straightforward development and recapitulation, a long coda ends with a great crashing finale in which the horns and trumpets play a stirring version of the second theme.

Anton Bruckner

Anton Bruckner (1824–1896), an Austrian composer and organist, joined Brahms in the effort to retain classical forms within an expanded harmonic and structural framework. Bruckner was a simple and very religious man, deeply involved with Catholic mysticism. Symphonic in technique, his three Masses are of sufficient caliber to rank Bruckner as the most important church composer of the late nineteenth century.

Bruckner's nine symphonies show his kinship to classical tradition in their formal design, but their exceptional length and weighty orchestration mark them as romantic works. Wagner was one of Bruckner's idols, and Bruckner's emphasis on chromatic tones and shifting tonalities shows Wagner's influence. Bruckner, in turn, influenced later composers in his native Vienna, particularly Mahler and Schoenberg.

Gustav Mahler

The Austrian Gustav Mahler (1860–1911) was a conductor as well as a symphonic composer. His nine completed symphonies are immense and complex, and encompass a vast emotional range. Although the symphonies follow the classical outline and have separate movements, their style incorporates many elements from vocal music, including opera. His symphonies contain long, lyrical melodies, often treated contrapuntally; four of them have parts for voices as well as instruments. Mahler's works span the spectrum of emotions, from ecstasy to despair. He tried to make each symphony a complete world in itself, with all types of themes and techniques. These large-scale works are unified, to some extent, by the use of recurring themes and motives.

Mahler is also famous for his songs and song cycles; the *Kindertotenlieder* (*Songs on the Death of Children,* 1902) and *Das Lied von der Erde* (*The Song of the Earth,* 1908) are particularly outstanding. Themes from the songs are often quoted in the symphonic works. Mahler's last works—the Ninth Symphony, the unfinished Tenth, and *Das Lied von der Erde*—are in a more contrapuntal style than his earlier compositions. They also show a weaker sense of tonality and thus point toward the important developments in atonal music in the early twentieth century.

THE ROMANTIC CONCERTO

As we pointed out in chapter 12, romantic audiences were dazzled by exhibitions of virtuosity. All through the romantic era there was a steady growth of virtuoso technique, particularly on the piano and the violin. The trend was begun by Beethoven, whose works were considerably more difficult to play than Mozart's. It was spurred on in 1820 by the arrival on the European concert stage of Niccolò Paganini (1782–1840); this phenomenal Italian violinist astounded and enchanted all who heard him by the incredible speed and brilliance of his playing.

The concerto for solo instrument and orchestra, with the improvised quality of its cadenza section, lent itself especially well to displays of technical skill. Composers wrote very difficult solo parts in their concertos. Unfortunately, many second-rate

MENDELSSOHN *(1809–1847)*

Unlike most of the great composers of his generation, Felix Mendelssohn not only achieved artistic success but also lived a life of relative ease and financial security. Born into a wealthy and cultured Jewish family—his father was a banker, his grandfather, Moses Mendelssohn, a distinguished philosopher—he and his brother and two sisters were brought up as Christians. The remarkable musical abilities of Felix and his elder sister Fanny were quickly recognized by the children's mother, Leah, who began teaching the children piano when they were quite young. After the family moved to Berlin in 1812, Felix and Fanny's formal musical training was entrusted to Carl Zelter, an eminent composer, teacher, and head of the famous *Singakademie*.

The Mendelssohn home was the meeting place for musicians and poets at which concerts of chamber music were organized and directed by Leah Mendelssohn. Felix and Fanny's earliest compositions were performed at these musicales.

By 1821 Felix had composed trios, quartets, sonatas, and operettas. His debut as a concert pianist had been made even earlier—at the age of nine—and he mastered both violin and viola while still in his teens. The first striking demonstration of Felix's genius as a composer was the overture to Shakespeare's *A Midsummer Night's Dream*, written in 1826 when he was seventeen. Three years later he made his mark as a conductor when he revived J. S. Bach's *St. Matthew Passion*. This performance of the Passion, a great triumph for Mendelssohn, was the first given since Bach's death almost eighty years earlier and began a wide-scale revival of Bach's music.

Early in the 1830s, Mendelssohn traveled extensively throughout Europe. He conducted his concert overture *Fingal's Cave* (*The Hebrides*) in London and met Hector Berlioz in Italy. Returning to Berlin in 1833, Mendelssohn decided to seek a permanent post and applied for the directorship of the *Singakademie*. He was turned down—one of his few failures—but in the same year he was asked to become town musical director and conductor at Düsseldorf. Two years later he accepted an offer to become conductor of the famous *Gewandhaus* Orchestra in Leipzig.

Figure 13.3 A child prodigy, Mendelssohn made his debut as a concert pianist at the age of nine. His magical concert overture, *A Midsummer Night's Dream,* was written when he was seventeen.

In 1837 Mendelssohn married Cécile Jeanrenaud, the daughter of a French Protestant clergyman. In 1841 they moved to Berlin where, at the request of Kaiser Friedrich Wilhelm IV, Mendelssohn took charge of the music division of the newly established Academy of Arts. The position did not require close supervision and he was able to develop his plans for a conservatory at Leipzig. In 1843 the conservatory opened with a distinguished faculty in residence, and several years later Mendelssohn moved his family back to Leipzig.

Though his health began to deteriorate after 1846, Mendelssohn continued to immerse himself in his work. The death of Fanny, to whom he was deeply attached, was a major shock. Falling into a severe depression, he soon became bedridden and died in Leipzig at the age of thirty-eight.

Figure 13.2 Niccolò Paganini's unusual appearance—he was tall, pencil-thin, and habitually dressed in black—combined with his unearthly virtuosity gave rise to rumors that his violin was the devil's consort and that the phenomenal Italian violinist was the devil himself. The German poet Heine called him "a vampire with a violin."

romantic composers mistook virtuosity for substance; thus, the majority of romantic concertos were either pleasant pieces or bombastic tirades, full of technical acrobatics but essentially meaningless.

The master composers of the period, however, joined virtuoso technique to lyric and expressive writing. Robert Schumann, Johannes Brahms, Felix Mendelssohn, and Peter Ilyich Tchaikovsky all wrote outstanding concertos.

MENDELSSOHN'S WORK

Despite his relatively short life, Mendelssohn produced many works, ranging from large-scale symphonies and oratorios to intimate chamber works and lieder. His first published symphony (in C minor, 1824) was actually the thirteenth he had written. Of the four symphonies that still remain, one—apparently influenced by Beethoven's Ninth—is for chorus and orchestra, entitled *Lobgesang* (*Hymn of Praise,* 1840). The others are descriptive: no. 3 (*Scottish,* 1830–1842), no. 4 (*Italian,* 1833), and no. 5 (*Reformation,* 1830–1842). His imaginative and original *concert overtures* (see page 260) include *A Midsummer Night's Dream* (1826), *Calm Sea and Prosperous Voyage* (1830–1832), *Fingal's Cave* (*The Hebrides,* 1830–1832), and the overture to Victor Hugo's play *Ruy Blas* (1839).

Along with these major orchestral works, Mendelssohn composed many chamber pieces, the octet for strings (opus 20, 1825) being one of his most original and delightful works.

Mendelssohn's long-standing appreciation of Bach's music shows up in his several collections of preludes and fugues for piano. The bulk of his piano music, however, consists of short character pieces in a highly romantic vein. The most popular of these are the eight collections of *Songs Without Words,* published between 1829 and 1845. His finest large-scale work for piano is the *Variations sérieuses* (opus 54, 1841).

Though he composed a great many religious works and an equally substantial number of art songs, Mendelssohn's reputation as a vocal composer rests on his two oratorios, *St. Paul* (1836) and *Elijah* (1846). In them, Mendelssohn incorporated elements of Bach's Passion style and of Handelian oratorio form. They are generally considered the most successful nineteenth-century works of their kind.

MUSIC OF THE ROMANTIC ERA

Many of Mendelssohn's later works, composed in the 1840s, appear to be somewhat uninspired. In one work, however, he fully recaptured the magical verve of the *Midsummer Night's Dream* overture: the incidental music he wrote for the same play in 1842, including the famous "Wedding March," stands as a fitting companion to his youthful masterpiece. And one of his greatest concertos is the Violin Concerto in E Minor (opus 64, 1844).

Mendelssohn's violin concerto retains the fast-slow-fast movement structure of the classical concerto except for the fact that there is no definite break between the first and second movements. The work is scored for solo violin and orchestra of modest proportions, consisting of two flutes, two oboes, two clarinets, two bassoons, two horns, two trumpets, timpani, and strings.

MENDELSSOHN: VIOLIN CONCERTO IN E MINOR (OPUS 64)

First Movement (Allegro molto appassionato)

Exposition   The first movement is in sonata form but does not include the orchestral introduction involved in the classical double exposition. Rather after only a few measures of orchestral introduction the violin enters with a statement of the first theme in which the violin is prominent against an unobtrusive orchestral accompaniment.

Example 13.8

The bridge is quite long and provides for considerable display of violinistic virtuosity in the midst of modulating to G major for the statement of the second theme.

The theme is introduced by the winds and then taken up and extended by the violin.

Example 13.9

Here again, Mendelssohn is careful to maintain a careful balance between the solo instrument and the orchestra so that the expressive violin melody is foremost in the listener's mind.

Development   Much of the development section is characterized by orchestral statements of parts of the first theme against brilliant and rapidly moving violin figurations. Of particular interest is the placement of the cadenza and its relationship to the development and recapitulation. In essence, the cadenza grows out of the development and blends into the beginning of the recapitulation where the orchestra begins the first theme while the violin continues to play the material of the cadenza.

Solo Violin   End of Cadenza   Recapitulation

1st Violin, Oboe, Flute

Example 13.10

The dramatic division between development and cadenza, and cadenza and recapitulation found in the classical tradition are thereby blurred and the music takes on a more continuous character.

Recapitulation The bridge in the recapitulation is divided between orchestra and solo instrument (in that order) and modulates to E major in which the second theme appears in an expanded version. What follows is a rather long coda which is very reminiscent of Beethoven in that it contains an additional development of the first theme.

The end of the coda is characterized by an increase in tempo leading to the dramatic end of a well-crafted piece of music.

Second Movement (Andante)

The first movement appears to end but doesn't—not really. A single note from the final chord played by the bassoon "hangs over" and forms a suspenseful link to the next movement.

The slow movement is in the key of C major and is a three-part alternating form—ABA—with coda.

Section A consists of a beautifully spun melody for the solo violin with quiet support provided by the strings.

Example 13.11

Solo Violin

In section B the orchestra and solo instrument alternate in stating phrases of the new thematic material. This section includes a good deal of modulation through a variety of keys, eventually returning to C major for the return of section A. As is often the case in romantic music, this is not a literal repetition of the initial material. Rather the theme is rearranged and shortened and leads to a short coda, drawing a compact and expressive movement to a close.

Third Movement (Allegro non troppo—allegro molto vivace)

SIDE 7/SELECTION 1
LISTENING GUIDE ON
PAGE 266

Introduction   The use of a short, slow introduction preceding a sonata form movement was a frequent occurrence in the classical period, and Mendelssohn uses it in the final movement of this concerto. This introductory section for solo violin and strings also serves the purpose of modulating from C major, the key of the second movement, to E major for the last movement.

Exposition   The beginning of the last movement proper retains an introductory flavor in which the orchestra and solo violin alternate in leading to the first theme.

Example 13.12

After a bridge based upon elements of the first theme, the orchestra introduces the second theme which is then taken up by the solo violin.

Example 13.13

Development   The design of the first part of this development section is similar to that found in the first movement—against a light orchestral background consisting of fragments of theme 2, the solo violin executes brilliant solo passages.

New thematic material not found in the exposition is introduced by the violin,

Example 13.14

and is taken up by the orchestra while the violin develops the thematic material leading to the recapitulation.

Recapitulation   The first and second themes are linked by a shortened bridge. The second theme leads to a new development section followed by a coda to bring the movement to a close resulting in the overall form:

Slow Intro   Exposition   Development   Recapitulation   Development   Coda

Throughout this concerto, Mendelssohn maintains a good balance between virtuosity and musical substance which are integrated into a musical work of enduring value and popularity among performers and audience alike.

THE ROMANTIC TRADITIONALISTS   **259**

CONCERT OVERTURE

Prior to the nineteenth century, the overture had been an instrumental piece that functioned as an introduction to a longer musical work (such as an opera or oratorio) or, in some instances as "incidental music" to spoken drama. Although this type of overture continued to be written during the nineteenth century, the romantic period gave rise to a new type of overture, one that was not an introduction to something else. The **concert overture** was a one-movement, self-contained musical work intended for performance in the concert hall. As such, it took its place alongside the symphony and the concerto as one of the major symphonic forms of the period.

Some concert overtures were written for specific festive occasions. Beethoven's *Consecration of the House* is one such work. Others, such as Mendelssohn's *Hebrides Overture,* attempted to evoke some aspect of nature. And still others, including Brahm's *Tragic Overture,* expressed a generalized mood or human condition.

Many concert overtures have programmatic and descriptive elements and in some respects resemble the symphonic poem. But unlike the symphonic poem, the concert overture retains the strong musical organization embodied in sonata-allegro form. In this respect the concert overture is much like the first movement of a symphony, except that it is complete in itself.

One of the most popular concert overtures written during the romantic era, *Romeo and Juliet,* was composed by the Russian Peter Ilyich Tchaikovsky.

During the romantic period there were two schools of musical thought in Russia. The nationalists (who will be discussed in chapter 15) attempted to create a music that was totally Russian in character and style. The cosmopolitans, on the other hand, looked to the Western European tradition for their inspiration and composed in the general romantic style. Tchaikovsky was the outstanding composer of the cosmopolitan school and the first Russian composer to gain an international reputation.

TCHAIKOVSKY'S WORK

Tchaikovsky's best-known works are his last three symphonies, his three ballets, his two symphonic fantasies, his violin concerto, his concert overtures, and his first piano concerto. He composed his first three symphonies between 1866 and 1875. The fourth was completed in 1877, the fifth in 1888, and the sixth (the *Pathétique*) in 1893.

Although Tchaikovsky followed traditional procedures in his symphonies, his main efforts were directed at creating beautiful melodies and brilliantly orchestrated textures. The Fourth Symphony has an elaborate program wedged into the traditional symphonic format. Tchaikovsky's Fifth Symphony uses a single theme to link the four movements, much as Beethoven and Brahms had done in the symphonies previously studied.

His ballets—*Swan Lake, The Sleeping Beauty,* and especially *The Nutcracker* (1891–1892) (fig. 13.5)—remain among the most celebrated works of their kind, and the orchestral suites drawn from them are basic items in present-day repertoire as well.

LISTENING GUIDE

Tchaikovsky: Romeo and Juliet

Single Movement: tempo varies (slow introduction; fast)
quadruple meter
sonata form with introduction

Full Romantic orchestra
Review: Example 13.15 (feud theme)
Example 13.16 (love theme)
Example 13.17 (love theme with countertheme)
Example 13.18 (theme associated with love music)
Outline of program, pp. 262–64

Introduction

Friar Laurence	1a	hymn-like, homophonic theme softly in clarinets and bassoons
	b	foreboding fragments begin in low strings, build to winds with harp arpeggios
	c	strings pizzicato, Friar Laurence theme more agitated in woodwinds
	d	foreboding music returns, then with harp arpeggios
	2a	timpani roll introduces intense, threatening motives climaxing in loud, fast passage
	b	timpani, threatening motives: woodwind-string echoes build directly to:

Exposition

Theme 1: Feud between Montague and Capulet families	1a	agitated feud theme in orchestra; strings rush up and down; agitated feud theme; rising three-note motive tossed between strings and winds
	b	fragments of feud theme and rushing strings combined, developed with three-note motive; full orchestra with cymbal crashes in loud chords and rushing strings build to climax
	c	feud theme explodes in full orchestra; transition with rushing strings; feud theme builds to close
Bridge	2	energy released in woodwind development of three-note motive; low strings take over
Theme 2: Love of Romeo and Juliet	3a	flowing love theme in English horn and muted violas, pulsating French horns accompany; harp arpeggio introduces muted strings with tender love music
	b	flutes and oboes surge upward to love theme with countertheme in French horn creating a love duet; greatly extended with lush orchestration

Closing	*4*	harp chords and soft tones in strings and winds subside to restful close
Development	*1*	fragments of feud theme; fast scales in strings accompany Friar Laurence theme intoned softly in French horn; theme extended and developed
	2	three-note motive interrupts in cellos and basses, with fragments of feud theme; downward rushing strings added and builds to climax
	3	cymbal crash, full orchestra develops feud theme fragment; Friar Laurence theme combined forte in trumpet; rushing strings with loud chords in orchestra lead directly into:
Recapitulation *Theme 1*	*1*	agitated feud theme in full orchestra with cymbal crashes; strings rush downward
Theme 2	*2a*	tender love music in oboes and clarinets; intensity grows as other winds enrich the sound; strings rise intensely upward into:
	b	love theme soars in strings and flute with countertheme in French horn and throbbing woodwind accompaniment; grows to full, rich orchestration
	c	love theme fragment in cellos answered by flute; extended with fragments and horns answered by flute; strings begin love theme but it dissolves
Coda	*3*	fragments of feud and love themes vie with each other in full orchestra; feud theme emphatically takes over, then combined with Friar Laurence theme in brass; extended development as feud music takes over; furious activity decreases to ominous timpani roll
	4a	drumbeat continues as in a funeral march; fragments of love theme sound brokenly in strings, drumbeat ceases as woodwinds answer with a variation of tender love music; rising harp arpeggios signal union of the lovers; strings yearningly sing fragment of love theme
	4b	drum roll crescendo to strong final chords, recalling the feud theme

••

SUMMARY

A stream of classical thought continued to flow through the romantic period. Although some composers discarded the classical forms, one group cultivated and expanded them in both orchestral and chamber music settings. The leading composers in this group were Schubert, Mendelssohn, Brahms, and Tchaikovsky.

Nearly all of the early romantic composers were influenced by Beethoven, either by his use of the orchestra or by his expansion of form. Brahms, the greatest of the late romantic symphonists, retained the four-movement symphonic structure. He continued to expand sonata-allegro form, to enlarge the orchestra, and to define structures by means of dynamics and instrumental colors.

The interest of romantic audiences in virtuosity encouraged composers to write concertos which contained very difficult solo parts. While many romantic concertos were second-rate, those written by Schumann, Brahms, Mendelssohn, and Tchaikovsky were outstanding.

The romantic era gave rise to a new type of overture, one which did not introduce a longer work but was instead a self-contained work in one movement, intended for performance in the concert hall. The concert overture, exemplified by Tchaikovsky's *Romeo and Juliet,* often had programmatic elements, but retained the sonata-allegro form of organization.

NEW TERMS

false recapitulation
concert overture

SUGGESTED LISTENING

Brahms, Johannes

Piano Quintet in F Minor op. 34. A wonderful example of romantic chamber music.

Variations on a Theme of Haydn, op. 56a. A fascinating set of eight variations and a finale on a simple theme *(Chorale St. Antonio)* probably not by Haydn. Each variation is not merely a reworking of the theme but an emotional transformation of the original melody. The orchestration is brilliant.

Mendelssohn, Felix

Hebrides Overture (Fingal's Cave). In this concert overture, Mendelssohn describes his impressions of a sea journey to Fingal's cave. The interplay of the two main themes—one restless, the second severe—evoke the play of wind and sun on water.

14 PROGRAM MUSIC

he romantic era gave rise to the establishment of a fascinating type of music which has become known as program music. In program music, musical materials and techniques are employed with the intent of depicting or portraying some extramusical phenomena such as a dramatic incident, a poetic image, a visual object, or some element in nature. Poems, dramatic plots, visual objects, and natural phenomena provided for the composer not only the general suggestive impulse for pieces of music but also became the dominating idea, determining the specific flow and form of the composition. Program music was thus contrasted to absolute music—music conceived of by the composer and understood by the listener *without* reference to extramusical features. As we shall see, however, much absolute music is subject to programmatic interpretation by the imaginative listener and the best program music can be understood and appreciated in purely musical terms without an awareness of the extramusical element.

Neither the principle nor the techniques of descriptive or program music originated in the romantic period. In fact, they extended back into the medieval and Renaissance eras. For example, we have already encountered Clement Jannequin's *Chant des oiseaux* (page 100) in which human voices imitate bird calls. In the baroque period, Antonio Vivaldi's *The Seasons* depicted the scenes and activities of each season of the year in the context of a violin concerto. Beethoven's Sixth Symphony *(Pastoral)* with its descriptive title for each movement is regarded as a type of program music. But these pieces were rare and isolated examples.

In the romantic period, program music became a major branch of musical composition engaging the imagination and energy of many of the finest composers of the era, among them Hector Berlioz, Franz Liszt, and Richard Strauss.

BERLIOZ (1803–1869)

*H*ector Berlioz grew up in a small town near Grenoble, France. Hector was expected to follow his father's profession and was sent to medical school in Paris. However, by his own inclinations he was drawn to the opera and the music library. When he appeared in class, he would annoy his fellow students by humming at the dissecting table. Finally, to the fury of his father, he quit the study of medicine to become a composer.

At twenty-three Berlioz began what he called "the great drama of my life." At a performance of *Hamlet* he was overwhelmed, both by "the lightning-flash" of Shakespeare's genius and "the dramatic genius" of Harriet Smithson, who played Ophelia. Berlioz tried to meet the actress, but his wild letters convinced her that he was a lunatic.

In 1830, on his fifth attempt, Berlioz won the Prix de Rome—a composition prize offered at the Paris Conservatory. In that year he also wrote the *Symphonie Fantastique,* the outpouring of his passion for Harriet Smithson. When the composition was performed in Paris two years later, Harriet Smithson was in the audience. Realizing that the music was about her, she felt (according to Berlioz) "as if the room reeled." They were married a year later, but the romantic dream faded and several years later they separated.

Although he had become successful, Berlioz had difficulty getting his work performed. His music soon ceased to appeal to most of "the frivolous and fickle public." Both to support his family and to promote an understanding of the kind of music he advocated, Berlioz wrote musical criticism. He also wrote a fascinating prose autobiography. In it he emerges as a romantic hero, falling in love, scheming murder, talking politics, passionately composing. He conducted performances of his own works throughout most of Europe, but in Paris he was ignored

Figure 14.1 In his passionate emotionalism, daring experimentation, and rich imagination, Berlioz epitomized the nineteenth-century romantic spirit.

for various honors and conducting posts. Increasingly bitter, his energies spent, he did not compose during the last seven years of his life.

BERLIOZ'S WORK

Perhaps Berlioz's greatest contribution to music was in the art of orchestration. In his music, tone color was as prominent an element as melody or harmony. He experimented extensively with individual instruments and devised many unusual blends, combining bells with brasses and directing violinists to strike the strings with their bow sticks. In 1844 he wrote his treatise on orchestration, the first comprehensive text on the subject and a work that is still in use today.

Berlioz's ideas were grandiose, and he wanted to carry them out on a grandiose scale. The first performance of *Symphonie fantastique* was thwarted because there were not enough chairs and music stands for the performers. At a time when orchestras usually numbered sixty players, Berlioz's ideal (never realized) was an orchestra of 240 strings, thirty harps, thirty grand pianos, and wind and percussion to scale!

Berlioz's major works are immense and dramatic. He usually composed from a literary text, favoring plays, epic poems, and novels. Works inspired by Shakespeare include the "dramatic symphony" *Romeo and Juliet* (1839), the *King Lear* Overture (1831), and the opera *Beátrice et Bénédict* (1860–1862). The *Waverly* and *Rob Roy* overtures (c. 1827 and 1832) are based on the novels of Sir Walter Scott, and *Harold in Italy* (1834), a symphony, is based on the poem by Byron.

BERLIOZ: SYMPHONIE FANTASTIQUE

The *Symphonie Fantastique* is a program symphony in five movements. It is based upon a program, supplied by Berlioz out of his personal experience:

Program of the symphony

A young musician of morbidly sensitive temperament and fiery imagination poisons himself with opium in a fit of lovesick despair. The dose of the narcotic, too weak to kill him, plunges him into a deep slumber accompanied by the strangest visions, during which his sensations, his emotions, his memories are transformed in his sick mind into musical thoughts and images. The loved one herself has become a melody to him, an *idée fixe* as it were, that he encounters and hears everywhere.

Part I.
Reveries, passions

He recalls first that soul-sickness, that *vague des passions,* those depressions, those groundless joys, that he experienced before he first saw his loved one; then the volcanic love that she suddenly inspired in him, his frenzied suffering, his jealous rages, his returns to tenderness, his religious consolations.

Part II.
A ball

He encounters the loved one at a dance in the midst of the tumult of a brilliant party.

Part III.
Scene in the country

One summer evening in the country, he hears two shepherds piping a *ranz des vaches* in dialogue; this pastoral duet, the scenery, the quiet rustling of the trees gently brushed by the wind, the hopes he has recently found some reason to entertain—all concur in affording his heart an unaccustomed calm, and in giving a more cheerful color to his ideas. But she appears again, he feels a tightening in his heart, painful presentiments disturb him—what if she were deceiving him?—One of the shepherds takes up his simple tune again, the other no longer answers. The sun sets—distant sound of thunder—loneliness—silence.

Part IV.
March to the scaffold

He dreams that he has killed his beloved, that he is condemned to death and led to the scaffold. The procession moves forward to the sounds of a march that is now somber and fierce, now brilliant and solemn, in which the muffled sound of heavy steps gives way without transition to the noisiest clamor. At the end, the *idée fixe* returns for a moment, like a last thought of love interrupted by the fatal blow.

Part V.
Dream of a witches' sabbath

He sees himself at the sabbath, in the midst of a frightful troop of ghosts, sorcerers, monsters of every kind, come together for his funeral. Strange noises, groans, bursts of laughter, distant cries which other cries seem to answer. The beloved melody appears again, but it has lost its character of nobility and shyness; it is no more than a dance tune, mean, trivial, and grotesque: it is she, coming to join the sabbath.—A roar of joy at her arrival.—She takes part in the devilish orgy.—Funeral knell, burlesque parody of the *Dies irae,*[1] *sabbath round-dance.* The sabbath round and the *Dies irae* combined.

The five movements are linked together by the use of one melody which represents the hero's image of his beloved. This melody, the **idée fixe** ("fixed idea"), appears in each movement of the symphony in various transformations—in the second movement it is a waltz tune; in the fourth it appears fleetingly just before the fall of the executioners blade; and in the fifth movement it becomes a grotesque witches' dance combined with the medieval chant *Dies irae* ("Day of Wrath"). The technique of theme transformation intensifies the effectiveness of the musical representation of the program and lends a purely musical unity to the symphony.

---

1. Hymn sung in the funeral rites of the Catholic Church.

Example 14.1

First Movement: Allegro agitato e appassionato assai

Second Movement: Flute and Oboe

Third Movement: Adagio / Flute and Oboe in octaves

Fourth Movement: Clarinet — Axe (full orchestra)

Fifth Movement: Allegro / E-flat Clarinet

Throughout the work, Berlioz's masterful use of the orchestra portrays a wide range of images and emotional states—from the fluctuating dream-like introduction to the grotesque and macabre Witches' Sabbath.

FRANZ LISZT

Franz Liszt's (1811–1886) (fig. 14.2) major achievement as an orchestral composer was his development of the **symphonic poem** or **tone poem,** an extended single movement programmatic work. In the symphonic poem, Liszt abandoned altogether old

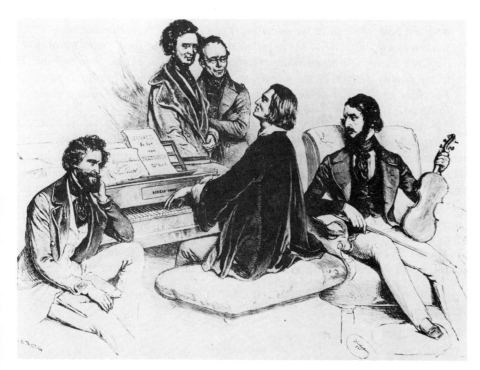

Figure 14.2 Liszt, a virtuoso artist of great physical attractiveness and personal charm, enthralled audiences of the nineteenth century as a movie or rock star does today.

forms such as sonata-allegro and relied instead on the principle of **theme transformation** as an organizing technique. His symphonic poem, *Les Préludes,* uses a three-note motive as the basis of themes depicting a variety of situations: in one section used to suggest love; in another a pastoral theme; in still another it takes on a march-like character.

In his rejection of the traditional multimovement organization and sonata-allegro form in favor of the single movement with flexible form based upon theme transformation, Liszt charted a new course that had a substantial impact upon the romantic period and beyond.

Les Préludes was originally written as the orchestral overture to a choral work but Liszt later decided to publish it separately. Looking for a suitable program, he was struck by the parallel construction of one of Alphonse de Lamartine's *Méditations poétiques.* He translated it freely and adopted it as the program for his composition.

LISZT:
LES PRÉLUDES
SIDE 8/SELECTION 2
LISTENING GUIDE ON
PAGES 281–82

Préludes
What is our life but a series of Preludes to that unknown song, the first solemn note of which is sounded by Death? The enchanted dawn of every existence is heralded by Love, yet in whose destiny are not the first throbs of happiness interrupted by storms whose violent blasts dissipate his fond illusions, consuming his altar with fatal fire? And where is to be found the cruelly bruised soul, that having become the sport of one of these tempests

does not seek oblivion in the sweet quiet of rural life? Nevertheless, man seldom resigns himself to the beneficient calm which at first chained him to Nature's bosom. No sooner does the trumpet sound the alarm, than he runs to the post of danger, be the war what it may that summons him to its ranks. For there he will find again in the struggle complete self-realization and the full possession of his forces.

Liszt composed *Les Préludes* for a full romantic orchestra—flutes, oboes, clarinets, bassoons, four horns, trumpets, trombones, tuba, timpani (three drums), harp, and strings. For the finale (the section analogous to the call to battle), a side drum, cymbals, and a bass drum are added. The manner in which the orchestra is used is also typically romantic; the winds are often used as solo instruments; the French horn, a favorite romantic instrument, is particularly prominent; fluctuations in tempo and dynamics occur frequently.

The stages of life mentioned in the poem correspond to the sections of Liszt's piece. It opens with a brief introduction, built on a three-note motive

Example 14.2

that will later be used in the construction of most of the themes in the composition. The opening is slow and tentative. The motive gradually expands by enlarging its second interval

Example 14.3

and eventually leads to the first theme. It is an expansive and majestic melody, vaguely related to the opening motive. The accompanying figure includes a direct statement of the motive.

Example 14.4

Russia is the classic example of a nation that was suddenly exposed to Western civilization and became culturally dependent before first having a chance to find its own national voice. Prior to the reign of Peter the Great (1672–1725), Russia had been isolated from the West; Peter forced Western customs and ideas on his people and eliminated national traditions. This pressure created the beginnings of a cultural division between the liberal, Western-oriented aristocracy and the more traditional, conservative masses. The split was reflected almost immediately in Russian literature and gradually appeared in music as well.

European music was introduced to Russia late in the seventeenth century, and Italian opera was particularly popular at the Imperial Court. Music was definitely a luxury in Russia, imported for the upper classes and monopolized by foreigners. But in the nineteenth century, a new sense of national pride began to grow, demanding that there be something "Russian" about the music produced for Russian consumption. At about this time, the first significant Russian composer, Glinka, appeared.

Mikhail Glinka

Although Mikhail Glinka (1804–1857) studied with German and Italian musicians, he became closely associated with the members of a nationalistic literary movement in St. Petersburg. At their urging, he wrote a "national opera," which he filled with the spirit and melody of the Russian people. His opera *A Life for the Tsar* was first performed in 1836. Russia had a vast supply of folk music and liturgical chant (for the Orthodox church), and Glinka was one of the first to draw on these resources.

The Split between Nationalists and Cosmopolitans

About the time of Glinka's death the Russian musical world divided into two camps. Some Russian composers wanted to be completely independent of the West, writing Russian music addressed to Russians only. Others were convinced that Slavic culture should be abandoned for the cosmopolitan culture of Western Europe. This split was paralleled in literary circles, in which the novelist Dostoyevsky was a leading nationalist, while Turgenev represented the more conservative faction. The outstanding composer of the cosmopolitan school was Peter Ilyich Tchaikovsky, who was discussed in chapter 13.

The Russian "Five"

The leaders of the nationalistic school of composition in Russia, who professed to have no interest in the music of the West, were a strange group. Known as the "Five," they were not professional musicians, except for the leader and teacher of the others, Mili Balakirev (1837–1910). The rest were professionally employed in other fields: Alexander Borodin (1834–1887) was a chemistry professor at a medical school; César Cui (1835–1918) was a military engineer; Modest Mussorgsky (1839–1881), an army officer; and Nikolai Rimsky-Korsakov (1844–1908), a naval officer. The most significant of these composers were Borodin, Rimsky-Korsakov, and Mussorgsky. Borodin's best works are an opera, *Prince Igor* (1890), and a symphonic sketch, *In the Steppes of Central Asia*. The music for the Broadway musical *Kismet* is taken from his work. Rimsky-Korsakov, who employed opulent and overwhelming orchestrations, is best known for his orchestral tone poem *Schéhérazade* (1888).

MUSSORGSKY *(1839–1881)*

M odest Mussorgsky, the outstanding composer of the Russian nationalistic school, is often called the founder of modern musical realism. Mussorgsky was born in Pskof to an aristocratic family. His mother gave him his first piano lessons, and at thirteen, Mussorgsky studied with one of the better piano teachers in St. Petersburg. He acquired facility on the piano and became familiar with German music, but received no training in musical theory. At seventeen, Mussorgsky became an army officer, indulging in such regimental pastimes as boasting, drinking, and wenching. He soon resigned his post to devote full time to composing, but when the emancipation of the Russian serfs in 1861 left his family in financial trouble, Mussorgsky became a government clerk, a position he held almost until his death.

At twenty-one, Mussorgsky became a pupil and friend of Balakirev. However, Balakirev never completely trusted Mussorgsky's judgment—either musically or personally—and eventually the two grew apart.

Some of Mussorgsky's earliest nationalistic feelings were expressed in a letter to Balakirev on his first trip to Moscow. He was equally moved by the tombs of the Tsars and by the common people, who had, he said, "a strange demeanor, a nimbleness of motion . . . I was a cosmopolitan; now I feel reborn, and quite close to all that is Russian." Increasingly, Mussorgsky began to base his music on Russian themes—its literature, legends, folk songs, and the memories of his own childhood.

At twenty-nine Mussorgsky began his greatest work, the opera *Boris Godunov*. He wrote the libretto himself, basing it loosely on Pushkin's drama of Boris, who became Tsar in 1598 by arranging the murder of the child heir to the throne. The opera was finally performed in 1874. It was acclaimed by the public, but panned by most critics, especially by César Cui, Mussorgsky's old friend. It was dropped from the repertory shortly after his death, but revived some years later.

Figure 15.1 Mussorgsky's new kind of music—based on Russian themes and full of dissonance and rhythmic variety—initially met considerable resistance from musical conservatives. But his harmonic and rhythmic innovations pointed the way for later composers.

Mussorgsky's life became more and more disordered. Periods of happiness and productivity alternated with periods of depression and bouts of drinking. He felt increasingly isolated from his friends, and in 1881 he died at the age of forty-two.

Figure 15.2 Costume designs for Mussorgsky's unfinished opera *Khovanshchina* (first performed five years after his death) reflect the distinctly Russian flavor of the work.

MUSSORGSKY'S WORK

"My music," Mussorgsky wrote, "must be an artistic reproduction of human speech in all its finest shades, that is, the sounds of human speech, as the external manifestations of thought and feeling, must, without exaggeration or violence, become true, accurate music . . ."

This credo helps to explain Mussorgsky's disdain for the conventions of the conservatory. His music is full of strange dissonances and rhythmic innovations that seemed to his contemporaries inexplicable and crude. But with these sounds Mussorgsky attempted to evoke Russian speech, folk music, and real and imagined happenings—bells clanging for Boris's coronation, a witches' sabbath, the laughter of peasant girls.

Mussorgsky strove for complete realism in his music. His programmatic orchestral suite *Night on Bald Mountain* retells the legend of St. John's night, when witches assembled to glorify Satan and hold their sabbath. His song cycle *The Nursery* describes different aspects of the life of an aristocractic child. His program work for piano (now more familiar in its orchestral version), *Pictures at an Exhibition,* descibes both particular paintings and the composer's thoughts as he looks at them. In *Boris Godunov,* the realism is evident on all levels. His vocal lines follow the accents of natural speech, and his portrayal of crowd scenes is intensely real. On a deeper level, he expresses musically the deep and often unutterable sufferings and passions that rage in the human soul.

The drama, which contains a Prologue and four acts, centers on the character of Boris, his psychological disintegration and eventual death. We see Boris become Tsar after arranging for the murder of the rightful heir to the throne. We watch him from the moment of his coronation to his death, tormented by hallucination, fear, and guilt from within and political intrigue from without.

But aside from the powerful figure of Boris and the realistic dramatization of his spiritual and physical deterioration, at the heart of the opera is the other central protagonist—the Russian people. Indeed, they are the drama's real hero. In choral sections and solo arias, Mussorgsky realistically depicts a variety of Russian types and sympathetically evokes the struggle and suffering of an oppressed people.

SIDE 9/SELECTION 1

One of the opera's most powerful scenes in this regard is the brilliant *Coronation Scene,* which occurs in the Prologue to act 1. As the Prologue begins, it is clear that Boris, the son-in-law of the Tsar, has devised the murder of the child Dmitri, the rightful successor to the throne. Upon the death of Tsar Feodor, Boris pretends to withdraw into seclusion but secretly contrives for the police to arouse the people to implore him to assume the throne. Thus the stage is set for the *Coronation Scene.*

The scene opens with a clamorous orchestral introduction based on the alternation of two dissonant chords. As bells peal, the curtain rises on a courtyard of the Kremlin with the Cathedral of the Assumption and the Cathedral of the Archangels at either side. The people kneel between the great churches, and a procession of brilliantly dressed boyars (noblemen) and churchmen moves across the courtyard toward the Cathedral of the Assumption. From the cathedral porch, Prince Shuiski turns to proclaim, "Long life to Tsar Boris Feodorovich." The crowds (prodded by police) and the boyars respond by singing a hymn of praise based on a Russian folk tune.

Example 15.1

As the chorus and orchestra reach the height of a crescendo, Boris, accompanied by his two children and robed in magnificent cloth of gold, appears before the kneeling throng.

The atmosphere changes to one of quiet intensity. In an introspective monologue, Boris sings of the anguish, guilt, and fear that grip his heart. He invokes the aid of his departed father to help him rule justly and with glory. Then, singing a stronger, more resolute melody, Boris bids the people, boyar and beggar alike, to be his guests at a royal feast.

To the renewed peals of the great bells, the royal procession moves on to the Cathedral of the Assumption. The people arise and again sing in praise of Boris. The chorus and orchestra surge to a climax and the scene ends with the continued reverberation of the cathedral bells.

Prince Shuiski

Da zdrávstvuyet Tsar Borís
Feódorovich!

Long life Tsar Boris Feodorovich!

Chorus

Zhiví i zdrávstvui, Tsar nash
bátyushka!

Long live the Tsar, our little father!

Prince Shuiski

Slávte!

Glory to you!

Chorus

Uzh kák na nébe sólntsu
krásnomu,
Sláva!
Uzh i sláva no Rusí Tsaryú
Borísu!
Sláva!

*Even as glory to the radiant sun in the
sky,*
Glory!
So glory to Tsar Boris in Russia!

Glory!

(An imperial procession from the Cathedral. Police officers keep the people in line on both sides of the procession.)

Zhivi i zdrávstvui!
Ráduisya, veselísya pravoslávnyi lyud!
Velichái Tsaryá Borísa i sláv!

*Long live the Tsar! Rejoice and make
merry, all ye faithful of the
Russian church, and glory to the
great Tsar Boris.*

Nobles

(from the porch)

Da zdrávstvuyet Tsar Borís
Feódorovich!

All hail to Tsar Boris Feodorovich!

Chorus

Da zdrávstvuyet!
(Boris now appears and crosses the stage.)
Uzh, kák na Rusí tsaryú Borísu!
Sláva, sláva, Tsaryú!
Sláva, sláva, sláva!

All hail!

Glory to Tsar Boris in all Russia!
Glory, glory, to the Tsar! Glory,
glory, glory!

Boris

Skorbít dushá!
Kakói-to strákh nevólnyi
Zlovéschim predchúvstviyem
Skovál mne sérdtse.
O právednik, o mói otéts derzhávnyi!
Vozzrí s nebés na slyózy vérnykh slug
I nisposhlí ty mné
svyaschénnoye na vlást
Blagoslovénye.
Da búdu blag i práveden kak tý,
Dá v sláve právlyu svói naród.
Tepér poklónimsya pochíyuschim
Vlastítelyam Rusíyi.

*My soul is torn with anguish!
Involuntary fears and sinister
forebodings clutch my heart. Oh,
righteous and sovereign Father,
look down from heaven and behold
the tears of these your faithful
servants! Bestow Thy sacred
blessings upon me and my
dominion! Help me to be kind and
just like Thyself, and rule over my
people in glory! And now let us bow
in homage to the great departed
rulers of Russia. Then let us*

A tám szyvát naród na pir,
Veskh, ot boyár do nischevo
sleptsá,
Vsem vólnyi vkhod, vse gósti dorogíye.

*summon the people, from the noble
to the blind beggar, to a feast. All
are free to come and be my dear
and welcome guests.*

(Bells are rung on stage as the procession continues to the Archangels Cathedral.)

Chorus

Zhiví zdrávstvui Tsár nash bátyushka.

Long live the Tsar, our little father!

(Police officers try to restore order, but the people break away and dash towards the Archangels Cathedral.)

Uzh kák na nébe sólntsu
krásnomu,
Sláva, sláva!
Uzh, kák na Rusí Tsaryú Borísu,
Sláva, sláva, i mnógaya léta!

*Even as glory to the radiant sun in the
    sky,
Glory, Glory!
So glory to Tsar Boris in Russia!
Glory, glory and a long life!*

(Great commotion. The police officers struggle with the people. Boris emerges from the Archangels Cathedral and proceeds to his chambers.)

The *Coronation Scene* has achieved great popularity in its own right and is frequently performed in concert form (without costumes or scenery) as an independent concert piece.

NATIONALISM IN OTHER COUNTRIES

The distinctive nature of Russian folk music and Slavic culture made the nationalist movement there very obvious. But Russia was not the only country in which nationalistic forces influenced the musical scene. Jean Sibelius in Finland, Edvard Grieg in Norway, Isaac Albéniz, Enrique Granados, and Manuel de Falla in Spain each drew in some way on the folk idioms of their native countries.

The forces of nationalism also influenced musical developments in Bohemia. Bohemia (an area which is now part of Czechoslovakia) had been an Austrian colony for centuries, and thus had always been in touch with the mainstream of European music. Many fine musicians were produced in this region, but until the romantic era no distinctively Czech national style had developed. Even when a nationalist movement did arise, no extreme effort was made to avoid Western influence.

The two composers who led in the formation of a national style were Bedřich Smetana and Antonín Dvořák. Both were fully trained in traditional methods: Smetana's style was closely related to Liszt's, while Dvořák's was much closer to that of Brahms.

SMETANA'S WORK

Aside from his operas, Smetana is best known for his famous cycle of symphonic poems, *Má vlast* (*My Country,* 1879). The six works in this cycle celebrated his country's legendary past, its splendid rivers and hillsides, and great moments in Bohemian history. One of the finest of the six is called *Vltava* (*The Moldau*). It traces musically the course of the river Moldau from its sources through central Bohemia to Prague and on to join the Elbe.

SMETANA *(1824–1884)*

Regarded as the founder of the Czech national school, Bedřich Smetana was a composer dedicated to merging the spirit of Bohemian folk music with the innovations of the European musical pioneers of his day. A gifted pianist from childhood, Smetana performed the works of the classical masters. His traditional orientation was supplanted, however, when on a visit to Prague, he had the opportunity to hear Liszt and Berlioz. Smetana came to share with these men not only a fascination with progressive musical ideas but a spirit of nationalism, to which his dream of a Bohemia free from Austrian rule responded.

The spirit of Czech nationalism was widespread in Austrian-ruled Bohemia, and rising unrest culminated in the revolution of 1848. The uprising was a failure and left in its wake a long period of repression which Smetana eventually found unbearable. In 1856 he traveled to Sweden, where he worked as a teacher and conductor. He returned to his homeland after six years, this time finding a new and dynamic liberalism in the air. Shortly after his return a Czech national theater for opera, drama, and ballet was established, and Smetana began work on an opera in the Czech language.

Over the next twenty years the composer produced ten operas, eight of them on patriotic themes. *The Bartered Bride* (1866), which told of a village romance and recounted the comic antics of local Bohemian peasants, was instrumental in establishing his reputation.

In 1874 Smetana suddenly became deaf. But, like Beethoven before him, he continued to compose until nearly the end of his life.

Although *The Moldau* is just one part of a large work and has some thematic relationship to other parts of the cycle, it stands complete in its own right and has become one of the most popular works in symphonic repertoire. The piece is a reflection of the composer's love for his country and an expression of the Czech national character. In addition, it is a good example of program music.

SMETANA: VLTAVA (THE MOLDAU)

As Smetana himself indicates in the score, the work consists of eight sections. It begins with (1) a depiction of the two sources of the river, played by the flutes, which

Example 15.2

are joined by clarinets and lower strings, gradually flowing into (2) the river itself, represented by the following melody in E minor:

Example 15.3

Beneath this flowing melody (the Moldau theme) the sixteenth-note motive that began the piece continues (example 15.2). In fact, with two notable exceptions, this "swirling" water motive acts as a unifying element throughout the work, continuing as a background against which events of greater importance take place.

The river flows through a hunting forest (3) where the French horns and trumpets sound hunting calls above the swirling water figure.

In the course of the river's flow the forest is replaced by (4) a rustic village in which a wedding celebration is taking place. The celebration is represented by joyous, dancelike music.

Example 15.4

In this section the sixteenth-note motive that has characterized the piece thus far is absent and, as a result, there is a feeling of repose.

The simple wedding scene gives way to an even more serene, almost unearthly section (5), "moonlight and the dance of the water sprites." The sixteenth-note figure now appears in an entirely different guise—as a gently rippling accompaniment to the "moonlight" theme played by the high strings, which are muted and have a shimmering effect.

Example 15.5

In the midst of this quiet and relaxed section the horns and trombones slip in, almost without notice, repeating the "water sprites dance" motive pianissimo. The serenity and quiet intensity of this section offer the perfect foil for the excitement and drama that follow.

As the water-sprite dance section draws to a close, the "swirling" motive begins to assert itself; the strings and brass contribute to a general increase in momentum, and the "river" theme (again in E minor) appears afresh (6). Then, abruptly, the entire orchestra interrupts the serene melodic flow with a theme suggesting great turbulence. We have reached St. John Rapids (7). Here Smetana uses the full resources of the romantic orchestra to evoke swirling rapids of chaotic and frightening proportions.

Soon, however, the rapids give way to the most beautiful and expansive part of the river (8). The "river" melody appears in its most stirring form, this time in E *major,* played forte by the full orchestra. At its broadest point the river flows past the Vysihrad, the glorious castle which symbolizes Bohemian grandeur, proclaimed

This driving phrase is the germ out of which the A section is built and which reappears throughout the movement. The B section is more lyrical and flowing.

Example 15.15

The trio also consists of two contrasting sections.

Example 15.16

Example 15.17

But instead of following the usual pattern of

Scherzo	Trio	Scherzo
ABA	ABA	ABA

Dvořák varies this structure again, using cyclical technique. Between the first scherzo and trio there appears a short transition, like a bridge, which employs not only the materials of the scherzo movement but also the motive obviously derived from theme 1 of the first movement.

Example 15.18

In the coda he again features this material from the first movement in an obvious and dramatic way, combining it with the 𝅘𝅥 𝅘𝅥𝅮 𝅘𝅥 𝅘𝅥 scherzo motive. Thus he achieves unusual unity; motives from the first movement not only permeate that movement but also lend coherence to the second and third movements.

Fourth Movement

The fourth movement is an enormous sonata-allegro in E minor, returning to a fast tempo (allegro con fuoco—fast, with fire). A short, fiery introductory section leads to the first theme, which is strong and marchlike.

Example 15.19

The contrasting second theme is tender in nature. It is stated first by the clarinet and immediately taken up by the strings, leading to a third and final theme straight out of a Czech village dance.

Example 15.20

At first the development concentrates on the marchlike first theme, but as the section progresses, themes from *all three* previous movements are introduced in various combinations and rhythmic alterations.

Example 15.21

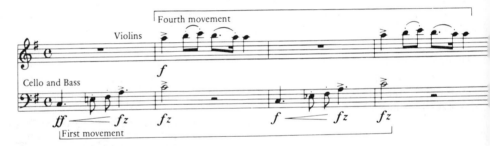

Perhaps the most dramatic moments in the symphony occur in the coda, when these two ideas are combined in climactic fashion.

Example 15.22

There follows the final drive to the end which, surprisingly, fades away to the softest possible sound on the last chord.

As we have seen, the use of themes from the earlier movements in the later ones lends great unity to the work. This procedure is used most strikingly in the last movement, which includes themes from all four movements. Even more importantly, one idea—the opening phrase of theme 1 of the first movement—is central throughout the symphony. Partly due to its original appearance, but also because of its treatment in the later movements, this motive, particularly its rhythmic structure ♩. ♪♪♩ | ♩. ♪♪♩. is the strongest unifying factor in the work.

The "New World Symphony" was immediately popular at the time of its creation and has remained so to this day. The world of music is richer for the fact that a Czech by the name of Dvořák came to the New World.

SUMMARY

Nationalism was most evident in countries that did not have strong musical traditions of their own.

Russia began early in the nineteenth century to produce music in a unique national idiom. Mikhail Glinka drew from his country's vast supply of folk music and liturgical chant to write the opera *A Life for the Tsar,* first performed in 1836. A group of Glinka's successors formed a nationalistic school known as the "Five." The outstanding members of this group were Alexander Borodin, Nikolai Rimsky-Korsakov, and Modest Mussorgsky. Mussorgsky, composer of the opera *Boris Godunov,* is often considered to be the founder of modern musical realism.

The forces of nationalism were also felt in other European countries. In particular, a national style developed in Bohemia through the efforts of Bedřich Smetana and Antonín Dvořák, and nationalistic influences were felt also in Spain, Finland, and the Scandinavian countries.

NEW TERMS

Cyclical treatment

SUGGESTED LISTENING

Dvořák, Antonín

Symphony no. 9 ("The New World"). See pages 294–99.

Smetana, Bedřich

The Moldau. See pages 291–93.

Sibelius, Jean

Finlandia. Finland's greatest composer is best known for his many symphonies and tone poems, many of which were inspired from Finnish mythology. *Finlandia* was written during the Russian domination of Finland and became a symbol for Finnish nationalism and independence.

ROMANTIC OPERA AND CHORAL MUSIC

O pera was one of the most important musical genres of the romantic period. In the eighteenth century each of the three leading countries of musical Europe—France, Italy, and Germany—had its own operatic style. These national styles became even more distinct during the romantic period.

FRENCH OPERA

During the first half of the romantic era, Paris was the operatic capital of Europe. Beginning in about 1820, with the rise of a large and influential middle class, a new type of opera developed. Called **grand opera,** it concentrated on the spectacular elements of the production: crowd scenes, ballets, choruses, and elaborate scenery. The integrity of the drama and the music was often sacrificed for these special effects. Giacomo Meyerbeer (1791–1864), a German composer who had studied and worked extensively in Italy before coming to France, introduced grand opera to Paris with such operas as *Les huguenots* (1836) and *Le prophète* (1849). One of the longest grand operas of the early romantic period was *Guillaume Tell* (*William Tell,* 1829) by an Italian, Gioacchino Rossini. The overture to *William Tell* remains popular today.

Although grand opera received the lion's share of Parisian attention, the less pretentious **opéra comique** (comic opera) continued to be popular. The distinguishing feature of opéra comique was its use of *spoken* dialogue rather than sung recitative. Both the music and the plot tended to be simpler than in grand opera. Despite the word "comique," many operas in this form had serious plots.

Later in the nineteenth century, a new form developed as a compromise between the overwhelming spectacle of grand opera and the lightness of opéra comique. Called **lyric opera,** it evolved from the more serious type of opéra comique. Using plots taken from romantic drama or fantasy, these works relied primarily on the beauty of their melodies. One of the finest lyric operas of the period, Charles Gounod's *Faust* (1859), was based on the first part of Goethe's famous play.

Naturalism

Toward the latter part of the century a new literary movement, **naturalism,** developed in France. Naturalist writers rebelled against the romantic tendency toward escapism and emphasis on individual feeling. They sought to depict life as it is, objectively and truthfully. Often they portrayed characters from the lower classes whose lives were controlled by impersonal social forces as well as by their own passions.

Georges Bizet (1838–1875) introduced naturalism to opera in his masterpiece *Carmen* (1875). Where grand operas often portrayed historical and mythological figures, with the performers using stylized gestures to express their feelings, Bizet's main character was a gypsy girl whose fiery temper and passionate nature were dramatized realistically. Bizet's brilliant orchestration and his vital melodies and rhythms effectively complement the characterization and dramatic action.

BIZET (1838–1875)

Born and brought up in Paris, Georges Bizet entered the Paris Conservatory at the age of ten, and by seventeen had written his first symphony. His work revealed such talent and ingenuity that he was awarded the Prix de Rome, enabling him to study at the Italian capital. Unfortunately, this brilliant beginning was soon clouded by the cold reception of his audiences, who were startled and offended by the boldness of his realism and the starkness of the emotions displayed in his early operatic works.

Following his youthful compositions, Bizet created three operas: *The Pearl Fishers* (1863), *The Fair Maid of Perth* (1867), and *Djamileh* (1872). Of the three, only *The Fair Maid of Perth* was well received, but Bizet's skill in orchestration and musical structure began to build his reputation. Success came in 1872 when he composed the incidental music for *L'Arlésienne,* a piece filled with exotic harmonies and bold orchestration. This won him an offer to do an opera based on a libretto adapted from Prosper Mérimée's novel about a fiery gypsy girl.

The realism of the libretto, dealing as it did with earthy figures and driving passion, was a perfect vehicle for Bizet's imagination and love of folk melodies. He undertook the assignment, and the opera, entitled *Carmen,* was produced in 1875. The subject scandalized the audience, and the themes of desire, love, and hate proved too bold for its time. The touch of scandal that surrounded it, however, kept the opera running for several months, and Bizet was subsequently offered a contract for his next work.

But the opera's reception was a great blow to the composer, and emotionally exhausted by so many months and years of work, he was stricken by a heart attack and died. At the age of thirty-eight he had created the greatest French opera of his century and now one of the best-loved operas in the world. His inspired vocal ensembles, his use of the orchestra to comment on the action on stage, his pounding rhythms, his masterly scoring, and his eminently singable melodies assured him musical immortality. Five years after its unfavorable reception in Paris, *Carmen* returned to that city and was received with great enthusiasm.

ITALIAN OPERA

By the nineteenth century, opera was virtually the only important musical form being cultivated in Italy. The distinctions between *opera seria* and *opera buffa* were still maintained, although both were influenced by French grand opera. The orchestra began to play a more important and colorful role and the chorus was also used more effectively.

Rossini, Donizetti, and Bellini

The most outstanding Italian opera composer of the early part of the nineteenth century was Gioacchino Rossini (1792–1868). His sense of melody and effective staging made him an instant success. Opera buffa seemed to be a natural outlet for his talents, and *Il barbiere di Siviglia* (*The Barber of Seville*, 1816) ranks with Mozart's *The Marriage of Figaro* as a supreme example of Italian comic opera. As with Mozart's work, the skillful treatment of ensembles and the exposition of comic situations and characters make *The Barber of Seville* an exceptional opera.

In his thirty-two operas and oratorios, Rossini sought to cultivate the aria to its highest possible level. Its function was to delight audiences with melodious and spontaneous music. This **bel canto** style, which emphasized beauty and purity of tone and an agile vocal technique, was also exemplified in the work of two of Rossini's contemporaries: Gaetano Donizetti (1797–1848), composer of some seventy operas, including *Lucia di Lammermoor* (1835); and Vincenzo Bellini (1801–1835), whose lyric and expressive style is particularly evident in his *La Sonnambula* (*The Sleepwalker,* 1831) and *Norma* (1831).

The greatest Italian opera composer of the second half of the nineteenth century was Giuseppe Verdi.

VERDI'S WORK

Verdi's style is frequently contrasted with that of his German contemporary Richard Wagner. While each of these composers brought romantic opera to its height in his native country, each did so by using quite different approaches. Wagner's plots usually involved larger-than-life, mythological characters whose activities were meant to symbolize underlying philosophical issues. Verdi's favored real people cast in dramatic, action-filled situations. Although Wagner's plots are more strictly ordered, Verdi's are notable for spontaneity and a sure sense of drama.

Verdi and Wagner disagreed on the relative importance of the singers and the orchestra. Wagner used orchestration to convey his philosophical ideas, sometimes overshadowing the singers, whose role was to move the surface action along. By contrast, Verdi's operas are dominated by the singing voice. Melody is the vehicle for expressing a vast range of emotions, and singers rarely compete with the orchestral background.

VERDI *(1813–1901)*

*B*orn of a poor family in a little hamlet in Bussetto, Italy, Giuseppe Verdi began his musical training as the apprentice of the local church organist. His hard work and talent were rewarded with a stipend contributed by his town to enable the continuation of his studies at the Milan Conservatory. He was subsequently turned down by the examiners, but through the financial aid of a friend continued his studies by means of private lessons.

Verdi's first opera, *Oberto* (1839), written when he was twenty-six, was an instant success. To this musical triumph he added another, with the presentation of his third opera, *Nabucco,* in 1842. It was this work that brought him not only musical recognition, but national fame. The story dealt with the plight of the Jews in Babylon, but the parallel with the Milanese crusade for freedom from Austrian rule was so striking that Verdi was exalted as a patriot and champion of the Italian cause. His name soon became linked with the cry for independence, and his evident sympathies, as they were reflected in his works, brought him under police suspicion.

After producing a number of successful works, Verdi settled on a country estate in 1849. There he continued to pursue his political activities and produced, in succession, three of his best-known works: *Rigoletto* (1851), *Il trovatore* (1853), and *La traviata* (1853). These productions are regarded as the culmination of his first creative period.

Years of intensive muscial productivity followed, during which such memorable works as *Un ballo in maschera* (*A Masked Ball,* 1859), *La forza del destino* (*The Force of Destiny,* 1861), and *Don Carlos* (1867) were created. In 1872, Verdi's masterpiece of spectacular grand opera, *Aida,* was written. With its cohesive dramatic structure, wealth of melodic, harmonic, and orchestral color, and subtle characterizations, this work is regarded as the height of his second creative phase.

Following this triumph, Verdi did not produce another operatic work for sixteen years. Then, in 1893, *Otello,* an opera unlike any he had previously written, was

Figure 16.1 Verdi was beloved not only as an operatic composer but also as a champion of the cause of Italian freedom.

performed in Milan. Regarded by many critics as the pinnacle of Italian tragic opera, its sense of continuity surpasses that of his earlier works, while its orchestration never obscures the singing voices. Verdi's last opera, *Falstaff,* written in 1893 when the composer was nearly eighty, is one of the finest in the comic opera genre.

The *Verismo* Movement

Toward the end of the nineteenth century, a movement toward naturalism and realism took place in Italian literature, similar to the movement in France. Called **verismo** (realism), it quickly penetrated Italian opera. Bizet's *Carmen* served as a model for the three Italian composers who led the movement: Giacomo Puccini (1858–1924), Ruggiero Leoncavallo (1858–1919), and Pietro Mascagni (1863–1945). Leoncavallo is remembered for *I pagliacci* (*The Clowns,* 1892), and Mascagni for *Cavalleria rusticana* (*Rustic Chivalry,* 1890). Puccini, the most successful of the *verismo* composers, effectively united grand opera and realism.

PUCCINI'S WORK

Puccini's operas reflect his realistic bent and his fascination with exotic settings. *Madame Butterfly,* for example, is set in Japan and *Turandot* in China. The opera that brought him international acclaim, *La Bohème,* combines rich and sensuous romantic melodies with realistic details of plot and characterization.

PUCCINI (1858–1924)

One of the most celebrated and successful of Italian opera composers, Giacomo Puccini was descended from a line of musicians that stretched back over five generations. During most of his childhood, Puccini showed only a modest talent for music; nevertheless, his mother insisted that he continue his studies, and by the age of sixteen he was composing in earnest—chiefly organ music for church services.

In 1880, Puccini obtained a scholarship to enter the Milan Conservatory. Once graduated from the Conservatory, he entered an opera competition with *Le Villi* (*The Vampire,* 1884), a work based on a Slavonic legend. He failed to win the contest, but the opera was produced in Milan on May 31, 1884. The success of the premiere persuaded the well-known publisher Giulio Ricordi to commission a second opera by Puccini. Largely because of a poor libretto, *Edgar* (1884–1888) was not a success; however, Ricordi continued to support the composer, and both men worked over the book for the next work, *Manon Lescaut.* Its premiere on February 1, 1893, was an immense triumph.

Although *Manon Lescaut* made Puccini famous in Italy, his next opera, *La Bohème* (*Bohemian Life,* 1893–1896), brought him worldwide fame. He completed the work in his magnificent new villa next to Lake Massaciuccoli in northern Italy.

Puccini's only serious failure was, ironically, his favorite opera, *Madame Butterfly* (1904). Despite the hisses and catcalls of the premiere, however, the work became quite popular outside Italy. His next opera, *La fanciulla del west* (*The Girl of the Golden West,* 1910), was based on a play by David Belasco, as was *Madame Butterfly.* Its premiere at the Metropolitan Opera in New York was one of the most glittering events of 1910, with Arturo Toscanini conducting and Enrico Caruso singing the lead male role.

During World War I Puccini remained in Italy, working quietly on more operas. His last work, *Turandot,* was left incomplete at his death. In 1923 he began suffering from what turned out to be cancer of the throat, and the following year he died of a heart attack. The task of finishing the final scenes of the work was entrusted to Franco Alfano, a distinguished younger composer. The opera was produced under Arturo Toscanini at La Scala, Milan, on April 25, 1926.

Figure 16.2 A scene from *La Bohème*.

PUCCINI:
LA BOHÈME

The Plot

The opera is set in the Latin Quarter of Paris (the artists' district on the Left Bank) in the 1830s. Rodolfo (a struggling young poet) and his friend Marcello (a painter) are freezing in their garret studio on Christmas Eve. Suddenly a friend enters with money, groceries, and firewood, and insists they all go out to celebrate. Rodolfo stays to finish an article he is writing but is interrupted by a knock at the door. The caller is Mimi, a neighbor, whose candle has blown out. She asks for a light, and he invites her in. She is ill and faints. When she feels strong enough to leave, they discover that her key has fallen. As they search for it on the floor, their hands meet, and they give up the search to wait for more light from the moon. Rodolfo tells Mimi about his life and hopes. She describes her life as a maker of artificial flowers and her longing for spring and sunshine. Rodolfo declares his love and Mimi responds passionately. As the act ends, they leave to join his friends at the cafe.

The next act opens with a holiday crowd in the streets near the cafe. Marcello sees his old flame, Musetta, with a wealthy old codger in tow. She tries to attract Marcello's attention, embarrassing her escort and amusing the spectators. Finally she sings a provocative waltz and, having sent her escort off on a fool's errand, leaps into Marcello's eager arms.

Some months later, Rodolfo's jealousy has caused Mimi to leave him. She seeks out Marcello to ask his help and tells him of Rodolfo's unbearable behavior; Rodolfo arrives and Mimi hides. He starts to complain to Marcello of Mimi's flirting, but admits that he is actually in despair over her failing health. When Mimi's coughing reveals her presence, Rodolfo begs her to stay with him until spring, and she agrees.

Act 4 is set in the garret the following fall. Rodolfo and Marcello are in the studio. Their fellow artists arrive for dinner and a hilarious evening begins. Musetta interrupts their gaiety, announcing that Mimi has collapsed on the stairs. They carry her in; all except Rodolfo leave to pawn their treasures to buy medical supplies. Rodolfo and Mimi recall their first meeting; their friends return and Mimi drifts off to sleep. She dies, and Rodolfo embraces her while the others weep.

The Music

The music of *La Bohème* follows the natural inflections of the words of the libretto. Although almost every word is sung, Puccini attempts to give the impression of normal spoken conversation in a kind of recitative style. Much of the action is delivered in short phrases, often sung on one or two notes. Characters constantly interrupt one another. Little musical ornamentation is used. Very often the orchestra has the most important melodic material and creates subtle transitions between recitative and aria, introducing new harmonies and hints of melodies to be sung.

All of this is illustrated in the last half of act 1. Mimi and Rodolfo are searching in the dark for her key. Mimi is very nervous, keeping up a steady volley of apologies and questions:

Mimi:
Importuna è la vicina . . .   *Your neighbor is troublesome . . .*

Rodolfo:
Cosa dice, ma le pare.   *What are you saying, don't mention it.*

Mimi:
Cerchi?   *Would you look?*

Rodolfo:
Cerco.   *I am looking.*

Mimi:
Ove sarà?   *Where can it be?*

Rodolfo:
Ah!   *Ah!*

(Rodolfo pockets the key)

Mimi:
L'ha trovata?   *Have you found it?*

Rodolfo:
No.   *No.*

Mimi:
Mi pareve . . .   *I thought . . .*

Rodolfo:
In verità.   *Honestly.*

Mimi:

Cerca?   *Are you looking?*

Rodolfo:

Cerco!   *I am looking!*

Puccini sets each of these phrases according to its character. Mimi's apology is a plaintive melodic line, while "I am looking" and "Where can it be?" are set on only one note. Rodolfo's "Ah!" is spoken, highlighted by a sudden pizzicato from the string section. The orchestra quietly advances the tension throughout, tossing in snatches of staccato melody while the low strings keep a steady beat.

While Rodolfo is groping toward Mimi's hand, the orchestra is preparing a change of mood. The staccato phrases become legato, the short notes give way to sustained ones, and the harmony begins to modulate in preparation for Rodolfo's aria. By the time Rodolfo has captured Mimi's hand, his aria flows naturally out of the preceding music.

Example 16.1

RODOLFO Che ge - li - da ma - ni - na, se la la - sci ris - cal - dar
(What a frozen little hand, let me warm it)

Rodolfo goes on to tell Mimi about his life and hopes, and the aria builds to a climax as he is swept up in a wave of emotion.

Example 16.2

Ta - lor   dal mio for - zie - re —— ru-ban tut-ti i gio -

iel - li   due la - dri: gli oc - chi bel - li.

*("Now and then two thieves will rob me of all the jewels from my strongbox:
two beautiful eyes.")*

Mimi responds with her own lovely aria, "Mi chiamano Mimi" ("They call me Mimi"). She lives by herself, she tells Rodolfo, and longs for the coming spring and the fragrant scent of rose blossoms. As Mimi ends her aria, Rodolfo's friends shout to him from the street, momentarily breaking the spell and allowing the audience a brief respite before the passionate closing duet.

As Rodolfo turns from the window he is transfixed by the sight of Mimi bathed in the glow of moonlight. He begins to sing and soon Mimi joins him in a love duet based on the climactic phrase of Rodolfo's aria (compare example 16.3 with example 16.2).

Example 16.3

This sensuous melody becomes the love theme of the opera. The duet ends in a kiss and act 1 closes as the lovers sing the word "amor."

They both grope on the floor for the key.

SIDE 9/SELECTION 2

Mimi:

Importuna è la vicina . . .   *Your neighbor is troublesome. . . .*

Rodolfo:

Cosa dice, ma le pare.   *What are you saying, don't mention it.*

Mimi:

Cerchi?   *Would you look?*

Rodolfo:

Cerco.   *I am looking.*

Mimi:

Ove sarà?   *Where can it be?*

Rodolfo:

Ah!   *Ah!*

Rodolfo finds the key and furtively slips it into his pocket.

Mimi:

L'ha trovata?   *Have you found it?*

Rodolfo:

No.   *No.*

Mimi:

Mi parve. . . .   *I thought . . .*

Rodolfo:

In verità.   *Honestly.*

Mimi:

Cerca?   *Are you looking?*

Rodolfo:

Cerco!   *I'm looking!*

Pretends to continue searching, and gropes his way nearer to Mimi; finally he manages to touch her hand in the darkness.

Mimi:

Ah!   *Ah!*

Surprised, she stands up.

Rodolfo:

Che gelida manina, se la lasci   *What a frozen little hand, would you*
riscaldar. Cercar che giova? Al buio   *let me warm it? What's the good of*
non si trova. Ma per fortuna, è una   *searching? We won't find it in the*
notta di luna . . . e qui la luna,   *dark. But by luck it is a moonlit*
l'abbiamo vicina. Aspetti, signorina,   *night, and we'll have the moon near*
le dirò con due parole chi son, chi   *us here. Wait, miss, and I'll tell you*
son, e che faccio, come vivo. Vuole?   *in a couple of words who I am—*
Chi son? Chi son? Sono un poeta.   *who I am, and what I do, how I*
Che cosa faccio?   *live. Would you like that? Who am*
Scrivo. E come vivo? Vivo. In   *I? Who am I? I'm a poet. What do*
povertà mia lieta scialo da gran   *I do? I write. And how do I live? I*
signore rime ed inni d'amore. Per   *live. In my poverty I feast as gaily*
sogni e per chimere e per castelli in   *as a grand lord on rhymes and*
aria l'anima ho millionaria. Talor   *hymns of love. For dreams and*
dal mio forziere ruban tutti i gioielli *fancies and castles in the air, I have*
due ladri: gli occhi belli. V'entrar   *a millionaire's soul. Now and then*
con voi pur ora, ed i miei sogni   *two thieves rob all the jewels from*
usati, e i bei sogni miei tosto si   *my strongbox: two beautiful eyes.*
dileguar! Ma il furto non m'accora   *They came in with you, just now,*
poichè—poichè v'ha preso stanza la   *and my old dreams, my beautiful*
dolce speranza! Or che mi   *dreams, quickly dissolved. But the*
conoscete, parlate voi, deh! Parlate!   *theft doesn't hurt me, since—since*
Che siete? Vi piaccia dir!   *such sweet expectation has taken its*
                                        stead. Now that you know me,
                                        come, you speak. Who are you?
                                        Please tell!

Rodolfo releases Mimi's hand, and she drops into a chair.

Mimi:

Si. Mi chiamano Mimì, ma il mio   *Yes. They call me Mimi, but my name*
nome è Lucia. La storia mia è   *is Lucia. My story is brief. I*
breve. A tela o a seta ricamo in casa   *embroider silk or linen at home and*
e fuori. Son tranquilla e lieta ed è   *outside. I'm contented and happy,*
mio svago far giglie e rose—Mi   *and it's my pleasure to make lilies*
piaccion quelle cose che han sì dolce   *and roses. I like those things that*
malia, che parlano d'amor, di   *have sweet charm, that speak of*
primavere, che parlano di sogni e di   *love, of springtimes, that speak of*
chimere—quelle cose che han nome   *dreams and fancies—those things*
poesia—Lei m'intende?   *that are called poetry. Do you*
                                        understand me?

Rodolfo:

Si.

Yes.

Mimì:

Mi chiamano Mimì, il perchè non so.
   Sola, mi fo il pranzo da me stessa.
   Non vado sempre a messa ma prego
   assai il Signor. Vivo sola, soletta, là
   in una bianca cameretta: guardo sui
   tetti e in cielo, ma quando vien lo
   sgelo il primo sole è mio—il primo
   bacio dell'aprile è mio! Il primo sole
   è mio! Germoglia in un vaso una
   rosa. Foglia a foglia la spiro! Cosi
   gentil il profumo d'un fior! Ma i fior
   ch'io faccio, ahimè, i fior ch'io
   faccio, ahimè, non hanno odore!
   Altro di me non le saprei narrare:
   sono la sua vicina che la vien fuori
   d'ora a importunare.

*They call me Mimi, but I don't know
   why. All alone, I make dinner for
   myself. I don't always go to Mass,
   but I often pray to the Lord. I live
   alone, all by myself, in a little
   white room over there. I look on the
   roofs and into the sky, but when the
   thaw comes, the first sunshine is
   mine—the first kiss of April is
   mine. The first sunshine is mine! A
   rose opens in a vase. Leaf by leaf I
   sniff its fragrance. So lovely is the
   perfume of a flower. But the
   flowers that I make—alas! the
   flowers that I make—alas! have no
   odor. I wouldn't know anything else
   to tell you about myself—I'm your
   neighbor who comes at this odd
   hour to trouble you.*

Voices are heard from outside.

Schaunard:

Ehi! Rodolfo!

Hey! Rodolfo!

Colline:

Rodolfo!

Rodolfo!

Marcello:

Olà! Non senti? Lumaca!

Hey there! Don't you hear? Snail!

Colline:

Poetucolo!

Paltry little rhymester!

Schaunard:

Accidenti al pigro!

Confound the slowpoke!

Rodolfo goes to the window and calls down.

Rodolfo:

Scrivo ancor tre righe a volo.

*I still have three lines to write in a
   flash.*

Mimi comes to the window beside Rodolfo.

Mimì:

Chi son?

Who are they?

Rodolfo:

Amici.

To Mimi. Friends.

Schaunard:

Sentirai le tue!

You'll get yours!

Marcello:

Che te ne fai li solo?

What are you doing up there all alone?

Rodolfo:

Non son solo. Siamo in due. Andate a Momus, tenete il posto, ci saremo tosto.

I'm not alone. There are two of us. Go to Momus, hold a place, we'll be there soon.

Marcello, Schaunard and Colline:

Momus, Momus, Momus, zitti e discreti, andiamocene, via!

Momus, Momus, Momus, quiet and discreet, let's get away from here, away!

Schaunard and Colline:

Momus, Momus!

Momus, Momus!

Marcello:

Trovò la poesia!

He found poetry!

Their voices fade into the distance.

Schaunard and Colline:

Momus, Momus, Momus!

Momus, Momus, Momus!

A moonbeam shines through the window on Mimi. Rodolfo, turning, sees her.

Rodolfo:

O soave fanciulla—

O gentle girl—

Marcello:

Trovò la poesia!

From far away. He found poetry!

Rodolfo:

O dolce viso di mite circonfuso alba lunar, in te ravviso il sogno ch'io vorrei sempre sognar.

O sweet face surrounded by mild white moonlight, the dream I would always dream comes to life in you.

The following is a duet.

Mimi:

Ah! tu sol commandi, amor!

Ah! love, you alone may rule!

Rodolfo:

Fremon già nell'anima—le dolcezze estreme—

Already extreme joys are thrilling in my soul—

Mimi:

Tu sol commandi, amore!

Love, you alone may rule!

Rodolfo:

Fremon nell' anima—

Are thrilling in my soul—

Mimi:

Oh! Come dolci scendono le sue lusinghe al core, tu sol commandi, amor!

Oh! How sweetly your soft words sink into my heart, love, you alone may rule!

ROMANTIC OPERA AND CHORAL MUSIC

Rodolfo:

—dolcezze estreme—fremon dolcezze estreme, nel bacio freme amor.

He kisses Mimi.

—*extreme joys—extreme joys are thrilling, love thrills in the kiss.*

Mimi:

No, per pietà!

She frees herself.

No, please!

Rodolfo:

Sei mia!

You're mine.

Mimi:

V'aspettan gli amici.

Your friends are waiting for you.

Rodolfo:

Già mi mandi via?

You send me away already?

Mimi:

Vorrei dir, ma non oso—

I'd like to ask, but I don't dare—

Rodolfo:

Di!

Ask it!

Mimi:

Se venissi con voi?

If I could come with you?

Rodolfo:

Che? Mimi! Sarebbe così dolce restar qui. C'è freddo fuori—

What? Mimi! It would be so pleasant to stay here. It's cold outside—

Mimi:

Vi starò vicina.

I'll stay near you.

Rodolfo:

E al ritorno?

And on returning?

Mimi:

Curioso!

Coquettishly. Inquisitive!

Rodolfo:

Dammi il braccio, mia piccina.

Gallantly. Take my arm, my little one.

Mimi:

Obbedisco, signor!

They exit, arm in arm; remainder of duet is heard from outside.

I obey, sir!

Rodolfo:

Che m'ami, di!

Say that you love me!

Mimi:

Io t'amo.

I love you.

Rodolfo and Mimi:

Amor! Amor! Amor!

Love! Love! Love!

Translation from: Bleiler, Ellen H., trans. *Denver Opera Guide and Libretto Series.* (New York: Dover Publications, 1962).

Both thematically and musically, *La Bohème* is unified by recurring motives. The last act is in many ways the mirror image of the first. In the same garret Rodolfo and the dying Mimi relive their first meeting. As in their first encounter, Mimi's hands are cold, but a muff is quickly bought and as she drifts into her last sleep she murmurs, "My hands are all warm. . ."

Although in the last act they sing parts of their opening arias, Rodolfo and Mimi never again sing their love duet. Its melody is present in the orchestra, shifting with the mood of the drama. By the very end, its lilting affirmation has changed to a forbidding minor cadence.

Example 16.4

GERMAN OPERA

While the Italian *verismo* composers were influenced by the realist movement in literature, nineteenth-century German opera drew much of its inspiration from the ideals of the romantic movement.

The first significant composer of German romantic opera was Carl Maria von Weber (1786–1826). A nationalist and romanticist, he built his style on the legends and songs of the German people and on romantic elements. His opera *Der Freischütz* (*The Freeshooter,* 1821) incorporates aspects of the supernatural, a typically romantic fascination.

German romantic operas, such as *Der Freischütz,* tended to stress mood and setting. Nature was represented as a wild and mysterious force, and supernatural beings mixed freely with ordinary mortals. Human characters often symbolized supernatural forces of good and evil, and the hero's victory meant salvation or redemption. Harmony and orchestral color were the primary means of dramatic expression, with the voice often relegated to a secondary role.

In the latter part of the nineteenth century, one of the most powerful personalities in the history of music emerged—Richard Wagner. In his works, German romantic opera reached its highest point.

WAGNER'S WORK

Although his most significant works were his operas and music dramas, Wagner also wrote some orchestral and choral music. His most important instrumental piece is the *Siegfried Idyll,* a short work composed for Cosima's birthday celebration of December 25, 1870. His most outstanding non-operatic vocal work is a collection of five settings of poems by Mathilde Wesendonk, with whom Wagner had a passionate love affair in the late 1850s. Composed during 1857–1858, the collection is known today as the *Wesendonk Lieder.*

WAGNER *(1813–1883)*

Born in Leipzig, Richard Wagner was the son of a clerk in the city police court who died when his son was only six months old. Richard's mother soon after married Ludwig Geyer, a gifted actor, playwright, and painter. It was rumored that Geyer was the composer's real father, and Wagner himself considered this likely. Wagner was a precocious child who showed an early interest in literature, writing a tragedy in the style of Shakespeare at the age of fourteen. In his formal musical training he was among the least systematic of the great nineteenth-century composers. He began piano lessons at age twelve, but never became a first-rate performer on any instrument. Like that of Berlioz, his great French contemporary, his music brought into play the full resources of the orchestra.

Lack of adequate preparation did not prevent him from early attempts at composition. By 1832 several of his works—including two overtures and a symphony—had been performed publicly. The following year—at age twenty—he began his professional career, becoming chorus master for the Wurzburg theater. Positions at Magdeburg, Königsberg, and Riga followed in succession, and he began composing operas.

While in Königsberg, he married the actress Minna Planer and began work on an opera based on Bulwer-Lytton's historical novel, *Rienzi, Last of the Tribunes*. The years 1839 to 1842 were spent in Paris, where he tried vainly to have the work performed. His financial situation became desperate, partly because of his increasingly spendthrift ways, and the first serious breakdown in his marriage occurred.

Rienzi was finally accepted, not in Paris but in Dresden, Germany, and Wagner returned to Germany to supervise the production. The success of both *Rienzi* (1842) and his next opera, *Der fliegende Holländer* (*The Flying Dutchman,* 1843), led to his appointment as conductor to the King of Saxony. For the next six years Wagner busied himself producing operas and writing two more himself: *Tannhäuser* (1842–1844) and *Lohengrin* (finished in 1848). Wagner's active participation in the revolutionary uprising of 1848–1849 forced him to flee to Switzerland.

Figure 16.3 An informal photograph of Wagner taken when he lived in Switzerland. He often posed for at-home pictures in the velvet jacket and beret.

While in exile, he turned to literary activity and wrote a number of essays, the most influential of which were *Das Kunstwerk der Zukunft* (*The Art-Work of the Future,* 1850) and *Oper und Drama* (*Opera and Drama,* 1851). In these he laid the foundations for "music drama," the term he used for his unique type of opera.

During his ten years in Switzerland, Wagner began putting his artistic theories into practice. By 1852 he had completed the poems of an epic cycle of four music dramas, entitled *Der Ring des Nibelungen* (*The Ring of the Nibelung*). The music for the first two dramas—*Das Rheingold* (*The Rhine Gold*) and *Die Walküre* (*The Valkyrie*)—

and for part of the third—*Siegfried*—was completed by 1857. The entire cycle was completed seventeen years later, in 1874, with the composition of *Die Götterdämmerung* (*The Twilight of the Gods*). These works place heavy demands on the performers, and since the individual dramas last three to five hours each, the whole tetralogy requires four separate days for its performance.

In the intervening years, Wagner wrote two other works that remain perhaps his most popular and most frequently performed: *Tristan und Isolde* (1856–1859) and *Die Meistersinger von Nürnberg* (*The Mastersingers of Nuremberg*, 1862–1867).

Although highly prolific, Wagner experienced great difficulty in arranging performances of his works. Most were formidable in scale, requiring theatrical and musical resources beyond the means of even the largest opera houses. As he approached the age of fifty, he became discouraged. His debts continued to pile up, and he separated from his wife and even contemplated suicide.

Then in 1864 his fortunes changed. The new king of Bavaria, Ludwig II, a devoted admirer of Wagner's music, invited the composer to Munich with the promise of financial and artistic support. At this time, Wagner fell in love with Cosima von Bülow, the daughter of Franz Liszt and wife of one of Wagner's close associates. Cosima left her husband to join Wagner, completely devoting herself to his career. They were finally married in 1870, and together raised enough money to build an opera house devoted exclusively to producing his works. Located in the small Bavarian town of Bayreuth, the *Fëstspielhaus,* as it was called, was the scene of the first complete performance of the Ring cycle, in 1876 (see fig. 16.4). One of the great artistic events of the century, this performance was the fulfillment of Wagner's lifelong dream. He completed one more work, *Parsifal* (1882), before illness forced him to travel to Italy in hope of regaining his health. He died quite suddenly, in Venice, on February 13, 1883.

Wagner's early operas—*Die Feen* (*The Fairies,* 1833), *Das Liebesverbot* (*Love Prohibited,* 1836), and *Rienzi* (1842)—were written under the influence of Meyerbeer, Bellini, and Donizetti, the masters of grand opera whose works dominated the European opera houses of the early nineteenth century. His next three operas—*The Flying Dutchman, Tannhäuser,* and *Lohengrin*—represent a culmination of the German romantic opera tradition that Wagner inherited from Carl Maria von Weber.

In the Ring cycle Wagner began to apply his innovative theories of operatic style and structure. The plots of the Ring cycle (all of which were his own creations, not those of a librettist) dealt with German mythology or historical legend. Underlying the surface plot were philosophical issues that he considered to be of fundamental importance: the struggles between the forces of good and evil and between the physical and spiritual, and the idea of redemption through unselfish love. In the Ring cycle Wagner attempted to symbolize the corruption of modern society through characters drawn from Teutonic mythology: giants, dwarfs, gods, and warriors.

His Style

Wagner believed that a music drama should be a *Gesamtkunstwerk* (universal artwork) combining elements from all the arts. The most important element should be drama, with the music serving to reinforce the dramatic expression. This view was directly opposed to that held by many earlier opera composers, including Mozart, who believed that the drama should serve as a framework for the music.

In Wagner's works the music is essentially continuous throughout each act, with one section moving smoothly into the next. In place of the traditional arias and recitatives, Wagner developed a musical line he called *Sprechsingen* (singing speech). This style combined the lyric quality of the aria and the speaking quality of the recitative and permitted a continuous musical flow which Wagner termed "endless melody."

The voices and orchestra each play a specific role in conveying several levels of meaning. The singers have the lesser role; through their actions and words, they explain the surface events of the drama. The orchestra is used to express the inner meaning of the events, which the characters themselves often do not understand. In addition, the orchestra serves as the major unifying force of the opera. The fabric of the orchestral music is held together by the use of the **leitmotif** (leading motive), a melodic fragment that represents a specific character, object, or idea; it is a kind of musical label that sounds every time its object appears in the drama. This technique was not original with Wagner; Verdi, Puccini, Weber, and Berlioz had used recurring themes to unify their works. But Wagner used the leitmotif much more consistently.

Apart from identifying characters or objects, leitmotivs are also used in more subtle ways. As musical phrases, they can be varied or developed in the usual symphonic fashion; with every variation and every change of context, they take on added shades of meaning. Wagner also uses them to suggest ideas to the audience. For example, the connection between two objects may be suggested by a similarity between their leitmotivs.

Figure 16.6 The colossal romantic choral style is humorously depicted in this 1850 caricature of Berlioz conducting an immense chorus.

Gioacchino Rossini. Verdi's *Requiem,* in memory of the author Alessandro Manzoni, is a large and dramatic setting of the moving requiem text.

In three great works, *The Damnation of Faust* (1846), the *Requiem* (*Grande messe des morts,* 1837) and the *Te Deum* (1855), Hector Berlioz reached the epitome of the colossal romantic choral style. The musical forces involved in these works are gigantic. The *Requiem* was written for 210 voices, a large orchestra, and four brass bands positioned in various locations and representing the calls to the Last Judgment. The *Te Deum* requires two choruses of one hundred singers each, six children's voices, and an orchestra of 150 players. The effects Berlioz achieved with his masterful skill at orchestration were truly dazzling.

BRAHMS

Johannes Brahms composed some of the most enduring choral music of the romantic period. He wrote for a wide variety of choral combinations and in diverse styles. Smaller works include a cappella choruses for various voice combinations, motets, canons, part songs, and psalm settings, many employing various types of instrumental accompaniment. One of the most popular of these works is the *Liebeslieder Walzer* (*Lovesong Waltz,* 1868–1869) for piano, four hands, and either mixed solo quartet or chorus. Brahms composed several large works for chorus and orchestra, some with several soloists. Among these are the cantata *Rinaldo* (opus 50), the incomparable *Schicksalslied* (*Song of Destiny,* opus 54) for chorus and orchestra, and *Triumphlied* (*Song of Triumph,* opus 55). The most important of his large-scale choral compositions was one of his early works, *Ein Deutsches Requiem* (*A German Requiem,* opus

45). It was composed over a period of eleven years and was finished in 1868 when Brahms was thirty-five. It not only preceded much of his other choral writing, but was written a full eight years before his first symphony.

BRAHMS: EIN DEUTSCHES REQUIEM (A GERMAN REQUIEM, OPUS 45)

Unlike the Requiems of Mozart, Berlioz, Verdi, and later Fauré, Brahm's setting does not employ the traditional Latin text, which is actually a Mass for the Dead (Missa pro defunctis). Rather, it is a setting of nonliturgical German texts which Brahms selected from the Lutheran Bible. A comparison of the Brahms text with the Roman Catholic liturgy shows a marked difference in intention and feeling: the Latin text prays for the soul of the dead, while Brahm's text is designed to console the living.

The opening words of the two texts confirm this:

ROMAN CATHOLIC TEXT	BRAHMS TEXT
(**Missa pro defunctis**)	(**Ein Deutsches Requiem**)
Requiem aeternam dona eis Domine	Selig sind, die da Leid tragen, denn sie sollen getröstet werden
(*Give them eternal rest, O Lord*)	(*Blessed are they that mourn, for they shall be comforted*)

Brahm's entire composition conveys this pervasive feeling of consolation in both the text and the music.

The work consists of seven movements and is scored for chorus, soprano and baritone soloists, and a large orchestra. The chorus and orchestra participate in all seven movements, although the orchestration varies somewhat from movement to movement. The role of the soloists is minimal, with the baritone appearing in the third and sixth movements and the soprano appearing only in the fifth.

FIRST MOVEMENT

Selig sind, die da Leid tragen,
  denn sie sollen getröstet werden.

*Blessed are they that mourn, for they
  shall be comforted.*
MATTHEW 5:4

Die mit Tränen säen, werden mit
  Freuden ernten.
Sie gehen hin und weinen und
  tragen edlen Samen, und
  kommen mit Freuden und
  bringen ihre Garben.

*They that sow in tears shall reap in
  joy.*
*They that go forth and weep, bearing
  precious seed, shall come again
  with rejoicing, bringing their
  sheaves with them.*
PSALM 126:5–6

This movement is an excellent example of Brahms's sensitive use of the orchestra; the instruments create a dark, somber tone quality that reflects the mood of the text. Brahms achieved this effect by omitting the high, bright sound of the violins and by dividing the lower strings into several parts: violas into two sections and cellos into three.

The work begins with a short orchestral introduction in which the upper cello and viola parts enter imitatively with an expressive melodic fragment over a pedal tone in the bass.

Example 16.9

This and the following choral section serve as principal unifying elements, which recur in the middle and at the end of the movement.

The contrasting section is built on the text beginning *"Die mit Tranen";* it expresses the tears (*Tranen*) with a falling melodic line, then climaxes at *"werden mit Freuden"* with a joyful rising motive and comes to a quiet conclusion at *"ernten."* The music of the opening section returns, and the chorus takes up the imitative entries with the words *"Sie gehen hin und weinen."*

After a short stretch of new material, the music set to *"werden mit Freuden"* returns, now with the text *"kommen mit Freuden."* Then the opening material is restated in its entirety, with the first two lines of text also repeated. A short coda, which decreases in intensity and volume, ends the movement.

Example 16.10

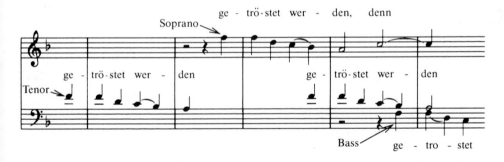

This section has greater significance than might appear, since Brahms repeats it almost literally at the end of the seventh movement, thus unifying the entire Requiem.

SECOND MOVEMENT

Denn alles Fleisch ist wie Gras und
    alle Herrlichkeit des Menschen wie
    des Grases Blumen.
Das Gras ist verdorret und die Blume
    abgefallen.

For all flesh is as grass, and all the
    glory of man as the flower of grass.
The grass withers, and the flower falls
    away.
I PETER 1:24

So seid nun geduldig, leiben
Brüder, bis auf die Zukunft
des Herrn.
Siehe, ein Ackermann wartet auf die
köstliche Frucht der Erde und ist
geduldig darüber, bis er empfange
den Morgenregen und Abendregen.

*Now therefore be patient, dear
brethren, until the coming of the
Lord.*
*Behold, the farmer waits for the
precious fruit of the earth and is
patient over it until it receives the
early and the late rain.*

JAMES 5:7

Aber des Herrn Wort bleibet in
Ewigkeit.

*But the word of the Lord endures
forever.*

I PETER 1:25

Die Erlöseten des Herrn werden wieder
kommen, und gen Zion kommen mit
Jauchzen; ewige Freude wird über
ihrem Haupt sein;
Freude und Wonne werden sie
ergreifen und Schmerz und Saufzen
wird weg mussen.

*The ransomed of the Lord shall return
and come to Zion with rejoicing,
everlasting joy shall be upon their
heads;*
*Joy and gladness shall they obtain,
and sorrow and sighing shall flee
away.*

ISAIAH 35:10

This movement calls for the full orchestra. The tempo is slow and the opening has the character of a funeral march. The upper strings are muted, maintaining the subdued tone of the first movement.

In the section based on the text *"So seid nun geduldig,"* the tempo is somewhat faster and the choral and string statement is echoed by the winds. The section ends with the same text that began it.

A sudden and startling contrast takes place at the words *"Aber des Herrn Wort,"* leading to a fast section with a fugal treatment of the text *"Die Erlöseten des Herrn."* After a contrasting section with many sudden changes of dynamics, the fugue subject returns in stretto—first in the winds, then in the chorus, strings, and brasses; it builds to a huge climax at the words *"kommen mit Jauchzen."* The coda, marked "Tranquillo," is in sharp contrast to the frenzy of the preceding section. The movement dies away, ending with a series of soft, descending scales in the orchestra.

THIRD MOVEMENT

Herr, lehre doch mich, dass ein Ende
mit mir haben muss, und mein
Leben ein Ziel hat, und ich davon
muss.
Siehe, meine Tage sind eine Hand breit
vor dir, und mein Leben ist wie
nichts vor dir.
Ach wie gar nichts sind alle Menschen,
die doch so sicher leben.

*Lord, make me to know my end, and
what is the measure of my days,
that I may know how frail I am.*

*Behold, my days are as a handbreadth
to Thee, and my lifetime is as
nothing before Thee.*
*Surely, mankind walks in a vain show,
their best state is vanity.*

CHARACTERISTICS OF ROMANTIC MUSIC

Tonality	Major-minor system with less firm sense of tonal center
Texture	Largely homophonic
Rhythm	Frequent fluctuations in tempo; use of rubato
Pitch	Greatly expanded pitch range
Harmony	Use of chromatic harmonies Modulations to distant keys Complicated chords Harmony used as expressive element
Tone Color	Fascination and experimentation with instrumental color; color rivals other elements in importance
Melody	Lyrical, expressive, flowing; sometimes ornamented
Dynamics	Wide range of dynamics Frequent fluctuations in dynamic level Dynamics used as structural element
Small Works	Art song (lied) Character pieces and miniatures for piano
Large Works	Concerto, symphony, program symphony, symphonic poem (tone poem), opera, choral works, chamber works, concert overture
Instruments	Piano was favorite instrument; large orchestra; unusual instrument groupings; emphasis on orchestration and color
Performance Style	Steady growth of virtuoso technique
Formal Innovations	Carefully constructed classical forms were freely manipulated and expanded; cyclical procedure; theme transformation; development of programmatic and descriptive music as manifested in the program symphony and tone poem; *verismo* movement in opera; development of nationalism in music.

The final movement of the Requiem marks a return to the spirit of the first movement, and to much of its musical material as well. Brahms has unified the entire work by linking the outer movements both textually and musically.

This movement is in ABA form with a coda; the first theme of the A section, *"Selig sind,"* is drawn almost directly from the coda of the first movement, where it was used for the words *"getröstet werden."*

Example 16.14

Se - lig sind die To-ten, die in dem Her-ren ster - ben von nun an, von nun an.

The B section begins with *"Ja, der Geist spricht,"* which is set for low voices singing in octaves, with trombones and horns; this leads to a tender section with the text *"dass sie ruhen,"* in which the winds play a very active part in the imitation. The material of the B section is then repeated, although in a somewhat abbreviated fashion, leading to a return of the opening material.

The opening theme is stated only once this time (by the tenor section), and the choral section is again repeated. The coda begins with a phrase in the alto and tenor sections that recalls the beginning of the return to original material from the first movement. It comes again, this time in another key, and leads directly into a literal restatement of the entire coda of the opening movement.

Ein Deutsches Requiem, like the great sacred choral works by Schütz and Bach in the baroque period, was inspired by a deep concern for the state of the human soul; the more humanistic orientation of the romantic age led Brahms to direct his words to the mourners rather than to the deceased. The texts of consolation and hope that he chose have an eloquent beauty of their own, and his music enhances this beauty still more.

SUMMARY

During the early part of the romantic era, Paris was the operatic capital of Europe. French opera concentrated on spectacular productions, featuring crowd scenes, ballets, choruses, and fantastic scenery. These grand operas, however, gradually gave way to lyric operas that emphasized romantic plots and beautiful melodies. Toward the end of the century a naturalistic style developed, of which Georges Bizet's *Carmen* is a prime example.

In Italy, Gioacchino Rossini was the outstanding composer of the early part of the nineteenth century. His *Barber of Seville* is an excellent example of the Italian *opera buffa*. The dominant figure in Italian opera during the second half of the century was Giuseppe Verdi. His realistic, action-filled plots were dominated by the singing voice, which became the primary vehicle for emotional expression. Toward the end of the century a movement toward naturalism penetrated Italian opera. Called *verisimo,* it is best exemplified in the works of Giacomo Puccini.

Romantic opera in Germany was strongly influenced by the romantic movement itself. The composer who first established a genuinely Germanic style was Carl Maria von Weber. German opera reached its highest point in the works of Richard Wagner, who sought to write "music dramas" that would encompass all the arts in a unified whole. To Wagner, the most important element was the drama, with the music serving the dramatic expression. Dramatic unity was enhanced by the use of leitmotivs, or melodic fragments associated with persons, objects, or ideas. Wagner's use of chromatic harmonies represented a significant step toward the development of new tonal systems in the twentieth century.

The lush sound of a large chorus was well-suited to the romantic style, and nearly every composer of the period wrote choral music in some form. Hector Berlioz frequently utilized a large chorus combined with an enormous orchestra in his works. Oratorios and settings of Catholic liturgical texts were written by such composers as Mendelssohn, Liszt, Berlioz, Schubert, Bruckner, and Verdi. Choruses also were used in programmatic symphonic works.

Some of the most enduring choral music of the romantic era was written by Johannes Brahms. The greatness of his most significant work, *Ein Deutsches Requiem,* rests on its masterful and eloquent marriage of the music and texts. In contrast to the traditional Catholic funeral Mass, Brahms' *Requiem* uses texts from the Old and New Testaments which give a message of comfort and consolation to the bereaved mourners.

NEW TERMS

grand opera   bel canto
opéra comique   verismo
lyric opera   leitmotif
naturalism

SUGGESTED LISTENING

Berlioz, Hector

Requiem (Grande messe des morts): Mass for the Dead. This monumental Mass for the dead requires over two hundred voices in the chorus and an immense orchestra with eight pairs of timpani and four brass ensembles scattered around the stage. Berlioz—a superb orchestrator—uses this huge force to the best effect, supporting the drama of the texts in this powerful work.

Bizet, Georges

Carmen. This *opéra comique* is based on Prosper Merimée's tragic novel about a fiery, beautiful, amoral gypsy woman and the tormented soldier who gives up everything for her. Bizet's last work is his greatest and, despite its initial failure (which directly contributed to his death), has become one of the most popular operas in the repertoire.

Leoncavallo, Ruggiero

I pagliacci (The Clowns)

Mascagni, Pietro

Cavalleria rusticana (*Rustic Chivalry*).

These two short, powerful operas are almost always presented together. Both are in *verismo* style and both deal with love betrayed and its tragic revenge. *I pagliacci* contains one of the most famous arias of Italian opera, "Vesti la giubba," in which the betrayed husband pours out his grief.

Mendelssohn, Felix

Elias (*Elijah*). This oratorio is Mendelssohn's most important choral work, incorporating elements of Bach's Passion style and Handel's oratorio form. Written for an English music festival, *Elias* had a brilliant premiere and remained extremely popular for a number of years. It remains one of the best known oratorios due to its inspired blending of musical and dramatic elements.

Rossini, Gioacchino

Il barbiëre di Siviglia (*The Barber of Seville*). This opera, based on the famous Beaumarchais play, is an example of *opera buffa* at its finest. It tells of the wooing of the beautiful and rich Rosina by Count Almaviva in spite of the opposition of Rosina's old guardian who wants to marry her himself. Love finds a way with the help of the crafty barber Figaro, whose comic opening aria is the famous "Largo al factotum."

Verdi, Giuseppe

La traviata (*The Fallen Woman*). This opera, which had a dismal premiere, became one of Verdi's best-known works. Based on the famous *La Dame aux Camélias* by Alexandre Dumas, it is the story of the ill-fated affair of the wealthy and fragile Parisian courtesan Violetta and her lover Alfredo. Verdi's lyrical music always reflects and amplifies the mood of the characters.

Wagner, Richard

Die Meistersinger von Nürnberg. This work remained one of Wagner's most popular and accessible operas. The libretto, by Wagner himself, is based on historical figures from the sixteenth-century Nuremberg guild of Mastersingers. The famous overture is frequently performed as a concert piece.

BRIDGING THE GAP
BETWEEN CENTURIES

T oward the end of the nineteenth century the center of cultural activity in Europe was Paris. Two different musical styles were current. One was the basically German-Italian late romantic style, strongly influenced by the monumental achievements of Richard Wagner. The leaders of this pan-European style of music in Paris were César Franck (1822–1890) and his pupils. The other was the specifically French tradition, as cultivated by Camille Saint-Saëns (1835–1921), Jules Massenet (1842–1912), and Gabriel Fauré (1845–1924). The underlying spirit of the French tradition was more classical and orderly than romantic and expressive. The music was subtle and understated, full of lyric melodies and carefully wrought details.

IMPRESSIONISM AND SYMBOLISM

The musical culture of France was closely connected to the other arts, particularly painting and literature. One of the outstanding artistic movements of the turn of the century was **impressionism,** in which painters sought to capture the visual impression, rather than the literal reality, of a subject. Though their work and methods were at first ridiculed by the critics, the impressionists persisted in their exploration of the play of light and in their use of patches and dabs of color to build up an image. They also continued their habit of working out-of-doors and of utilizing bright afternoon light; mood and atmosphere and the richness of nature were among their major inspirations. Meanwhile, **symbolist** poets were experimenting with rhythm, sound, and the clustering of images to suggest moods or emotions.

Coming slightly later than the movements in art and literature, the impressionist movement in music was similarly characterized by experimentation and by the rejection of past viewpoints. It, too, emphasized mood and atmosphere more than structure, and it, too, adopted nature as a frequent subject. Impressionist music was recognizable by its fragile and decorative beauty, its sensuous tone colors, its subdued atmosphere, its elegance and refinement. It cast off the more pompous, heavy, and serious quality of the German tradition. The influence of impressionism extended to England, Spain, Italy, and America, but France produced the most important composers: Claude Debussy and Maurice Ravel.

DEBUSSY *(1862–1918)*

*C*laude Debussy was born in St. Germain-en-Laye, near Paris, and was educated at the Paris Conservatory, where he received traditional training in the cosmopolitan late romantic style. He absorbed it well enough to win the Prix de Rome at the age of twenty-two, but soon after he began to reject the Germanic tradition in general and Wagner's philosophy in particular.

Debussy was put off by the grand themes and ponderous quality of German romantic music. For him the primary goal of music was to give pleasure, to appeal to the senses. An incisive critic, Debussy wrote articles on music which were published in the leading French journals. His reaction to Wagner's use of the leitmotif is characteristically witty and caustic: "Remember, [Wagnerian characters] never appear unless accompanied by their damnable leitmotiv, and there are even those who sing it! It's rather like those silly people who hand you their visiting cards and then lyrically recite key information they contain."

Opera was one of Debussy's lifelong interests, and his operatic style was very much a reaction against Wagner's influence. *Pelléas et Mélisande* (1902), which Debussy worked on over the decade of the 1890s, is taken from a symbolist play, and the vague references and images of the text are matched by the strange harmonies and restrained colors of the music. Throughout the work the voices dominate over a continuous orchestral background. The first performance of the opera met a mixed reaction, with some critics attacking it for its lack of form and melody and its unconventional harmonies and others enchanted by its subtle, elusive quality. The opera caught on and established Debussy as the leader of the impressionist movement in music.

Debussy was deeply devoted to his country, and the onset of World War I disturbed him so profoundly that for a time he felt incapable of writing music. But his sense of

Figure 17.1 Debussy broke with the German romantic style to create evocative impressionistic music characterized by its sensuous tone colors, elusive chromatic harmonies, and freedom of form.

nationalism impelled him to return to his art and he began composing again with furious energy—an effort spurred on by the fact that he was slowly dying of cancer. His death came in March, 1918, as Paris was being bombarded by German artillery.

DEBUSSY'S WORK

Debussy's compositions for piano are among the most significant works for that instrument written during the present century. His early (nonimpressionistic) works include the *Suite bergamasque* (1893) and a suite *Pour le piano* (1901). *Clair de lune* (*Moonlight*, 1890) is perhaps his best-known work for piano. The impressionistic style is fully evident in works published between 1903 and 1913: *Estampes* (*Engravings*), two collections of *Préludes,* and two of *Images.*

Debussy's important orchestral works are all impressionistic, beginning with the *Prélude à l'après-midi d'un faune* (*Prelude to the Afternoon of a Faun,* 1894), and continuing with the three *Nocturnes—Nuages* (*Clouds*), *Fêtes* (*Festivals*), and *Sirènes* (*Sirens*)—and *La mer* (*The Sea,* 1905), a set of symphonic sketches. In chamber music his greatest achievement was the Quartet in G Minor for Strings (1893). The first performance of this work left its audience puzzled and critics complaining of an "orgy of modulations." A forerunner of his musical impressionism, it came to be recognized in the twentieth century as one of the most important string quartets since those of Brahms.

Although Debussy loved opera, he completed only one of the many operatic projects he started, *Pelléas et Mélisande.* He also wrote incidental music for a play as well as art songs set to poems by Mallarmé, Villon, Verlaine, Baudelaire, and others.

His Style

The music of Claude Debussy is programmatic, but in a very general way; there is little attempt to tell a story or express specific feelings. Rather, his music creates a "mood" or atmosphere to correspond with its subject or program.

Although Debussy's style is unique, many influences can be seen to have helped form it. Most important were the romantic pianists Chopin and Liszt and the composers in the French tradition. Paris was a center for Russian music, and Mussorgsky's idiom pointed Debussy in new directions. His interest in exotic music was stimulated by the Javanese orchestra (called a *gamelan*), which he heard at the Paris Exposition of 1889.

One of the strongest influences on Debussy's style was not musical at all, but literary; he was closely associated with a group of artists centered around Stéphane Mallarmé, the symbolist poet. Through this connection Debussy became interested in expressing the unique sounds and rhythmic patterns of the French language in music. French generally avoids strong accents, making use of vowels of different lengths for rhythm and stress. Debussy's choice of subject matter for many of his pieces also reflects his close association with this important literary movement.

Debussy was the first European composer to break with the old system of tonality, and the new language he developed had a profound influence on almost every other composer of the twentieth century. His music is organized around sound patterns; he works with blocks of color and shifts from one to another very subtly. The harmonic basis of his music is entirely new, building on the symmetrical patterns of the whole-tone scale.

Example 17.1

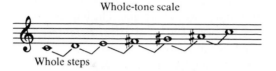

Whole-tone scale

Whole steps

Notice that the *dominant* (G♮) and the *leading tone* (B) are not included in the whole tone scale. Thus, instead of relying on the traditional tonic-dominant-tonic sequence of harmonies, he often uses a series of chords built on adjacent degrees of the scale. These parallel chains of chords leave the piece without any clearly defined tonal center for extended periods. Other elements of the music must therefore function as form-building devices—particularly rhythm, dynamics, texture, and instrumental timbre.

In one sense, of course, Debussy's style is clearly an offshoot of the romantic movement; the emphasis on color and the lack of interest in traditional forms and procedures are evidence of this, as are the literary associations of most his works. But in another sense, Debussy represents the beginning of the new and radically different music of the twentieth century. His use of nonfunctional harmonies took music into new and uncharted areas, and his freer forms and concentration on timbre influenced almost all later composers.

DEBUSSY: PRÉLUDE À L'APRÈS-MIDI D'UN FAUNE (PRELUDE TO THE AFTERNOON OF A FAUN)
SIDE 10/SELECTION 3 LISTENING GUIDE ON PAGE 345

This brief work was inspired by Mallarmé's poem *L'après-midi d'un faune,* published in 1876. Debussy first intended to write an opera based on the poem but soon abandoned this project for a smaller one; he described the *Prélude* as a "very free illustration of Mallarmé's beautiful poem." The faun of the title is the sensual forest deity of pagan mythology, half man, half goat. Awakening from sleep, his mind befuddled by wine, the faun recalls two nymphs he had seen earlier in the day. Did he carry them off to his lair or was it only a fantasy? "Is it a dream that I love?" he asks. But the afternoon is warm, the effort to remember too great, so once again he drifts off to sleep. Without following the events of the poem literally, Debussy evokes a musical impresson of each scene.

In the *Prélude,* which was his first orchestral work, Debussy had not completely broken with traditional ideas of form; the piece is very roughly in an AA'BA'' pattern, although there is no literal repetition. However, the character and significance of the work lie, not in its formal structure, but in those elements which give it its impressionistic quality.

The choice of instruments is in itself unusual and indicative of the nature of the piece. The winds consist of three flutes, two oboes, English horn, two clarinets, and two bassoons; there are four French horns, but the rest of the brasses (trumpets, trombones, and tuba) are omitted and the percussion is limited to a pair of tiny "antique cymbals," which produce a delicate rather than a smashing sound. Two harps and strings complete the instrumentation.

Debussy also departs from the standard orchestral practice in his *use* of these instruments. Virtually all the main melodic material is assigned to solo winds, primarily flute and oboe, with the French horn also playing an important role. The strings are often muted and divided. The use of the harps helps evoke the langorous atmosphere which is the essence of the piece.

The opening theme is a sensuous melody first played by the solo flute and heard later in various transformations throughout the work.

The lyric theme of the middle section is first located in the wind instruments in unison and repeated later by the strings.

In general the piece has a delicate, restrained, dreamlike quality. The dynamic level is subdued, only occasionally rising to a forte or fortissimo. There are frequent subtle changes of tempo and dynamics, a relaxed, almost vague rhythmic movement without a strong beat, and many dissonant harmonies, which provide color more than a strong sense of progression. All of these contribute to the floating, evocative nature of the work.

Along with Debussy's later orchestral works, the *Prélude* had a profound and lasting effect on the subsequent development of orchestral music.

MAURICE RAVEL

Maurice Ravel (1875–1937) is often linked with Debussy as the other major figure who most fully realized the possibilities of musical impressionism. But Ravel's music, especially the compositions written in his later years, combines the sonorous impressionism of Debussy with a classical orientation toward form and balance.

Philosophically, Ravel had much in common with Debussy. Both composers agreed that music should serve an aesthetic purpose, that the creation of beautiful sound was the ultimate aim. They considered themselves rebels against German romanticism and the Wagnerian school. They shared an attraction to the medieval modes and the novel scales employed by nationalistic composers of other countries. The rhythms of Spanish dance music also intrigued them, as did Oriental modes and colors.

But the similarities between the two composers were limited. While Ravel made use of all the impressionist devices, his compositional procedures were quite different in a number of ways from those of Debussy. There is less use of the whole-tone scale and sparing use of dissonance in Ravel's work. His use of orchestral color is more brilliant and dynamic than Debussy's. For musical texture, he relied on melodic lines rather than on the parallel blocks of sound which Debussy favored. Ravel also displayed a firmer sense of key and employed broader melodies, more distinct harmonic movement, and more emphatic rhythms than his predecessor.

Ravel created many compositions for the piano. *Pavane pour une infante défunte* (*Pavane for a Dead Princess,* 1899), *Jeux d'eaux* (*Fountains,* 1901), and *Miroirs* (1905) are among the works that earned him his reputation as one of the outstanding composers of piano music of the twentieth century.

Songs were also a source of fascination to Ravel, and he continued their composition until the end of his life. *Schéhérazade* (1903) is a song cycle for voice and orchestra. Ravel also succeeded in combining chamber music with voice, as in the *Trois poemes de Stéphane Mallarmé* (1913) and the sensuous *Chansons madécasses* (*Songs of Madagascar,* 1926).

Despite his popular repertoire of piano works, songs, and chamber music, Ravel is unquestionably best-known for his orchestral works. His *Rapsodie espagnole* (*Spanish Rhapsody,* 1907) remains a favorite today. So, too, does his *Mother Goose Suite* (1912) for orchestra, adapted from his own piano composition. One of his most ambitious undertakings was *Daphnis et Chlöe* (1912), a ballet from which were taken two frequently performed orchestral suites. Two of his most enduring compositions are *La valse* (1920) and *Boléro* (1928). In both, the artist made use of unusual elements. *La valse* is notable for its unusual combination of traditional waltz rhythms and arresting and disturbing harmonic and textural elements. *Boléro,* drawing its inspiration from the Spanish dance of the same name, employs a gradual uninterrupted crescendo and a repetitive single melody. To this great body of work must also be added the famous Piano Concerto in G (1931) and the Concerto for the Left Hand (1931), two virtuosic masterpieces.

OTHER TRENDS IN THE EARLY TWENTIETH CENTURY

The effects of Debussy's musical innovations were lasting. Conceptions of tonality broadened in the wake of his break with the harmonic tradition that culminated in the romanticism of the music dramas of Richard Wagner. However, by 1918, the year of Debussy's death, impressionism was giving way to other styles.

A group of young French composers known as "The Six," Georges Auric, Louis Durey, Arthur Honnegger, Darius Milhaud, Francis Poulenc, and Germaine Tailleferre, shared the common goal of creating lighthearted, "simple" music, free of the emotional intensity of romanticism and the vague qualities of impressionism.

Each member of "The Six" composed in a variety of forms and styles. Honnegger's and Poulenc's music became conservative as their careers progressed. Milhaud remained an experimenter. He explored polytonality, incorporated jazz elements, and, late in his career, wrote electronic music. Tailleferre was not an innovator. Her works remained within the original boundaries of the group. She cultivated a style characterized by simple melodies and uncomplicated harmony and rhythm. Auric achieved distinction as a composer of film scores and Durey turned to musicological research instead of composing.

The mentor who brought The Six together was Eric Satie (1866–1925). Like his younger colleagues of The Six, Satie created "unserious" music which was antisentimental and displayed an ironic sense of humor. The objectivity and simplicity of his style are exemplified in his piano music.

In contrast to the objectivity and wit of Satie are the compositions of Lili Boulanger (1893–1918). Her vocal works are passionate settings of themes of humility, sadness, and despair. Her religious works include Psalm settings for various combinations of vocal soloists and orchestra. Her last work, *Pie Jesu* (1918), is scored for solo voice, string quartet, harp, and organ.

Much of her music employs typical romantic techniques such as use of leitmotivs in combination with impressionistic harmonies and flexible rhythmic progressions. Boulanger's song cycle, *Clairières dans le ciel* (*Rifts in the Sky*), is a 1914 setting of thirteen poems from symbolist poet Francis James's poetic cycle *Tristesses* (*Sadnesses*). Boulanger won the Prix de Rome in 1913 for her cantata *Faust et Heline*. Her music was championed by her older sister, Nadia Boulanger, the great recitalist, conductor, and teacher.

Frederick Delius

An English impressionistic composer was Frederick Delius (1862–1934), a man of German extraction who spent much of his adult life in Paris. His style is lush and chromatic, with constantly shifting harmonies. His melodies, however, are rather simple, tonal, and even reminiscent of folk songs. In England, a country which had not been a significant force in music for almost two hundred years, the twentieth century marked the beginning of a musical Renaissance. A few composers early in the century, particularly Edward Elgar and Delius, had adopted the techniques and styles of the continental mainstream, but it remained for Ralph Vaughan Williams to use them in a uniquely English manner.

Ralph Vaughan Williams

Ralph Vaughan Williams (1872–1958) was influenced by Debussy's ambiguous tonalities and emphasis on tone color. He studied orchestration with Ravel. But his interests also extended to English folk music and to the music of the English Renaissance. Moreover, he felt that music was a democratic cultural phenomenon; it belonged to the common people and had to reflect their interests. Vaughan Williams's emphasis on choral music in his early years is a part of the centuries-old tradition of choral singing in Great Britain.

The nationalistic aspect of Vaughan Williams's music is not merely a matter of quoting folk songs; it is a philosophical position that is indirectly expressed in the music. His symphonic style involves a nontraditional approach to tonality, but a generally romantic idiom. His nine symphonies and his other large orchestral works are balanced by an extensive collection of vocal music ranging from simple folk-song settings to large operas, songs, and many choral works, including some with orchestral accompaniment. One of the finest of these is *Dona Nobis Pacem* (1936), whose text is drawn from passages in Walt Whitman, John Bright's "Angel of Death" speech, Latin liturgical prayer, and the Old and New Testaments.

Ethel Smyth

Ethel Smyth (1858–1944) was an English composer who was active in literature and politics as well as music.

Against strong opposition from her parents, Smyth became the first woman to study composition in the Leipzig Conservatory. Her first compositions were so well received that she was quickly accepted into musical circles that included Brahms and Clara Schumann. She wrote her first major work, the Mass in D, in 1891 after which she devoted herself almost entirely to writing operas. Between 1894 and 1925, she wrote six operas including *The Wreckers* (1904), a tragedy about the evil villagers of an isolated Cornish seacoast community. In collaboration with her friend, Henry Brewster, she wrote the libretto in French. She then had it translated into German and finally English in the attempt to make the work acceptable in various opera houses throughout Europe.

Smyth was an interesting writer. Between 1919 and 1940, she published ten books including *A Final Burning of Boats,* containing fascinating accounts of musical life in Europe and England in the late nineteenth and early twentieth centuries.

Manuel de Falla

A Spanish composer who was first influenced by Debussy but later displayed a more classical spirit was Manuel de Falla (1876–1948). His earliest works were strongly nationalistic and employed the idioms of Andalusian folk music and dance very effectively. De Falla spent his last years in South America. His best-known works are the ballet *El amor brujo* (usually translated as *Love the Magician,* 1915), which features the ritual Fire Dance, and *Noches en los jardines de España* (*Nights in the Gardens of Spain,* 1916) for piano and orchestra, which effectively blends the impressionist style with native Spanish musical elements.

Ottorino Respighi

Impressionism also made its mark on an Italian composer, Ottorino Respighi (1879–1936), who studied with Rimsky-Korsakov in Russia before returning to his native land to teach and compose. Both instrumental and vocal music interested him; his most successful opera was *La Fiamma* (1934). He is best known today for his trilogy of nationalistically oriented symphonic poems: *Fontane di Roma* (*The Fountains of Rome,* 1917), *Pini di Roma* (*The Pines of Rome,* 1924), and *Feste Romane* (*Roman Festivals,* 1929).

LISTENING GUIDE

Debussy: *Prélude à l'après-midi d'un faune (Prelude to the Afternoon of a Faun)*

Single Movement: changing tempo
meter irregular and unclear
modified ternary form

Orchestra with modified instrumentation

Review: Example 17.2 (A theme)
Example 17.3 (B theme)
Outline of program, pp. 340–41

A	languid, sensuous flute melody floats down and up; horn calls and harp glissandos; sensuous melody again in flute with quiet tremolo in strings; crescendo in orchestra as intensity builds, then fades away
A'	sensuous melody, flute, with added decoration, accompanied by occasional harp arpeggios
Bridge	splashes of instrumental color through the orchestra grow in volume and animation, suggest faun's awakening senses, then subside; slow, dream-like clarinet solo with delicate strings introduces:
B	lyric, long-breathed melody in woodwinds with gently pulsing string accompaniment; suddenly soft as lyric melody repeats in strings with harp arpeggios and pulsing woodwinds
Bridge	fragments from previous bridge in strings, then in various woodwind colors; solo violin longingly sings beginning of lyric melody
	harp arpeggios accompany flute in anticipation of sensuous melody; woodwind fragments of melody and staccato chords interrupt; harp arpeggios accompany opening of sensuous melody in oboe; again soft interruptions
A''	sensuous melody in flutes, with the delicate ring of antique cymbals and subdued tremolo in strings, yearning solo violin counterpoint; melody repeated in flute and cello, flute wanders drowsily off, melody completed by oboe
Coda	harp and strings in floating, static notes, fragment of sensuous melody in horns, ringing antique cymbals, pizzicato in low strings

SUMMARY

Around the turn of the century the musical culture of France was closely related to the other arts. Two of the dominant movements at the time were impressionism in painting and symbolism in literature, both of which influenced the development of impressionism in music. Impressionist music is characterized by its fragile beauty, sensuous tone colors, subdued atmosphere, and elegance. It cast off the more pompous, heavy, and serious quality of the German tradition. Claude Debussy is the composer primarily associated with impressionistic style. His use of nonfunctional harmonies and free forms led to the development of organizational procedures built around sound patterns and blocks of color. Other organizational devices used by Debussy are rhythm, dynamics, texture, and instrumental color. Maurice Ravel, who is often linked with Debussy, incorporated many impressionistic devices in his music, but also displayed a classical orientation towards form and balance.

Debussy's innovations had a profound impact on a number of composers. By the time of Debussy's death, some composers were rejecting both the vague qualities of impressionism and the emotional intensity of romanticism. Eric Satie and the group of French composers known as "The Six" created light-hearted, antisentimental, and sometimes ironic compositions. Lili Boulanger in France, Frederick Delius, Ralph Vaughan Williams and Ethel Smyth in England, Manual de Falla in Spain, and Ottorino Respighi in Italy all used impressionistic techniques in their music.

NEW TERMS

impressionism
symbolism

SUGGESTED LISTENING

Boulanger, Lili

Clairières dans le ciel (*Rifts in the Sky*). This work is a setting of the thirteen poems from symbolist poet Francis James's poetic cycle *Tristesses* (*Sadnesses*). The songs are about a poet's despair as he mourns the disappearance of his lover. (Leonarda Productions).

Debussy, Claude

Pelléas et Mélisande. An opera in five acts based on a medieval legend. It epitomizes the subtlety of impressionism—each act is a continuum of musical narrative employing leitmotivs.

DeFalla, Manuel

Noches en los jardines de España (*Nights in the Gardens of Spain*). One of the composer's best-known works, this piece for piano and orchestra blends the impressionist style with native Spanish musical elements.

Ravel, Maurice

Daphnis et Chlöe. Ravel's most ambitious work, this "ballet symphony" was commissioned for the Russian ballet.

Vaughan Williams, Ralph

Dona Nobis Pacem. This large work for chorus, soloists, and orchestra is an effective antiwar piece, the text of which draws on poetry by Walt Whitman.

Plate 23 Horace Walpole built Strawberry Hill (1748–72) in the Gothic style, a design favored by romantics because of their fascination with the mystery and heroism of the Middle Ages. The Gothic Revival, especially in church building, continued into the twentieth century. (Rosenthal Art Slides.)

Plate 24 This painting by Henry Fuseli, *Night-Hag Visiting Lapland Witches* (1741–1825) reflects the romantic preoccupation with dreams, fantasies, and hallucinations. The romantics were interested in the "exceptional" rather the "reasonable" side of human nature. (The Metropolitan Museum of Art, purchase, bequest of Lillian S. Timken by exchange, Victor Wilbour Memorial Fund, The Alfred N. Punnett Endowment Fund, Marguand and Curtis Funds, 1980.)

Plate 25 Eugene Delacroix (1798–1863), the leader of the French romantics, rejected the neoclassical style of David and instead used the bright colors and forms of Rubens as his models. He was especially attracted by action-packed scenes in exotic, foreign locales, as shown in this late example, *The Lion Hunt* (1861). (© 1988 The Art Institute of Chicago; Potter Palmer Collection. All rights reserved.)

Plate 26 William Turner's painting of a Swiss avalanche (*The Fall of an Avalanche in the Grisons,* 1810) is typical of his explosive, highly abstracted scenes that reflected the power of nature. His practice of painting light and atmosphere in patches of pure color anticipated the impressionists by about forty years. (The Tate Gallery, London.)

Plate 27 The Arc de Triomphe (1833–36) was a huge monument to the victories of Napoleon, modeled after the imperial arches of ancient Rome. (© John S. Flannery/Bruce Coleman, Inc.)

Plate 28 When Claude Monet's *Impression: Sunrise* was exhibited in 1874, one critic who was appalled by its "unfinished" qualities denounced the new style and coined the term "impressonism" in disgust. (Scala/Art Resource.)

Plate 29 In the 1880s French artists, using impressionism as a starting point, developed far more radical designs. Vincent van Gogh's late paintings of the dazzling light and color of the Provençal countryside—as in *The Starry Night* (1889)—demonstrate the agitation and emotional power of his highly individual style. (Collection, The Museum of Modern Art, New York; acquired through the Lillie P. Bliss Bequest.)

Plate 30 Pablo Picasso's *Les Demoiselles d'Avignon,* painted in 1907, fractures and dislocates form into planes and geometrical blocks. Early critics dubbed the new style cubism. The figures on the right reflect the influence of African sculpture. (Collection, The Museum of Modern Art, New York; acquired through the Lillie P. Bliss Bequest.)

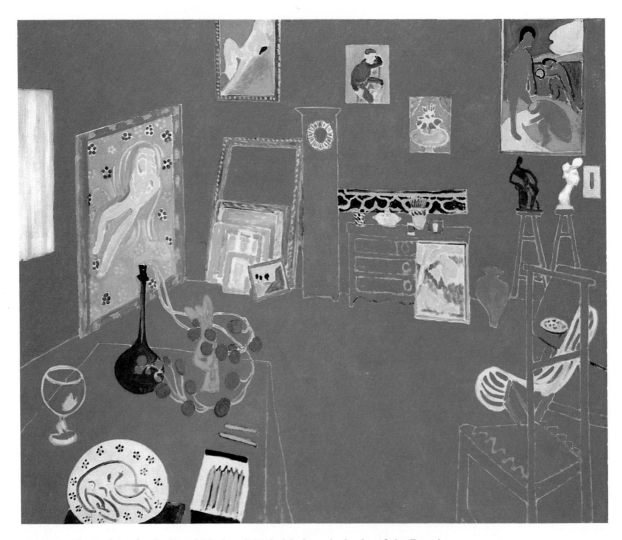

Plate 31 *The Red Studio,* by Henri Matisse (1911). Matisse, the leader of the French expressionists, painted through a long career in bright, decorative color. He said he wanted an art "of purity and serenity, devoid of troubling or depressing subject matter." (Collection, The Museum of Modern Art, New York; Mrs. Simon Guggenheim Fund.)

Plate 35 *The Last of the Buffalo* (ca. 1885), by Albert Bierstadt. In the nineteenth century, Americans living in Eastern cities provided artists with an enthusiastic audience for exotic and dramatic scenes of Western life and landscapes. In 1800 the American frontier was just beyond the Appalachians; by 1900 it was gone. (Corcoran Gallery of Art; gift of Mrs. Albert Bierstadt, 1909.)

Plate 36 Augustus Saint-Gaudens's *Memorial to Robert Shaw,* a relief depicting a triumphant Civil War colonel and his black regiment, was erected in 1897 and reveals the American taste for patriotic and commemorative sculpture at the end of the nineteenth century. (R. Avery/Stock Boston.)

Plate 37 As shown in his *Early Sunday Morning* (1930), Edward Hopper painted harsh, simplified forms in flat, bright light. Although his paintings have an "abstract" quality, Hopper remained distant from the experiments of such European innovators as Picasso and Matisse. (Collection, Whitney Museum of American Art; Purchase with funds from Gertrude Vanderbilt Whitney.)

Plate 38 Frank Lloyd Wright designed the Kaufman House at Bear Run, Pennsylvania (1936–37) as an organic extension of nature. Massive cantilevers support the floors that hover above the waterfall; a skeleton of concrete, glass, and native rock further integrates the house with the landscape. (Western Pennsylvania Conservancy/Art Resource.)

Plate 39 *Janitor's Holiday,* by Paul Starrett Sample (1936). This gentle scene of a New England countryside is an example of the nostalgic regionalism of many American painters in the 1930s. Their work celebrated, often in sentimental fashion, purely American subjects. (The Metropolitan Museum of Art; Arthur Hearn Fund, 1937.)

Plate 40 The Breakers at Newport, Rhode Island (1893–95), built by McKim, Mead, and White for the Vanderbilt family, was the grandest of all the palaces commissioned by American industrialists in the late nineteenth century. (Photo by Richard Cheek/The Preservation Society of Newport County.)

Neoclassical composers often avoided the huge romantic orchestra in favor of smaller instrumental combinations. They preferred absolute music, which received its impetus from purely musical ideas, to the descriptive elements so prevalent in romantic and impressionistic music. They looked on musical composition as an intellectual challenge to be approached systematically and rationally, with irrelevant emotions held in check. The neoclassical composers were especially attracted to the forms of the baroque and classical periods. But they did not simply resurrect these old forms; they varied them to develop a new and distinctly modern idiom.

STRAVINSKY'S WORK

Stravinsky's work constitutes a unique variety of styles, genres, musical forms, and instrumental combinations. By and large his most popular works continue to be the music he composed for three early ballets, written before World War I. These works, which include Russian and Oriental elements, are characterized by exotic and colorful melodies and harmonies, glittering orchestration, and striking, often primitive-sounding rhythmic patterns.

Most of the works that he wrote between 1913 and 1923—including three ballets as well as some short piano pieces, songs, and chamber music—were scored for small instrumental ensembles of various types. One of his most popular works for stage composed during this period is *L'histoire du soldat* (*The Soldier's Tale*, 1918), "to be read, played, and danced"; it is scored for a chamber ensemble of only seven instruments.

His ballet *Pulcinella* (1919), based on music by the eighteenth-century composer Giovanni Battista Pergolesi, and the *Octet for Wind Instruments* (1923) began his neoclassical period, which lasted until 1951. His compositions during this long creative period incorporate references to many older materials and styles, all transformed in a uniquely Stravinskian way. Many of these works demonstrate an austere style, clear—even dry—texture, and meticulous craftsmanship. Some show the influence of jazz; others make a deliberate return to baroque or classical models; still others represent an attempt to strip music of any subjective or emotional appeal whatever. The opera *Oedipus Rex* (1927) is based on the ancient Greek tragedy. *The Rake's Progress* (1950), titled after a series of engravings by the English artist William Hogarth and structured after the conventions of Italian opera, represents the essence of neoclassicism.

The most important orchestral works to come out of Stravinsky's neoclassical period include Symphonies of Wind Instruments (1920), Concerto for Piano and Wind Orchestra (1924), *Dumbarton Oaks Concerto* (Concerto in E-flat, 1938), Symphony in C (1940), and Symphony in Three Movements (1945).

Stravinsky's first major choral work, an undisputed masterpiece, was the *Symphony of Psalms* (1930), written for chorus and orchestra. This three-movement setting of three psalms exhibits several innovations in tonality and rhythm. Instead of being based on traditional functions (such as the tonic-dominant relationship), the tonality is established by the frequent repetition of a particular pitch as a center of reference. An important structural technique is the simultaneous use of several different *ostinato* patterns (persistently repeated figures) as building blocks; these patterns overlap and produce shifting accents and conflicting rhythms.

During the early years of the twentieth century, many artists and intellectual leaders became fascinated with nonliterate, "primitive" cultures. Henri Matisse and Pablo Picasso incorporated into their early paintings the stylized forms of African sculpture (see plate 30). Similarly, Stravinsky's imagination was stirred by the frenzied, irregular rhythms found in non-Western music. *The Rite of Spring,* the third in the series of ballet scores written by Stravinsky for Diaghilev's Ballets Russes, is perhaps the premier example of musical **primitivism.** Subtitled *Pictures of Pagan Russia,* it depicts the cruelty of the primitive Russian peasants' rites to celebrate the coming of spring, culminating in the sacrifice of a young virgin, who dances herself to death while the tribal elders watch.

The Rite of Spring was a revolutionary landmark in the history of musical style. Its unconventional use of the large orchestra, its dramatic rhythmic complexities and its consistent use of dissonant harmonies made the ballet a wild and exciting piece of music—one that confounded the Parisian audience at its first performance in 1913 and one that greatly influenced successive generations of composers.

The instrumentation for which Stravinsky composed *The Rite of Spring* is unusually large[1] consisting of:

2 piccolos	8 French horns
3 flutes	5 trumpets
1 alto flute	1 bass trumpet
4 oboes	3 trombones
2 English horns	4 tubas
4 bassoons	large percussion section
2 contrabassoons	very large string section

Stravinsky draws upon the richness and variety of sounds available to him in such a large ensemble to portray the quality of primitive ceremonies his imagination conjured up—"I saw in imagination a solemn pagan rite: wise elders, seated in a circle, watching a young girl dance herself to death. They were sacrificing her to propitiate the god of spring." As was the case with Hector Berlioz in the romantic period, Stravinsky's orchestration was an integral part of the process of composition and Stravinsky exploits the lowest and highest registers of the instruments (particularly woodwinds) to produce unorthodox sounds in portraying primitive actions and scenes.

The rhythmic complexity in *The Rite of Spring* was an aspect of the work that confused and alienated early audiences but fired the imagination of musicians and composers. Very often the number of beats in the measure changes resulting in a series of measures of *different* sizes:

$$\frac{7}{8} \ \frac{3}{8} \ \frac{5}{8} \ \frac{3}{8} \ \frac{4}{8} \ \frac{5}{8} \ \frac{6}{8} \ \frac{5}{8} \ \text{etc.}$$

[1]In order to facilitate performance of *The Rite of Spring* by orchestras of moderate size, a revised edition with reduced instrumentation was published in 1974.

An even greater degree of rhythmic complexity results when the value of the beat itself varies—

$$\frac{7}{8} \quad \frac{3}{4} \quad \frac{6}{8} \quad \frac{2}{4} \quad \frac{6}{8} \quad \frac{3}{4} \text{ etc.}$$

—a complexity that is often compounded by the use of syncopation.

Its rhythmic complexity combined with a high degree of harmonic dissonance and vagueness of tonality mark *The Rite of Spring* as a forerunner in the development of twentieth-century music.

The piece is laid out in two large parts, each of which has several contrasting movements (scenes) that follow each other without pause. The first half is called "Worship of the Earth"; after a slow introduction, the scenes are "Auguries of Spring—Dances of the Young Girls," "The Ritual of Abduction," "Roundelays of Spring," "Contest of Rival Clans," "Cortege of the Sage," and "The Sage—Dance of the Earth." The second part, "The Great Sacrifice," opens with a long slow introduction ("The Pagan Night") followed by five movements entitled "Mystic Circle Dance of the Young Girls," "Glorification of the Chosen One," "Evocation of the Ancestors," "Ritual Dance of the Ancestors," and "Sacrificial Dance."

SIDE 11/SELECTION 1
LISTENING GUIDE
ON PAGES 337–78

Part I Worship of the Earth

A. Introduction   The introduction is dominated by woodwinds, French horns and trumpet; the strings have a minor role; the rest of the brass and percussion are not involved at all. It begins with a solo bassoon in its highest register

and is immediately followed by English horn.

Example 18.2

Example 18.1 From Igor Stravinsky, *Le sacre du printemps.* Copyright 1921 by Edition Russe de Musique. Copyright assigned 1947 to Boosey & Hawkes, Inc. Reprinted by permission of Boosey & Hawkes, Inc.

Additional prominent melodic materials are added as the movement progresses.

Example 18.3

Example 18.4

Example 18.5

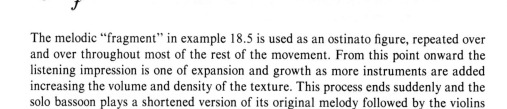

The melodic "fragment" in example 18.5 is used as an ostinato figure, repeated over and over throughout most of the rest of the movement. From this point onward the listening impression is one of expansion and growth as more instruments are added increasing the volume and density of the texture. This process ends suddenly and the solo bassoon plays a shortened version of its original melody followed by the violins stating a figure which links the introduction to the next movement.

Example 18.6

This violin figure becomes an ostinato figure throughout most of the second movement; at times quite prominent, at other instances barely audible as part of the general background.

    B. Auguries of Spring—Dances of the Young Girls   A strong rhythmic pattern is established by the strings repeating the same dissonant chord with strong, irregular accents (>) which are intensified by the French horns.

Example 18.7

During the first portion of this movement, the material in example 18.7 is used as the constant part of an alternating scheme. Each time it appears it becomes background against which new melodic material is introduced.

Example 18.8

The second phrase of the melody introduced by bassoons (example 18.8) is used contrapuntally by bassoons, trombones, and oboes, bringing the music to a surprising halt.

For the rest of the movement, the violin motive (♪♩ ♩♪) in one form or another is used as an ostinato figure, repeated over and over, against which other melodic material is added:

Example 18.9

and finally:

Example 18.10

The rest of the movement is one huge crescendo to the "end," which is the "beginning" of the next movement. Here again, the movement does not end in the normal sense. It simply "gives up" in suspense and we go on to something else.

C. The Ritual of Abduction   The beginning of this section comes as the climactic end of the previous movement. In fact, the listening impression interprets movement C as a kind of fast coda of movement B, leaving it to the dancers on stage to define the character of this stretch of music (C) as a separate structural unit.

The music of "The Ritual of Abduction" is very fast (presto) and loud and changes both the beat and measure frequently—

9 4 5 7 3
8 8 8 8 4—

and uses the full orchestra.

Again there is increasing momentum to the end of the movement which of course, again, does not really end but is tied into the beginning of the next movement.

D. Roundelays of Spring   Like much of Stravinsky's music, this movement is sectional and makes extensive use of repetition as a form-building technique, as a method of exploiting short rhythmic/melodic ideas and as a way of creating tonal centers.

"Roundelays of Spring" clearly consists of four distinct sections—1, 2, 3, and 1a. Sections 1 and 1a are virtually identical and unify the entire section into one complete whole. Sections 2 and 3 provide strong contrasts with each other and with 1.

The way in which these sections relate to each other can be seen in example 18.11.

Example 18.11

	Section 1	**Section 2**	**Section 3**
Length	brief (6 measures)	long (36 measures)	short (13 measures)
Tempo	moderately slow	moderate	very fast (Vivo)
Dynamic Level	piano	piano-fortissimo	fortissimo
Texture	thin	moderate to thick	moderate
Instrumentation	flutes & clarinets	partial to full	thin to full
Mood	calm	insistent/growing	whirlwind

Section 2 is a fascinating example of Stravinsky's practice of using repetition as a way of expanding rhythmic/melodic ideas. It begins with a small "germ" consisting of one measure in which an E-flat chord is played on the downbeat by lower strings and winds, followed by a chord played by upper strings on beats 2, 3, and 4 against a syncopated figure played by cellos, violas, and bass clarinets.

Example 18.12

With the exception of two brief instances when contrasting material is introduced, the entire second section consists of the repetition and expansion of this germinal idea. In the first part of the section, the idea is expanded as follows:

Example 18.13

With each statement the idea grows in length and in expressiveness.

After a brief exchange with the previous contrasting material, the full orchestra takes up the lengthened phrase. Increased volume and harmonic dissonance convey rising tension and excitement climaxing in a suspenseful lingering on a long chord ƒ after which the third section begins its whirlwind drive to the reappearance of section 1a, ending the movement.

The kind of thematic "development" encountered in the second section of this movement is quite different from the development sections in the sonata-allegro movements of Mozart, Beethoven, and Brahms. With Stravinsky it is not a matter of manipulating the theme through various development processes. Rather it is a matter of constant and insistent *repetition* that intensifies and expands the thematic material, all the while building to greater levels of emotional tension and excitement. In addition it is often the case that Stravinsky establishes and maintains a tonal center not through the dominant-tonic relationship of the major-minor system but through repetition. For instance, in section 2 of "Roundelays of Spring," the first beat of each measure is occupied by an E♭ chord, anchoring everything that happens to E♭ as the tonic.

The culminating movement of this exciting work is, of course, the finale of part 2, the "Sacrificial Dance" in which the chosen one dances herself to death. Stravinsky's use of the musical materials to create and sustain the frenzied atmosphere demanded by the ballet plot is masterful. What on first hearing may seem chaotic, is in fact a carefully crafted piece of music. Cast in five part alternating form ABAC²A, the movement employs and epitomizes the techniques already encountered in the work: sectionalization, repetition, rhythmic complexity, harmonic dissonance, obscure tonal center, and unconventional use of the orchestra.

Although *The Rite of Spring* was conceived of as a ballet, today it is most often performed as a tone poem, a concert piece for orchestra without dancers. As an artistic conception it stands as an early twentieth-century masterpiece; one that had a profound impact on generations of composers.

²Section C includes a brief quotation from section A.

The leading German composer of the first half of the twentieth century was Paul Hindemith. He was born in the town of Hanau, just outside of Frankfurt, Germany.

He began violin lessons at nine, learned to play other instruments, and was soon composing in a steady stream that was to make him among the most prolific of twentieth-century composers. At the Conservatory in Frankfurt he became close friends with the violin teacher Adolf Rebner, who helped him obtain a position as violinist in the Frankfurt Opera orchestra, which was conducted by Ludwig Rottenberg. In 1924, Hindemith married Rottenberg's daughter, Gertrude.

During his years with the opera orchestra, Hindemith gradually began to break with the highly chromatic styles of Wagner and Strauss. His song cycle *Das Marienleben* (*The Life of Mary,* 1923) was a landmark in his development as a composer, revealing a style devoid of romantic traits. During the late 1920s he became interested in creating music that amateurs could not only listen to, but also play and sing. He began composing in a technically simple, melodically appealing style which came to be termed *Gebrauchsmusik* ("use music") because it was intended to be played (used) in the home by amateurs rather than by professional virtuosos.

Following the performance of his large-scale opera *Cardillac* at Dresden in 1926, Hindemith's reputation as a composer spread throughout Germany. The following year he took a teaching position at the Berlin Hochschule für Musik, which he held until 1935.

With the rise of the Nazi party in Germany in the 1930s, Hindemith found himself under attack as a "cultural Bolshevik" and as an associate of Jewish musicians. When the performance of his opera *Mathis der maler* (*Matthias the Painter,* 1932–1935) was banned in Germany, the premiere of this work took place in Zürich, Switzerland, in 1938.

Hindemith made his first appearance in America in 1937 and toured the country from 1938 to 1939. In 1940, when he was appointed to the music faculty of Yale University, he decided to settle in this country, becoming an

Figure 18.3 In addition to composing works in virtually all the traditional genres, Hindemith made an extremely valuable contribution as a teacher of composition and music theory.

American citizen six years later. He did not return to Germany until 1949, when he conducted the Berlin Philharmonic in a performance of his own works. In 1953 he moved back to Europe, teaching at the University of Zürich and conducting concerts throughout Germany and Austria. He died in Frankfurt on December 23, 1963, at the age of sixty-eight.

HINDEMITH'S WORK

In many respects, Hindemith's music is conservative. Tonality, harmonic tension (consonance/dissonance), rhythmic patterns, and texture (homophony/polyphony) were calculated to serve the formal plan of the work. For the most part, Hindemith conceived his music in terms of traditional formal procedures: contrasting themes in different tonalities often connected by transitions (bridges), development, and confirmation of thematic materials. Much of his music employs traditional contrapuntal devices as part of the theme or as a method of developing thematic material. His music is a rational combination of traditional formal concepts with new harmonic, tonal, and rhythmic elements characteristic of twentieth-century music.

Hindemith wrote in virtually all traditional genres of music and contributed important works to the twentieth-century repertoire of almost all musical instruments. He wrote extensively for the piano including several sonatas and *Ludis Tonalis,* subtitled "Studies in Counterpoint, Tonal Organization, and Piano Playing."

His ten operas include *Mathis der maler* (*Matthias the Painter*). The orchestra suite of excerpts from this opera and the *Symphonic Metamorphosis on Themes by Weber,* and the dance compositions, *The Four Temperaments* and *Nobilissima Visione* on St. Francis of Assisi, are his best known works for orchestra. His vocal works include *Das Marienleber* (*The Life of Mary*), a song cycle for soprano and piano and the large-scale choral-orchestral work, *When Lilacs Last in the Dooryard Bloom'd,* an American requiem with text from Walt Whitman.

Hindemith's chamber music is extensive and includes sonatas for solo instruments, duos and trios, seven string quartets, and a series of works for miscellaneous instrumental ensembles, the most well-known of which is *Kleine Kammermusik* for five wind instruments.

This quintet from Hindemith's set of miscellaneous chamber works written in 1922 is one of his most delightful pieces and illustrates his early style. It is written for the traditional woodwind quintet instrumentation: flute (piccolo), oboe, clarinet, French horn, and bassoon.

The piece consists of five contrasting movements. The outer movements are fast, the second is a waltz and the fourth is very short and humorous. The middle movement is slow and lyrical.

First Movement (Jolly)

Like much of Hindemith's music, this movement has clearly recognizable themes which are developed in a fairly traditional manner. The first section of the movement is based upon the theme first put forth by the clarinet.

**HINDEMITH:
KLEINE
KAMMERMUSIK FÜR
FÜNF BLÄSER
(*LITTLE CHAMBER
MUSIC FOR FIVE
WINDS*) OP. 24, NO. 2.**

*SIDE 11/SELECTION 2
LISTENING GUIDE
ON PAGE 379*

Example 18.14

Against this melodic material in the clarinet, the horn and bassoon joined by the oboe have a rhythmical accompaniment based upon ♩♫. This rhythmic figure is constant throughout most of the movement. The first theme is taken up and extended by the oboe, climaxing with the entrance of the flute which eventually states the full first theme. This is followed by a short bridge in which the rhythmic and melodic activity is reduced, preparing for the entrance of the second theme played by the oboe and then the oboe and flute together.

Example 18.15

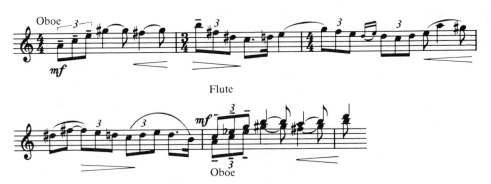

This leads directly into the development of elements from themes 1 and 2, with a slowing down of tempo, a decrescendo, and thinning of instrumental texture followed by an increase of tempo while the clarinet picks up a fragment of theme 1. What sounds at first like a recapitualtion is in fact more development followed by what sounds like a "real" recapitulation of the first theme played by the oboe. The first theme is shortened and gradually fragmented coming to a complete stop.

After this pause, the bassoon enters in a slow and free tempo on the first part of theme 2 joined to material from the first theme. This is followed by a surprise entry of the clarinet in fast tempo with a final thematic fragment.

Example 18.16

Second Movement: Waltz

This lilting waltz is divided into several short sections in an alternating scheme: AA′BCBA′ coda. The first section (A) features the clarinet.

Example 18.17

MUSIC OF THE EARLY TWENTIETH CENTURY

A′ is essentially a repetition of A except that the piccolo replaces the flute in this movement. The short B section features the oboe and prepares the way for the lyrical C section in which the French horn is prominent with a rhythm that conflicts with the waltz's *one*-two-three, *one*-two-three.

Example 18.18

Clarinet and Bassoon

This conflict in rhythmic pattern imparts a subtle tension to what seemed to be a simple dance tune.

After a brief interval in which the oboe is prominent, the beginning of C is repeated with the addition of a rhythmic pattern:  added by the oboe. This leads smoothly into the reappearance of the B section which in turn moves gently into the A′ section in which the piccolo is the primary instrument.

The coda is characterized by a slowing of tempo to "lento" (very slow) paving the way for a surprise when the tempo is suddenly fast to end the movement.

Third Movement (Quietly)

The strong contrast between movements is intensified by the third movement, the elegant, soft, slow movement, providing a beautiful example of Hindemith's skill in spinning out long and fascinating melodies.

In broad outline the movement is an alternating form: A B bridge A coda. Both large sections (A and B) are sectionalized:

A	B	bridge	A	coda
aba′c	dd′		ac	a(d)

The primary material of A (a and a′) is:

Example 18.19

Flute

the b material is an interlude between the statements of a and a′, and the c material is a modulating transition to the second large section, B, which begins after a slight pause.

Section B consists of a quiet ostinato figure for flute, clarinet, and muted French horn:

Section B

against which the oboe plays a long, expressive melody.

Example 18.20

This is immediately followed by an exact repetition of the same music with the addition of the bassoon doubling the oboe two octaves below.

A short bridge in which the flute is prominent takes us back to the A section which this time consists only of a and c. After a short pause, the muted French horn takes up a shortened version of the previous ostinato figure while the upper winds concentrate on several statements of the beginning of the A theme.

Fourth Movement (Fast)

This very brief movement is based on a very simple plan: a short and pounding two-measure ritornello

Example 18.21

alternates with solos for each instrument in turn; flute, bassoon, clarinet, oboe, and French horn. The solo passages are very well suited to the particular characteristics of each instrument.

Fifth Movement (Very Fast)

The final movement is a dramatic climax to this chamber piece. Its length, dynamic range, extreme pitch registers, degree of dissonance, and structure make it the culmination of everything before. It is organized around several contrasting thematic ideas in the following plan:

A B bridge C B A bridge coda

The A theme is itself a small aba complex consisting of a loud emphatic phrase (a) with strong accents followed by a soft legato passage (b) and a return to (a).

Example 18.22

The B section is characterized by the rhythmic tension between a syncopated melody in the upper parts against a very regular bass line.

Example 18.23

The music dwells on this rhythmical complex for some time with both gradual and abrupt changes of dynamics. A sudden change to piano marks the beginning of the long bridge

Example 18.24

which makes a smooth transition to the C section. C consists of two ideas which alternate. The first is a solo flute melody against a smooth ostinato in the lower parts.

Example 18.25

The second alternates with the first and provides a transition to the return of B.

The movement ends convincingly with repeated chords expressing a clear tonic that imparts a sense of finality.

Figure 18.4 Although
Benjamin Britten
composed a good deal of
instrumental music, his
finest compositions are
those for voices, either
solo or in chorus.

BENJAMIN BRITTEN

The most outstanding English composer of the twentieth century was Benjamin Britten (1913–1976). In spite of a considerable output in instrumental music, Britten's best works were composed for voices or voices and instruments. Indeed, Britten is widely regarded as a master at setting English texts to music, in the tradition and, at times, the manner of his great English predecessor, Henry Purcell. His operas, particularly *Peter Grimes* (1945), are among the best twentieth-century works in the traditional operatic format.

Britten's style bears an original stamp. Superficially, his music is rather simple and appealing, with a wide variety of forms and procedures and an essentially tonal harmonic language. But beneath the surface lie complex and carefully worked out structures.

Britten's *War Requiem* (1963) is an outstanding example of the elaborate forces that may be involved. This work juxtaposes the Latin text of the Mass for the Dead with antiwar poems in English by Wilfred Owen, a young soldier-poet who wrote and died during World War I. This contrast is reflected in the orchestration: the traditional Latin text is performed by full orchestra, chorus, boys' choir, and solo soprano; the English poetry is assigned to tenor and baritone soloists (representing soldiers) and a separate chamber orchestra. The styles employed range from Gregorian chant to fugue to aria. The result is a highly dramatic work depicting the horror of war in a unique and very moving way.

Almost all of Britten's major works involve voices, either solo or chorus. Some are on a large scale, particularly the *Spring Symphony* (1949), and *Ballad for Heroes* (1939) an unusually effective antiwar piece for large orchestra, chorus, and soloist.

One of Britten's best-known works is *A Ceremony of Carols,* written in 1942. The piece was originally composed for boys' chorus (SSA) and harp but was later arranged for mixed chorus (SATB), also with harp. In it Britten welded together an exquisite selection of medieval carol texts in the form of choruses, a recitative, a solo movement, a duet, and an interlude for harp solo. All these pieces are framed by a processional and recessional consisting of an unaccompanied chant sung by the soprano section of the chorus at the beginning and end of the composition. The general character of the piece is joyous and festive, qualities that have made *A Ceremony of Carols* an extremely popular piece, particularly at the Christmas season.

A CEREMONY OF CAROLS

Britten made several important contributions to the literature of orchestrally accompanied song, the best known of which is *Serenade for Tenor, Horn, and Strings,* op. 31 composed in 1943. The piece was written for the virtuoso hornist, Dennis Brain, and tenor, Peter Pears, an intimate associate of Britten.

BRITTEN: SERENADE FOR TENOR, HORN, AND STRINGS, OP. 31

For this work, Britten combined six poems by different authors: Ben Jonson (1572–1637), Charles Cotton (1630–1687), William Blake (1775–1827), John Keats (1795–1821), Alfred Tennyson (1809–1892), and an anonymous poet of the fifteenth century. Although different in style and historical period, these poems have in common aspects of night, the prevailing theme of the song cycle.

Throughout his life, Britten was sensitive to words and challenged by the task of setting them to music. The musical setting he provided for these separate poems galvanized them into one unified expressive whole.

The settings of the poems are framed by a Prologue and Epilogue played by the solo horn, on stage at the beginning, off stage from a distance at the end. Although these sections are exactly the same, they differ greatly in impact—the Epilogue is colored by all the music that separates it from its twin, and it comes from a distance, as an echo of the Prologue, enhancing the emotional flavor of the conclusion.

SIDE 12/SELECTION 1

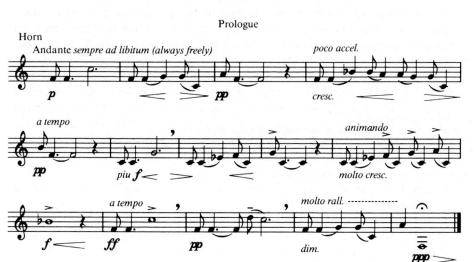

Example 18.26
Examples 18.26–18.35 from *Serenade, Opus 31, for Tenor, Horns and Strings* by Benjamin Britten. © Copyright 1944 by Hawkes and Son (London) Ltd.; copyright renewed. Reprinted by Boosey & Hawkes, Inc.

PASTORAL

(COTTON)

The Day's grown old; the fainting Sun
Has but a little way to run,
And yet his Steeds, with all his skill,
Scarce lug the Chariot down the hill.

The shadows now so long do grow,
That brambles like tall cedars show;
Molehills seem mountains and the ant
Appears a monstrous elephant.

A very little, little flock
Shades thrice the ground that it would stock;
Whilst the small stripling following them
Appears a mighty Polypheme.[3]

And now on benches all are sat,
In the cool air to sit and chat,
Till Phoebus,[4] dipping in the West,
Shall lead the way to rest.

Pastoral centers on night as the ending of the day—the fading sun with distorting shadows, closing with the god of light dipping in the west, leading the world to rest. Britten represents the day-ending flavor effectively. Out of the four stanzas of the poem, he fashions a three-part musical form:

A	B	A
stanzas one & two	stanza three	stanza four

The pastoral mood is established by muted strings which provide a gently syncopated introduction which continues as background against which the tenor sings a melody that beautifully reflects both the inflection and the spirit of the words. The downward movement of the voice on "The Day's grown old" is echoed by the horn.

---

[3]Cyclops—one-eyed giant
[4]Phoebus Apollo—Olympian god of light; originally a god of shepherds and flocks.

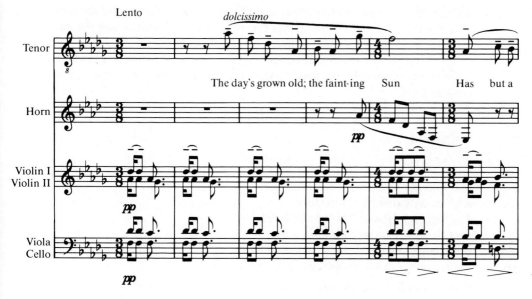

Example 18.27

The horn continues to interject this sunset motive throughout the A section and into the B section.

At the beginning of the B section, the tempo becomes faster, the strings have contrasting material played pizzicato (plucked), and the voice takes on a playful character while the horn continues to dwell on the sunset motive

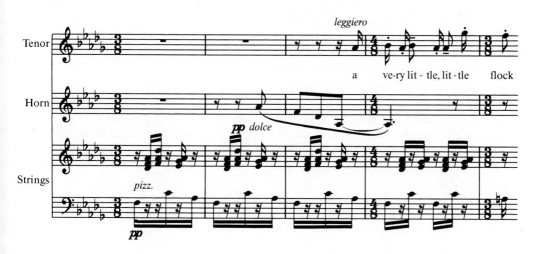

Example 18.28

until it is used to characterize the words "appears a mighty Polypheme" by sounding a low tone which is held and rearticulated through the rest of the B section and through the repeated A section to the very end of the piece. Meanwhile the tenor and strings, at the words, "And now on benches, . . ." resume the music of section A, the violins taking over the sunset motive in place of the horn. At the very end of the movement, after the voice is finished, the strings return to the initial motive and the horn "sets the sun" one final syncopated time to close the movement.

It is typical of Britten that tempo, texture, rhythmic patterns, melodic contour, consonance/dissonance, and tonality serve the essence of the poetry in a well balanced musical form.

SIDE 12/SELECTION 1   **NOCTURNE**

(TENNYSON)

The splendor falls on castle walls
And snowy summits old in story:
The long light shakes[5] across the lakes,
And the wild cataract[6] leaps in glory;
Blow, bugle, blow, set the wild echoes flying,
Bugle, blow, answer, echoes, answer, dying.

O hark, O hear! how thin and clear,
And thinner, clearer, farther going!
O sweet and far from cliff and scar[7]
The horns of Elfland faintly blowing!
Blow, let us hear the purple glens replying:
Bugle, blow; answer, echoes, answer, dying.

O love, they die in yon rich sky,
They faint on hill or field or river:
Our echoes roll from soul to soul
And grow for ever and for ever.
Blow, bugle, blow, set the wild echoes flying,
And answer, echoes, answer, dying.

Britten takes ingenious advantage of the structure of this poem: the first three lines of each stanza receive similar but not identical melodic treatment; each fourth line ends with the tenor singing a fanfare-like figure which leads to a cadenza in which the voice and horn answer each other, the horn adopting the fanfare in response to the voice.

[5]trembles
[6]waterfall
[7]bare rocks on the side of a mountain

Example 18.29

and the wild cat-ar-act leaps in glo - ry: Blow bu-gle,

p accel.------- rit.

blow,   set the wild ech-oes fly-ing,   Bu-gle, blow,

più f

In each stanza the cadenza increases in intensity (tempo and volume), climaxing at "answer, echoes, answer," after which the music subsides through successive "dying, dying, dying."

With the exception of this dynamic pattern in the cadenza, the second stanza is pianissimo and, in the cadenza, the horn is muted, intensifying the contrast of the second section to the first and last.

ELEGY

SIDE 12/SELECTION 1

(BLAKE)

O Rose, thou art sick;
The invisible worm
That flies in the night,
In the howling storm,
Has found out thy bed
Of crimson joy;
And his dark secret love
Does thy life destroy.

Britten exploits the interval of the half step and the fluctuation between major and minor harmony to symbolize the intense images in Blake's grim poem. In particular, he manipulates the half step between G and G♯ as it distinguishes an E *major* chord with a G♯ or an E *minor* chord with a G♮.

The movement is laid out as a three-part plan:

A	B	A
horn and strings	*voice and strings*	*horn and strings*
	recitative	*exact repetition of A*
		with a short extension

The A section features the solo horn playing a long melody that employs the extremes of the horn range and makes repeated use of the half step in establishing and maintaining the sentiment of the poem.

Example 18.30

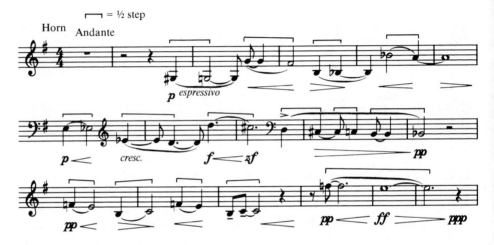

The voice takes up the half step progression (G♯–G♮) at the beginning of the recitative on "O Rose," changing the underlying E chord from major to minor. And at the end on "life destroys" the reverse, G♮–G♯, prepares the way for the reentrance of the horn with its G♯–G♮ to begin the repetition of A.

Example 18.31

MUSIC OF THE EARLY TWENTIETH CENTURY

The emotional quality of this movement is intensified at the very end when the horn dwells on the half step motion:

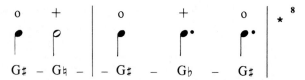

finally ending the movement in E major.

DIRGE

(ANONYMOUS, 15TH CENTURY)

This ae[9] nighte, this ae nighte,
Every nighte and alle,
Fire and fleet[10] and candle-lighte,
And Christe receive thy saule.[11]

When thou from hence away art past,
Every nighte and alle,
To Whinny-muir[12] thou com'st at last;
And Christe receive thy saule.

If ever thou gav'st hos'n and shoon,[13]
Ever nighte and alle,
Sit thee down and put them on;
And Christe receive thy saule.

If hos'n and shoon thou ne'er gav'st nane,[14]
Every nighte and alle,
The whinnes[15] sall prick thee to the bare bane;[16]
And Christe receive thy saule.

From Whinny-muir when thou may'st pass,
Every nighte and alle,
To Brig o'Dread[17] thou com'st at last;
And Christe receive thy saule.

[8]o = open bell
 + = stopped bell by right hand of player, producing a muffled, eerie sound
[9]ae—one
[10]fleet—should be *sleete* for salt, a plate of which was placed on the breast of the corpse as a symbol of enduring life and to keep away the devil.
[11]saule—soul
[12]Whinny-muir—a moor of prickly plants
[13]hos'n and shoon—stockings and shoes
[14]nane—none
[15]whinnes—prickly plants
[16]bane—bone
[17]Brig o'Dread—Bridge of dread

From Brig o'Dread when thou may'st pass,
Every nighte and alle,
To Purgatory fire thou com'st at last;
And Christe receive thy saule.

If ever thou gav'st meat or drink,
Every nighte and alle,
The fire sall never make thee shrink;
And Christe receive thy saule.

If meat or drink thou ne'er gav'st nane,
Every nighte and alle,
The fire will burn thee to the bare bane;
And Christe receive thy saule.

This ae nighte, this ae nighte,
Every nighte and alle,
Fire and fleet and candle-lighte,
And Christe receive thy saule.

The half step G♮–G♯ ending *Elegy* is recast as G♮–A♭ (the same half-step notated differently) and used to generate the melodic material that begins *Dirge*.

Example 18.32

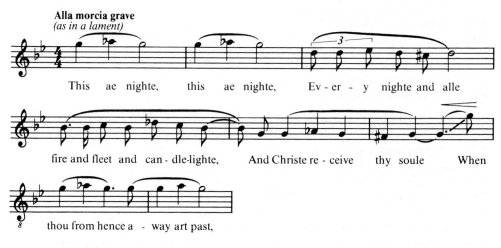

All nine stanzas are sung to this melody. Against it, Britten writes an instrumental fugue using as a subject:

Example 18.33

MUSIC OF THE EARLY TWENTIETH CENTURY

The fugal process of successive entrances and development of the subject increases the momentum which climaxes with the entrance of the fugue subject by the horn at "From Brig o'Dread" in the tenor. This is followed by a gradual relaxation until only the tenor and string basses with a fragment of the fugue subject remain to end the movement, pianissimo.

HYMN

(BEN JONSON)

Queen and huntress,[18] chaste and fair,
Now the sun is laid to sleep,
Seated in thy silver chair,
State in wonted manner keep:

Hesperus[19] entreats thy light,
Hesperus entreats thy light,
Goddess, goddess, goddess, excellently bright.

Earth, let not thy envious shade
Dare itself to interpose;
Cynthia's[20] shining orb was made,
Heav'n to clear when day did close:

Bless us then with wishèd sight,
Bless us then with wishèd sight,
Goddess, goddess, goddess, excellently bright.

Lay thy bow of pearl apart,
And thy crystal shining quiver;
Give unto the flying hart
Space to breathe, how short so ever:

Thou that mak'st a day of night,
Thou that mak'st a day of night,
Thou that mak'st, Thou,
Goddess, goddess, goddess, excellently bright.

This scherzo-like movement is very fast and humorous. Throughout, the strings provide a light pizzicato background for the voice-horn interchange. Each segment of this ABA plan ends with a spectacular bit of melismatic tone painting on "excellently bright." The brisk pace and light-hearted brilliance of this movement is calculated to give the last movement extreme contrast.

[18]Diana, goddess of the sun.
[19]Greek for Venus, the evening star.
[20]Cynthia—the moon personified.

SONNET

(KEATS)

O soft embalmer of the still midnight,
Shutting with careful fingers and benign
Our gloom-pleas'd eyes, embower'd from the light,
Enshaded in forgetfulness divine:

O soothest Sleep! if so it please thee, close
In midst of this thine hymn my willing eyes,
Or wait the "Amen" ere thy poppy throws
Around my bed its lulling charities.

Then save me, save me, or the passèd day will shine
Upon my pillow, breeding many woes,
Save me, save me from curious Conscience, that still lords
Its strength for darkness, burrowing like a mole;

Turn the key deftly in the oilèd wards,
And seal the hushèd Casket of my Soul.

Britten's sensitivity to poetry and his mastery of setting it to music are nowhere better illustrated than in his rendering of Keat's sonnet as the last movement of this fine work.

The horn is absent,[21] leaving the strings (often divided into many parts) and the voice to interpret the dream-like poem. The music is through-composed, its unity ensured by the frequent appearance of a distinctive harmonic progression with which the movement begins and ends

Example 18.34

firmly establishing and confirming the prevailing tonality of D major.

The inspired joining of music to words so that they enrich each other is a profound testament to Britten's craftmanship and artistry.

---

[21]In part, to allow the player to get off stage for the epilogue.

Adagio tranquillo e liberamente

Example 18.35

O soft__ em-bal-mer of the still mid-night, Shut-ting with care-ful

fin-gers and be - nign__ Our gloom-pleas'd eyes,__ em-bower'd from the light,__ en -

sha-ded__ in for - get - - - ful-ness di - vine:

O sooth - est Sleep!__ if__ so it please thee,__

close in midst of this thine hymn__ my will - ing eyes, or wait the "A-men"__

ere thy pop-py throws A-round my bed its lul - - - -

ling char-i - ties. Then save__ me, save__

__ me, or the pass-èd day will shine up-on my pil-low, breed-ing man-y woes,

Save me, save me from cur-ious Conscience, that__ still lords__ It's strength for

dark-ness, bur-row-ing like a mole; Turn the key deft-ly__ in the oil-èd wards,__

__ And seal the hush-èd cask - et of__ my soul!__

375

The ethereal closing of the sonnet is followed by a distant echo of the beginning of the *Serenade*—from the horn—off stage.

BÉLA BARTÓK

Béla Bartók (1881–1945) was the most significant composer to come out of eastern Europe in the early twentieth century. As a young musician he developed a strong interest in creating a national music and began collecting Hungarian folk songs, an activity he shared with Zoltán Koldály (1882–1967), another prominent Hungarian composer. Bartók's interest in folk music had a profound effect on his own music; side by side with the most current compositional techniques appeared folk-derived rhythms and melodic patterns.

The political turmoil of the late 1930s, brought on by the expansionist policies of Nazi Germany, convinced Bartók that he had to leave Hungary. He immigrated to the United States in 1940 where he lived and worked until his death five years later.

Bartók was primarily an instrumental composer; with a few exceptions almost all of his music falls into one of the following categories: music for solo piano, chamber music for strings (often with piano), concertos, orchestral works of various types, and stage works.

His works for piano range from technical studies and beginners' pieces to difficult recital pieces and concertos. His major contribution to piano literature is the six-volume *Mikrokosmos* (1926–1937), a collection of 153 pieces graded in order of difficulty.

Among his chamber works, the most outstanding pieces are the six string quartets. Since they span a large portion of his creative life, they offer a comprehensive picture of his development as a composer. In particular the Fifth String Quartet, written in 1934, is considered to be a pivotal point in his stylistic development, after which his music assumes qualities that make it much more accessible to the listener. The Sixth String Quartet (1939) is in many ways the culmination of Bartóks life and work; it displays the ingenuity and self-discipline which are the hallmarks of his style. Taken as a whole, Bartók's quartets rank among the finest contributions to the literature in the modern era.

His ten concertos are all major works and most of them remain essential items in twentieth-century repertory. The Second Concerto for Violin (1937–1938) is one of the finest in the modern idiom.

Bartók's stage works include a one-act opera and two ballets. His one major choral work, the *Cantata profana* (1930), based on a Hungarian legend, requires a double mixed chorus, tenor and baritone soloists, and a large orchestra.

Kossuth, an orchestral tone poem and Bartók's first major work for orchestra, was highly acclaimed at performances in England and in Budapest. The much later *Concerto for Orchestra* (1943) was his orchestral masterpiece and one of the great works of this century. Two other popular works, both written for smaller forces, round out his orchestral music—*Music for Strings, Percussion, and Celesta* (1936), and the *Divertimento for String Orchestra* (1939).

SERIALISM

I n their efforts to create a new kind of "tonality," it occurred to many twentieth-century composers that they might be able to avoid the traditional concept of tonality completely. But the idea of the tonal center was so fundamental to musical organization that it could not simply be dropped. Rather, it had to be replaced by an organizing principle of equal strength and validity. The search for such an alternative was the life work of several Viennese composers early in this century. Their work took place at the same time that Stravinsky, Bartók, Hindemith, and others were expanding the idea of tonality. These two simultaneous developments determined the course of musical composition for the first half of the century.

SCHOENBERG'S WORK

Schoenberg's work—amounting to fifty opus numbers, several early unpublished pieces, and three unfinished compositions—includes stage works, art songs, choral pieces, works for piano, a number of orchestral compositions, and an extensive variety of chamber music. His early works, up through the first years of the century, stand in the late German romantic tradition of Wagner, Brahms, and Mahler. They are tonally based and use many of the romantic forms. The tone poem *Verklärte Nacht* (*Transfigured Night,* 1899), written for string sextet and later revised for string orchestra, is based on a literary program and uses a recurring theme to link the sections of the work. The harmonic style is related to that of Wagner's *Tristan and Isolde.* His symphonic poem *Pelléas und Mélisande* was inspired by the same Maeterlinck drama that interested Debussy. The symphonic cantata *Gurrelieder* (*Songs of Gurre,* 1900–1901) is a gigantic and complex work for soloists, chorus, and huge orchestra.

SCHOENBERG *(1874–1951)*

Figure 19.1 One of the most important and innovative figures in twentieth-century music, Schoenburg also enjoyed painting.

*A*t the start of his career, Arnold Schoenberg was closely allied with late German romanticism, although he moved farther from it than almost any of his contemporaries. Together with two of his students, Alban Berg and Anton von Webern, Schoenberg took the fateful step of rejecting the concept of tonality completely, and wrote in what is called an atonal style. He later developed a new system of musical organization to replace tonality which involves setting the twelve chromatic tones in a chosen order, and then using them in various ways. This system is called **serialism, twelve-tone technique,** or **dodecaphony.**

Almost single-handedly Arnold Schoenberg effected a radical and significant change in basic concepts of music. His development of the twelve-tone technique opened the door to new methods of composing and new ways of constructing harmonic relationships. He himself viewed his new method of composing not as a dramatic, revolutionary gesture against the past but as a logical consequence of nineteenth-century chromatic developments in harmony. He developed his method over many years through a number of compositions, each of which explores new techniques. Some of these techniques were to form part of his serial procedures.

Schoenberg was born into a Viennese middle-class family; although his parents both loved music, neither provided much guidance in his early training. While in

Atonality and Expressionism

Beginning in about 1905, Schoenberg evolved radically different procedures that were regarded by his contemporaries as quite revolutionary. Two different terms are often used to describe his new approach. The first, **atonality,** refers to the systematic avoidance of any kind of tonal center. This is accomplished by excluding simple, familiar chords, major or minor scales, and octave leaps. When these principles are combined with dissonance and a rapid succession of chords, the ear cannot find any stable point (tonic) to use as a center of reference. In this way the twelve tones of the chromatic scale are made equal, rather than consisting of seven "belonging" to the key of a piece and five others "not belonging."

As previously noted, Schoenberg considered his new harmonic style to be a logical extension of tendencies already apparent in late German romanticism. In the music of Wagner and Strauss, brief atonal passages can be found, although they are embedded in a tonal context. Schoenberg simply increased the amount of dissonance and chromaticism in his music until the listener could no longer perceive the difference between stable tones ("belonging") and unstable tones ("not belonging"). Since grammar school he studied the violin and cello and was soon composing and playing in chamber ensembles. When Schoenberg was in his late teens, a friend, Alexander von Zemlinsky, who directed an amateur orchestral society, first interested him in serious musical study; and after working several years as a bank employee, Schoenberg decided in 1895 to embark on a musical career.

The two great influences in his early composition were the giants of late nineteenth-century German music: Brahms and Wagner. During the 1890s he wrote several string quartets and piano works and a small number of songs. In 1901 he married his friend's sister, Mathilde von Zemlinsky. Shortly afterward he was engaged as a theater conductor in Berlin. There he became acquainted with Richard Strauss, who helped him obtain a teaching position and expressed great interest in his work. In 1903 Schoenberg returned to Vienna to teach musical composition. Gustav Mahler became a supporter of his music, and, more importantly, he took on as students two younger men, Alban Berg and Anton von Webern. Both pupils would later adopt Schoenberg's twelve-tone methods, would develop them in their own individual ways, and Webern would influence decisively the future course of music.

During the first decade of the twentieth century, Schoenberg began turning away from the late romantic style of his earlier works and gradually developed his new twelve-tone method. Although his name spread among composers and performers, public acclaim eluded him. His famous song cycle *Pierrot lunaire* (*Moonstruck Pierrot*), which drew invectives from critics but praise from avant-garde sympathizers, employed a half-sung, half-spoken technique called **Sprechstimme** (literally, "speech voice").

Schoenberg's reputation was beginning to grow when his career was interrupted by World War I, in which he served with the Austrian army; but soon after he was again active as a composer, lecturer on theory, and teacher. The 1920s marked a new direction. He went to Berlin in 1925 to teach composition at the State Academy of the Arts, taking with him his second wife, Gertrude Kolisch. (His first wife had died in 1923.)

In 1933 Schoenberg's career again took another direction. When the Nazi party assumed power, Schoenberg, being a Jew, was dismissed from his post and emigrated first to France, then to the United States. Although his reputation as a teacher and as a "modernist" preceded him, he nevertheless had financial difficulty. After working in Boston and New York, he joined the faculty of U.C.L.A. He died in Los Angeles at the age of seventy-seven.

dissonances were no longer resolved in the traditional manner, they became "emancipated." The ordering of successive intervals, not the traditional relationship of dissonance to consonance, became the chief organizing principle.

The second term used to describe Schoenberg's works in the period from 1905 to about 1912 is **expressionism.** Borrowed from the field of art criticism, the term refers to a school of German artists and dramatists who tried to represent the artist's innermost experience. Often expressionist artists used unusual, even revolutionary, methods—such as harsh colors and distortion of the human image—to achieve an intense emotional effect. The subject matter of expressionism was modern humanity in its varied psychological states: isolated, irrational, rebellious, tense. The artist did not attempt to produce beautiful or realistic art, but only to penetrate and reveal inner feelings. Schoenberg shared the goals of the expressionistic artists; his atonal music was the stylistic means of reaching those goals.

The problem that Schoenberg eventually had to face, having abandoned tonality, was the loss of the form-building properties that the old stysem had provided. Without tonal centers and modulations, the traditional forms could not really exist. Without such simple but useful devices as the dominant-tonic chord progression, there was no harmonic guide to help distinguish a cadence from any other point in a phrase.

At first Schoenberg found only temporary solutions. He wrote short pieces and depended heavily on outside material (either literary or dramatic) to impose form on the music. In addition, he used intricate motivic development and contrapuntal procedures to unify his "free" atonal compositions. These devices had been part of his romantic style, but they became even more important as this expressionistic style emerged. Some of his works from this middle period are characterized by the dominance of a particular interval. Others contain canons and ostinato figures.

Schoenberg creates incredible variety within each piece of his music. Rarely is the same texture maintained for more than a single phrase. Instead, contrapuntal patches are interspersed with accompanied melody. Rhythm and dynamics are also subject to the same rapid variation. Two consecutive phrases are rarely equal in length. Schoenberg almost never uses literal repetition or any other formal symmetry, even when a repeated text in vocal music invites such treatment.

An excellent example of Schoenberg's expressionistic style is *Pierrot lunaire* (1912), a setting of twenty-one surrealistic poems for vocalist, piano, flute, clarinet, violin, and cello. Schoenberg provides for further variety by having some players switch to other instruments: piccolo, bass clarinet, and viola. The singer (a woman) uses the *Sprechstimme* technique. Both the rhythms and the pitches are precisely notated. The pitches, however, are points which the singer may center on, then fall away from. The effect of *Sprechstimme* in *Pierrot lunaire* is haunting and eerie.

Development of the Twelve-Tone Method

Schoenberg continued to be very much aware of the limitations his free atonal style placed on him; he wanted to write longer pieces, but lacked a formal framework on which to build them. Form was very important to Schoenberg. He believed that some underlying organization was essential, no matter what radical changes took place in the harmonic idiom.

Gradually he evolved a system he described as a "method of composing with twelve tones that are related only with one another, not to a central tone: a tonic." The rudiments of this method are simple: the composer arranges the twelve pitches of the chromatic scale in a particular order (example 19.1).

Example 19.1

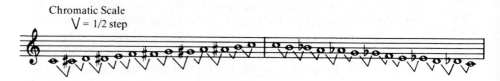

Chromatic Scale
V = 1/2 step

This is known as a **tone row,** or **series,** or **set,** for a specific piece. The row can be transported to any pitch level, and used upside down (*inversion*), backward (*retrograde*), or upside down and backward (*retrograde inversion*).

The original form of the row below is taken from the opening of the choral melody of Schoenberg's *A Survivor from Warsaw.*

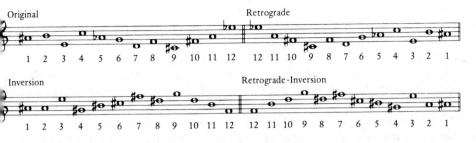

The notes of the series (or any of its variations) are sometimes used sequentially, both in full or in segments, to form a melody or theme, and are also used simultaneously in clusters to form chords. The system does not impose limits on rhythm, dynamics, or textures that the composer will choose, so it is not a mechanical music-producing method, as it might seem at first. A composer who writes with the serial technique is no more limited than one who chooses to write tonally. The basic tone row provides some coherence, in the same way that tonality does, but there is still room for tremendous variety.

Schoenberg had formulated his twelve-tone method by 1923, and he used it in most of his compositions thereafter. It was applied in part to the *Five Piano Pieces* (opus 23, 1923) and the *Serenade for Seven Instruments and Bass Voice* (opus 24, 1923). The *Suite for Piano* (opus 25, 1924), which uses baroque forms, and the *Wind Quintet* (opus 26, 1924) use the system throughout.

No longer expressionistic, the works written in the 1920s have a marked air of confidence and playfulness. A traditional spirit is also evident. In a way, Schoenberg could not be called a neoclassicist. He used forms resembling classical ones—theme and variations and sonata form, for instance—and contrasted his themes in a classical manner, while continuing to write in a very dissonant idiom with serial techniques.

In 1928 Schoenberg completed the powerful *Variations for Orchestra* (opus 31), a serial work for full orchestra. He also used the twelve-tone system in a number of important works written in the United States during the 1930s and 1940s, including the Concerto for Violin and Orchestra (1936), the String Quartet no. 4 (1937), the Concerto for Piano and Orchestra (1942), and *A Survivor From Warsaw* (1947), a cantata for speaker, chorus, and orchestra. His death left uncompleted his major opera, *Moses und Aron* (begun in 1931).

*Used by permission of Boelke-Bomart, Inc., Hillsdale, N.Y. 12529.

*SIDE 13/SELECTION 1
LISTENING GUIDE ON
PAGES 394–96.*

Example 19.3 Examples 19.3–19.6 used by permission of Belmont Music Publishers, Pacific Palisades, California 90272. Copyright 1928 by Belmont Music Publishers.

Variations for Orchestra is scored for a large orchestra with a full complement of winds, harp, celesta, mandolin, the usual strings, and a very extensive percussion section, including glockenspiel and xylophone. The piece consists of an introduction, a theme and nine variations, and a finale.

The basic series for this work is:

The introduction presents this series gradually in its opening measures; it is not yet used thematically, since that would anticipate the function of the theme section. After a slow beginning and a more emphatic central section, a quiet closing rounds it off. The trombone introduces a motive that will be heard occasionally throughout the piece.

Example 19.4

In the German system for naming notes, our B-flat is called B, and our B is called H—thus these four notes spell BACH. Johann Sebastian Bach used this motive as the subject of one of his organ fugues, and other composers have been intrigued by it since. In *Variations for Orchestra,* the BACH motive is always treated motivically in fairly long note values.

The theme section introduces the row as a theme; it is played by the cellos with a soft chordal accompaniment. What sounds like one long melody is actually the row, first in its original form, then in retrograde inversion, then in retrograde, and finally in inversion. At the end of the movement it is treated contrapuntally, with the cellos playing the original version while the violins play its inversion (see example 19.5).

In the variations that follow, the row is always present in a melodic form, but is not used with the same octaves or rhythms as in the theme, making it somewhat difficult to identify. Moreover, the entire row theme is not always the most important melodic material in each variation. Other motives also derived from the row are presented and developed; rhythmic ideas are elaborated; and varied instrumentations and contrapuntal textures are often the focus of attention. In a sense the conflict between the row as an underlying structural force (a substitute for tonality) and as thematic material is the basis of the piece.

One way to describe the variations is to locate the "theme" (meaning some continuous melodic variant of the basic series) and show how it it used. We can illustrate this most easily by giving the various rhythmic treatments of the theme in some of the variations (see example 19.6).

Example 19.5

Example 19.6

THEMA

Cellos

VAR. I

Basses

VAR. III

Horns

VAR. V

Basses

Var. VII

Glockenspiel and piccolo with varied rhythm

VAR. IX

Piccolo   Original

Tpt.

Inversion   Viola

VARIATION I. The theme stays in the lowest bass instruments, with the full orchestra playing very short motives above.

VARIATION II. The inversion of the theme is presented in canon by the violin and oboe. The texture is complicated by simultaneous canons on other subjects. The movement is scored very lightly, for only solo instruments, which help clarify the complex contrapuntal texture. The BACH motive is heard in the trombone.

VARIATION III. The theme is played mostly by the horns, but it is not particularly important. The first motivic material is a dotted arpeggio figure; a repeated-note group later turns out to be the central idea.

VARIATION IV. The harp, celesta, and mandolin play the theme as an accompaniment to contrapuntal wind and string parts. The instrumental colors are quite unusual because of the choice of instruments.

VARIATION V. The basses again have the theme, but attention focuses on the large leaps they make after each thematic note. These leaps are taken up by the other instruments and characterize the variation.

VARIATION VI. The theme is hidden in the solo part, but the more interesting material is first in the clarinet, and then in the other winds.

VARIATION VII. The piccolo and glockenspiel play the theme in a very high register and entirely off the beat. The winds are featured again, and the rapid changes of instrumental color are notable. Toward the end of this rather long variation, the rhythmic patterns are quite exciting.

VARIATION VIII. For the first time, the theme is not used melodically at the beginning of a variation. The texture provides the primary interest, with contrapuntal wind parts contrasted with rhythmic ostinatos in the strings. The theme appears in the flute and violin toward the end of the variation.

VARIATION IX. The theme itself is the dominant feature of this variation. It is treated contrapuntally at the beginning, with short interludes between presentations; later only fragments of it are used.

FINALE. The BACH motive opens the last movement and proves to be of great importance. It is interspersed with various versions of the row theme and several other motives derived from row material. There are many changes of tempo and texture in this concluding movement.

ALBAN BERG

Alban Berg (1885–1935) adopted most of Schoenberg's methods of construction but used them with a great deal of flexibility. His works allow for a sense of tonality and combine Schoenbergian techniques with established formal procedures from earlier musical periods, including the suite, the march, the rondo, and the passacaglia. His music has a warmth and lyricism that stems from the romantic tendencies in Schoenberg. In addition, such elements as his ability to sustain large forms and his use of large orchestras reinforce the romantic aspect of his style. As a result much of Berg's music is more accessible to the listener than some of Schoenberg's and most of Webern's.

Berg's principal works are his *Lyric Suite for String Quartet* (1926), his *Violin Concerto* (1935), and his two operas, *Lulu* (1929–1935, uncompleted) and *Wozzeck*. *Lulu* was not allowed to be completed until after the death ofl his widow in 1976, and it was not until 1979 that the completed version by Friedrich Cherha was premiered.

Wozzeck is considered by many to be his greatest work. It was written between 1917 and 1921 and was unquestionably influenced by the environment created in Europe by World War I. In its psychological probing of the unconscious and its presentation of a nightmarish world, it is the finest manifestation of expressionism in opera form.

The central character is Wozzeck, the soldier who represents "We poor people." He is belittled and abused by his superior, the captain; used as a hired guinea pig in medical "experiments" by his doctor; betrayed by his mistress, Marie; and eventually driven to murder and suicide by a completely hostile society.

Berg himself constructed the libretto, fashioning it from bits and pieces of a drama by Georg Bückner (1813–1837). Only a musician with substantial mastery of his craft could have formulated such a libretto. As designed by Berg, the opera has three acts which follow the scheme:

Act 1 Exposition
Act 2 Development
Act 3 Catastrophe

Each act consists of five scenes and is organized along the lines of a specific musical form. For example, act 2 (the longest) takes the form of a symphony in five movements, the individual scenes of which are:

Sonata Movement (scene 1)
Fantasia and Fugue (scene 2)
Largo (scene 3)
Scherzo (scene 4)
Rondo with introduction (scene 5)

Acts 1 and 3 are organized along similar lines.

Actually there is continuous music throughout each act. The intervals between scenes are filled with short orchestral transitional passages which function either as a coda to the scene just finished or as an introduction to the ensuing scene.

Each of the musical structures (scenes) is used as the vehicle through which the plot of the opera is advanced and the spirit of the action is portrayed. The "delivery" of the lines of the libretto by the actor/singers and their stage actions take place within this musical framework.

The vocal style of *Wozzeck* depends heavily on the *Sprechstimme* technique, which in *Wozzeck* alternates with ordinary speech and conventional singing in an extremely expressive manner.

The prevailing mood of *Wozzeck* is one of cynicism, irony, helplessness, and depression. Partly in spite of this feeling and partly because of it, *Wozzeck* is an extremely exciting theater piece that speaks forcefully to our own troubled times.

Figure 19.2 Like his teacher, Schoenberg, Webern achieved little recognition during his lifetime. Yet a decade after his death he came to be regarded as one of the principal influences on contemporary composers.

ANTON VON WEBERN

Anton von Webern (1883–1945) was also a pupil of Arnold Schoenberg in Vienna. While Berg came to represent a link to the past among the followers of Schoenberg, Webern represents a more radical denial of and departure from established compositional procedures and concepts. His mature works crystalize the serialist constructionist approach to musical composition inherent in the twelve-tone technique as originally postulated by Schoenberg.

While Berg was writing in long forms for large musical forces, Webern was striving for economy of material and extreme compactness of form. He was preoccupied with the idea that each individual note in a composition was in itself important; nothing was added for "general effect." As a result of this preoccupation, most of his works take on the quality of "miniatures." Indeed, Webern's music is the epitome of clarity, economy of material, spareness of texture, and brevity.

It is not surprising, then, that Webern wrote very little music and that all his works tend to be quite short, some individual pieces lasting less than a minute and some of the "largest" works not exceeding ten minutes. Recently his complete output was recorded on four long-playing records, which means that his entire creative effort produced perhaps four hours of music.

Webern's compositions are about equally divided between vocal and instrumental pieces. His vocal music includes collections of solo songs with various types of instrumental accompaniment, the choral work *Das Augenlicht* (*Light of the Eyes,* 1935), and two cantatas for soloists, chorus, and orchestra. The most important instrumental works are the *Symphonie,* op. 21 (1928) for nine solo instruments; String Quartet, opus 28 (1938); the Concerto for Nine Instruments, op. 24 (1934); and the Piano Variations, op. 27 (1936).

Almost without exception, Webern's works are on the scale of chamber music, another manifestation of economy of means and compactness. His instrumentation often includes highly unorthodox combinations of instruments such as in his *Quartet,* op. 22 (1930), which is scored for clarinet, saxophone, violin, and piano.

As we noted before, Webern's music depends heavily on serialism. His style is essentially contrapuntal and is marked by an exceptional sensitivity to instrumental color. Often a single melodic line, derived from a twelve-tone row, is divided among several instruments, each assigned only one or two notes at a time; the changes of timbre from instrument to instrument give the melody an added interest.

The beginning of the first movement of the *Symphonie,* opus 21, demonstrates the spareness of Webern's style and the distribution of the melodic line over a number of instruments.

SYMPHONIE (OP. 21)

Example 19.7
From Anton von Webern, *Symphonie,* Op. 21. Copyright 1929 by Universal Edition. Copyright renewed. All Rights Reserved. Used by permission of European American Music Distributors Corporation, sole U.S. and Canadian agents for Universal Edition.

Webern suffered the same lack of recognition by the general public during his lifetime as Schoenberg did, but his music, like that of his teacher, has become increasingly influential since World War II. In particular, in the last twenty years many young composers, captivated by the lean character of his style and his isolation of the single note as an important musical event, have adapted features of his music and expanded the techniques of serialism to suit their own purposes. It now seems inevitable that the twelve-tone technique initiated by Schoenberg and advanced by Berg and Webern will continue to be a powerful force in the world of music.

ELIZABETH LUTYENS

Elizabeth Lutyens (1906–1983) appears to be the first British composer to adopt atonality as a compositional principle. Independently from the work of Schoenberg, Berg, and Webern, she experimented with the use of all twelve tones, discarding such devices as the dominant-to-tonic relationship. Her *String Quartet no. 2* (1938) and *String Trio* (1939) are among the most important of her atonal works.

CHARACTERISTICS OF TWENTIETH-CENTURY MUSIC (TO WORLD WAR II)

TONALITY	Major-minor system retained by some composers, but methods of establishing tonal centers altered; other composers employed atonal systems including serialism
TEXTURE	Both homophonic and contrapuntal textures employed; variety of textures within a single work
RHYTHM	Complex rhythms; rhythmic patterns used to build form; frequent absence of well-defined beat; frequent change of meter

SUMMARY

The development of the atonal style was led by Arnold Schoenberg, a Viennese composer who, along with Igor Stravinsky, has been the dominant figure in twentieth-century music. Schoenberg rejected the concept of tonality completely and devised a new system, ultimately called serialism, to organize his works.

Schoenberg's early works are in the late romantic tradition and are tonally based. During the first decade of the twentieth century he began to develop a "free" atonal style that systematically avoided any tonal center, thereby equalizing all twelve tones. He depended heavily on literary or dramatic material, motivic development, and contrapuntal procedures to impose form and organization. His works from 1905 to about 1912 are also described as expressionistic, reflecting his association with the school of German artists and dramatists who were attempting through their art to represent the psychological experience of modern humanity.

Schoenberg was aware that the free atonal style placed certain limitations on his work. Tonality had provided a means of making structural distinctions. In its absence he needed to develop a formal framework on which to build. His solution was to arrange the twelve pitches of the chromatic scale in a particular order known as the tone row, series, or set for a specific piece. The twelve tones of the series could be used in sequence, forming a melody or theme, or simultaneously in groups to form chords. Furthermore, the system did not impose limitations on rhythm, dynamics, or texture. As a result the tone row provided coherence in the same way that tonality does, but still left room for great variety. Schoenberg had formulated his twelve-tone method by 1923 and used it in most of his compositions thereafter.

Although he received little recognition during his lifetime, Schoenberg has had a major influence on contemporary composition. Much of that influence has been transmitted through the music of his pupil and colleague Anton von Webern. Webern and Alban Berg represent the further development of two divergent aspects of Schoenberg's style: Webern the abstract constructionist, Berg the romanticist. The British composer Elizabeth Lutyens also experimented with twelve-tone techniques and atonality.

NEW TERMS

serialism (twelve-tone technique, dodecaphony)
Sprechstimme

atonality
expressionism
tone row (series, set)

SUGGESTED LISTENING

Berg, Alban

Wozzeck. The opera *Wozzeck* is considered by many to be Berg's greatest work. See page 389.

Schoenberg, Arnold

A Survivor from Warsaw, op. 46, for narrator, men's chorus, and orchestra. Schoenberg fashioned his text from reports of the Warsaw ghetto uprising after hearing that his niece had been murdered in a Nazi death camp. The narrator recites the account of horror in the first person against a dramatic orchestral background. In this 1947 work, a late example of expressionism in the composer's twelve-tone output, the row is divided into units which function as fragments of melody and harmony. At the climax, the chorus breaks into the ancient Hebrew prayer *Shema Yisroel* (*Hear, O Israel*), the first clear melodic statement of the row. *A Survivor from Warsaw* is among Schoenberg's most gripping works, one of a series inspired by his experience as a Jew living through the twentieth-century nightmare.

Webern, Anton von

Symphonie, op. 21. After composing a series of short pieces, Webern wrote this symphony in two movements: the first, in sonata-allegro form; the second, a theme and variations. The symphony is scored for clarinet, bass clarinet, two French horns, harp, and a small string section. See page 391.

MUSIC IN AMERICA

Illustration from "BILLY THE KID" (Aaron Copland)
used by permission of Boosey & Hawkes, Inc.

AMERICAN CULTURE BEFORE WORLD WAR II

*I*n the seventeenth century Europeans colonized and settled the eastern seaboard
  of North America. By 1700, there were more than a million colonists scattered
  up and down the Atlantic coast, living mainly on farms, sometimes in villages,
occasionally in trading towns like Boston, New York, or Charleston. In the eighteenth century the imperial health of England depended more and more on American shipbuilding and exports of agricultural commodities. To many Europeans the
economic promise of the New World seemed limitless.

*The cultural record of the American colonies is more spare. There is some rather
naive local portraiture and some expressive tomb sculpture; the architecture, modeled on that of European masters like Palladio and Wren, is sometimes outstanding.
On balance, however, there is little in American art of the seventeenth and eighteenth
centuries to stand beside the masterwork across the Atlantic.*

*On the other hand, the American colonies had a rich local tradition in the crafts:
even today the names Paul Revere and Duncan Phyfe suggest excellence in silver-
smithing and furniture-making. Likewise, native composers, mainly self-taught,
traveled the countryside, organizing singing assemblies and getting tune-books published. These singing masters, of course, were most inclined toward choral music
and hymn singing.*

*American painting came into its own in the late eighteenth century. The best
American painters, though, had to leave the colonies and go to London to make their
reputations. John Singleton Copley (1738–1815) moved to England in 1774, and
Benjamin West (1738–1820) became President of the Royal Academy and Court
Painter to George III. Purely American scenes did not become fashionable until the
early nineteenth century. Then, painters of the untraveled West found a large and
enthusiastic audience. George Caleb Bingham (1811–1879) painted scenes of flat-
boatmen, river ports, trappers, and local elections in Missouri. Hudson River landscapists like Thomas Cole (1801–1848) and Asher Durand (1796–1886) began a*

school of American nature painting that celebrated the wonder of the wilderness—in a more and more melodramatic way as the nineteenth century progressed. The paintings of later landscapists like Frederic Church (1826–1900) and Albert Bierstadt (1830–1902, plate 35) were sometimes first displayed in the manner of the contemporary film premiere and were immensely popular, even if these works gave many Easterners a distorted and grandiloquent vision of Western topography.

In its pantheism and nature worship, early nineteenth-century American painting reflected elements of the romantic movement. So also did literature, as Washington Irving, James Fenimore Cooper, and Edgar Allen Poe wrote tales of the wild, exotic, and supernatural. Not until 1830, however, did New England enter its greatest literary period. The brilliant speculations of transcendentalist Ralph Waldo Emerson, the radical primitivism of Henry David Thoreau, and the thoughtful fiction of Nathaniel Hawthorne and Herman Melville created a rich literary environment of far-reaching significance.

Achievements in American music came late and were more modest. The most notable composer in the United States before the Civil War came out of the slightly vulgar realm of the minstrel show. Stephen Foster (1826–1864), a dreamer and outcast who destroyed himself with alcohol, wrote more than two hundred songs, including tunes like "Camptown Races" and "Oh! Susanna" that have formed the bedrock of American popular music. The first American composers to achieve a reputation abroad were Edward MacDowell (1861–1908) and Amy Beach (1867–1944) who composed in the style of the German romantics at a time when the romantic mode was no longer in the European avant-garde. Even in the late nineteenth century most American composition continued to respond to European fashion. It was Charles Ives (1874–1954) who broke away from European tradition and helped to initiate an independent American avant-garde. Ives's extraordinarily original compositions were far ahead of their time, and it was not until World War II that his work gained wide critical acceptance. Since then his influence has been extensive, and composers today continue to draw inspiration from his bold experimentation.

When the colonies achieved independence in the late eighteenth century, the country had begun to outgrow its character as a collection of separate, often competing provinces and to move toward greater centralization. But it was not until the end of the Civil War (1865) that federal supremacy was assured. Then, with the rise of great railroad networks came the emergence of new corporations that delivered manufactured goods to rapidly growing cities all over the continent. With the settlement of the American interior from coast to coast, the United States became an urban, industrial power very different from the land of yeoman farmers that Thomas Jefferson had dreamed of at the beginning of the nineteenth century.

Significantly, American industrial captains of the nineteenth century collected art to decorate their great townhouses and country estates (plate 40). Just as significantly, they were much more interested in buying Renaissance and baroque work by established masters than in commissioning work that reflected American realities! Most American designers, especially architects, emulated (sometimes with slavish reverence) the models of the French academicians and l'École des Beaux-Arts (the pretigious French school of fine arts). A few farsighted collectors bought *the controversial work of the impressionists; most connoisseurs, however, were attracted to the culturally "safe" style dictated by the well-entrenched art establishment in Paris. The distinction between "local color" and the "made-in-Europe" label was visible in music as well, as the upper class that built majestic concert halls and subscribed to operas and symphonies clearly demonstrated its preference for the imported styles.*

At the turn of the century the favored painter in the United States was John Singer Sargent (1856–1925), whose handsome portraits of the landed, powerful, and financially secure were eagerly sought and displayed in the best New York and Boston townhouses. At the same time a very different style of art was being produced by the Ashcan School, so called after its raw, graphic scenes of proletarian New York. These paintings disturbed the average art patron, who felt that vulgarity and low life were not proper subjects for the painter. The European avant-garde was threatening, too. In 1913 a large exhibition of European art, including the cubist work of Pablo Picasso and the fauvist work of Henri Matisse, stupefied and revolted most of New York's influential critics—in the same way the impressionists had scandalized Paris thirty years earlier. Nevertheless the Armory Show, as it was called, began to redirect American painting, and Europe's new modernism became a force that no serious painter could ignore.

Most American architecture of the early twentieth century was historical in concept, using a diverse vocabulary of styles that were revived from antiquity, the Middle Ages, the Renaissance, and the baroque. Two architects broke this mold, and in so doing, they created the prototypes for many of the buildings seen in America today. Louis Sullivan (1856–1924) rejected highly ornamented details when he built impressive skyscrapers whose lines clearly echoed their steel skeletons, and Frank Lloyd Wright (1869–1959) invented the low, relatively rustic residence that has since become a standard style of housing in suburban America (plate 38).

The building of cities slowed or halted during the Great Depression, although some projects, like Rockefeller Center in New York, went forward. In the 1930s the federal government, as part of its public works program, also commissioned murals and decorations for public buildings. These were primarily in the regional style (plate 39), of which Thomas Hart Benton and Grant Wood were leaders. Although the work of Benton and Wood was more abstract than earlier American art, it reflected a nostalgic realism that was uneasy with European experiments. Edward Hopper (1882–1967) understood the structural logic of cubism, but his great talent lay in evoking the mystery inherent in commonplace aspects of American life (plate 37). In the 1930s painters were also drawn to political subjects; some idealized the worker as the backbone and real hero of the American people.

Between the two world wars some American painters, especially in New York, were aware of concurrent French work; and in the 1930s the Museum of Modern Art was founded in New York. New York, however, did not outshine Paris until after 1945. Then the United States, which despite its commercial power had remained on the periphery of Western art, would become the cultural center of the Atlantic Community.

AMERICAN MUSIC BEFORE WORLD WAR II

‖S‖ triking contrasts run through the history of music in the United States. Imitation of European models has contrasted with attempts to produce a more uniquely American idiom; conservative and radical strains have alternated or vied for dominance; concert music, jazz, and popular music have tended to go their separate ways, though occasionally cross-fertilizing. As America has grown in expanse and population, so has the breadth and significance of her musical expression. In the twentieth century, American music, written in the many different musical languages which characterize our multicultural nation, stands in the forefront of important and influential artistic movements throughout the world.

THE SEVENTEENTH CENTURY

The religious dissenters who settled New England in the early seventeenth century had come from a world rich in music and the other arts. The Pilgrims, for example, loved and practiced music, but had little time to spare for entertainment in their new land. Their music was functional and used mostly for worship, in church and at home. It consisted primarily of psalms and hymns, with tunes taken from older hymns or folk songs brought over from England and Holland.

The first book printed in the Colonies was a new rhymed translation of the psalms, called the *Bay Psalm Book* (1640), to which music was added in a 1698 edition. Its publication underscores the strong ties between music and religion in early America.

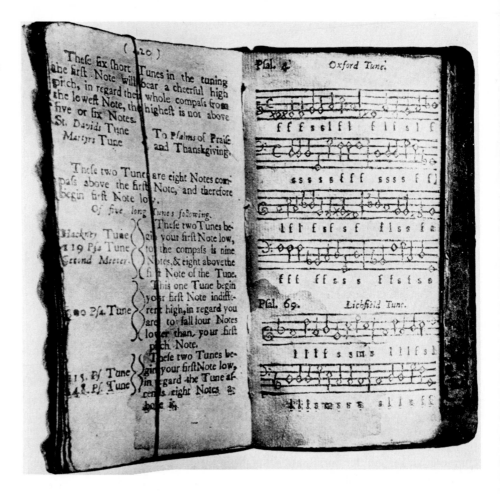

Figure 20.1 A page from the Bay Psalm Book, the first book printed in the American colonies.

THE EIGHTEENTH CENTURY

Secular music began to flourish in the Colonies during the eighteenth century, particularly in such major cities as New York, Boston, Philadelphia, and Charleston. Through shipping and trading, the people in these cities remained in close contact with the artistic life of Europe. As the cities prospered, the growing middle class acquired both the leisure and the money to support the arts.

Beginning in the 1730s, there were concerts, operas, and other musical events that featured immigrant musicians. These professionals worked both as performers and as "professors" of music. They taught music to gentlemen amateurs who, in turn, supported the rapid growth of music in America. The supporters included Thomas Jefferson, one of the outstanding patrons of music of his day and an amateur violinist himself, and Benjamin Franklin, who served capably as a performer, inventor of an

Figure 20.2 Eighteenth
Century Boston.

FANEUIL HALL, BOSTON.

instrument (the glass harmonica), and music critic. Another of the gentlemen amateurs, Francis Hopkinson (1737–1791), who wrote genteel songs, claimed to be the "first native of the United States who has produced a musical composition."

By 1770 there was a group of native American composers with enough in common to be considered a school. Led by William Billings (1746–1800), these composers produced music with a simple, rugged hymn style, angular, folklike melodies, and stark harmonies. Not feeling bound by the European traditions of composition, they created their own style. One of the favorite devices of Billings and his contemporaries was the "fuguing tune," a hymn or psalm tune with brief polyphonic sections that have imitative entrances. Billings and the others of this school felt that these pieces were "twenty times as powerful as the old slow tunes."

Unfortunately, however, this virile new style was soon abandoned, and native American music returned to a position of subservience to the European style. The original style created by the New England composers was considered crude by comparison with that of the European masters; and Americans were becoming self-conscious about their lack of sophistication and cultural heritage.

THE NINETEENTH CENTURY

The musical culture of nineteenth-century America was marked by two significant phenomena. The first was the division between what we now call "classical" and "popular" music. Classical music was meant either for serious study and listening or

Figure 20.3 Stephen Foster composed many popular songs many of which are still familiar and sung today. (Attributed to MMK Major and Knapp lithography co., active 1864–1871, after photo lithograph with tintatone $7^3/_5 \times 6^5/_8$ in. National Portrait Gallery, Smithsonian Institution, Washington, D.C.)

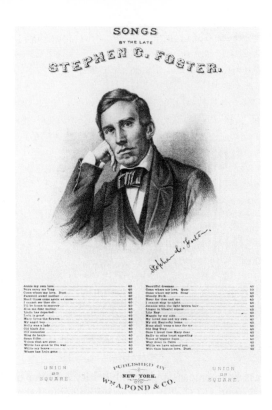

for religious purposes, while popular music aimed only to entertain. Earlier music had served both functions. For example, the eighteenth-century fuguing tunes were written for worship and enlightenment, but learning and singing them was also an enjoyable social function.

The second phenomenon of nineteenth-century music was the imitation of German music by American composers, a trend that became most evident after the Civil War. By that time the pattern of immigration to the United States had changed, as more people came from the European continent and fewer from Great Britain. The Europeans brought to America the ideas of romantic movement, which was strongest in Germany. Soon romanticism influenced every area of American musical life.

American Composers before the Civil War

In the years preceding the Civil War, many extremely sentimental songs were written and published primarily for use by amateurs in their homes. The one great songwriter of the period did not follow in the European tradition, but wrote for the parlors and minstrel shows of America.

Stephen Foster (1826–1864) wrote music that appealed to a large segment of the American population—those who were from neither the sophisticated Eastern cities nor the frontier. He articulated the uneasy feelings of dislocation and transition in a rapidly changing country.

Although his formal musical training was not extensive, he had an unmistakable gift for melody. Many of his songs are filled with nostalgic yearning, often for an unattainable love; both the text and music of his best-known songs, like "I Dream of Jeanie," are gentle and tender. Foster also wrote many songs for the minstrel shows that were a popular form of entertainment in the North, both before and after the Civil War. The music of minstrel shows had a robust quality that was missing from the household songs of the period. Dance tunes and songs using the dialects of black Americans were the basis of the shows, and Foster contributed many of the latter, including his well-known "Oh! Susanna" and "Camptown Races."

While Foster wrote in a vernacular style and drew from uniquely American experience, composers of sacred music centered their attention on European styles. The Civil War and Reconstruction years were marked by a growing taste for hymns adapted from the music of the great European composers, from Palestrina to Mendelssohn. Lowell Mason (1792–1872) composed and adapted many such hymns. His efforts also brought music education into the public school curriculum for the first time.

Much American music—original compositions, arrangements of songs and dances, and sets of variations on well-known tunes—was written for the piano, the favorite instrument of the romantic era. American piano builders became some of the best in the world. One of the most colorful and talented figures in American music before the Civil War was a virtuoso pianist from New Orleans, Louis Moreau Gottschalk (1829–1869), who adopted many of the mannerisms of Liszt. He composed numerous works for both piano and orchestra, many of exaggerated sentimentality, and also made use of such exotic musical materials as Afro-Caribbean rhythms and Creole melodies.

Most of the music performed by American orchestras was by European composers, although the works of the American George Bristow (1825–1898) were sometimes performed. Bristow wrote six symphonies in a style almost identical to Mendelssohn's. The New York Philharmonic, of which he was a member, was founded in 1842. A typical orchestral program in this period carefully mixed "heavy" music (single movements of symphonies, never complete ones) and lighter music (marches and overtures).

After the Civil War

From the end of the Civil War to World War I, German romantic music had its greatest influence. Symphony orchestras were formed in many of the major cities, and large concert halls were built, including Carnegie Hall in New York (1891). Conservatories were established, and music departments appeared in colleges and universities.

A group of romantic composers formed in Boston under John K. Paine (1839–1906), a conservative and serious craftsman who became the first professor of music at Harvard. Other talented members of the Boston group were Horatio Parker (1863–1919) of Yale and George Chadwick (1854–1931). These men composed instrumental and choral music: symphonies, sonatas, chamber music, and oratorios. Stylistically, they were closely allied with the early German romantics, such as Schubert, Mendelssohn, and Schumann.

Amy Beach (1867–1944) also lived in Boston and composed in the conservative romantic tradition. Her output included more than one hundred songs, short piano pieces, sacred and secular choral works, a piano quintet, and a symphony (1894). Her works for chorus and orchestra, *Three Browning Songs* (1900) and *The Canticle of the Sun* (1928), were among her most popular works. Beach was recognized as a gifted pianist and composer both in the United States and Europe which she toured from 1910 to 1914. Beginning in 1885, much of her music was published by Arthur P. Schmidt, an early champion of American composers including such women as Beach, Margaret Ruthren Lang, Helen Hood, Clara Kathleen Rogers, and others.

Beach very much admired the work of the English poet, Robert Browning (1812–1889). In 1900 she set three of his poems to music and dedicated the music to the Browning Society of Boston. The group of three songs begins with "The Year's at Spring" with its famous line "God's in His Heaven, all's right with the world!," and ends with an effective musical rendering of "I send my heart up to thee." As a center piece, Beach chose the poem "Ah, Love, but a day."

BEACH:
AH, LOVE, BUT A
DAY
SIDE 13/SELECTION 2

As example 20.1 shows, the composer manipulated the text by repeating certain words and lines to facilitate the musical structure she designed to convey the overall quality of the poem. The piece consists of two larger sections. Each begins quietly, builds to a climax, then subsides. Between them is a brief refrain, on the words:

"Ah, Love, but a day
And the world has changed!"

Example 20.1

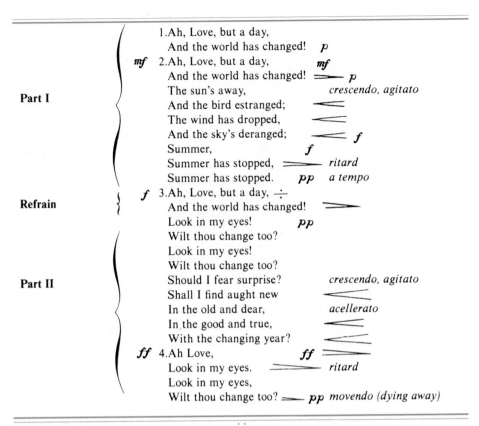

Part I	1. Ah, Love, but a day,
	And the world has changed! *p*
	mf 2. Ah, Love, but a day, *mf*
	And the world has changed! ⎯ *p*
	The sun's away, *crescendo, agitato*
	And the bird estranged;
	The wind has dropped,
	And the sky's deranged; *f*
	Summer, *f*
	Summer has stopped, ⎯ *ritard*
	Summer has stopped. *pp* *a tempo*
Refrain	*f* 3. Ah, Love, but a day,
	And the world has changed!
	Look in my eyes! *pp*
Part II	Wilt thou change too?
	Look in my eyes!
	Wilt thou change too?
	Should I fear surprise? *crescendo, agitato*
	Shall I find aught new
	In the old and dear, *acellerato*
	In the good and true,
	With the changing year?
	ff 4. Ah Love, *ff*
	Look in my eyes. ⎯ *ritard*
	Look in my eyes,
	Wilt thou change too? ⎯ *pp movendo (dying away)*

In addition to the dynamic pattern of each individual section, there is a musical progression that transcends the separate segments and ties them into a larger dynamic structure. This progression consists of the differing musical treatments of the words "Ah, Love."

Example 20.2

Each successive setting of "Ah, Love" is heard as an increase of musical energy, growing toward a climax. The second "Ah, Love" is louder and higher than the first; the third is louder and longer; the fourth, the loudest, longest, and highest, is the climax of this progress and of the entire song.

The craftsmanship exemplified in "Ah, Love, but a Day" made Beach a respected and popular composer during her life time.

Edward MacDowell (1861–1908) also came under the influence of German romanticism, but avoided the established instrumental forms in favor of program music. Having studied in Germany, he went on to achieve success there as a pianist, composer, and teacher. In contrast to the Boston group, MacDowell allied himself with the tradition of Wagner and Liszt. He wrote several tone poems for orchestra, a well-known piano concerto (in D minor), and many songs and choral pieces. But this American "tone poet" became primarily the composer of small character pieces for piano, most with programmatic titles. His *Woodland Sketches,* containing "To a Wild Rose" and "To a Water Lily," and *New England Idyls* are among his best-known works in this vein.

Late in the century a few American musicians began to react against the domination of German ideals and attitudes. Some American composers decided to make use of American Indian and Negro themes—a challenge put forth by Czech composer Antonín Dvořák on his visit to America from 1892 to 1895. Arthur Farwell (1872–1951) was an American composer who accepted Dvořák's challenge and concentrated on using Indian themes in his works. Those who reacted against the German influence also took interest in the new musical ideas from France and Russia. Charles T. Griffes (1884–1920), whose creative talents were cut short by his premature death, showed in his early works the influence of Debussy, Ravel, and Stravinsky. He also developed an interest in Oriental music, and his last works, especially the *Sonata for Piano* (1918, revised 1919) and the *Poem for Flute and Orchestra* (1919), contain the seeds of a synthesis of his various interests.

THE EARLY TWENTIETH CENTURY

During the first two decades of the twentieth century, as we have just noted, the German romantic tradition continued to hold sway within the American musical "establishment"—among the concert-going public and in academic circles. Eventually, the influence of French impressionism made some inroads via the music of Charles T. Griffes. Later, French traditions and the neoclassicism of Stravinsky would be transmitted to American composers through influential French teachers and would supplant German attitudes.

But American musical pioneers were at the same time beginning to discover and invent new and radical kinds of music of their own, independently of and in some cases even before their European counterparts. From about 1900 to 1920, in such widely separated places as Danbury, Connecticut, and San Francisco, California, a few Americans were tinkering with an assortment of "ultramodern" sounds and methods of composition.

One of these bold figures was Charles E. Ives, one of the most extraordinary and original composers that America has produced. Not only did Ives use such advanced techniques as atonality, free dissonance, and extreme rhythmic complexity, he dipped into home-grown music as well. Indeed, his music contains elements drawn from the entire gamut of his musical and personal experience, from popular American songs and marches to hymn tunes to quotations from famous European classics. In a statement reflecting his open-minded approach, Ives said, "There can be nothing '*exclusive*' about a substantial art. It comes directly out of the heart of experience of life and thinking about life and living life." Thus, even within the same composition, Ives might shift from atonality to simple, hymnbook harmonies for evocative purposes. Ives, with his acceptance of all musical sources as valid and his rejection of dogmatic and exclusive methods, continues to influence composers here and beyond our borders.

IVES (1874–1954)

*C*harles Ives was raised in the small town of Danbury, Connecticut, where his father was town bandleader, church organist, music teacher, and composer. His father had an unusual interest in musical experimentation and a fascination with unconventional sounds, which he transmitted to his son. This was undoubtedly one of the most important musical influences in Ives's life.

The young Ives studied music at Yale and then launched a successful career in life insurance. He deliberately chose to earn his living in an enterprise separate from his composing on the theory that both efforts would be better for it, and he never regretted the decision. He composed furiously during evenings and weekends, storing his manuscripts in his barn. Ives's music was totally unknown until he published his *Concord* Sonata, a volume of songs, and a collection of essays in the early 1920s. Even then, his works were not readily accepted; only since World War II has his music become widely performed, published, and recorded. As his works became better known, Ives's influence increased, and successive generations of composers still draw inspiration from various aspects of his wide-ranging musical language. His work is considered to be so important among musicians and his popularity with the concert-going public is such that the one hundredth anniversary of his birth was widely celebrated in 1974.

The musical isolation in which Ives worked led to the development of an unusual philosophy of music. Ives idealized the strength and simple virtue of ordinary people. He had little regard for technical skill, either in composition or in performance, but placed high value on the spirit and earnestness with which amateurs sang and played their

Figure 20.4 Charles Ives, perhaps the boldest and most original of American composers, drew his musical elements and inspiration from the entire stage of his musical and personal experiences.

popular hymns and songs. The freedom that Ives permitted himself in the choice of musical materials he extended to performers of his works. Undismayed by an enthusiastic but inaccurate performance of *Three Places in New England* (1903–1914), Ives remarked approvingly, "Just like a town meeting—every man for himself. Wonderful how it came out!"

IVES'S WORK

Ives wrote several engaging orchestral works, including his four numbered symphonies, another symphony titled *New England Holidays,* and *Three Places in New England.* The latter contains the famous musical representation of two marching bands coming down Main Street on July Fourth, each playing in a different rhythm and key! Ives produced a considerable amount of chamber music as well, some for such traditional combinations as string quartet. But he also enjoyed creating new and unusual groupings of instruments. In *The Unanswered Question* (1906), a solo trumpet "asks the question" with an atonal melody, four flutes attempt an answer in successive flurries of confusion, all against a tonal background played by offstage strings. In *Hallowe'en* (1907?), for string quartet, piano, and optional bass drum, each of the strings plays in a different key. Ives wrote over one hundred songs, several violin sonatas, and works for piano, including the great Second Sonata (1909–1915), subtitled *Concord Mass., 1840–60.*

Like much of his music, *Variations on "America"* displays an intriguing sense of humor. The piece was composed for organ in 1891 but is best known today in the transcription for symphony orchestra made in 1963 by the American composer, William Schuman.

IVES:
VARIATIONS ON
"AMERICA"
SIDE 14/SELECTION 1

A typical theme and variation begins with the statement of a theme allowing the listener to become sufficiently familiar with the basic musical material in order to follow and appreciate it as it is varied in subsequent sections of the composition. On the assumption that just about everyone in the United States knew the tune of "America" ("My country 'tis of thee"), Ives dispensed with this traditional process and began the piece not with a simple statement of the theme but with an introduction which is in itself a kind of variation of segments of the melody.

Example 20.3

Each section of the ABA plan of the introduction begins with this variant of the beginning of "America." The second A ends on a dominant chord $f\!<$ $_{.ff}$ which resolves into a statement of the entire melody with its traditional harmonization in the clear-cut key of F major. The instrumental tone quality of the theme, however, is anything but traditional. In order to match the strange sound Ives wanted from the organ, the transcriber uses muted trumpets and trombones combined with strings played not with the *hair* of the bow but the *wood* of the bow drawn over the strings (*col legno—with wood*), producing an eerie sound from the string section. To heighten this effect, bells make unexpected entrances at the end of each phrase of the tune. The effect of this familiar and simple tune combined with such strange and unorthodox orchestration provides an overall impression that can best be described as wierdly incongruous.

In variation I, the theme is presented by the strings against rapid decorative material played by oboes, clarinets, bassoons, and xylophone, with trumpets and snare drum coming in with a finishing touch. In this variation, the theme itself is not altered.

Variation results from the new and varied material played *against* the theme. The key of F major is clearly maintained.

Variation II is quite different in several interesting aspects. While the overall tonic key of F major is maintained, the harmonic vocabulary is much richer and more complex than that normally associated with this simple tune. This is particularly true at the end of each section where the style is reminiscent of "barbershop harmony."

The sectional nature of the tune is emphasized by the orchestration. In the first section, the tune (somewhat simplified) is played by solo clarinet, doubled by solo horn, accompanied by strings. The instruments employed in the second section creates an entirely different tone quality. In it, the tune (somewhat fragmented) is played by muted solo trumpet accompanied by horns, trombones, and tuba (all muted), with the solo clarinet making a surprise entrance at the very end. A change in dynamic level, *pp* in section one, *mf* in section two, intensifies the contrast between sections.

Thus far, the introduction, the theme, and variations I and II have maintained the key of F major as the prevailing tonic. Variation III is quite clearly in a different key—D-flat major. In between variation II (F major) and variation III (D♭ major), Ives inserts an interlude in which both F major and D♭ major are used simultaneously, a device known as **polytonality.** In this polytonal texture, Ives employs *canon,* an imitative contrapuntal device in which flutes, oboes, clarinet, trumpets, and violins play the tune in F major, followed one measure later, by the tune in D♭ major played by horns, trumpet, and trombones.

Example 20.4

The dissonance which normally results from polytonality is well illustrated in the interlude's final chord which consists of a combination of the chords of F major and D♭ major.

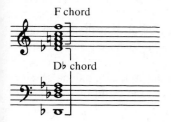

Example 20.5

While the tone F is common to both chords, the D♭ and A♭ of the D♭ chord and the A♮ and C of the F chord clash harshly so that the overall sound is quite dissonant. The interlude is further set off from its two neighbors (variations II and III) by its *fff* dynamic level.

The fun begins in earnest when variation III provides relief of comic proportions after the harsh and loud interlude. The change of key from F major to D♭ major keeps company with a switch in meter, from $\frac{3}{4}$ to $\frac{6}{8}$. The melody is transformed into a lively "dance tune" played by the oboe against a repeated jocular figure in the cello.

Example 20.6

The rest of the strings provide pizzicato accompaniment. The first statement by the tune ends 🎵 followed by a deliciously flippant phrase by solo flute.

Example 20.7

The second time around, the clarinet, and second violin have the tune, the first violins add increased rhythmic activity.

Example 20.8

In the second half of the tune, the glockenspiel adds to the *ff* level—the flippant ending is played by the trumpet and extended by the piccolo ⟶ *p* to close a jolly musical episode.

Without pause we are launched into variation IV in the style of a polonaise. The tune is played in F minor by solo trombone and tuba against the traditional polonaise rhythm provided by strings, horns, and percussion.

Example 20.9

MUSIC IN AMERICA

The second half of the tune is repeated by oboes, clarinets, and bassoons while the flutes, piccolo, and trumpet enliven the background by adding ♪ ♪♪ ♪ ♪ | ♪. The combination of the tune in a minor key against such a "foreign" background makes the movement grotesquely funny.

A very brief interlude, in which the brass section confirms the key of F minor, prepares for variation V, the last, longest, and most brilliant, to finish the piece majestically. Variation V consists of two statements of the theme, the second of which is extended and climaxes in a surprise return of the original introduction. The introduction in turn, leads to a coda, with full orchestra, fortissimo, ending the composition.

Example 20.9

Variations on "America" gives us an intriguing glimpse of one aspect of a unique and fascinating musical personality, one that continues to grow in stature as a figure in the history of American music.

EARLY CONSERVATIVES

In addition to Charles Ives, many other American composers were working out their techniques and developing their styles during the early years of the twentieth century. A number of them came under the influence of a remarkable teacher, Nadia Boulanger (1887–1979).

Nadia Boulanger was born in Paris where her father was a professor of violin and composition at the Paris Conservatory. It was there that she began her studies with Gabriel Fauré whose influence on her was strong and lasting. A talented composer in her own right, she nevertheless devoted herself primarily to teaching and in 1921, joined the faculty of the American Conservatory at Fontainebleau.

In the 1930s, Boulanger achieved distinction in the United States as a conductor as a result of guest appearances with leading American orchestras such as the Boston and Philadelphia Symphonies and The New York Philharmonic. During World War II, she lived and taught in the United States. She returned to France in 1946 and became director of the American Conservatory at Fontainebleau in 1950.

She had great admiration for Stravinsky and his music and rejected serialism. Although she held up Stravinsky as a model, she encouraged young composers to develop their own individual styles of composition. During her long teaching career, she had as pupils many American men and women who later became prominent composers. Among them were Nathaniel Dett, Roy Harris, Ulysses Kay, Thea Musgrave, Julia Penny, Walter Piston, Howard Swanson, Louis Talma, Virgil Thomson, and George Walker, all of whom have contributed to American music.

Figure 20.5 Nadia
Boulanger, influential
teacher of many
American composers,
with Sir Yehudi
Menuhin, violinist and
conductor.

AARON COPLAND

Aaron Copland (b. 1900) was the first of this stream of Americans who traveled to
France to study with Boulanger. He developed an abstract, neoclassical style. Among
his works in this style are the brilliant *Piano Variations* (1930) and the rhythmically
complex *Short Symphony* (1933).

By the mid-1930s, however, Copland began to be dissatisfied with the growing
distance between the concert-going public and the contemporary composer. "I felt
that it was worth the effort to see if I couldn't say what I had to say in the simplest
terms possible," Copland wrote. Increasingly thereafter he drew on themes of regional America. His best-known scores are three ballets: *Billy the Kid* (1938) and
Rodeo (1942) use actual cowboy songs; *Appalachian Spring* (1944) depicts life in
rural Pennsylvania and is among the most beautiful and enduring representatives of
Americana in our musical heritage.

Copland also wrote film scores during this period, among others *Of Mice and
Men* (1939), *Our Town* (1940), and *The Red Pony* (1948). Several patriotic works,
including the *Lincoln Portrait* (1942) and *Fanfare for the Common Man* (1942),
were occasioned by the entry of the United States into World War II. Almost all these
works used American subjects and were aimed at the wider audience provided by
such media as film. Like Stravinsky, Copland turned to serial composition after 1950.
The *Connotations for Orchestra* (1962) adapts the twelve-tone technique to his special musical style. For the past several decades Copland has spent much of his time
conducting concerts of his own music all over the world.

Figure 20.6 One of Aaron Copland's abiding concerns has been to bridge the gap between the concert-going public and the modern composer.

Appalachian Spring, the last of Copland's three ballets on American frontier themes, was written on commission for Martha Graham's modern dance company. The work, choreographed by Miss Graham, premiered in October, 1944.

Scored originally for a chamber orchestra of thirteen instruments, the ballet was later revised by Copland as a suite for symphony orchestra and is best known today in this form. The ballet itself is virtually plotless, having for its characters a young bride (originally danced by Miss Graham), her farmer husband-to-be, an older pioneering woman, and a preacher with his followers.

The music, evoking a simple, tender, and pastoral atmosphere, is distinctly American in its use of folklike themes suggesting barn dances, fiddle tunes, and revival hymns. Only one is actually a genuine folk tune: the Shaker song "Simple Gifts," which forms the basis for a set of five variations. Not only his melodic material, but also Copland's compositional techniques suggest a native American musical style. The orchestral texture is, by and large, open and transparent, with the different instrumental choirs—string, woodwind, brass, and percussion (chiefly piano and harp)—scored as individual units and juxtaposed with one another. The vigorous, four-square rhythmic patterns, particularly in the music for the revivalist preacher and his followers, could not have originated anywhere but in the folk music of the American frontier.

The orchestral suite falls into eight distinct sections, set off from one another by changes in tempo and meter. The opening section, marked "very slowly," introduces the characters, one by one. Over a luminous string background, solo woodwind and

COPLAND:
APPALACHIAN
SPRING

SIDE 14/SELECTION 2
LISTENING GUIDE
ON PAGES 422–23

brass instruments enter one by one—paralleling the balletic action—with slowly rising and falling figures that outline different major triads. It is not until the solo flute and violin enter that these triadic figures coalesce into any kind of definite "theme:"

Example 20.10
Examples 20.10–20.15 from Aaron Copland, *Appalachian Spring,* © 1945 by Aaron Copland, Renewed 1972. Reprinted by permission of Aaron Copland, copyright owner, and Boosey & Hawkes, Inc., sole publishers and licensees.

(Solo Violin doubles an octave higher.)

The serene mood of the introduction is suddenly broken by a vigorous, strongly accented theme sounded in unison in the strings and piano.

Example 20.11

The action of the ballet now gets under way. The theme—initially built on the notes of an A-major triad—is soon broken down into smaller motives with the rhythmic figure ♪♩ predominating.

Musical development intensifies as these motives are passed back and forth between different orchestral choirs and solo instruments. Constant changes in meter and shifts in rhythmic accents add to the increasing momentum of this section.

Then follows a *pas de deux* (a dance for two performers) for the bride and her husband-to-be, and their mixed feelings of tenderness and passion are expressed in a lyrical melody originating in the clarinet.

Example 20.12

The melody gradually expands and takes a definitive shape through numerous changes in tempo, culminating in a statement divided among the oboe, clarinet, and flute.

The revivalist preacher and his followers take over, announced by a cheerful tune that seems to have come right out of a country fiddlers' convention. Though heard first in the oboe and then the flute, the tune is not given fully until the entry of the violins.

Example 20.13

As in the second section, the rhythmic aspects of the tune soon prove to be more important than the melodic ones. The pace becomes more frenetic, cross-accents and syncopations soon predominate, and the section ends in a very Stravinskian manner with alternating meters of 2/4 and 5/8.

An extended solo for the bride follows, in which she expresses extremes of joy and fear, and exaltation at her coming motherhood. A presto theme forms the basis for most of this section,

Example 20.14

but toward the end a lyrical theme—very much like that of the earlier *pas de deux*—enters in the solo violin and oboe, gradually leading into a short recapitulation of the introduction.

A solo clarinet presents the melody of the Shaker song "Simple Gifts."

Example 20.15

The action of the ballet at this point, scenes of daily activity for the bride and her intended, seem perfectly reflected in the tune. The text of the song runs as follows:

'Tis the gift to be simple,
'Tis the gift to be free,
'Tis the gift to come down where we ought to be,
And when we find ourselves in the place just right,
'Twill be in the valley of love and delight.
When true simplicity is gain'd,
To bow and to bend we shan't be asham'd,
To turn, turn will be our delight
'Till by turning, turning, we come round right.

The five variations following the statement of the tune present the melody in a variety of contrasting textures and accompanimental figures, often with new lines of counterpoint. At the end, the full orchestra blazes forth in a broad choralelike setting of the tune.

In the final section, the bride takes her place among her neighbors, and they depart quietly, leaving the young couple alone. Once again the luminous sonorities of the introduction return, and the work concludes in the atmosphere of serenity with which it began.

To the list of conservative American composers of the early twentieth century should be added William Schuman (b. 1900) and the neoromanticists Samuel Barber (1910–1981) and Gian Carlo Menotti (b. 1911), known primarily for his operas for both stage and television.

Other composers in the beginning of the century were taking more radical approaches to compositional techniques and musical style.

Henry Cowell (1879–1965), a West Coast composer, experimented with many radical compositional procedures which would later have considerable influence. His most well-known device, found mainly in his piano works, is the **tone cluster.** This dense, indistinct sound can be produced by playing a large group of adjacent notes on the piano with the flat of the hand. It is said that Béla Bartók wrote Cowell asking permission to use this "invention" of his American colleague. Cowell wrote energetically about and published modern music as well, especially promoting the work of Charles Ives and Edgard Varèse.

EDGARD VARÈSE

Edgard Varèse (1883–1965) was born in Paris, but came to New York to live in 1915 and became one of the most innovative and influential composers of the twentieth century. Varèse challenged conservative musical traditions by defining music as "organized sound." This meant *all* sound, including some previously classified as nonmusical noises, such as Cowell's tone clusters.

Many of Varèse's compositions employ unusual combinations of instruments, which often play at the extremes of their registers. The musical idiom is characterized by violent, screechingly dissonant, and blocklike chords spanning many octaves. Varèse's titles often reflect an interest in science: *Hyperprism* (1923), *Intégrales* (1925), *Ionisation* (1930–1933), and *Density 21.5* for solo flute (1936). The sound of the music tends to recall the noises of mechanized society. *Ionisation,* written for percussion ensemble, employs a huge battery of standard orchestral percussion and exotic instruments as well, such as the "lion's-roar" (a primitive kind of friction drum), and three sirens. The sirens illustrate Varèse's passion for expanding sound resources beyond those of the normal orchestra. Later, the development of more sophisticated electronic means was to inspire Varèse to write such masterpieces as *Desérts* (1949–1954) and *Poème électronique* (1957–1958).

Wallingford Riegger (1885–1961) adapted serial procedures freely in such works as *Dichotomy* for chamber orchestra (1932) and his Third Symphony (1948).

Ives, Charles

Three Places in New England. Each of the three movements of this work illustrates a different facet of the composer's highly individualistic technique: the first (The "St. Gaudens" in Boston Common) presents a subtle and complex use of traditional American melodies; the second ('Putnam's Camp,' Redding, Connecticut) depicts a lively Fourth of July celebration, complete with colliding brass bands; the last ("The Housatonic at Stockbridge") is a wonderfully evocative tone poem portraying a quiet New England river.

Schuman, William

New England Triptych. In this piece for symphony orchestra, Schuman used three works by the early American composer, William Billings, "Be Glad Then, America," When Jesus Wept, and the hymn tune, "Chester." Each piece forms the basis for one of the movements.

Seeger, Ruth Crawford

String Quartet (1931). This work is recognized as one of the most outstanding works in American chamber music. In it the composer employs a number of compositional techniques which came into vogue much later in the century. The third movement features "dynamic counterpoint" in which the listener's attention moves from one voice to another because of dynamic level rather than melodic interest. The fourth movement is an example of "total serialization" in which all aspects of the piece (pitches, rests, rhythm, and dynamics) are serialized.

Swanson, Howard

Short Symphony. Howard Swanson is one of the first blacks to be recognized in the first half of the twentieth century. His *Short Symphony* (1948) is probably his best known work.

Varèse, Edgard

Ionization. This is one of the first pieces of Western music scored entirely for solo percussion instruments (including sirens, piano, gong, bongos, bass drums, maracas, and chimes).

MUSIC OF THE LATE TWENTIETH CENTURY

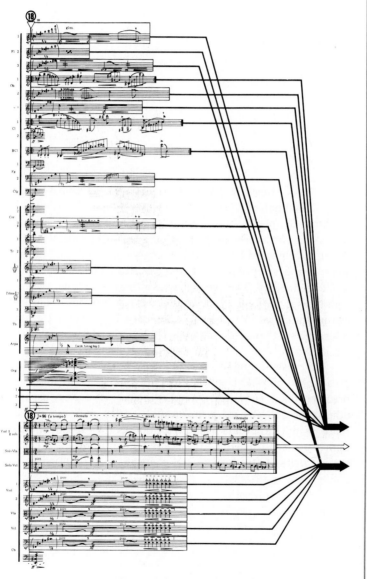

"Windows" by Jacob Druckman. © 1974 by MCA Music
Publishing, a division of MCA, Inc., New York, NY.
Used by permission. All rights reserved.

CHAPTER 1

MUSIC IN THE SECOND HALF OF THE TWENTIETH CENTURY

|M| usic after World War II continued and extended trends originated during the first half of the twentieth century. These trends included atonality, serialism, rhythmic complexity, and the use of unconventional sounds as valid musical materials. Along with this continuation, new and more radical notions about the way music might be composed became increasingly important, and the rapidity with which new ideas were developed and put into practice was accelerated by the intrusion of electronic technology. The development of magnetic tape, the long playing record, and high-quality playback equipment influenced the mode of musical communication from live performance in the direction of recording. The later availability of computer-controlled synthesizers made possible entirely new ways of composing and performing music.

The years immediately following World War II produced two opposing approaches to musical composition. One approach was **total serialism**—the complete, predetermined, and ultrarational organization of every aspect of a composition. The other approach was **indeterminacy**—the free, unpremeditated, and irrational occurrence of musical events which were deliberately meant to lie beyond the composer's immediate control. Other terms for indeterminacy are **chance music** and **aleatory music** (*alea* is Latin for game of chance).

TOTAL SERIALIZATION

The French composer and conductor Pierre Boulez (b. 1925) described the feelings of younger post-war composers: "After the war we all felt that music, like the world around us, was in a state of chaos. Our problem was to create a new musical language . . . We went through a period of seeking out total control over music."

Arnold Schoenberg's twelve-tone technique applied only to pitch and did not impose a similar mode of organization on rhythm, dynamics, tone color, or texture. It was the lean, lucid, and compact serial technique of Anton Webern that became the model for young composers in the pursuit of total serialism.

The first composer to apply serial procedures to all aspects of music was the American composer, Milton Babbitt (b. 1916). Babbitt extended the system of organizing pitch (melody and harmony) to the systematization of rhythm, tempo, dynamics, and timbre. His Second String Quartet (1954) is considered to be a model of serial organization.

At about the same time the French composer and teacher at the Paris Conservatory, Olivier Messiaen (b. 1908), was experimenting with total serialization. His students, Pierre Boulez and Karlheinz Stockhausen (b. 1928), became two of the most important figures on the international music scene. Other prominent serial composers of the 1950s were the Hungarian György Ligeti (b. 1923), the Italians, Luigi Nono (b. 1924) and Luciano Berio (b. 1925), and the American, Gunther Schuller (b. 1925).

Figure 21.2 Milton Babbitt at the huge RCA Mark II Synthesizer. In several important works, including the rigorously serial *Philomel,* Babbitt has pitted a singer against recorded sound.

CHANCE MUSIC (INDETERMINACY)

The years immediately following the war saw the rise of chance music. In chance music, elements such as pitches, rhythmic values, and dynamic levels are determined by various extramusical methods such as throwing dice or tossing coins. Another type of chance music takes place in the performance in which the performer determines aspects of the flow of the music.

JOHN CAGE

The chief figure in chance music is the American composer, John Cage (b. 1912). His 1951 piano piece, *Music of Changes,* was the first work based in large part on random procedures. For it, Cage tossed coins and used the results to determine musical materials from the *I Ching,* (Chinese *Book of Changes*). The map of the heavens supplied the note heads for *Atlas Eclipticalis* (1961–1962). This work consists of eighty-six instrumental parts "to be played in whole or part, any duration, in any ensemble, chamber or orchestral."

Cage has been one of the great innovaters in the twentieth century. The role of silence and of the unpredictable background noises that are always present is embodied in *4'33'',* Cage's famous 1952 example of pure "nonmusic." The piece consists

Figure 21.3 John Cage's experiments in indeterminacy have had enormous impact on the new music. Many current composers, including leading serialists, have adopted aspects of this "music of chance."

entirely of whatever environmental sounds happen to be present during its performance, in which a pianist sits quietly before an open piano for four minutes and thirty-three seconds, then leaves the stage. The point of this gesture is to focus attention on the sounds around us furthering the premise that any sound or no sound at all is as valid or "good" as any other.

Cage's pieces are all radically different from one another, but they have things in common: they are programmed activities with certain boundaries set by the composer who has only a limited control over the outcome of the piece. Like the wind blowing a mobile and thereby changing its shape, the performers make decisions on the spur of the moment, thus avoiding rational control.

Cage's impact has been and continues to be great. Many serialist composers such as Boulez and Stockhausen as well as younger composers such as Pauline Oliveros (b. 1932) have adapted aspects of chance music in varying degrees.

ELECTRONIC MUSIC

The development of advanced electronic technology in the 1950s and 1960s made possible radical changes in the way music can be composed and performed. Magnetic tape, synthesizers, and computers allow the composer to control every aspect of music and made possible accurate rendition of the music without relying on live performers. The tape is both the piece of music *and* its performance.

Figure 21.4 Karlheinz Stockhausen, one of the foremost exponents of total serialism, has also made use of chance elements and minimalist techniques.

Musique Concrète

An example of electronic music is **musique concrète.** Any kind of sound may be used in musique concrète, such as street noise, sounds from nature, human singing and speech, and usual or unusual sounds from traditional musical instruments, all of which can be manipulated and recombined on tape. After prerecording, sound alteration, cutting, and splicing are finished, the piece has been both composed and performed by the composer in a permanently accurate version. Early masterpieces of musique concrète are Stockhausen's *Gesang der Junglinge* (*Song of the Youths,* 1956), *Poeme électronique* (1958) by Edgard Varèse, and Berio's *Omaggio a Joyce* (*Homage to Joyce,* 1958).

Music for Synthesizer

Because the medium of tape offered complete and accurate control over both the piece of music and its "performance," it attracted serialists such as Babbitt and Stockhausen, whose music had become incredibly difficult to execute by performers. These composers went beyond the sounds of musique concrète. Using the synthesizer they invented entirely *new* sounds. Important synthesized electronic works of the 1950s and 1960s are Stockhausen's *Electronic Studies I and II,* Babbitt's *Composition for Synthesizer, Silver Apples of the Moon* by Morton Subotnick (b. 1933) and *Time's Encomium* by Charles Wuorinen (b. 1938).

Figure 21.5 Philip Glass, an early minimalist who became widely known for his opera, *Einstein on the Beach*.

Tape and Live Performers

Taped sounds in combination with live performers has yielded many interesting and beautiful works. Edgard Varèse used such a combination in his *Déserts* (1954) in which music for winds, brass and percussion alternates with taped musique concrète. Mario Davidovsky (b. 1934) with his series of *Synchronisms* (1963–1977) and Jacob Druckman (b. 1928) with his *Animus* series have created brilliant works for live performance with prerecorded tape. Barbara Kolb (b. 1939) has produced a string of interesting works including *Looking for Claudio* (1975) scored for seven guitars, mandolins, vibraphone, chimes, and three humming voices. All but one solo guitar are provided by prerecorded tape. During the performance, the solo guitar part is supplied live, along with the tape.

MINIMALISM

Partly as a reaction against the extreme complexities that characterized much music of the twentieth century a new style developed in the 1960s. This new style, dubbed **minimalism,** began as a trend toward musical simplicity, and was essentially an American phenomenon. Its early advocates were four young American composers, La-Monte Young (b. 1935), Terry Riley (b. 1935), Steve Reich (b. 1936), and Philip Glass (b. 1937).

In the music of the minimalists, we hear seemingly endless repetitions of short musical fragments or patterns. This basic material changes only gradually and over long time spans, and the listener loses a sense of "real time" due to the hypnotical

Figure 21.6 Minimalist composer John Adams at a rehearsal of his opera *Nixon in China,* 1987.

repetition and slow rate of gradual, almost imperceptible change. Terry Riley's *In C* (1964) was one of the first pieces of music to be called minimalist. In it each member of a musical ensemble is given short musical fragments numbered from one through fifty-three. Each player plays all fifty-three fragments in order. However, each performer is free to repeat each fragment any number of times at his or her discretion. These fragments are played against the constant pulsating of the tone C played on the piano throughout the entire piece. The effect of this procedure is one of endless repetition with very subtle change over a long stretch of time.

Steve Reich's minimalist compositions include *It's Gonna Rain* (1965), *Piano Phase* (1967), and *Music for 18 Musicians* (1976). Philip Glass is best known for his opera *Einstein on the Beach* (1975).

The new generation of minimalist composers is headed by John Adams (b. 1947), whose *The Desert Music* (1984) is a large symphonic setting of poems by William Carlos Williams. More recently his opera, *Nixon in China,* received its first performance in 1987.

Atonality, serialism, chance music, electronic music, musique concrète, minimalism, and music that fits into none of these categories reflect the rich diversity of musical thought, techniques, and styles that characterize music of the second half of the twentieth century. This stylistic pluralism is well illustrated in the music of four American composers.

MILTON BABBITT

Milton Babbitt (b. 1916) is one of the most influential composers of the second half of the twentieth century. He was attracted to serial music early in his career and was the first composer to apply serial techniques to all aspects of a composition in such works as Three Compositions for Piano (1947), Composition for Four Instruments (1946), and Composition for Twelve Instruments (1948). Babbitt was a pioneer in electronic music and has composed a number of works using tape and synthesizer. Many of his tape works include live performers. Among these works are *Vision and Prayer* (1961), *Philomel* (1964), and *Phonemena* (1974), all for tape and soprano.

Phonemena is a short serial work the title of which refers to *phonemes*—the smallest sound unit of speech. For this piece, the composer arranged twenty-four consonants and twelve vowels into a "text" that forms part of the comprehensive serial organization. (The phonemes are not organized into words; they are used merely as sounds.) The work is a virtuoso piece for singer and is an elegant example of Babbitt's style.

BABBITT: PHONEMENA SIDE 14/SELECTION 3

TERRY RILEY

Along with La Monte Young, Steve Reich, and Philip Glass, Terry Riley was a founding father of minimalism. His piece *In C* (1964) was a ground breaking work in the minimalist movement. As a result of a recording contract with CBS, *In C* was issued in 1968 and Riley has continued to record his music throughout his career.

A Rainbow in Curved Air, one of Riley's early works, is an excellent example of early minimalism. It is written for multiple keyboards; one provides a constant background over which the others improvise.

RILEY: RAINBOW IN CURVED AIR SIDE 15/SELECTION 1

JOHN CORIGLIANO

John Corigliano (b. 1938), distinguished Professor of Music at Lehman College in New York City, is in the midst of a highly varied career. Since completing his formal music training at Columbia University, he has held a number of posts and has been active in highly disparate endeavors. He has been a music programmer for prominent radio stations, and an associate producer of musical programs for CBS television. He has arranged rock music for record companies and in 1970 composed *The Naked Carmen,* an "electric rock opera" after Bizet. His music for the movie *Altered States* won an Academy Award nomination in 1980.

He has written some of the most accessible and enjoyable music in the second half of the twentieth century beginning with his *Violin* Sonata which won a prize at the Spoleto Festival. He is best known for his concertos for Piano (1968), Oboe (1975), Clarinet (1977) and Flute, *Pied Piper Fantasy* (1981). His most recent major work is the opera, *A Figaro for Antonio,* commissioned by the Metropolitan Opera Company in New York.

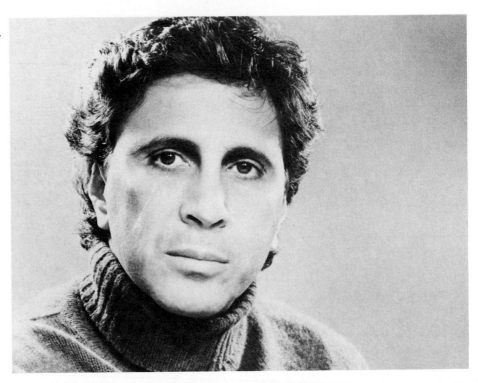

Figure 21.7 John Corigliano, composer of a variety of works, including concertos, operas, and film music.

CORIGLIANO:
TOURNAMENTS
OVERTURE
SIDE 15/SELECTION 3
LISTENING GUIDE ON
PAGES 438–39

Corigliano's first piece for full orchestra is *Tournaments* Overture composed in 1965. The composer calls it a "contest piece" in which sections of the orchestra and individual players compete with one another in virtuoso playing.

MIRIAM GIDEON

Miriam Gideon (b. 1906) is an inventive and effective composer of works for solo voice and instrumental accompaniment. In much of her vocal music she employs the unusual practice of setting the text bilingually, alternating between English and another language or languages. *Mixco* (1957) was her first song of this kind. In it each verse is sung first in English, then in Spanish. *The Condemned Playground* (1963) was written for soprano, tenor, flute, bassoon, and string quartet and is set in four languages—Latin, Japanese, French, and English.

Songs of Youth and Madness, on poems by the German poet Friedrich Hölderlin, is a substantial work composed in 1977 on a grant from the National Endowment for the Arts. The piece is scored for soprano and orchestra and consists of four poems set to music in both English and German versions. "To Diotima," the second song in the cycle, illustrates Gideon's bilingual approach to vocal music.

TO DIOTIMA

Beautiful being, you live as do
Delicate blossoms in winter;
In a world that's grown old,
Hidden, you blossom alone.

Lovingly outward you press
To bask in the light of the springtime;
To be warmed by it still,
Look for the youth of the world.

But your sun, the lovelier world,
Has gone down now,
And the quarreling gales
Rage in an icy bleak night.

Schönes Leben! du lebst
Wie die zarten Blüthen im Winter,
In der gealterten Welt
Blühst du verschlossen, allein.

Liebend strebst du hinaus,
Dich zu sonnen am Lichte des Frühlings;
Zu erwarmen an ihr
Suchst du die Jugend der Welt

Deine Sonne, die schönere
Zeit ist untergegangen
Und in frostiger Nacht
Zanken Orkane sich nun.

    The poem consists of two different statements of the same idea, first in English, then in German. The musical structure of the song corresponds to the two-part plan of the poem. A brief orchestral interlude divides the song in half; the first consisting of three stanzas in English, the second part having three stanzas in German. The language contrast between the English and German versions of the poem is enhanced by the musical setting in which the composer uses musical material to reflect the meaning, spirit, and particular inflections of each language. In both sections, the words are set syllabically so that they are always clear, almost as if spoken. The clarity of the text is aided by the relationship between the solo voice and the orchestra. For the most part, the voice is predominant; the orchestra is used to support the voice.

Corigliano: Tournaments Overture

Single Movement: tempo varies
meter varies
irregular alternating form

Large Orchestra

Germ Idea **(Introduction)**		emphatic three-note germ (pitch moves up a step, down a step), expanded to five notes, three-note "sparks of light," dissolve
A	*la*	theme 1 (begins with germ idea) gently, imitated throughout woodwinds and strings; brass, faster rhythms; strings return, gently, then woodwinds, trumpet, extended imitation, low strings join
	b	horns, forte, transition to:
	2a	piccolo and double basses in unison, jaunty statement of theme 1, short string interruption
	b	woodwinds, jaunty statement, imitation; piccolo and double basses; woodwinds join, brass, crescendo, two drumbeats
A		doodle-doodle horn accompaniment, whirlwind development of germ idea in woodwinds, plunging string scales, trumpet calls, mounting excitement, crescendo; xylophone fragments; snare drum, trombone smears, trumpet and horn calls; xylophone; full orchestra, trombone smears, snare drum builds into:
Germ Idea		broad statement of three-note germ, dissolve extended through low piano, bass clarinet; pause
B	*la*	clarinet, swaying dance-like theme 2 (inversion of theme 1 idea), flute, strings; violins and woodwinds, pause
	b	muted solo viola, muted solo cello, flute, bassoon, other instruments enter gradually
	c	brasses enter, tempo quickens; texture fragments to flute alone
	2	dance-like, woodwinds, then strings, horns; gradually slowing to single note high in violins
C		low strings, leaping melody, rise in pitch; woodwinds develop fragments; smooth swaying statement; leaping accompaniment in low strings; texture breaks up; fragment descends through flute, oboe, clarinet, bassoon, clarinet, bassoon
C'		loud chords; motive of leaping theme developed, strings; winds and horns; snare drum, trombones, directly into:

A		brass, triumphant statement of theme 1; repeated, extended, ends with drumbeat, forte
A'		doodle-doodle horn accompaniment, whirlwind development of germ idea in woodwinds, plunging string scales, trumpet calls, mounting excitement; xylophone fragments; snare drum, builds into:
Germ Idea:		three-note germ, expanded to five notes, three-note "sparks of light," dissolve
B	a	dance-like theme imitated among woodwinds, strings, horn; activity decreases gradually
	b	oboe descends in leaps, fragments echo through woodwinds, continue as:
C		low strings, leaping melody, rise in pitch; snare drum roll, rising transition to:
C'		trumpets, horns, strings, develop leaping theme; snare drum, trombones directly into:
A		brass, triumphant statement of theme 1; repeated; activity falls apart in fragments, pause
Coda		brass, forte, lead to piccolo and double basses, in jaunty statement, strings add triumphant statement; full orchestra joins, mounting excitement moves quickly to climax; trumpets emerge holding chord, full orchestra ends

••

SUMMARY

Music after World War II continued trends originated earlier in the century as well as developing new, radically different ideas and techniques. One of the new approaches was total serialism, in which every aspect of a composition is predetermined by the composer. This technique was used by such prominent composers as Pierre Boulez, Milton Babbitt, and Karlheinz Stockhausen. Another approach was indeterminacy (chance or aleatory music) in which most of the musical events of a piece lie beyond the immediate control of the composer. John Cage, one of the great innovators of modern music, is well-known for his chance compositions.

Electronic technology in the form of magnetic tape, synthesizers, and computers had a powerful impact on music composition. Musique concrète utilizes naturally occurring sounds which are then manipulated on magnetic tape. Synthesizers are used to create entirely new sounds and to accurately control aspects of a composition. Tapes and synthesizers are frequently used with each other as well as with live performers.

Minimalism developed in the 1960s as a reaction against the complexities of much modern music. In minimalist music, short musical patterns are repeated over long time spans with only gradual change. La Monte Young, Terry Riley, Steve Reich, and Philip Glass are considered the founders of minimalism.

Some composers, such as John Corigliano and Miriam Gideon, have developed their own individual styles without being adherents to any specific technical approach.

NEW TERMS

total serialism
indeterminacy (chance music, aleatory music)
electronic music

musique concrète
minimalism

SUGGESTED LISTENING

Babbitt, Milton

Philomel (1963–1964). The text of this work is by poet John Hollander, and is drawn from Greek myth. Babbitt's ingenious setting is scored for live soprano, prerecorded soprano, and synthesized sounds. *Philomel* defies the notion that total serialism produces music that is any less communicative than that produced by other techniques.

Boulez, Pierre

Improvisation sur Mallarmé II, "Une dentelle s'abolit" ("A piece of lace disappears," 1958). Boulez incorporated this ten-minute piece, written for soprano and nine keyboard and percussion players, into his large-scale *Pli selon pii* (1957–1962). Both versions illustrate the composer's tempering of pointillism with lacy, bell-like sounds and almost Debussian colors.

Cage, John

Concerto for Prepared Piano and Chamber Orchestra (1951). The delicate percussive sounds of Javanese gamelan music inspired Cage's "preparation" of the piano. Chance operations determined many of the musical events.

Messiaen, Olivier

Turangalila-Symphonie for piano, ondes Martenot, and orchestra (1946–1948). This immense and extravagant work employs many of the composer's stylistic traits, including sumptuous harmony, personalized uses of serial and ostinato procedures, and bird calls (especially in the sixth movement—"The garden of the sleep of love"). The piano and the electronic instrument known as the ondes Martenot are given featured roles.

Riley, Terry

In C for any combination of instruments (1964). This attractive example of minimalism is open to performance by almost everyone, for the "score," consisting of small fragments of melody played over and over, is printed right on the record album.

Stockhausen, Karlheinz

Gesang der Junglinge (*Song of the Youths* 1955–1956). A landmark "electroacoustical" work, combining sung sounds with electronically produced sounds. The sung sounds—though often distorted in various ways—become comprehensible words from time to time. The text is based on the Biblical account of Shadrach, Meshach, and Abednego being cast into the fiery furnace (Daniel 3).

Subotnick, Morton

Silver Apples of the Moon, electronic sounds on tape (1967). One of several albums commissioned specifically for recordings, this work illustrates the composer's rich and colorful palette of electronically produced sounds.

JAZZ AND ROCK

© M. Simpson/FGP International

JAZZ AND ROCK

||J|| azz is considered by many to be America's greatest contribution to music. Its impact on American society has been enormous and its influence on world culture has been far reaching. Its message has been direct, vital, and immediate, enabling it to hurdle cultural, linguistic, and political barriers.

ORIGINS OF JAZZ

The precise origins and early history of **jazz** cannot be chronicled because early jazz was neither notated nor recorded—it was *improvised* and existed only in performance.

It is clear, however, that what we now call jazz was rooted in southern America, inspired by experiences of black slaves and resulted from the interaction of several cultures—African, white and black American, and European.

When Africans, brought to this country as slaves, began to acquire aspects of American culture, particularly the Christian religion, a new kind of music began to emerge. To the European harmonies of the Christian hymns, the Afro-Americans added aspects of African rhythm, vocal inflection, and the pattern of *call and response*. In this pattern a leader "calls" (sings) a first line followed by an improvised answer sung by the chorus. Out of these various elements grew a body of black folk music consisting of work songs, spirituals, and dances. The emotional content of this music, its use of improvisation, and its forceful rhythms all figured in the emergence of the **blues.**

THE BLUES

The unique style of music known as the **blues** is the common strain running through virtually all American popular music. The style and phrasings of the blues can be found in the early music of the black churches, in country and western music, in songs by George Gershwin and other Broadway composers, and in current rock styles. But more than all else, the blues have influenced jazz styles, from the earliest to the most recent.

The blues are an intensely personal form of expression. Drawing on real experiences and deeply felt emotions such as loneliness, loss, and despair, the blues explore the frustrations of black American life.

By around 1900 the blues featured a highly structured style, with distinct forms for both the lyrics and the melodies. The standard lyrical pattern consisted of two rhyming lines of poetry with the first line (aab) as in the following example:

Now listen baby, you so good and sweet,
Now listen baby, you so good and sweet,
I want to stay 'round you, if I have to beg in the street.

The form of the blues is typically based on a twelve-bar harmonic progression in three phrases of four measures each. Only three chords are involved: tonic, dominant, and subdominant. The blues are usually played in 4/4 time. So-called **blue notes,** produced by flatting the third fifth, or seventh notes of a major scale, are used extensively. These notes can be manipulated by allowing the performer to slide into them, rather than hitting them solidly. The result is "bent" or "glided" pitches that produce a highly distinctive sound.

Early blues were created by vocalists, but many instrumentalists soon adopted blues techniques and devices. One of the most influential blues vocalists and interpreters of this art was Bessie Smith (1895–1937), whose powerful, emotional, and poetic style is legendary. The musicians who accompanied her used their instruments to wail, sob, and growl in imitation of the pathos of her blues technique. Other fine vocalists who have sung blues include Ella Fitzgerald, Billie Holiday (see biography), and Sarah Vaughan.

BILLIE HOLIDAY *(1915–1959)*

Women have usually played a part in jazz only as singers. Although there have been a few exceptions over the years (such as virtuoso pianist Mary Lou Williams and composer/bandleader Toshiko Akiyoshi), by far the widest avenue for women to enter the field has been as vocalists, and that remains the case even in our own "liberated" age.

Most of the leading jazz singers of the past few decades were greatly influenced by the classic female blues singers, such as Ma Rainey, Bessie Smith, and Ethel Waters. But the vocalist who brought the special art of the blues singer to its greatest heights and had the greatest influence on future jazz vocal styles was Billie Holiday (1915–1959).

Holiday was raised in the poorest section of Harlem, the daughter of a jazz guitarist with Fletcher Henderson's band who displayed little interest in Billie or her mother. She had a small, fragile voice and no musical training. Holiday got her start as a singer in 1933 at a club in Harlem, where her emotional rendition of "Body and Soul" had the customers in tears.

Shortly after she landed this job the eighteen-year-old Holiday was discovered by talent scout John Hammond (who later uncovered such talented contemporary performers as Aretha Franklin and Bob Dylan). Hammond arranged for her to record with Benny Goodman. Although these early records were disappointing, in 1936 she recorded with an all-star band that included Roy Eldridge, Ben Webster, Benny Goodman, and Lester Young. It was Young who gave her the nickname that stuck, "Lady Day." The 1936 recordings and subsequent ones, such as

Lady Day (Columbia CL 637), *Golden Years,* Vol. 1 (Columbia C 3L 21), and *The Billie Holiday Story* (MCA 4006E), demonstrate eloquently the unique vocal style that became her trademark.

After "paying her dues" as a band singer, first with Count Basie and then—as the first black female singer in a white band—with Artie Shaw, Holiday made a breakthrough as a single attraction. Throughout the 1940s, her personal life began to deteriorate but her fame continued to spread. She performed such standards as "He's Funny That Way," "Crazy He Calls Me," and "Stormy Weather," and she also wrote her own material, including the deeply felt "God Bless The Child." The last became a pop hit in the late 1960s for the rock group Blood, Sweat and Tears. But by then Lady Day had passed from the scene, a victim of drug addiction, alcoholism, police harassment, and her own tragic self-destructiveness. Although she did record extensively for producer Norman Granz during the 1950s, in general her career as well as her personal life had been deteriorating steadily, and on July 17, 1959, she died at the age of 44.

The events that surround her premature death have added a sordid luster to the legend of Billie Holiday and to some extent have obscured the very real contributions that she made to jazz. Where most vocalists sang the music "straight," Holiday made each song her own, improvising on the basic melody, changing the beat of a phrase, investing the song with her unique inflections and emotional quality. As she herself once put it, "I don't think I'm really singing. I feel like I'm playing a horn. I try to improvise like Les Young, like Louis Armstrong, or someone else I admire. What comes out is what I feel."[*]

[*] Dan Morganstern, *Jazz People* (New York: Abrams, 1976), p. 240.

between a bass note and a chord played an octave or more above the bass, giving the effect of "striding" back and forth, while the right hand played the melody. The stride style, which was applied to blues, popular songs, and show tunes, allowed ample opportunity for improvisation.

Boogie-woogie was a blues piano style which used a rhythmic ostinato bass of eight notes to the measure in the left hand, while the right hand played a simple, often improvised melody. Typical left-hand patterns were

The percussive bass part gave the sound and feel of the left hand "walking" over the piano keys. For this reason boogie-woogie is sometimes called the "walkin' bass."

Among the finest of the early jazz pianists were James P. Johnson (1891–1955), Willie "The Lion" Smith (1893–1973), and Thomas "Fats" Waller (1904–1943). Another innovative jazz pianist was Earl "Fatha" Hines (1905–1983), who early in his career worked with Louis Armstrong. Hines was influenced by Armstrong's inventive cornet style, which he translated into the "trumpet style" for keyboard. In this style, the right hand played a melody line (much as a trumpet player or any single-line player might do) while the left hand played chords in flurries, punctuating and complementing the solo line. Pianists of the later bebop era drew from and expanded on the trumpet style of playing.

SWING

By the mid-1930s, with the economy slowly recovering, larger ensembles began to make a comeback. Gradually jazz moved out of the saloons and into white as well as black ballrooms and dance halls. The big band sound, as it became known, soon reached an ever larger audience via radio. During this period New York, which had become the cultural and communications center of America, replaced Chicago as the major jazz city. Thus began the *swing* era, which lasted roughly from 1935 to 1950.

Swing featured big bands of perhaps fifteen to seventeen players, with the old New Orleans front line of cornet, clarinet, and trombone increased dramaticaly to include whole brass sections of trumpets and trombones, as well as woodwind sections of clarinets and saxophones. The rhythm section included piano, string bass, guitar, and drums.

Stylistically the big bands evolved in two directions. One style, which was shaped primarily by black bandleaders, was built around the solo performer. In a departure from traditional jazz, which was mostly improvised, loose arrangements of pieces were written down. Yet these arrangements were often modified by the bandleader to showcase the special talents of individual performers. A characteristic technique of these bands was the use of a riff, a short melodic line, usually rhythmic, which can be repeated over and over to form either the main melody or the background for improvised solos. The musical repertoire included many blues tunes and many original compositions.

Figure 22.5 Duke Ellington, an important and highly innovative pioneer in big band jazz.

The first of a long line of talented black bandleaders was Fletcher Henderson, an important innovator in band arranging in the 1920s and Benny Goodman's chief arranger in the late 1930s. But perhaps the most original contributions to big band jazz were made by Edward Kennedy "Duke" Ellington (1899–1974), a bandleader/ composer/pianist/arranger who brought out the best in his soloists with music so masterfully arranged that it created the effect if not always the fact of improvisation. During his long career, which spanned nearly half a century, he composed many popular standards ("Mood Indigo" "Take the 'A' Train," "It Don't Mean a Thing If You Ain't Got That Swing") as well as other works of great inventiveness, sophistication, and variety. Two other outstanding black musicians who gained fame in the swing era were William "Count" Basie, pianist and leader of a popular band, and saxophonist Lester Young, one of Basie's great soloists.

The other big band style is represented in the work of white bandleaders such as Benny Goodman, Harry James, Glenn Miller, Artie Shaw, Tommy Dorsey, and Woody Herman, all of whom drew on the black style but modified it for their predominantly white audiences. Their intricate, special arrangements were calculated to achieve a consistent and "characteristic" sound. Often the leader was showcased as the star personality and sometimes as the star soloist. A few other "star" soloists might also be featured, but the main emphasis was on the overall sound of the band as a unit. The standard bill of fare served up by this type of big band consisted of smooth, polished arrangements of popular tunes. The aim was to please the listening and dancing audience, a goal that tended to produce music that was commercially successful but not artistically innovative.

Figure 22.6 The great popularity of Benny Goodman as a jazz clarinetist and band leader led to the title, the "King of Swing."

BOP

At the height of the swing era, many jazz musicians rebelled against the big band style and its commercialization. These young rebels began to organize small "combos" that offered more opportunity for individual expression. The result was **Bebop** or just **Bop.**

It was in special after-hours clubs that young, adventurous, experimental musicians like guitarist Charlie Christian (1919–1942), pianist Thelonious Monk (see biography), and drummer Kenny Clarke (1914–1985) found the freedom to explore their personal potential. These and other musicians, notably trumpeter John "Dizzy" Gilliespie (b. 1917) and saxophonist Charlie "Bird" Parker (1920–1955), would work all night with the swing bands in Manhattan nightclubs and ballrooms, then ride north to Minton's Play House in the early morning to participate in "jam sessions" where they experimented with free-form solo work and harmonic improvisation. The new style they developed was given the name bebop (later shortened to simply bop). The bop combo consisted of one to three soloists supported by a rhythm section of drums and bass and sometimes piano or guitar.

Bop musicians sought to achieve a totally new sound by experimenting with various devices: wide leaps in melody, phrases of uneven lengths, and rhythmic variety. Kenny Clarke introduced an extraordinary rhythmic innovation with his technique of "dropping bombs"—that is, placing unanticipated bass drum accents before or after the beat. Almost singlehandedly, Clarke sniffed the focus of jazz drumming away from the objective of simply keeping time. Now drummers worked around an implicit rather than a stated beat, and whatever timekeeping was necessary in the bop group usually fell to the bass player.

Another difference between bop and jazz styles that preceded it was its exploration of chromatic harmonies, an innovation that expanded the range of harmonic possibilities.

Improvisation continued to be an integral part of bop. Among those who gained fame for their improvisations were Charlie Parker and Charlie Christian. Christian was a natural musician who first popularized the use of amplified guitar as a jazz instrument. In his improvisations, however, he inspired later horn players as much as later guitarists, because he did much of his solo work on a single string. Ironically, Christian died in 1942 at the age of 24, only three years after the public debut of the music he helped shape. Good examples of Christian's single-string solo work occur in "I Found a New Baby" and "Blues Sequence," both recorded with the Benny Goodman Sextet (*Smithsonian Collection of Classic Jazz,* P11894).

THELONIOUS MONK *(1917–1982)*

Jazz musicians in general (and bop players in particular) have never been noted for their conformity. Even among such strongly individualistic personalities, however, pianist Thelonious Monk (1917–1982) stands out. Monk was his own man. Primarily a self-taught musician, he played in a manner that was totally "wrong" in standard pianistic technique—his fingers were practically unbending—yet it somehow worked for him. He pounded out his music in a syncopated, percussive style that was too unusual and individualistic for many; thus, the New York-bred musician often had difficulty gaining employment, even in his hometown.

For years he worked only sporadically, playing obscure Harlem nightclubs and an occasional "downtown" job arranged by fellow musicians and admirers like Coleman Hawkins. It was not until 1947, when Monk was already thirty, that he made his first recording with Blue Note Records. This and later recordings, such as *Genius of Modern Music,* Vols. 1 and 2 (Blue Note 81510, 81511) created a storm of critical comment, both pro and con, concerning Monk's unorthodox and unpredictable style, which utilized constant rhythmic variations and startling harmonic improvisations as well as an understated sense of humor. Despite the success of his recordings, he nevertheless continued to have trouble finding steady work.

Yet Monk did enjoy the respect and admiration of his peers, including bandleader Miles Davis, who asked Monk to record with him in 1954 (though he insisted that Monk refrain from playing during his solos, since his style was too distracting). Finally, in the mid-1950s, Monk began to gain some measure of popular acceptance with regular gigs

Figure 22.7 Thelonious Monk, whose unorthodox piano technique and unpredictable music style made him one of the outstanding individuals in the bop era.

at the Five Spot Club in the Bowery, which became a haven for all those interested in exploring the challenges of the new music known as bop.

By 1964, Monk's career had progressed to the point that he was featured on the cover of *Time* magazine. Thelonious Monk had finally become established in the jazz world's hierarchy. Despite ill health, Monk made a triumphant return to the Newport Jazz Festival in 1975 and gave a brilliant Carnegie Hall recital in 1976.

A NEW ATTITUDE

Besides being musically advanced, bop was one manifestation of a larger social protest movement whose members later became known as the "beat generation." Part of the "beat" attitude was an insistence on a "cool," detached manner. No longer did bandleaders extend the customary amenities to the audience, such as announcing song titles or hamming it up between tunes. The early bop players, though not outwardly rude to their audience, intended to make no concessions or commercial compromises with their music.

At least part of the detached attitude and the militant image of the bop musicians was due to changes in the way they saw themselves. At the same time as traditional swing music structure was being abandoned, many black musicians were undergoing a shift in consciousness. Whereas older black players had been forced to play the sometimes unwanted role of "entertainer" for the amusement of their predominantly white audience, the newer generation of players asumed a more self-assertive stance. As John Lewis of the Modern Jazz Quarter once put it:

> This revolution, or whatever you want to call it, in the 1940's took place for many reasons, not only musical ones . . . For the younger musicians, this was the way to react against the attitude that Negroes were supposed to entertain people. The new attitude was: "Either you listen to me on the basis of what I actually do or forget it."*

POST BEBOP

The flexibility of jazz and its ability to adapt to trends is evident in the period following World War II. There was a revival of interest in Dixieland and Chicago Style, and a number of swing bands were able to survive and are still active today. Bebop continued as the main stream of jazz development, evolving in the 1950s into a style known as hard bop. Hard bop is still today the basic style of pure jazz. Alongside these styles, new styles took their places; the most popular of these are cool jazz, free jazz, and rock-jazz (fusion).

Cool Jazz

Cool jazz came about as a reaction to bop. The frenzied quality of bop was countered by a cool and detached sound. The leaders of this new style were pianist Lennie Tristano (1919–1978) and Miles Davis (b. 1926). It was Davis' nine-piece band that set the general style of cool jazz in the recordings known as *Birth of the Cool* in 1949–1950. Davis' group consisted of a French horn, trumpet, trombone, tuba, alto and baritone saxophone, piano, string bass, and drums, an ensemble that approximated the mellow sound of the Claude Thornhill orchestra.

* Nat Hentoff, *Jazz Is* (New York: Random House, 1976), pp. 259–260.

Figure 22.8 Miles Davis, an outstanding trumpet player, has retained a lyric style in his "cool jazz" and "rock jazz" music while incorporating some of the avant-garde's modal and improvisatory techniques.

Another group that contributed to the style was the Modern Jazz Quartet headed by pianist John Lewis (b. 1920). This group incorporated classical forms such as the rondo and fugue into jazz, even playing actual classical compositions with a jazz flavor. In addition, the Dave Brubeck Quartet made excursions into odd-metered music in such compositions as "Take Five" in 5/4 meter and "Blue Rondo a la Turk" in an irregular 9/8. And the American composer, Gunther Schuller (b. 1925) made what is sometimes called "Third Stream" music; music consisting of the combination of jazz and classical music.

Free Jazz

Free jazz was the most radical departure from previous styles. It is the result of the work of several jazz musicians, particularly John Coltrane (1926–1967) and Ornette Coleman (b. 1930). John Coltrane became an influential jazz figure after he joined Miles Davis' organization. Moving beyond bebop, he explored complex harmonies and modal scale systems. He extended the possibilities of the saxophone through flights into extreme registers of the instrument. His efforts to expand the frontiers of jazz improvisations were shared by Ornette Coleman.

Figure 22.12 One of the most important figures in the history of rock, Chuck Berry's aggressive and driving songs, innovative guitar techniques, and striking stage presence made him one of rock's earliest stars.

Grammy awards from the National Academy of Recording Arts and Sciences in the same year, one for the best classical recording of the year (for performances of trumpet concerts by Haydn and Hummel), and one for the best jazz recording.

Since its inception aroud the turn of the century, jazz, in its many styles has been integral to American culture and has represented America in many parts of the world. Its flexibility and adjustability will undoubtedly ensure its continued growth in the future.

ROCK

In 1955 the movie *Blackboard Jungle* featured the song "Rock Around the Clock." Almost overnight rock culture was born and the rock generation was on its way. Rock music in its many forms became a major force in the musical, social, and political upheaval that occupied young people in the 1960s.

While rock music became popular virtually overnight in 1955, it had developed over a considerable period of time. As was the case with jazz, much of rock's early history was the work of black musicians such as Chuck Berry and Little Richard. Black **rhythm and blues** supplied an essential ingredient for rock—an insistently heavy beat, hard driving sound, and earthy vocals with electric guitar. The other main component came from **country and western** music representing the white American folk tradition popularized in the "Grand Ole Opry" broadcasts and by such popular figures as Gene Autry and Roy Rogers.

Figure 22.13 Elvis Presley, whose popularity as a rock performer created a cult that continued beyond his death.

Elvis Presley

The first period of rock music culminated in the personality and music of Elvis Presley (1935–1977), the most important rock artist to appear in the middle 1950s. Presley gained enormous popularity and was regarded as "king of **rock 'n' roll**" for almost ten years.

The Presley craze opened the floodgates for rock music and musicians. A number of other white rockers became popular, among them Jerry Lee Lewis ("Great Balls of Fire,") Carl Perkins ("Blue Suede Shoes,") and Buddy Holly ("That'll be the Day"). Black performers such as Chuck Berry ("Maybelline"), Little Richard ("Tutti Frutti"), and Fats Domino ("Blueberry Hill") began to see their records "cross over" from the rhythm and blues charts to gain acceptance from the white audience.

Soul and Motown

Gospel-style singing, with its dynamic emotion, combined with blues, jazz, and rhythm and blues to form **soul** music. Soul had been popular for years with black audiences but didn't become popular with whites until the mid-1960s. The Rolling Stones and other groups who recorded black soul tunes introduced white Americans to the sounds of soul and made it easier for black artists to gain widespread acceptance. Among the most popular soul artists are Aretha Franklin ("Respect"), Otis Redding ("I Can't Turn You Loose"), James Brown ("Papa's Got a Brand New Bag"), and Wilson Pickett

Figure 22.14 Aretha Franklin, whose roots are in gospel music, has successfully performed rock, jazz, rhythm and blues, and soul. Her powerful vocal style has earned her the title "Queen of Soul."

("The Midnight Hour"). Soul is as much an attitude as a style, but it is always spirited, raw-edged music and frequently features wailing vocals and hard-driving rhythm and brass sections.

Another development in popular music of the 1960s was the Motown sound—so called because the headquarters of Motown Records was in Detroit, the "motor city." Berry Gordy, the head of Motown Records, was largely responsible for the development of Motown's musical personality, which is represented by groups like the Supremes ("Stop in the Name of Love") and the Temptations ("My Girl") and by solo performers like Stevie Wonder ("I Was Made to Love Her") and Marvin Gaye ("How Sweet It Is").

The difference between Motown and soul is the difference between satin and burlap. In contrast to the wailing, visceral sound of soul, the Motown sound features intricate, highly polished arrangements and relies on precise studio production for its smooth, elegant sound.

The Beatles

Four young Englishmen from Liverpool calling themselves the Beatles "invaded" the United States in 1964. Almost overnight, they changed the face of American popular music. Their first American recording, "I Wanna Hold Your Hand," sold a million copies after only ten days on the market. During 1964–65 they recorded albums and single recordings that represented virtually every style of rock music of the sixties:

Figure 22.15 The Beatles, in a recording session.

rhythm and blues, "Roll Over Beethoven" (Chuck Berry), "Money," and "She's a Woman"; country and western (rockabilly), "I've Just Seen a Face" and "Words of Love"; folk, "I'll Follow the Sun"; ballad, "And I Love Her," "If I Fell," and "Till There Was You."

The genius of the Beatles, particularly that of the songwriters John Lennon and Paul McCartney, emerged as they experimented with rock style. One of the best examples of such experimentation is their 1967 recording *Sgt. Pepper's Lonely Hearts Club Band*. In this, the first "conceptual" or "song cycle" rock album, each song relates to the next and to an over-riding theme. The cycle included a range of diverse elements—an English music hall song ("When I'm Sixty-Four"), new "psychedelic" sounds using advanced electronic devices ("Lucy in the Sky with Diamonds"), large orchestration, Indian instruments ("Within You Without You") and good, old-fashioned rock 'n' roll.

After five years of unprecedented success and popularity the Beatles disbanded in 1970.

Bob Dylan

Bob Dylan (Robert Zimmerman) gained a following in the early 1960s as a folk singer emulating the work of Woody Guthrie. Dylan's protest songs had strong appeal for young people. Such albums as *Highway 61 Revisited* and *Bringing It All Back Home* reflected concerns in the struggle for civil rights for blacks and later in the growing protest against the war in Vietnam. Dylan and other artists, including the Beatles, the Rolling Stones, and "psychedelic" San Francisco groups like Jefferson Airplane,

Figure 22.18 Michael Jackson, a multitalented singer, dancer, composer, actor, and producer, has been a rock star since the age of 11. His albums and music videos have gained enormous popularity.

Bruce Springsteen

Bruce Springsteen (b. 1949) was known only in the northeast before 1975 when he recorded the album *Born to Run* with his excellent rock ensemble, The E Street Band. The release of the album accompanied by an extensive public relations campaign and followed by a national tour catapulted Springsteen into rock stardom. The 1978 album, *Darkness at the Edge of Town,* and *The River,* released in 1980, confirmed his status as one of the most exciting rock personalities on the national scene. In particular, *The River*—included songs focusing on aspects of the automobile ("Stolen Car," "Wreck on the Highway," "Cadillac Ranch") and the hit song, "Hungry Heart"—was acclaimed as the best rock album of the year.

Springsteen's 1982 album *Nebraska* represents a pointed departure from his earlier recordings and *Born in the USA* which followed in 1984.

Nebraska

In both its lyrics and its sound, *Nebraska* evokes the folk-like qualities reminiscent of Bob Dylan and Arlo Guthrie. The singer/composer with his acoustic guitar and mouth harp replace the rock and roll character of Springsteen's other albums. The

Figure 22.19 Hailed in the 1970s as "the next Bob Dylan," singer/ songwriter Bruce Springsteen captured a large following with his driving music, perceptive lyrics, and kinetic live performances.

atmosphere of *Nebraska* is intimate and its message is direct and personal as it reflects upon contemporary society with its hopelessness and despair. All ten songs that make up *Nebraska* are imbued with compassion for the homeless, the unemployed, and the hopeless.

Perhaps the height of irony is achieved by the images in "Reason to Believe," the album's final song. A man at the side of a road tries to bring a dead dog back to life. A woman waits for her lover who left without notice. A child is baptized as an old man is buried. A young man waits in vain at the altar for his bride. Each verse ends with the ironic refrain:

"Struck me kinda funny, seems kinda funny sir to me
Still at the end of every hard-earned day people find some reason to believe."

Nebraska went against the current rock trends toward high tech electronics with synthesizers and computers, and professionals in the recording industry predicted low sales for the album. However, 800,000 copies were sold and the magazine *Rolling Stone* named *Nebraska* among its albums of the year. Springsteen won the designations artist of the year, top male vocalist, and best songwriter.

Born in the USA, released in 1984, represented a return to a more orthodox rock style for Springsteen. The E Street Band returned for this album which sold 11.5 million copies and seven of its ten songs achieved similar success on single records.

Both jazz and rock can be expected to adapt to new styles, and new personalities are bound to arise as America moves into the twenty-first century.

SUMMARY

Perhaps the most significant American contribution to music is jazz, a musical language which grew out of the black experience in America. Among its early ancestors were the composed piano music known as ragtime and the improvisational vocal art known as the blues.

New Orleans or Dixieland jazz developed in the early 1900s and utilized a small jazz combo made up of front line instruments and a rhythm section. The outstanding feature of New Orleans jazz is collective improvisation. In the 1920s, Chicago style jazz emphasized the soloist as improviser. The Depression years saw the development of jazz piano styles of stride and boogie-woogie. As the economy recovered, big bands emerged and played swing style music and, for the first time, jazz became popular with white audiences and performers. At the height of the swing era, many jazz musicians rebelled against the big band style and its commercialization. They developed an innovative style for small combos called bop or bebop. Bop musicians experimented with unusual harmonies, rhythms, and improvisatory techniques.

The 1950s and 60s brought a new kind of jazz musician and more experimentation. Cool jazz, a reaction against the frenzied quality of bop, features a cool, detached sound and frequently incorporates features of classical music. Rock-jazz style combines the electric sound and beat of rock with the improvisatory nature of jazz. Free jazz, the most radical departure from previous styles, seeks to expand all the elements of jazz to their farthest frontiers.

Rock music has had a powerful impact on recent and current popular culture. Two of the major components in the development of rock were rhythm and blues, and country and western music. In the mid-1950s, rock, then known as rock 'n' roll, was popularized by such artists as Elvis Presley. From the late 1950s to the mid-1960s, a number of offshoots developed, notably the Motown sound and soul.

The arrival of the Beatles in 1964 changed the face of American popular music. The Beatles' late recordings are a fusion of current rock styles and a variety of other musical styles and elements. Important contributions to the social consciousness of the rock movement were made by folk/folk-rock artist Bob Dylan and others. While some believe that the golden age of rock came to a close in the early 1970s, a continuous stream of new artists, such as Bruce Springsteen, continue to develop new styles of rock music.

NEW TERMS

jazz	**boogie-woogie**
blues	**swing**
blue notes	**bop (bebop)**
ragtime	**cool jazz**
New Orleans style (Dixieland)	**free jazz**
front line	**rock-jazz (fusion)**
rhythm section	**rhythm and blues**
group improvisation	**country and western**
Chicago style	**rock 'n' roll**
stride	**soul**

SUGGESTED LISTENING

Smithsonian Collection of Classical Jazz.

Louis Armstrong,

The Louis Armstrong Story.
"S.O.L. Blues"; side 15, selection 4

Count Basie,

Moten Swing.

Charlie Christian,

Solo Flight.

Ornette Coleman,

Free Jazz.

John Coltrane,

A Love Supreme; Ascension.

Miles Davis,

The Complete Birth of the Cool; King of Blue; Bitches Brew.

Duke Ellington,

This Is Duke Ellington; Ellington at Newport.

Billie Holiday,

Lady Day; The Golden Years, Volume I.
"God Bless the Child"; side 15; selection 5

Scott Joplin,

Maple Leaf Rag.

Thelonius Monk,

Genius of Modern Music.
"Monk's Dream"; side 16, selection 1

Charlie Parker,

The Savoy Recordings.

Weather Report,

Birdland.

The Beatles,

"I Wanna Hold Your Hand"; Sgt. Pepper's Lonely Hearts Club Band.

Bob Dylan,

"It Ain't Me Babe"; "Blowin' in the Wind."

Bruce Springsteen,

Born in the USA, Nebraska.

JAZZ AND ROCK

SUGGESTED READINGS

GENERAL READING LIST

Apel, Willi, and R. T. Daniel. *The Harvard Brief Dictionary of Music.* Cambridge, Mass.: Harvard University Press, 1970. A succinct version of the *Harvard Dictionary of Music.*

Bowers, Jane, and Judith Tick, eds. *Women Making Music: The Western Art Tradition, 1150–1950.* Urbana: University of Illinois Press, 1986. A series of essays by noted scholars on the role of women composers and performers in Western art music.

Crocker, Richard L. *A History of Musical Style.* New York: McGraw-Hill, 1966; New York: Dover, 1986 (paper). Emphasis on the evolution of characteristic musical styles within major historical periods.

Einstein, Alfred. *A Short History of Music.* New York: Knopf, 1954; New York: Random House, 1954 (paper). One of the best concise histories of music, this work is a nontechnical chronological survey of important composers and musical genres from the Middle Ages through the nineteenth century.

Grout, Donald Jay. *A History of Western Music.* 3rd ed. New York: Norton, 1980. An excellent college-level text, with thorough coverage of European music from the end of antiquity through the early twentieth century.

Kinsky, George. *A History of Music in Pictures.* St. Clair Shores, Mich.: Scholarly Press, 1971. The standard one-volume pictorial history of music, arranged chronologically from antiquity to the early twentieth century.

Lang, Paul Henry. *Music in Western Civilization.* New York: Norton, 1940. A highly influential work which discusses music in the context of political, cultural, and social trends in Western civilization from ancient Greece through the nineteenth century.

Neuls-Bates, Carol, ed. *Women in Music: An Anthology of Source Readings from the Middle Ages to the Present.* New York: Harper & Row, 1982. A collection of writings by and about a variety of women musicians; arranged in chronological order.

Bandel, Don Michael, ed. *New Harvard Dictionary of Music.* Cambridge, Mass.: Belknap Press, 1986. A concise historical and bibliographical handbook of terms and concepts; biographical information is not included. Each major entry has a working definition, history, and bibliography.

Sadie, Stanley, ed. *New Grove Dictionary of Music and Musicians.* 20 vols. London: Macmillan, 1980. The most authoritative and comprehensive music reference tool in the English language. It is the first place to look for information on any music subject.

Strunk, Oliver, ed. *Source Readings in Music History.* 5 vols. New York: Norton, 1965. Each volume (Antiquity and Middle Ages, Renaissance, Baroque, Classic, Romantic) collects the writings of theorists, composers, teachers, critics, and musicians arranged in chronological order under topics.

GENRES

Cuyler, Louise Elvira. *The Symphony.* New York: Harcourt Brace Jovanovich, 1973. Traces the two hundred-year development of the symphony, citing and analyzing the most important, representative compositions from each period by country and composer.

Grout, Donald Jay. *A Short History of Opera.* 2nd ed. New York: Columbia University Press, 1965. The standard English-language history of opera, this book surveys the most significant works and the major developments in operatic style from its beginnings through the early twentieth century.

Hartmann, Rudolph. *Opera.* New York: Morrow, 1977. Beautifully produced book that links photographs of recent celebrated productions and interviews with designers and stage directors.

Stevens, Denis, ed. *A History of Song.* rev. ed. New York: Norton, 1970. A technical, historical, and geographic survey of secular song in Western countries with criticism and analysis.

Ulrich, Homer. *Chamber Music.* 2nd ed. New York: Columbia University Press, 1966. Ulrich defines and anlayzes the growth of chamber music to 1930, using the works of Haydn, Mozart, Beethoven, and the romantics as the core. Contemporary chamber music is also discussed.

PART I: FUNDAMENTALS OF MUSIC

A. GENERAL WORKS

Cooper, Grosvenor W. *Learning to Listen.* Chicago: University of Chicago Press, 1962. A compact survey of musical elements and concepts, including chapters on rudiments of theory and notation, rhythm, harmony, form, and style.

Copland, Aaron. *What to Listen for in Music.* New York: New American Library, 1964. A highly useful introductory guide to the elements of music, including chapters on basic structural forms (fugue, variation, sonata-allegro).

Erikson, Robert. *The Structure of Music: A Listener's Guide.* Westport, Conn.: Greenwood Press, 1977. Explores the nature of harmony, melody, and counterpoint from a nontechnical point of view.

B. MUSICAL INSTRUMENTS AND ORCHESTRATION

Baines, Anthony, ed. *Musical Instruments through the Ages.* 2nd ed. New York: Walker & Co., 1976. A brief chronological survey of the development of instruments and their performance capabilities.

Carse, Adam. *The History of Orchestration.* New York: Dover, 1964. A largely nontechnical survey of the orchestra and the art of orchestration from the sixteenth century through the late nineteenth century.

Sachs, Curt. *The History of Musical Instruments.* New York: Norton, 1940. An exhaustive evolutionary survey of instruments by history (from antiquity), period, country, and function.

PART II: THE MUSIC OF WORLD CULTURES

Béhague, Gerard. *Music in Latin America: An Introduction.* Englewood Cliffs, N.J.: Prentice-Hall, 1979. A survey of Western traditional music in Latin America from sixteenth century colonial times through the present. Much of the work concentrates on the twentieth century.

Collaer, Paul, ed. *Music of the Americas: An Illustrated Music Ethnology of the Eskimo and American Indian Peoples.* New York: Praeger, 1971. A survey of the music and instruments of North and South American Indians and Eskimos.

Hofmann, Charles. *American Indians Sing.* New York: The John Day Company, 1967. A study of the thought, religion, and culture of American Indians as revealed through their music, dances, and ceremonies. Well illustrated and very readable.

Malm, William P. *Music Cultures of the Pacific, the Near East, and Asia.* 2nd ed. Englewood Cliffs, N.J.: Prentice-Hall, 1977. Well illustrated with both drawings and musical selections, this volume explores the anthropological, historical, and musical aspects of the subject cultures.

Nettl, Bruno. *Folk and Traditional Music of the Western Continents.* 2nd ed. Englewood Cliffs, N.J.: Prentice-Hall, 1973. Describes in some detail representative folk music of Europe, America, and Africa south of the Sahara. The more general introductory chapters are especially valuable.

Nettl, Bruno, and Helen Myers. *Folk Music in the United States: An Introduction.* 3rd ed. Detroit: Wayne State University Press, 1976. An introducton to characteristics of folk music, its history, instruments, and singers.

B. INDIVIDUAL COMPOSERS

Copland

Dobrin, Arnold. *Aaron Copland: His Life and Times.* New York: Crowell, 1967. A short biographical sketch, including general discussion of the composer's ideas and musical activities.

Gershwin

Jablonski, Edward, and Lawrence Stewart. *The Gershwin Years.* New York: Doubleday, 1973. A pictorial biography of the composer-lyricist brother team of George and Ira Gershwin with critical bibliography, Gershwin compositions, discography, and performance notes.

Ives

Cowell, Henry, and Sidney Cowell. *Charles Ives and His Music.* New York: Oxford University Press, 1969. A biography of Ives written by two close friends of the composer. Approximately half of the book is devoted to a study of Ives's musical style and major works with many quotations from the composer that are not found elsewhere.

Perlis, Vivian. *Charles Ives Remembered: An Oral History.* New Haven: Yale University Press, 1974 (hard cover); New York: Norton, 1976 (paper). An illustrated oral biography of fifty-eight interviews with friends and musicians, with Ives's music discussed both anecdotally and analytically.

PART IX: MUSIC OF THE LATE TWENTIETH CENTURY

A. PERIODICAL LITERATURE

The most important source of information on contemporary music is periodical literature. Significant periodicals devoted to contemporary and avant-garde compositions are *Perspectives of New Music* (published by Princeton University Press) and *Die Reihe* ("The Row," a German periodical published in translation by Theodore Presser Company), *The Score* (London), the *Journal of Music Theory* (New Haven), and the *Music Quarterly* (New York).

Babbitt, Milton. "Who Cares if You Listen?" *High Fidelity,* vol. VIII. no. 2 (February, 1958). A personal and unusual statement by one of America's most influential composers defending his concepts of an esoteric and "cerebral" style of composition.

B. GENERAL WORKS

Cope, David H. *New Directions in Music.* 4th ed. Dubuque, Ia.: Wm. C. Brown, 1984. An introduction and general survey of avant-garde and post avant-garde music in the twentieth century. Contains many useful illustrations and photographs and lengthy bibliographies and discographies.

Lang, Paul Henry, and Nathan Broder, eds. *Contemporary Music in Europe: A Comprehensive Survey.* New York: Norton, 1965; 1968 (paper). This group of essays discusses postwar musical trends in each of the major European countries.

Salzman, Eric. *Twentieth-Century Music: An Introduction.* 3rd ed. Englewood Cliffs, N.J.: Prentice-Hall, 1988. This excellent and concise survey includes valuable chapters on avant-garde music through the early 1960s.

Schaefer, John. *A Listener's Guide to New Music.* New York: Harper & Row, 1987. An entertaining discussion of the various trends and movements in new music. Includes detailed listings of composers, works, and recordings.

C. INDIVIDUAL COMPOSERS

Boulez

Peyser, Joan. *Pierre Boulez.* New York: Schirmer Books, 1976. A chatty, controversial profile of the avant-garde composer, populated with famous friends and artistic figures, and enlivened by accounts of clashes of will and infighting.

Cage

Cage, John. *Silence.* Middletown, Conn.: Wesleyan Press, 1961. A collection of writings on experimental music, techniques of composition, and other miscellaneous topics. An invaluable source for the author's ideas on chance music.

PART X: JAZZ AND ROCK

Belz, Carl. *The Story of Rock.* 2nd ed. New York: Oxford University Press, 1972. A survey of the stylistic trends of rock music from the mid-1950s through the early 1970s. Includes a selected discography of classic rock records.

Collier, Graham. *Inside Jazz.* London: Quartet Books, 1973. A readable, entertaining, general introduction to the world of jazz.

Dahl, Linda. *Stormy Weather: The Music and Lives of a Century of Jazzwomen.* New York: Pantheon, 1984. A fascinating look at jazzwomen vocalists and instrumentalists from the 1890s through the present. Includes a lengthy discography.

Fanagan, Bill. *Written in My Soul: Rock's Great Songwriters Talk About Creating Their Music.* Chicago: Contemporary Books, 1986. A series of interviews with twenty-five rock composers from Chuck Berry to Sting.

Feather, Leonard. *The Encyclopedia of Jazz.* rev. ed. New York: Horizon, 1960. Feather's widely praised work has two thousand biographies, recommended records, and essay articles ("Anatomy of Jazz," "Guide to Jazz History," "Jazz and Classical Music"), as well as photographs and technical definitions.

Garland, Phyl. *The Sound of Soul: The History of Black Music.* New York: Contemporary Books, 1969. A detailed, sensitive study of the roots and forms of black music in America. A masterfully stated discussion of the music of the early years serves as a prelude to a more extended treatment of the major "soul" singers of recent years.

Gridley, Mark C. *Jazz Styles.* Englewood Cliffs, N.J.: Prentice-Hall, 1978. A guide to appreciating jazz as well as an introduction to most styles which have appeared on recordings. Includes a discography and a guide to record buying.

Helander, Brock. *The Rock Who's Who: A Biographical Dictionary and Critical Discography.* New York: Schirmer, 1982. Contains in-depth biographies and extensive discographies of some three-hundred rock artists and groups in rhythm and blues, soul, rockabilly, folk, country, easy listening, punk, and new wave.

Hentoff, Nat, and Albert J. McCarthy, eds. *Jazz.* New York: Rinehart, 1959. A collection of essays containing perspectives on the history of jazz by jazz critics and scholars.

Jones, Leroi. *Blues People.* New York: Morrow, 1971. Jones places the entire continuum of black music in the context of cultural history, following changes in musical style by social and economic events. An excellent and intriguing thesis.

Litweiler, John. *The Freedom Principle: Jazz after 1958.* New York: William Morrow, 1984. An overview of contemporary jazz trends and musicians in Europe and America. Includes a discography and a guide to record buying.

Morgenstern, Dan. *Jazz People.* New York: Abrams, 1976. Combines an excellent tracing of the origins and subsequent history of jazz with a number of finely etched personality profiles. Includes graceful and insinuating photographs by Ole Brask.

The New Rolling Stone Record Guide. Rev. ed. Eds. Dave Marsh and John Swenson. New York: Random House, 1983. One of the most comprehensive guides to pop music albums. Reviews and rates over twelve-thousand rock, pop, soul, country, blues, folk, and gospel albums.

Ostransky, Leroy. *Jazz City: The Impact of Our Cities on the Development of Jazz.* Englewood Cliffs, N.J.: Prentice-Hall, 1978. An interesting discussion of the possible reasons for the development and flourishing of jazz in New Orleans, Chicago, Kansas City and New York.

Pielke, Robert G. *You Say You Want A Revolution: Rock Music in American Culture.* Chicago: Nelson-Hall, 1986. Discusses the significance of rock music as a cultural phenomenon, including its impact on the media of radio, records, film, and television.

Rolling Stone (1967–present). The preeminent periodical of American rock and popular culture.

Rolling Stone Illustrated History of Rock and Roll. Rev. ed. Ed. Jim Miller. New York: Random House, 1981. A critical history, bringing together the work of the finest rock writers in a pictorial record of the history of rock 'n' roll, soul, and rock and blues. Unique photos and discographies.

Santelli, Robert. *Sixties Rock: A Listener's Guide.* Chicago: Contemporary Books, 1985.

Shapiro, Nat, and Nat Hentoff, eds. *Hear Me Talkin' to Ya.* New York: Dover, 1966. A collection of first-person reminiscences by many major figures from the richest years of jazz history.

Williams, Martin. *The Jazz Tradition.* rev. ed. Oxford: Oxford University Press, 1983. A clear and vivid narrative of developments in jazz from the early 1920s through the 1960s, with discussions of leading jazz figures from "Jelly Roll" Morton through Ornette Coleman.

CREDITS

GLOSSARY

A Cappella Designating choral music without instrumental accompaniment.

Absolute Music Music that is entirely free of extramusical references or ideas.

Accompanied Recitative A type of recitative in which the voice is accompanied by instruments in addition to continuo.

Accompaniment Musical material, usually instrumental, which harmonically supports a melodic line. See also *homophony.*

Alternation A principle for building musical form in which a main section (A) alternates with contrasting sections (B, C, D, etc.). Ternary form (ABA) is a simple example.

Aria A composition for solo voice and instrumental accompaniment.

Arioso A vocal style that is midway between recitative and aria. Its meter is less flexible than that of recitative, but its form is much simpler and more flexible than that of the aria.

Arpeggio A chord whose tones are played one after another in rapid succession rather than simultaneously.

Art Song A musical setting of a poem for solo voice and piano. The German words *lied* (song) and *lieder* (plural) became the standard terms for this type of song.

Atonal Lacking a recognizable tonal center of tonic.

Augmentation A rhythmic variation in which the original note values of a theme are increased.

Ballad (Vocal) A narrative poem set to music.

Ballade (Instrumental) A relatively large, free-form instrumental work. The term was apparently used first by Chopin.

Bar line The vertical line which separates the notes in one measure from those in the next.

Basso Continuo, Continuo Continuous bass. A bass part performed by (1) a keyboard player who improvises harmony above the given bass notes, and (2) a string player—usually cello or viola da gamba—who reinforces the bass line.

Basso Ostinato A short melodic phrase that is repeated continually as a bass line, above which one or more voices have contrasting material.

Battery The percussion section of an orchestra.

Bebop (Bop) A jazz style which emphasizes small ensembles, harmonic innovation, unusual chord structures, an implicit beat, and a "hard" sound.

Bel Canto "Beautiful song." A vocal technique emphasizing beauty and purity of tone and agility in executing various ornamental details.

Binary Form A basic musical form consisting of two contrasting sections (AB), both section often being repeated (AABB); the two sections are in related keys.

Blue Note In blues and jazz music, any of the notes produced by flatting the third, fifth, or seventh notes of a major scale.

Blues A lamenting, melancholy song characterized by a three-line lyrical pattern in AAB form, a twelve-bar harmonic progression, and the continual use of "blue notes."

Boogie-Woogie A blues piano style which uses a rhythmic ostinato bass in the left hand while the right hand plays a simple, often improvised melody.

Bridge In a musical composition, a section that connects two themes.

Cadence A point of rest at the end of a passage, section, or complete work that gives the music a sense of convincing conclusion. Also, a melodic or harmonic progression that gives the feeling of conclusion.

Cadenza A section of music, usually in a concerto, played in an improvisatory style by a solo performer without orchestral accompaniment.

Call and Response A song style found in many West African cultures (and black American folk music) in which phrases sung by a leader alternate with responding phrases sung by a chorus.

Canon A contrapuntal technique in which a melody in one part is strictly imitated by another voice or voices.

Cantata A choral work, usually on a sacred subject and frequently built upon a chorale tune, combining aria, recitative, chorus, and instrumental accompaniment.

Chamber Music Music written for a small group of instruments, with one player to a part.

Chanson French for "song." A type of Renaissance secular vocal music.

Character Piece A work portraying a single mood, emotion, or idea.

Chorale A German hymn, often used as a unifying theme for a cantata.

Chord A combination of three or more tones sounded simultaneously. See also *arpeggio*.

Chorus, Choir A vocal ensemble consisting of several voice parts with four or five or more singers in each section. Also, a section of the orchestra comprising certain types of instruments, such as a *brass choir*.

Chromatic Designating melodic movement by half steps.

Chromatic Scale The scale containing all twelve tones within the interval of an octave.

Church Modes A system of eight scales forming the tonal foundation for Gregorian chant and for polyphony up to the baroque era.

Clef Sign A sign placed at the beginning of a staff to indicate the exact pitch of the notes.

Coda The concluding section of a musical work or individual movement, often leading to a final climax and coupled with an increase in tempo.

Codetta The closing theme of the exposition in a sonata-allegro form movement.

Concert Overture A one-movement self-contained orchestral concert piece, often in sonata-allegro form.

Concertino The solo instrument group in a concerto grosso.

Concerto A work for one or more solo instruments and orchestra.

Concerto Grosso A multimovement work for instruments in which a solo group called the *concertino* and a full ensemble called the *ripieno* are pitted against each other.

Consonance A quality of an interval, chord, or harmony that imparts a sense of stability, repose, or finality.

Continuo See *basso continuo*.

Cool Jazz A restrained, controlled jazz style that developed during the 1950s.

Counterpoint A musical texture consisting of two or more equal and independent melodic lines sounding simultaneously. See also *polyphony*.

Countersubject In a fugue, new melodic material stated in counterpoint with the subject.

Country and Western A form of white popular music derived from the English/Scottish folk tradition of the Appalachian region and from cowboy ballads.

Cyclical Treatment A unifying technique of long musical works in which the same thematic material recurs in succeeding movements.

Da Capo "From the beginning." Indicates that a piece is to be repeated in its entirety or to a point marked *fine* ("end").

De Capo Aria An aria in ABA form; the original melody of A may be treated in a virtuosic fashion in the second A section.

Development In a general sense, the elaboration of musical material through various procedures. Also, the second section of a movement in sonata-allegro form.

Diminution A rhythmic variation in which the original note values of a theme are shortened.

Dissonance A quality of an interval, chord, or harmony that gives a sense of tension and movement.

Dodecaphony See *twelve-tone technique*.

Dominant The fifth note of a given scale or the chord built upon it (dominant chord): it is the note that most actively "seeks" or creates the expectation of the tonic note.

Drone A stationary tone or tones of constant pitch played throughout a piece or section of a piece.

Dynamics See *volume.*

Edge Blown Describing a woodwind technique in which the player funnels a narrow stream of air to the opposite edge of the mouth hole.

Electronic Music Music produced by such means as magnetic tape, synthesizer, or computer.

End Blown Describing a woodwind technique in which the air is blown into a mouthpiece.

Episode In a fugue, a transitional passage based on material derived from the subject or based on new material, leading to a new statement of the subject.

Etude A study piece for piano concentrating on a single technical problem.

Exposition The first section in sonata-allegro form, containing the statement of the principal themes. Also, the first section in a fugue, in which the principal theme or subject is presented imitatively.

Expressionism An artisitic school of the early twentieth century which attempted to represent the psychological and emotional experience of modern humanity.

Fantasia An improvised keyboard piece characterized by virtuosity in composition and performance; popular during the baroque era. Also, a virtuoso piece for lute; popular during the Renaissance.

Fermata (⌢) A notational symbol which indicates that a note is to be sounded longer than its normal time value; the exact length being left to the discretion of the performer.

Figured Bass, Thorough Bass A shorthand method of notating an accompanimental part. Numbers are placed under the bass notes to indicate the intervals to be sounded above the bass notes. See also *basso continuo.*

Flat (♭) A notational sign indicating that a pitch is to be lowered by a half step.

Form The aspect of music involving the overall structuring and organization of music.

Frequency The rate at which a sounding body vibrates, determining the pitch of a musical sound.

Front Line In jazz bands, the instruments that carry the melodic material.

Fugue A type of imitative polyphony based on the development of a single theme or subject.

Glissando A rapid sliding up or down the scale.

Grand Opera A type of romantic opera which concentrated on the spectacular elements of the production.

Gregorian Chant The music that accompanies the Roman Catholic Liturgy, consisting of monophonic, single-line melodies sung without instrumental accompaniment.

Half Step, Semi-tone One half of a whole step; the smallest interval in traditional Western music.

Harmonic Progression A series of harmonies.

Harmony A composite sound made up of two or more tones of different pitch that sound simultaneously.

Heptatonic Scale A seven-tone scale, used in both Western and non-Western music.

Heterophony Performance of a single melody by two or more individuals who add their own rhythmic or melodic modifications.

Homophony A musical texture in which one voice predominates melodically, the other parts blending into an accompaniment providing harmonic support.

Idée fixe A single, recurring motive; e.g., in Berlioz's *Symphony Fantastique,* a musical idea representing the hero's beloved that recurs throughout the piece.

Imitation The repetition, in close succession, of a melody by another voice or voices within a contrapuntal texture.

Impressionism A late nineteenth-century artistic movement which sought to capture the visual impression rather than the literal reality of a subject. Also, in music, a style belonging primarily to Claude Debussy, characterized by an emphasis on mood and atmosphere, sensuous tone colors, elegance and beauty of sound.

Improvisation The practice of "making up" music and performing it on the spot without first having written it down.

Incidental Music Music written to accompany a play.

Indeterminacy, Aleatory, or Chance Music Music in which the composer sets out to remove the decision-making process from his or her own control. Chance operations such as throwing dice are employed to obtain a random series of musical events.

Interval The distance in pitch between any two tones.

Inversion Modification of a theme by reversing the direction of the intervals, with ascending intervals replaced by descending intervals and vice versa.

Key Tonality; the relationship of tones to a central tone, the tonic.

Key Signature The group of sharps or flats placed at the beginning of each staff to indicate which notes are to be raised or lowered a half step. The particular combination of sharps or flats indicates the key of a composition.

Ledger Lines Short horizontal lines added above or below the staff to indicate notes that are too high or too low to be placed within the staff.

Legato "Linked, tied." Indicating a smooth, even style of performance, with each note connected to the next.

Leitmotiv "Leading motive." A musical motive representing a particular character, object, idea, or emotional state. Used especially in Wagner's operas.

Libretto The text of an opera or similar extended dramatic musical work.

Lied, Lieder "Song." See *art song.*

Lyric Opera A type of French romantic opera that relied on beautiful melodies for its effect.

Madrigal A polyphonic vocal piece set to a short poem; it originated during the Renaissance.

Major Scale A scale having a pattern of whole and half steps, with the half steps falling between the third and fourth and between the seventh and eighth tones of the scale.

Mass The most solemn service of the Roman Catholic Church. The parts of the Mass most frequently set to music are the Kyrie, Gloria, Credo, Sanctus and Benedictus, and Agnus Dei.

Mazurka In romantic music, a small piano piece based on the Polish dance form. Prominent in the works of Chopin.

Measure A unit of time organization consisting of a fixed number of beats. Measures are separated from one another by vertical bar lines on the staff.

Measured Rhythm Regulated rhythm in which precise time values are related to each other.

Melismatic Designating a melodic phrase in which one syllable of text is spread over several notes.

Melody A basic musical element consisting of a series of pitches of particular duration that sound one after another.

Meter The organization of rhythmic pulses or beats into equal, recurring groups.

Microtone An interval smaller than a half step.

Minimalism A late twentieth-century movement which seeks to return music to its simplest, most basic elements.

Minor Scale A scale having a pattern of whole and half steps, with the half steps falling between the second and third and between the sixth and seventh tones of the scale.

Minuet and Trio A form employed in the third movement of classical symphonies, cast in a stately triple meter and ternary form (ABA).

Modulation Gradual or rapid change from one key to another within a composition.

Monodic Style Designates a type of accompanied solo song that evolved in Italy around 1600 in reaction to the complex polyphonic style of the late Renaissance. Its principal characteristics are (1) a recitativelike vocal line, (2) an arioso with basso continuo accompaniment.

Monophony A musical texture consisting of a single melodic line without accompanying material, as in Gregorian chant.

Motet A polyphonic choral work set to a sacred text.

Motive A short melodic or rhythmic figure that reappears frequently throughout a work or section of a work as a unifying device.

Movement An independent section of a longer composition.

Musique Concrète "Concrete music." A musical style originating in France about 1948; its technique consists of recording natural or "concrete" sounds, altering the sounds by various electronic means, and then combining them into organized pieces.

Natural (♮) A notational symbol indicating that a pitch that has been sharped or flatted is to be restored to its basic pitch.

Neoclassicism In music of the early twentieth century, the philosophy that musical composition should be approached with objectivity and restraint. Neoclassical composers were attracted to the textures and forms of baroque and classical periods.

Nocturne "Night piece." A character piece for piano, of melancholy moods, with expressive melodies sounding over an arpeggiated accompaniment.

Octave An interval between two pitches in which the higher pitch vibrates at twice the frequency of the lower. When sounded simultaneously, the two pitches sound very much alike.

Opera A drama set to music and made up of vocal pieces such as recitatives, arias, duets, trios, and ensembles with orchestral accompaniment, and orchestral overtures and interludes. Scenery, stage action, and costuming are employed.

Opera Buffa Italian comic opera.

Opéra Comique (Comic Opera) A type of French romantic opera distinguished by its use of spoken dialogue rather than sung recitative. Many operas in this form had serious plots.

Opera Seria Italian opera with a serious (i.e., noncomic) subject.

Oratorio An extended choral work made up of recitatives, arias, and choruses, *without* costuming, stage action, or scenery.

Orchestration The arrangement of a musical composition for performance by an orchestra. Also, utilization of orchestral instruments for expressive and structural purposes.

Organum The earliest type of medieval polyphonic music.

Ostinato A musical phrase repeated persistently at the same pitch.

Overture The orchestral introduction to a musical dramatic work.

Pedal Point A long-held tone, usually in the bass, sounding through changing harmonies in other parts.

Passion A musical setting of the story of the suffering and crucifixion of Jesus Christ.

Pentatonic Scale A five-tone scale. Various pentatonic scales are commonly employed in non-Western music.

Phrase A musical unit consisting of several measures.

Pitch The highness or lowness of a musical tone, determined by the frequency of vibration of the sounding body.

Pizzicato A performance technique in which stringed instruments such as the violin are plucked with the fingers instead of bowed.

Plainsong, Plainchant See *Gregorian chant.*

Pointillism A term borrowed from the visual arts and used to describe a melodic line made from isolated tones or chords.

Polonaise In romantic music, a small piano piece based on the Polish dance form.

Polyphony Many voices. A texture combining two or more independent melodies heard simultaneously; generally synonymous with counterpoint.

Polyrhythm Two or more contrasting and independent rhythms used at the same time.

Polytonality The simultaneous use of two or more different keys.

Prelude A free-form piece that may introduce another piece or stand alone.

Primitivism In music, the use of frenzied, irregular rhythms and percussive effects to evoke a feeling of primitive power, as in Stravinsky's *The Rite of Spring.*

Program Music Instrumental music associated with a nonmusical idea, this idea often being stated in the title or in an explanatory program note.

Raga One of the ancient melodic patterns employed in Indian music.

Ragtime A composed music of the 1890s, usually for piano, characterized by steady, marchlike accompaniment in the left hand and a decorated syncopated melody in the right hand.

Recapitulation The third section of sonata-allegro form, which restates the entire exposition in the tonic key.

Recitative A form of "singing speech" in which the rhythm is dictated by the natural inflection of the words.

Rest A notational sign denoting the duration of silence.

Retrograde A melody read backwards, beginning with the last note and ending with the first.

Rhythm The element of music that encompasses all aspects of musical time.

Rhythm and Blues A form of black popular music which blends elements of jazz and the blues.

Rhythm Section In jazz bands, the instruments that supply the harmonic and rhythmic accompaniment.

Ricercar A type of Renaissance lute music, often polyphonic, that demonstrated the virtuosity of the performer.

Riff A short melodic line, usually rhythmic, which can be repeated over and over to form either the main melody or the background for improvised solos.

Ripieno The full ensemble in a concerto grosso.

Ritornello "Return." A characteristic form for the first and sometimes the last movement of the baroque concerto grosso. The thematic material given to the ripieno returns between the passages played by the soloists.

Rock 'n' roll (Rock) Popular music characterized by a heavy beat, electronically amplified instruments, simple melodies, and often using elements from country music and the blues.

Rondo An extended alternating form often employed in the fourth movement of classical symphonies; generally spirited and playful in character.

Rubato "Robbed." A term indicating that a performer may treat the tempo with a certain amount of freedom, shortening the duration of some beats and correspondingly lengthening others.

Scale The arrangement of adjacent tones in an order of ascending or descending pitches.

Scherzo "Joke." A sprightly, humorous instrumental piece, swift in tempo; developed by Beethoven to replace the minuet.

Secco Recitative A recitative with only continuo accompaniment.

Serialism See *twelve-tone technique*.

Sharp (♯) A notational sign indicating that a pitch is to be raised by a half step.

Sinfonia A short instrumental introduction to a baroque choral work.

Singspiel German comic opera that employed spoken dialogue.

Solo Concerto A multimovement baroque work differing from concerto grosso in that the concertino consists of only one instrument (most often the violin or piano).

Solo Sonata A sonata for one instrument with continuo accompaniment.

Sonata An instrumental work consisting of three or four contrasting movements.

Sonata-Allegro Form A musical form encompassing one movement of a composition and consisting of three sections—exposition, development, and recapitulation—the last often followed by a coda.

Sonata Da Camera "Chamber sonata." A baroque instrumental work, essentially a dance suite.

Sonata Da Chiesa "Church sonata." A baroque instrumental work in four movements (slow-fast-slow-fast).

Song Cycle A series of art songs that tell a story.

Soul A spirited, raw-edged form of rock music that features walling vocals and hard-driving rhythm and brass sections.

Sprechstimme "Speech voice." A vocal technique in which a pitch is half sung, half spoken. Developed by Arnold Schoenberg.

Staccato "Detached." Indicating a style of performance in which each note is played in a short, crisp manner.

Staff A graph, consisting of five lines and four intermediate spaces, on which music is notated.

Stopping Changing the pitch of, for example, a violin string by pressing the string against the fingerboard.

Stretto A type of imitation in which each successive voice enters before the phrase is completed in the previous voice; usually employed in fugues or fugal textures.

Stride A jazz piano style in which the left hand alternates between a bass note and a chord played an octave or more above the bass, giving the effect of "striding" back and forth, while the right hand plays the melody.

String Quartet A chamber ensemble consisting of a first and a second violin, a viola, and a cello. Also, the form which is a sonata for these instruments.

Strophic Designating a song in which all verses of text are sung to the same music.

Style Broadly, the manner of expression that distinguishes a particular work, composer, historical period, or artistic school.

Subject In a fugue, the principal theme, introduced first in a single voice and then imitated in other voices, returning frequently during the course of the composition.

Suite A series of instrumental movements, each based on a particular dance rhythm.

Syllabic Designating a musical phrase in which each syllable of text is given one note.

Symphonic poem See *tone poem*.

Symphony A sonata for orchestra.

Syncopation A deliberate disturbance of the normal metrical pulse, produced by shifting the accent from a normally strong beat to a weak beat.

Tala One of the ancient rhythmic patterns employed in Indian music.

Tempo The speed at which a piece of music moves.

Ternary Form A basic musical form consisting of three sections, ABA, the final A section being a repetition or slight variation of the first.

Texture The relationship between the horizontal (melodic) and vertical (harmonic) aspects of a piece of music. The principal classifications are monophony, homophony, and polyphony.

Theme A musical idea that serves as a starting point for development of a composition or section of a composition.

Theme and Variations A form based on a single theme and its subsequent repetition, with each new statement varied in some way from the original.

Theme Transformation The practice of varying a single theme or melody through the different sections of a piece; this procedure was used especially in romantic tone poems.

Thorough Bass See *figured bass*.

Through-Composed A term applied to songs in which new music is used for each successive verse.

Time Signature A numerical sign placed at the beginning of a composition to indicate the meter.

Toccata A baroque keyboard piece full of scale passages, rapid runs and trills, and massive chords.

Tonality The relationship of tones to a central tone called the tonic. See also *key*.

Tone A pitch having a steady, constant frequency.

Tone Cluster A chord produced by playing a large group of adjacent notes on the piano with the flat of the hand. The resulting sound is dense and indistinct.

Tone Color, Timbre The characteristic quality, or "color," of a musical sound as produced by a specific instrument or voice, by a combination of instruments.

Tone Poem, Symphonic Poem A single-movement programmatic work, relatively long and very free in form, usually involving a dramatic plot or literary idea.

Tone row (series, set) See *twelve-tone technique*.

Tonic The tonal center. The tone which acts as a musical home base, or point of rest and finality, in a piece of music.

Total Serialism The complete, predetermined, and ultrarational systemization of every aspect of a composition: pitch, tempo, dynamics, articulations, and timbre.

Transcription An arrangement of a composition for a medium other than that for which it was originally written.

Tremolo A "trembling" effect produced on string instruments when the bow is moved rapidly back and forth across the strings.

Trio sonata A sonata for two instruments with continuo accompaniment.

Tritonic scale A three-tone scale, generally used in non-Western music.

Twelve-Tone Technique, Serialism, Dodecaphony A system of composition developed by Arnold Schoenberg which consists of arranging the twelve pitches of the chromatic scale in a particular order (known as a tone row, series, or set).

Verismo "Realism." An Italian operatic point of view favoring realistic subjects taken from everyday, often lower-class, life.

Vibrato A slight fluctuation in pitch which increases the "warmth" of a tone.

Voice (Voice Part) A melodic line, either vocal or instrumental, in a contrapuntal piece such as a fugue

Volume (Dynamics) Relative degrees of loudness or softness.

Whole Tone Scale The scale in which the octave is divided into six consecutive whole steps.

Word Painting Representation of the literal meaning of a text through musical means.

INDEX

Head, of drum, 42
Heavenly City, 85
Heavy metal, 462
Hebrides, The. *See Fingal's Cave*
Henderson, Fletcher, 450
Hendrix, Jimi, 461
Heptatonic scale, 60, 70, 77
Herman, Woody, 450
Heterophonic style, 70
Hildegard of Bingen, 91; *Ordo virtutum,* 91; *Symphonia Armonie Celestrium Revelationum,* 91
Hillbilly band, 51
Hindemith, Paul, 51, 169, 336, 358, **359–63, 379;** biography, 358; *Kleine Kammermusik für fünf Bläser* (Little Chamber Music for Five Winds), **359–63, 379;** work, 359–63
Hindu culture, 64
Hines, Earl "Fatha," 449
Hölderlin, Friedrich, 436
Holiday, Billie, 443, 444; biography, 444
Holly, Buddy, 458
Holy Roman Empire, 154
Home base, 18
Home key, 28
Homophonic music, 26–27, 125
Homophony, 24, 26–27
Honnegger, Arthur, 342–43
Hood, Helen, 408
Hopkinson, Francis, 405
Hopper, Edward, 402
Horn Signal Symphony. *See* Symphony No. 31 in D
Hosho, 72
Huang chung, 61
Hubbard, Freddy, 456
Hugo, Victor, 240, 255
Huguenots, Les (Meyerbeer), 300
Hungarian Fantasia (Liszt), 241
Hungarian Rhapsodies (Liszt), 241
Hymn (Britten), 373
Hymn of Praise (*Lobgesang*). *See* Symphony No. 2 in B Flat
Hymn to Joy (Schiller), 261

Idée fixe, 272, 273
Idiophones, 71
Idomeneo (Mozart), 162, 189
Il ritorno de Ulisse in patria (Monteverdi), 114
Imitation, 25, 95
Impressionism, 29; and symbolism, 337–38
Improvisation, group, 446
Indefinite pitch, 41, 43

Independent melodic lines, in polyphony, 25
Indeterminacy, 428, 430
India: and instruments, 66–67; music of, 64–67; and performance, 66; and pitch, scales, harmony, and rhythm, 65
Industrial Revolution, 336
Innovations, formal: and Romantic music characteristics, 322; and twentieth-century characteristics, 393
Instrumental music: Baroque, 137–49; Medieval and Renaissance characteristics, 103; and Mozart, **162–70;** Renaissance, 101–3
Instruments: and Africa, 71–73; Baroque, 112, 137–49; bowed, 32–36; and characteristics of classical music, 179; and China, 63–64; electronic. *See* Electronic instruments; and ensembles, 31–55; harmonic, 46; and India, 66–67; Medieval and Renaissance characteristics, 103; melodic, 46; and Native American music, 78–79; plucked, 32, 36; and Renaissance, 101–3; and Romantic music characteristics, 322; string. *See* Strings; wind. *See* Woodwinds
Interval, 5; regular, 20
Introduction, and Mendelssohn, **259**
Inversion: and fugue, 138; and twelve-tone method, 384
Irving, Washington, 401
Isaac, Heinrich, 101
Israel in Egypt (Handel), 117
Italian opera, 302
Italian Renaissance, 87
Italian Symphony. *See* Symphony No. 4 in A
Ives, Charles, 29, 401, 410–11, **412–15,** 420; biography, 411; and polytonality, 413; *Variations on "America,"* 29, **412–15;** work, 412–15

Jackson, Michael, 462, 463
James, Francis, 343
James, Harry, 450
Jannequin, Clement, **100–101,** 146
Javanese orchestra, 339
Jazz, 446–47; cool, 453–54; electric, 456–57; free, 454–55; origins of, 442–45; and rock, 441–66, 454, 456–57; and syncopation, 21
Jazz band, 51
Jeanrenaud, Cécile, 256
Jefferson, Thomas, 401, 404
Jefferson Airplane, 460

Jemez Pueblo, 77
Jepthe (Carissimi), 115
Jericho, 88
Jesuit Order, 108
Jesus Christ, Superstar, 462
Jhaptal, 65
Jig. *See* Gigue
Joachim, Joseph, 248
Johnson, James P., 449
Joke. *See* Scherzo
Jonson, Ben, 365, 373
Joplin, Janis, 461
Joplin, Scott, 445
Joyce, James, 335
Judas Maccabaeus (Handel), 117
Judges, Book of, 115
Jupiter Symphony. *See* Symphony No. 41 in C

Kandinsky, Wassily, 335
Kappellmeister, 139, 169
Kassel, 139
Kay, Ulysses, 415
Keats, John, 228, 365, 374–76
Keller, Maria Anna, 169
Kettledrums, 42
Key, 17–18; home, 28
Keyboards, 31, 46–48, 137; Baroque, 137
Khovanshchina (Mussorgsky), 287
Kinderscenen (Scenes from Childhood)(Schumann), 239
Kindertotenlieder (Songs on the Death of Children)(Mahler), 254
King Lear Overture (Berlioz), 272
King of the Elves. *See* "Erlkönig" (Goethe) *and Erlkönig* (Schubert)
Kleine Kammermusik für fünf Bläser (Little Chamber Music for Five Winds)(Hindemith), **359–63, 379**
Köchel, Ludwig von, 162
Köchel's catalogue, 162
Koldály, Zoltán, 376
Kple, 70
Kyrie, 91, 92; and Haydn, **186**

La Bohème (Puccini), 304, **305–13**
La favola d'Orfeo (Monteverdi), 114
Lamb, Joseph, 445
Lang, Margaret Ruthren, 408
Large vocal works, Medieval and Renaissance characteristics, 103
Large works: and characteristics of classical music, 179; and Romantic music characteristics, 322
Largo, 21